The End of Meaning

The End of Meaning

Cultural Change in America since 1945

WILLIAM A. SIKES

◈PICKWICK *Publications* · Eugene, Oregon

THE END OF MEANING
Cultural Change in America since 1945

Copyright © 2024 William A. Sikes. All rights reserved. Except for brief quotations in critical publications or reviews, no part of this book may be reproduced in any manner without prior written permission from the publisher. Write: Permissions, Wipf and Stock Publishers, 199 W. 8th Ave., Suite 3, Eugene, OR 97401.

Pickwick Publications
An Imprint of Wipf and Stock Publishers
199 W. 8th Ave., Suite 3
Eugene, OR 97401

www.wipfandstock.com

PAPERBACK ISBN: 978-1-6667-8334-6
HARDCOVER ISBN: 978-1-6667-8335-3
EBOOK ISBN: 978-1-6667-8336-0

Cataloguing-in-Publication data:

Names: Sikes, William A., author.

Title: The end of meaning : cultural change in America since 1945 / William A. Sikes.

Description: Eugene, OR: Pickwick Publications, 2024. | Includes bibliographical references.

Identifiers: ISBN 978-1-6667-8334-6 (paperback). | ISBN 978-1-6667-8335-3 (hardcover). | ISBN 978-1-6667-8336-0 (ebook).

Subjects: LCSH: Popular culture—United States—History—20th century. | United States—Civilization—1945–. | Ethics.

Classification: E169.12 S58 2024 (print). | E169.12 (epub).

04/02/24

Scripture quotations marked KJV are from the King James or Authorized Version.

Scripture quotations marked NRSV are from the New Revised Standard Version, copyright @ 1989, Division of Christian Education of the National Council of the Churches of Christ in the United States in the United States of America. Used by permission. All rights reserved.

Scripture quotations marked RSV are from the Revised Standard Version of the Bible, copyright 1971 by the Division of Christian Education of the National Council of the Churches of Christ in the United States of America. Used by permission. All rights reserved.

*For my parents, who taught me
to value meaning, and for Jennie,
who brought so much of it into my life*

Men and women of our city, your costumes please us, close-fitting, colorless, fine; great city, your foods, your odors, your speedy sensuality, casual encounters begun, fiercely consummated, discontinued, we accept you all . . . factories, schools, places of entertainment and ill repute, our metropolis, thrive, thrive! You are our joy and we are yours and so we go together, between the rivers, towards an end beyond which there is no beginning, and beyond that, none, and the dawn city glistening in the sun.

But something befell us when the worlds were sealed off from each other. As the days lengthened into weeks, months, years, as the decades passed, and the centuries, something that once happened to us all every night, every one of us, every member of the greater "we" which we have all become, stopped happening. We no longer dreamt.

Salman Rushdie
Two Years Eight Months and
Twenty-Eight Nights

Contents

Overview: Meaning and Culture ... 1

PART ONE | MEANING FOR THE PHILOSOPHERS, POETS, AND PROFESSORS

1. Philosophers and Poets ... 17
2. Higher Education ... 28

PART TWO | SMALL IS MEANINGFUL

3. Everyday Objects and Experiences ... 43
4. Poetry and Art ... 65
5. Peak Experiences ... 87

PART THREE | MEANING WRIT LARGE

6. Family and Community ... 105
7. Labor ... 127
8. Death, War, and Politics ... 152
9. Sports and Religion ... 185

PART FOUR | STORIES OF MEANING

10. Music, the Novel, Drama, and Dance ... 221
11. Film ... 245
12. Romantic Love ... 263

PART FIVE | LIFE'S JOURNEY OF MEANING

Conclusion: American Dystopia and the Hero of Meaning   319

Bibliography   339

Overview: Meaning and Culture

WHEN SOMEONE COMPLAINS, "THINGS aren't as good as they used to be," someone else will often respond: "People have always said that. It doesn't mean anything." It is indeed likely that people have been saying that for a long time—certainly for generations, possibly for hundreds, if not thousands, of years. However, it doesn't follow that it doesn't mean anything. To the contrary, it may mean a great deal.

While fond memories will inevitably distort the past, in the view of many older Americans, things *were* better in the postwar years (c. 1945–65). I don't mean they were physically or materially superior. Americans then had more modest medical care and shorter life spans than they do today. Women had much more limited opportunities, while minorities and those with disabilities were often relegated to the fringes of society—as was the LGBTQ community, when its members didn't suffer outright persecution. The pace of life was slower in the postwar years, technology more primitive, and the pleasures of consumerism much more modest. Given all this (and more) it may seem strange that anyone would look fondly to the past. They are too old, we say. They have forgotten what it was like.

But while the many changes over the decades have brought longer life spans, greater individual freedom, technological sophistication, untold consumer riches and more, they have not brought more *meaning*. On the contrary, in the following pages we will find evidence that the vast majority of changes that typify the postmodern world (a world which, for us, began in the late sixties) exist in inverse relation to meaning in life.

The notion of "meaning" employed in this book will be spelled out in detail in our first chapter. Suffice it to say that by the term I do not have in mind its usage in everyday discourse—meaning, as it were, with a small *m*. I am thinking rather of deeper experiences, like those that arise from close-knit families and communities, from having a sense of vocation or purpose in life, from falling in love, reveling in the glories of nature, listening to great music and the like. It is in these experiences of "connection"—to other people, or to larger ideas or powers—that a deep and lasting sense of meaning in life is to be found. Meaning like this is chiefly a function of culture, which provides its inhabitants with such experiences and teaches them to recognize their value—or fails in this vital task. Indeed, any culture that lacks the capacity to provide and enhance experiences like these is almost certainly on its last legs.

If we wish to see where meaning flourishes, we might look to the Pueblo peoples of the American Southwest (like the Zuni and Hopi) as they still existed in the years between the two World Wars.[1] Here the "connections" we have in mind were everywhere. They included: common labor; intimate ties to nature; strong bonds to family and community; vital arts, crafts, stories, and songs (all of which gained meaning from their foundations in age-old values, styles and methods); a broader vision of life that embraced the wider universe and stretched back generations; and a notion of life's journey that gave meaning to each stage of individual existence—not only on earth, but beyond.

At the heart of these cultures was religion. C. G. Jung, the founder of analytical psychology, tells a story from his travels in the American West in 1925 that dramatizes this. Jung had sought out a man named Mountain Lake, who was a leader of the Hopi nation and one of a group of old men known as the "Keepers of the Faith." At the time, Pueblo religious practices were being harshly suppressed by the American government—a policy that took a turn for the better a few years later. Thus Mountain Lake was guarded in his conversations with Jung, and often vague regarding the deepest mysteries of his people's faith. However, at one point in their conversation, Mountain Lake can no longer contain his confusion and anger. Why won't the Americans leave us alone, he asks; don't they know that what we do benefits the entire world? When Jung probes a bit further, Mountain Lake gestures to the sun:

"After all," he said, "we are a people who live on the roof of the world; we are the sons of father Sun, and with our religion we daily help our father to go across the sky. We do this not only for ourselves, but for the whole world. If we were to cease practicing our religion, in ten years the sun would no longer rise. Then it would be night forever."

---

1. See Parsons, *Pueblo Indian Religion*; Dozier, *Pueblo Indians*; Wyaco, *Zuni Life*.

Jung continues:

> I then realized on what the "dignity," the tranquil composure of the individual Indian, was founded. It springs from his being a son of the sun; his life is cosmologically meaningful, for he helps the father and preserver of all life in his daily rise and descent. If we set against this our own self-justifications, the meaning of our own lives as it is formulated by our reason, we cannot help but see our poverty. Out of sheer envy we are obliged to smile at the Indians' naiveté and to plume ourselves on our cleverness; for otherwise we would discover how impoverished and down at the heels we are.[2]

The vital point here is the extraordinary sense of *meaning* that comes from an existence that includes assisting the life-giving powers of the universe. Our technology may do wondrous things, but it has never enabled the sun to rise—and it never will.

There is a steep price to be paid for such a life of meaning. Although the Pueblo, like all traditional peoples, have a relationship to nature that is not only meaningful but ecologically sound, it is one that discourages material advancement. Such a life also places severe limitations on the individuality and personal autonomy we regard as so essential today. Pueblo tradition puts significant restrictions on marriage, and the Pueblo divide labor according to patterns that are typical of small-scale societies (i.e., women usually work at home while men work abroad, clearing the land, hunting, trading and the like). The behavior of children is firmly controlled by elders, who will sometimes frighten a child into behaving by telling him he may be attacked by witches, or by bogeys who will spirit him away in a basket. Respect for elders is strictly enforced. Although customs differ somewhat among the tribes, Pueblo children may be expected to pause in play when an elder passes, to greet elders respectfully by a kinship term (never by name), and to take on a submissive posture (with arms behind their back) when waiting on them.

The most characteristic behavioral strictures for Pueblo of all ages are demands for social solidarity and cooperation, which commonly come at the expense of individual freedom and initiative. The traditional Pueblo home offers very little privacy. Moving from towns is discouraged, and those who must leave their home generally seek labor as nearby as possible. Disputes typically take place between groups rather than

---

2. Jung, *Memories, Dreams, Reflections*, 251–52.

individuals, while labor within the community is often a collective activity, according to the notion that all will at some point need the help of others. Community work includes hunting and gathering firewood, spinning wool and grinding corn, planting and gathering crops, and special projects, including care of the irrigation ditches that are vital to some of these communities. As we might imagine, these activities are rich in that social capital that adds enormously to meaning in life. In conjunction with religious ceremonies (which occupy entire weeks of the year) they are the bedrock of meaning-rich societies.

In the Pueblo communities, members who show originality or initiative are often disparaged. It is the one who is discrete and group-oriented, rather than the outspoken or even the most talented, who is generally chosen for important positions in the community. Elsie Clews Parsons says of the Zuni that the man "who thirsts for power or knowledge, who wishes to be, as they scornfully phrase it, 'a leader of his people,' receives nothing but censure and will very likely be persecuted for sorcery."[3] This lack of self-assertion carries over into little daily rituals. In his autobiography, *A Zuni Life*, Virgil Wyaco notes how Indian men lightly touch flesh when shaking hands, and refuse to look in the other's face, regarding a firm handshake and direct eye contact as aggressive actions. Wyaco adds that, in many contexts, even gentle questions may be considered aggressive, and that pointing is widely associated with witchcraft.[4]

Not only self-assertion but self-expression as we usually understand it is frowned upon. Creative endeavors like art, songs, or stories are expected to follow time-honored patterns rather than take form as creative expressions of individual talent or point of view. An underlying sacred purpose is evident in all, instilling them with meaning. As Parsons explains: "Poetry and song, dance music and steps, mask, figurine, fresco and ground painting, beautiful feather-work, weaving and embroidery, whatever else they are, also are measures to invoke and coerce, to gratify or pay, the Spirits."[5]

In the Pueblo villages, age-old myths are told and reenacted in ritual, while (at least prior to the advent of TV) the old stories are passed on from generation to generation at evening in the home. The character of songs also remains the same. This is typical of traditional peoples generally, as Ananda Coomaraswamy has characterized them: "New songs, yes; but

---

3. Parsons, *Pueblo Indian Religion*, 1:108.
4. Wyaco, *Zuni Life*, 10–11.
5. Parsons, *Pueblo Indian Religion*, 1:xxxiii.

never new kinds of music, for these may destroy our whole civilization."⁶ Coomaraswamy may not exaggerate. Writing as an old man at the end of the twentieth century, Wyaco cites the appearance of radio and TV—and especially the rock and roll music that became their staple—as the chief cause of the breakdown of Zuni culture in the fifties.⁷

In all this, the traditional Pueblo appear to be very different from us. And yet, their world is not so very different from the world of postwar America. Indeed, in many ways American culture then was closer to the Pueblo world than to our own.

The biggest criticism of postwar Americans was that they had lost the spirit of individualism that had been so vital to the nation's success. Beginning with *The Lonely Crowd* (1950),⁸ and proceeding through a number of both academic studies and popular films and novels, Americans of the era were depicted as a generation who took their cues from others rather than relying upon their own initiative. The many "yes men" in America's corporations (popularized in Sloan Wilson's 1955 novel, *The Man in the Grey Flannel Suit*) was the most obvious example of this. Many believed that men accustomed to taking orders during the war were now adopting the same approach in their work, politics and families—to the detriment of society. Women were no better. Popular culture of the day dictated that women marry young and assume the role of housewives, "smiling as they ran the new electric waxer over the spotless kitchen floor" in Betty Friedan's memorable phrase.⁹ Critics seemed unable to understand that a generation that had recently suffered war and deprivation were content to take meaning where they found it.

Close-knit communities and families were another salient feature of American society in the postwar years. In cities, ethnic communities were prominent, and, weather permitting, socializing took place long after dark on stoops or in popular establishments. America's countrysides then had twice as many farms in a nation with half the population, leaving plenty of woods, fields and vacant lots for children to explore. Those living in the postwar housing developments were noted (and often criticized) for their strong sense of community. This was evident from the dozens of community organizations in the big developments (more

---

6. Coomaraswamy, *Christian and Oriental Philosophy*, 11.
7. Wyaco, *Zuni Life*, 50.
8. Riesman et al., *Lonely Crowd*.
9. Halliwell, *American Culture in 1950s*, 40.

than sixty each in Park Forest, Illinois, and Levittown, New York[10]) and by the willingness of neighbors to share important items like lawn mowers, silver, and china. Small towns then had town centers, with hotels, restaurants, churches, and movie theaters. Cousins generally lived close to cousins, neighbor knew neighbor, and grandparents tended to be available for advice and to pass on family history. Homes were small by today's standards, and this, in conjunction with the baby boom, brought children closer together, while encouraging parenting by community. PTAs flourished, and both parents and schools stressed citizenship and getting along with others more than the athletic success and high test scores so valued today.

Young people who attended colleges and universities in the period were expected to broaden their horizons by studying the major writings of Western civilization and by reading the classics of English literature (Shakespeare especially). It was a time when college students often took advantage of available cultural activities on campus, like guest speakers or concerts of classical music. Most of the young regarded the college years not simply as a time for fun and career preparation, but as a rare opportunity to engage with those deeper issues that promised a greater sense of meaning in life. Such notions persisted into the late sixties, when some 86 percent of incoming college freshman said that "developing a meaningful philosophy of life" was either "essential" or "very important" to them.[11] This is about twice the number who find meaning important today.

Like the Pueblo, postwar Americans generally assigned some jobs to men and others to women. Labor then was not the socially disruptive force it so often is today. At a time when social stability was more important than personal success, most men in small towns sought employment in local businesses or became jacks of all trades, moving from one job to another as needs arose rather than uproot their families. Factory towns were relatively stable then, and those in industry found meaning in close-knit communities while taking pride in creating products that were expected to last. Big-city lawyers often regarded their work as a "calling," and enjoyed close ties to clients, partners, and associates without "billable hours" being the bane it is today. Teachers were respected members of the community, and could expect support for both teaching methods and objectives without the disruptive classroom behavior and social and

---

10. O'Neil, *American High*, 25.
11. E. Smith, *Power of Meaning*, 6.

political controversy so widespread now. Service jobs had the great virtue of bringing people into close contact with their neighbors and fellow employees. Both the workweek and commute times were shorter in the postwar era, leaving more time for family. Parents raised children together and socialized together at the popular bridge clubs, country clubs, PTAs, and churches.

Family time in the fifties consisted of two common meals and some family radio listening or TV watching. With one radio or TV in the house, programs were generally chosen by consensus. At the time, profanity, graphic violence, and sexual content of any sort were forbidden (even the menacing notes of the *Dragnet* theme were enough to send some little children scurrying off to bed). Music was a popular radio and TV choice and, prior to the emergence of rock and roll, children and parents usually enjoyed the same songs. These tended to be romantic tunes, thereby conveying to the young an exalted vision of love that was elsewhere prevalent on the silver screen. Other popular tunes referenced America itself—from Patti Page's "Old Cape Cod" to Perry Como's "Delaware," which mentions no fewer than fifteen states in its lyrics. Nat King Cole's "Route 66" took listeners on an excursion through eleven cities located along the fabled highway. Such entertainment not only helped unite the country, but (along with the popular TV jingle, "See the U.S.A. in your Chevrolet") encouraged Americans to get to know their nation in a way not possible before—nor after, when interstate highways and jets would render the American landscape a blur.

One of the most remarkable features of postwar America was the effort to provide ready access to serious culture. Popular periodicals of the day featured articles on prominent writers, classical musicians, and artists. This is not surprising given that, through the fifties, live performances of classical music, opera, and drama had an important place on radio and TV. In the period, creators generally managed to reconcile their own individuality with a broader culture that featured the Bible, the classics, the nation's history, and the distinctive character of its many regions. We see this, for example, in John Steinbeck and William Faulkner, Tennessee Williams and Henry Miller, Carl Sandburg and Robert Frost. Dancer Martha Graham, as great a creative genius as any, looked to American myth and history in her works. So did the foremost American composer of the era, Aaron Copland. Their great collaboration, *Appalachian Spring*, is both a masterpiece and pure Americana.

Through the forties, mature artists like Georgia O'Keeffe, Charles Burchfield, and John Marin were still painting the American landscape in forms that were easily discernible yet distinctively their own. And when abstract painting eventually took hold, many of these works found meaning by reference to Navaho sand painting or Native American totems and petroglyphs. Existential philosophy and the popular psychologies of the unconscious also played a role in giving meaning to the visual arts—the first, by regarding creative gesture as an heroic act; the second, by reading the artists' forms as manifestations of ideas and impulses as old as humanity itself. It was a time when the notion of the "spiritual" was not only widely accepted by the public, but by many arts figures, who sought meaning in their work as much, if not more, than fame and fortune.

As with the Pueblo, meaning in the postwar era took root in religion. Church affiliation in America rose from 43 percent of the population before the war to a remarkable 69 percent by 1960.[12] The Bible generally, and Christianity in particular, was everywhere. In the public schools, religion had an important place through prayer, story, and song, while the school year had Easter and Christmas holidays rather than the generic seasonal breaks of today. A series of powerful biblical epics (including *The Ten Commandments* and *Ben Hur*) appeared in movie theaters from the late forties into the early sixties, reinforcing basic principles of belief. In such an environment, a broad biblical reading of America's history and her values—which sociologists would dub "American civil religion"—naturally prospered. This was evident from the prominent place of the language of "civil religion" in political and religious spokesmen of the era, including men as ideologically different as Dwight Eisenhower and John Kennedy, Billy Graham and Dr. Martin Luther King Jr.

The last is an especially important point. In the fifties, Americans lived in fear of what most regarded as an inevitable nuclear conflict with the Soviet Union. Now, more than ever, religion came to be regarded as a vital tool in instilling national unity and courage. With resolve thus stiffened, pride in country and meaning in national life soared. All this, of course, is the very opposite of the American political landscape today. And here, especially, the Pueblo have much to teach us.

Among the Pueblo, disputes are never allowed to threaten community stability. Tradition is simply too important, and anyone who will not accept it generally leaves. Those who remain but still push for change

---

12. Fitzgerald, *Evangelicals*, 146.

make their case by appealing to time-honored traditions rather than by rejecting the past.

In this they remind us of Dr. Martin Luther King Jr., who emerges as one of the heroes in my narrative.

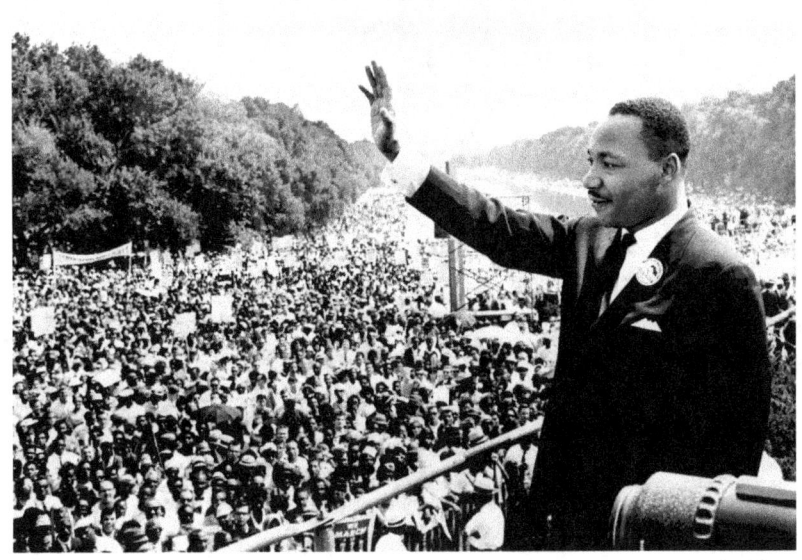

Dr. Martin Luther King Jr. waves to participants in the civil rights movement's March on Washington from the Lincoln Memorial. It was from this spot that he delivered his famous "I Have a Dream" speech on August 28, 1963.
Photo by © Hulton-Deutsch Collection/CORBIS/Corbis via Getty Images.

King was a poet of American civil religion and an expert in joining the language of the pulpit with the language of American history. In doing so, he opened up a world of meaning even his opponents often felt compelled to acknowledge. But King was much more than this. King's commitment to a higher moral standard—which led him to abhor violence of any kind, and to foreswear association with the divisive ideology of the Black Power movement—stands in sharp contrast to those political views and values that today fracture our society. It is worth noting that King's last major campaign, which was taking shape just prior to his death, involved a poor people's movement that joined blacks, Hispanics, Indians, and poor whites in common cause. In today's society, many whom King would have sought to bring into the fold find it necessary to look outside the political and cultural mainstream to preserve what little meaning they still have in their lives.

King's assassination on April 4, 1968, was the first of a series of events in that year that signaled a watershed in American history. The subsequent assassination of Democratic presidential frontrunner Robert Kennedy in June, the violence at the Democratic Convention in Chicago in August, and the eventual election of Richard Nixon in November marked the official end of postwar America. By now, other signs of momentous change were already in place.

The baby boomers whose appearance accompanied the end of War had entered a world of prosperity even their older brothers and sisters had not known. For a time, however, little seemed to change. The toys that were now in greater abundance beneath the Christmas tree bore a general similarity to those of an earlier generation, for whom they had served not only to delight but to instruct and to prepare the young for adulthood. The TVs that proliferated in the fifties simply replaced the radio as the center of family entertainment, while the presence of a second car in the driveway fueled a sociability and community involvement that would last well into the sixties. Only then would the glut of cars finally succeed in hollowing out the town centers of America—a development that would be one of the great losses in meaning of the era.

The first indications of change came in the Supreme Court decisions in *Engle v. Vitale* (1962) and *Abingdon v. Schempp* (1963), which marked the effective end of a strong alliance of religion and American culture that had a home in the nation's schools. Other court rulings led to a weakening of obscenity laws that was most visible in film, where, in 1966, the Production Code (forbidding profanity, sacrilege, sexually explicit, or gratuitously violent imagery) was summarily tossed aside. Millions of Americans responded to this change by abandoning the movie theaters, thus dealing a blow to one of the most meaning-rich institutions in the nation. Even the family was eventually impacted by legal shifts, as no-fault divorce laws began to proliferate following a California law in 1969. Coming in the wake of the sexual revolution (which was also heavily fueled by the courts), this dealt an enormous blow to what had been a bedrock of fifties society.

Like a drumbeat providing the backdrop to all this was war in Vietnam. For young Americans, the violence and destruction in Southeast Asia were ample justification for any and all excesses—political, sexual, or drug induced. In this project, they were aided by the colleges and universities, which, by the late sixties, were forsaking the role of in loco parentis and would soon dismantle the core curriculum—thereby coupling educational disaster with moral decline. Things might have been different with a JFK or RFK in the White House. However, having first extended the war, Nixon would partially redeem himself to the young by ending the military draft in 1973—thus erasing a link between young men and their country that had been in place for more than three decades. Now it appeared as if individual desires and needs would triumph over all the major bonds of meaning. For many Americans, the young were nothing but a long-haired, foul-mouthed, pot-smoking, country-hating band of hedonists.

Meanwhile—from public education to the economy, families to films, presidents to pop stars—America in the seventies had entered a decade of manifest decline and disillusion.

In the midst of all this, the counterculture attempted to provide its own sources of meaning (something that was apparent in the hippies but not so much in the political radicals who are the heroes of today's youth). At its center was a notion of "love" that hinted at metaphysical heights but more often became a justification for plain old-fashioned fooling around. On the other hand, the return to nature was a high point of the period, when it was apparent in everything from a love of flowers and a preference for more natural, colorful attire to a communal movement that strove for a simple, ecologically sound lifestyle—one that would join human beings to one another and to nature. Youth culture also had its own varieties of spirituality, which took form in everything from hallucinogenic drugs to the many gurus who journeyed to America in the late sixties and seventies only to lose their way. Simply put, America was neither willing nor able to support alien forms of spirituality. Thus the gurus adapted or abandoned their ambitions, leaving their followers with few alternatives but to look to themselves and turn to more tangible pursuits.

Referring to this change, in 1976, author Tom Wolfe characterized the seventies as the "Me Decade."[13] Looking back a few years later Christopher Lasch argued that a "culture of narcissism" had taken hold in the country.[14] Meanwhile, the forces of greed, materialism, scientism, the politicization of higher education, and all the rest were beginning to fill the vacuum left by the withdrawal of the forces of meaning, old and new.

13. T. Wolfe, "Me Decade."
14. Lasch, *Culture of Narcissism*.

In the coming years, meaning would increasingly find itself irrelevant and overwhelmed, as the tangible and the down-to-earth replaced the airy idealism of youth. Fifty years on, few young Americans recognize the spiritual longing that had been the quieter but more persistent voice of the counterculture.

Meanwhile, the eighties began with a pressing concern: what to do with the tens of millions of Americans who were now liberated from custom, country, and church, and seemed determined to pursue their own wants and needs. To this, American commerce in the eighties had the answer: provide them with millions upon millions of customized goods and services.

From the late eighties into the early twenty-first century, scholars were taking stock of the dramatic cultural decline in books proclaiming the "closing" of America's mind, the "collapse" of her communities, the "end" of her art, her education, and more.[15] What the works of authors like Harold Bloom, Robert Putnam, Donald Kuspit, and Neil Postman have in common is a (largely unacknowledged) recognition of meaning loss that was now apparent across the spectrum of American society. At the center of Bloom's broad cultural critique is the loss of the meanings available from a strong humanities education, while the decline of meaning-rich community bonds (and their consequences) is the theme of Putnam's equally acclaimed study. The shift from the meaningful languages of existentialism and depth psychology to the cool commercialism of pop art signaled the beginning of the end of art in Kuspit's work, while our inability to establish some meaningful narrative at the core of public education (one that can replace the old tales of our nation and its heroes) foreshadows its demise according to Postman.

In the twenty-first century, traces of the sixties are still with us. Some of these, like a tolerance for different lifestyles and a recognition of the central place of the environment in any future plans are clearly gains. However, the chief legacy of that era appears to be a political activism that so attacks opposing points of view that consensus is impossible. At the root of the current divide is the issue of meaning. On the one side are those who seek to retain what's left of a meaning-rich past; on the other are those who reject the past and look to a nebulous and mostly untried vision of meaning going forward.

---

15. Bloom, *Closing of American Mind*; Putnam, *Bowling Alone*; Kuspit, *End of Art*; Postman, *End of Education*.

Exacerbating this political conflict is a decline in meaning that has reached epic proportions. This is apparent from a 2023 *Wall Street Journal* poll comparing today's Americans with those of 1998 on the values they hold dear.[16] In 1998, 62 percent of Americans said religion was very important to them. By 2023, that number was down to 39 percent. Patriotism saw an even more dramatic drop in the period (70 percent to 38 percent) while the importance attached to having children and community involvement also declined—the first from 59 percent to 30 percent; the second, from 47 percent to 27 percent. And this decline is not only apparent in such traditionally "meaning-rich" institutions. Of the more than two dozen sources of meaning in America we will be examining, only sports and politics remain as meaningful as ever (indeed, more so, as they seem to be taking on meanings that might once have found a home elsewhere). But in sports there is always one more game, one more sport, one more season. There is only one country. In our era of meaning loss, political opponents today resemble nothing so much as two starving wolves fighting over one scrawny rabbit.

Politics is necessarily a minor theme in the following pages, which offer no easy answers to our dilemma. But if reconciliation is possible, it must begin by our understanding how we lost the old cultural values and cohesion, so that meaning began to die. The alternative is nothing less than the end of American culture and the birth of a new kind of being—one who, judged by past standards, is scarcely human.

16. Zitner, "Americans Pull Back."

PART ONE

Meaning for the Philosophers, Poets, and Professors

1

Philosophers and Poets

WHEN THE ISSUE OF meaning is raised in regard to our deepest thoughts and feelings, it usually appears in the form of the Question: "What is the meaning of life?" In recent years this question is most often associated with a variety of popular gag cartoons. In its most characteristic form, these cartoons depict a pilgrim who has, with apparent difficulty, finally ascended to the cave of a guru. The humor in the cartoons usually centers upon the fact that the guru's answer to the question of life's meaning is either trivial or nonsensical. Today, he is likely to respond with reference to one of the new technologies, where, presumably, the answer to this most difficult of questions is to be found.

While we all may find humor in cartoons like these, we might assume that the issue of the meaning of life still evokes serious thought in some quarters. Surely philosophers still deem the question worthwhile. In fact, the tendency of recent philosophy has been away from such Big Questions. Nor are those philosophers who take up the issue likely to do so in ways we find entirely helpful.[1]

Some philosophers argue that any notion of life's meaning must be based upon belief in a higher power who is the source of all things and who guides our life, giving it direction and purpose. These philosophers suggest that meaning like this is possible only through religious faith, and thus falls outside the purview of philosophy per se. Other philosophers go further, arguing that there is no reason to believe that life has any

1. See Klemke and Cahn, *Meaning of Life*.

real meaning at all. What significance life possesses, they reason, is found only within the natural universe, in the processes of birth, maturity, reproduction, and death that govern all living things. Apart from this, life is an absurdity—a cosmic joke we would be wise to acknowledge while drawing from existence what value we may.

Still other philosophers have argued that the question of life's meaning is itself meaningless. And, indeed, the sense of the term "meaning" in our question is altogether different from the significance of the term in the phrase "What is the meaning of that blinking yellow traffic light?" While the meaning of the light is clear enough to anyone familiar with the governing rules of traffic and traffic signs, the phrase "meaning of life" is ambiguous due to the enormous range of possibilities implied. Does the question refer to my life, to all earthly life forms or to the universe at large? By the term "meaning" do we really have in mind the notion of "purpose"? If so, what sorts of purposes? Are we referring to social or biological ends, to evolutionary processes, or to the ethical and spiritual potential of human beings? Perhaps we have much or even all of this in mind. If so, this is a lot of freight for a simple phrase to bear.

Aware of such difficulties, the contemporary philosopher may shift ground. The question "What is the meaning of life?," he or she tells us, should be amended to read: "How do I live a meaningful life?" or "How do I find meaning in my life?"

Here we are on firmer footing. However, the change from the search from some universal truth to a preoccupation with subjective experience raises issues of its own. Taken to the extreme, the subjective viewpoint leads to the notion that meaning is merely what we choose it to be. Surely meaning is more than this. Meaningful experiences are those that engage us in unique and potentially transformative ways, bonding us to others, to the larger worlds of culture or nature—perhaps even to some ultimate reality, which, inaccessible to mere reason, we may know as God.

Philosopher Irving Singer's *Meaning in Life: the Creation of Value* is one serious philosophical work that veers perilously close to a purely subjective point of view. This is disappointing, since the book begins with a powerful appraisal of an increasingly meaning-impoverished America. In his introduction, Singer characterizes the eighties as an era of "instant gratification," and he observes how, by the nineties, our culture's determination to fulfill all desires threatened to undermine society at its foundations. He continues:

It would be barbaric to suggest that people ought not to seek happiness. Nevertheless, we should consider the possibility that our current difficulties often result from a sense of meaninglessness to which favored human beings are commonly prone, and more so than those who struggle for mere survival. If this is true, pursuing and attaining happiness might appear to be paradoxically self-defeating. The happier we are, the harder it becomes to find the meaning in our lives that is essential for remaining truly happy.

Seen from this perspective, our contemporary concern about meaning is peculiar to the modern world. It arises from our relative wealth and freedom in a context of malaise, even despair, about man's ability to achieve lasting and genuine happiness.[2]

This is a good summation of our dilemma as understood within the larger context of human experience. It is all the more disappointing, then, that the bulk of Singer's book is taken up with a history of philosophical perspectives on meaning which, though certainly worth the reader's attention, are not entirely relevant to our current plight. A few of the thinkers Singer mentions (e.g., Tolstoy, Wittgenstein) eventually looked beyond philosophy to religious faith for an answer to life's meaning. However, Singer firmly rejects this option. "The challenge in our age," he observes, "is to understand how meaning can be acquired without dubious fantasying beyond the limits of our knowledge."[3] Having thus rejected any possibility of transcendence, Singer has no special place for the "higher" needs and strivings—that is, for meaning with a capital *m*. Meaningful behavior, he argues, is meaningful simply by virtue of the ends that matter to the individual. For Singer, this encompasses everything from the acts of the compulsive gambler to the ground mole's search for worms and roots.

Toward the end of the book, Singer betrays a sense that there is something missing in his argument. This leads him to consider the writings of his contemporary, philosopher Richard Taylor. Taylor has argued that a meaningful life is one devoted to good and noble purposes, and that it evolves as a creative expression of our distinctive talents and abilities. Singer takes exception to such an elevated tone, and to Taylor's exclusion of the "lesser" creatures. Still, he acknowledges that the meanings found in an heroic life are fundamentally different from those experienced in the

---

2. Singer, *Meaning in Life*, 4–5.
3. Singer, *Meaning in Life*, 72–73.

most basic everyday acts. Hence, Singer now adds the concept of "significance" to his notion of meaning, thereby distinguishing forms of meaning that embrace larger values from those limited to narrow self-interest.

More recently, Susan Wolf has taken up the question of meaning in life along the lines indicated by Singer and Taylor in her book *Meaning in Life and Why It Matters*. Wolf's little book is basically an extension of ideas sketched out by her predecessors. Still, it takes us a step closer toward our own understanding of meaning.

In her book, Wolf characterizes meaningful lives as those that are actively engaged "in projects of worth." She is aware that the phrase opens her to charges of "elitism." Nevertheless, she rightly defends it as necessary in distinguishing meaningful activities from those that are merely enjoyable or engaging. She also fleshes out her notion of "projects of worth," thereby giving badly needed substance to ideas that philosophers have often left vague:

> It is noteworthy what a broad and diverse range of projects and activities meet these standards. In particular, though it will include the projects and activities recognized as morally valuable by conventional standards, embracing both positive relationships with family and friends and engagement with political and social causes, the range extends far beyond that. Creating art, adding to our knowledge of the world, preserving a place of natural beauty all seem intuitively to deserve classification as valuable activities even if they do not bring about obvious improvement in human or animal welfare. So do efforts to achieve excellence or to develop one's powers—for example, as a runner, as a cellist, a cabinetmaker, a pastry chef.[4]

Wolf's views are clearly the most useful. Here, we get a strong sense of that "significance" Singer too late acknowledges while retreating a bit from the rarified air that mars Taylor's analysis. Still, a number of problems remain. In abandoning the view that life itself may have a larger meaning or purpose we have lost a great deal. From the sense of a possible connection to some all-encompassing power or truth we now seem to be chiefly left with the dilemma of choosing a worthwhile career or avocation.

However, there is another, more fundamental problem—and one that afflicts all the philosophers of meaning. From Singer's lowly mole digging in the soil to Taylor and Wolf's genuinely creative acts, the experience of meaning, for the philosophers, is primarily an individual

---

4. Wolf, *Meaning in Life*, 36–37.

endeavor. As the philosophers see it, meaning is something we attain rather than something that comes unbidden. It is a personal achievement rather than an inheritance. We may find meaning from writing a poem but not reading one, from creating a nature preserve but not walking through it. For the philosophers, meaning is a personal quest—much like the pilgrim's journey to the guru. Only there is no guru. Indeed, religion is notably absent here.

And this leads us to ponder: *When did the experience of meaning in life begin to depend so much upon individual choice and striving? And when did providing meaning cease to be a primary task—indeed, the primary task—of culture?*

By culture I have in mind both the ways the term is most commonly used. Broadly considered, *culture* includes the fundamental thoughts, values, habits and beliefs of a society, and the tangible forms these assume (e.g., in religion, politics, the popular arts, etc.). More narrowly, culture refers to "high" culture, which involves thoughts, values, habits, and beliefs rendered in forms of greater subtlety and complexity—forms that are usually intended for an educated or wealthy elite. In modern societies, the historical tendency has been to separate these two, with high culture being limited much as wealth and education are. However, as we observed in our overview, America in the postwar years sought to make high culture available to millions through government arts programs, the various new popular media, and the general education requirements of its institutions of higher learning. This was impossible previously and is inconceivable in a society that today acknowledges no common cultural heritage nor any lasting verities, but is preoccupied instead with financial success, political conflict, and bodily wants and needs.

But high culture in the postwar years benefited from more than greater accessibility. In traditional societies the arts are rooted in religion, which gives them their value and significance. The history of Western civilization is the story of the gradual separation of these, with the arts increasingly turning from the gods, a divinely ordered universe, and the rulers who embody this order and power, to everyday human beings and their struggles and strivings. However, even as the arts moved out of the shadow of myth and religious faith, they continued for centuries to look to philosophy and depth psychology, mysticism and metaphysics, for truths inaccessible to mere reason—truths that only some notion of the "spirit" could render. In the postwar years, there were still any number of creative figures who felt that art could articulate something of lasting value, and were therefore willing to make what George Steiner once called "a gamble on transcendence."[5] Our reluctance to any longer make such a gamble—whether through dreams, prayers, or the powers of the imagination—is a vital part of our story.

The above is by way of defining our approach to the question of meaning and of distinguishing it from that of the philosophers. In this book, we will primarily be looking at meaning from the outside in rather than the inside out. By this I mean that we want to see how meaning chiefly arises from experiences that our culture provides and to which it gives form. For us, meaning is not something we can fully attain on our own. For us, meaning is a series of *possibilities* that are rooted in our encounters with the world, which is chiefly known and understood through the lens of culture. It is culture that distinguishes the sage from the fool, the meaningful from the meaningless. It is culture that ultimately determines whether meaning will saturate our world or, as increasingly appears to be the case, disappear from it altogether.

The proud parent at a college graduation or a music lover listening to a symphony are examples of individuals engaged in the sort of meaningful encounters I have in mind. In each case, the meaning of the experience is aided by engagement with what I call *rituals of meaning*. By this notion I am thinking of standards and practices that both enhance meaning and provide ready access to it. A ritual of meaning includes everything from a suitable setting for meaningful activity to appropriate forms of dress and behavior, including a prescribed order of events and the ways we may be expected to respond to them. Rituals of meaning will naturally intersect with religious rituals in many cases. However, they extend far beyond religion to encompass a variety of activities that cultures establish and embrace as a way of giving heightened value to life.

In addition to such rituals of meaning there are what I call *languages of meaning*, which have to do with the specific forms by which the content of meaning is rendered. The speeches uttered at a graduation or the forms by which music expresses itself in a concert are examples of such languages, which range from the fairly straightforward to those that require greater experience and expertise. Of course, the lines distinguishing "languages" of meaning from "rituals" of meaning are not firm and fast. For example, the standard program notes that prepare the listener for a concert not only set the stage for the event but further our understanding of it.

---

5. Steiner, *Bluebeard's Castle*, 89.

In the graduation ceremony, the procession, speech, music, colorful robes, and banners, etc. all join to give meaning. So, too, does the surrounding atmosphere, which typically joins a serious mood (signifying both a recognition of the accomplishment and an awareness of the transition it marks) with an aura of joyful celebration of labor completed and the journey just begun. The atmosphere in the symphony hall is very different, the darkness and quiet of the hall encouraging listening and imaginative engagement. Of course, music has its own formal language of meaning, a knowledge of which adds enormously to the listener's experience. However, a receptive listener can get a great deal from a symphony without knowing the difference between an arpeggio and an archipelago.

In their careful and intelligible organization of parts, rituals and languages of meaning have a formal order and rules much like ordinary speech. Yet the two are very different. Were we to ask a symphony goer the or the parent of a college graduate what the experience "meant" to them, they are likely to profess their inability to clearly express their thoughts and feelings in words. In such circumstances they might simply say that they had a feeling of exaltation, a sense of awe or the like. To this they may add that the experience "made me think about . . ." or "reminded me of . . ."

This raises an important issue with regard to meaning, which lies in the fact that meaningful encounters draw upon thoughts and feelings in a unique way. In meaningful encounters, thought and feeling closely interact, our feelings triggering a range of associations, images, memories, and ideas that are themselves laden with emotional resonance. The struggle to express ourselves is important, because, by discovering the right words, we may be able to somehow grasp the experience and draw meaning from it in a way that is otherwise impossible.

In attempting to give verbal expression to meaningful experiences, we are much like the poets. In fact, a number of philosophers have observed a vital link between poetry and meaning. These include the great modern philosopher of language, Ludwig Wittgenstein, who praised poetry in his letters, going so far as to suggest that philosophy should be expressed in poetic language. Wittgenstein once bewildered a group of philosophers with whom he was meeting by reading the poetry of Rabindranath Tagore to them. In his view, it is poetry that is best suited to rendering the "unsayable"—by which he had in mind "ethics, value and the meaning of life."[6]

---

6. Janik and Toulmin, *Wittgenstein's Vienna*, 191. On Wittgenstein's major ideas, see also Brand, *Essential Wittgenstein*; Richter, *Historical Dictionary*.

Irving Singer's observations move in much the same direction. Questions regarding the meaning of life, argues Singer, must necessarily be vague because they seek to range beyond everyday experience. This does not render them unintelligible. It simply means that they must be treated as "metaphoric and symbolic rather than factual and literal"—that is, more like poetry than like science.[7]

The father of existential philosophy, Søren Kierkegaard, regarded himself as "a kind of poet," while his modern successor, Martin Heidegger, asserted that all genuine thought is poetic. Much of Heidegger's late writing was devoted toward developing a mode of discourse whereby the underlying relations between all things—for centuries concealed by science and technology—are laid bare.[8] More recently, the American philosopher Richard Rorty praised the virtues of poetry. In an essay published in *Poetry Magazine* (just before the author's death in 2007), Rorty professed that he regretted having not read more verse in his life. Rorty suggested that reading poetry, like having close friendships, made a person more fully human.[9]

Our discussion moves along similar lines. For our purposes, the chief value of poetry lies in its capacity to affirm the concreteness of the visible world even as it wrests words out of their everyday role to indicate more meaningful ways of knowing reality. Good poetry expands awareness, joining our little world to the larger universe and establishing connections across a broad range of experience.

Although poets have a number of ways of doing this, the most common is by employing imagery whereby thoughts and feelings are linked to natural forms of greater, more lasting, significance. The opening words of Shakespeare's well-known sonnet ("Shall I compare thee to a summer's day?") or William Wordsworth's famous poem ("I wandered lonely as a cloud") are notable examples. The first phrase allows the poet to render his deepest thoughts and feelings about his beloved by reference to the bounty of nature—and to find the latter wanting in comparison. The second, in comparing a solitary walker to the form of a cloud against a clear blue sky, enables the reader to experience something of that elevation of the spirit that may occur in nature's vast beauty—even as it prepares her for the poet's discovery of a glorious field of daffodils.

Perhaps it should come as no surprise to find that moments of poetic inspiration are foremost among the experiences of meaning in life.

7. Singer, *Meaning in Life*, 10–11.
8. Heidegger, *Poetry, Language, Thought*.
9. Rorty, "Fire of Life."

This is apparent from the famous preface to the second edition of *Lyrical Ballads*, where Wordsworth speaks of inspiration in ways that may sound familiar. Poetry, says Wordsworth, is "the spontaneous overflow of powerful feelings." But feeling is not enough. Wordsworth adds that good poetry can be written only by a poet who has "thought long and deeply." Says Wordsworth: "Our continuous influxes of feeling are modified and directed by our thoughts, which are indeed the representatives of all our past feelings; and, as by contemplating the relation of these general representatives to each other, we discover what is truly important to men."[10]

Wordsworth's words are telling. For what is "truly important" are those experiences in which thought and emotion come together in search of a certain coherence. Such interaction is vital to meaning.

But experiences like these are quintessentially meaningful in another important way. Wordsworth observes how, in good poetry, thought and feeling are connected to "important subjects." By this, Wordsworth has in mind subjects that are capable of expanding our everyday world and going beyond the merely temporary.

This is meaning as we understand it. For us, *meaning arises from the interaction of thought and feeling in experiences that connect us to something of greater and more lasting value than ourselves.*

Of course, meaning comes not merely from creating a poem. It also comes from *reading* one. Wordsworth points this out, too, noting how the poet should deal with significant subjects, and write in such a way that "the understanding of the reader must necessarily be in some degree enlightened, and his affections strengthened and purified."[11] Adam Kirsch makes the same point, observing that "the greatest poets are able to make us think boldly and feel strongly at the same time."[12] Kirsch adds that Emily Dickinson was a master of this kind of writing, and that she often used the classic meter of the hymnbook to pique the mind and stir the emotions, as in the following:

> I felt a Funeral in my Brain,
> And mourners to and fro
> Kept treading—treading—till it seemed
> That sense was breaking through—

---

10. Wordsworth, "Preface," 435.
11. Wordsworth, "Preface," 435.
12. Kirsch, "Poetry for the Pleasure," para. 8.

> And when they all were seated,
> A service, like a Drum—
> Kept beating—beating—till I thought
> My mind was going numb—[13]

Finally, the analogy to poetry is a reminder that the "reverie" that poets so often value is an important element in the achievement of meaning. By this I mean the capacity to quiet the busyness of everyday experience so that we may think and feel more deeply and consider our connection to our world and (perhaps) its Creator. Wordsworth (who was often painted in a contemplative posture) undoubtedly had such moments in mind when he said that poetry was born from "emotion recollected in tranquility."[14] This poet, an inveterate walker, found tranquility chiefly in England's Lake District, where he was born and spent most of his life. For Dickinson, it was abundant in the family home—where she spent her entire life, except for a year at Mount Holyoke Seminary and travels to a few big Eastern cities in her youth.

Sadly, places of tranquility are increasingly difficult to come by. The closest we come to peace and quiet today is likely to be in those venues where meaning is still thought to unfold—e.g., churches, libraries, museums. It is worth noting, however, that silence is not valued in these settings as much as it once was.

Today, most of our churches have lost that sense of awe that once defined encounter with the sacred. From mainline Protestant congregations to the new megachurches, the quiet, contemplative atmosphere of the past has been replaced by a more sociable, upbeat style of worship. Libraries, too, are increasingly places of social interaction rather than sites of quiet contemplation. As books have given way to computers, so are librarians prepared to "shush" loud interlopers becoming a thing of the past. Perhaps museums have fared worst of all. In an effort to popularize art and to break down the barriers between "high" culture and its patrons, museums today host parties of boisterous crowds, invite noisy children's groups into the inner sanctum, and give increasing visibility to bustling businesses where, in addition to the standard cards and posters, one may now purchase coasters, T-shirts, sleepwear, and socks bedecked with popular Monets and Van Goghs. This is undoubtedly one reason

---

13. Emily Dickinson, as quoted in Kirsch, "Poetry for the Pleasure," paras. 9–10.
14. Wordsworth, "Preface," 441.

museum visitors today spend only about ten seconds before a work of art—scarcely time to read the wall label.[15]

The loss of a quiet so essential to contemplation—not only in these settings but in our homes, hospitals, neighborhoods, and countrysides—is yet another clear indication of the withdrawal of meaning from our world.

---

15. Butterfield, "No Photos," para. 3.

2

Higher Education

ONE OBVIOUS INDICATION OF meaning's decline can be seen on America's college campuses. In the late sixties, an annual survey of college students revealed that 86 percent of incoming freshmen believed that developing a meaningful philosophy of life was "essential" or "very important." By 2004 that number had dropped to 41 percent.[1] In recent years, the percent of freshmen who think it important to develop a meaningful philosophy of life has remained in the forties—or about half what it was in the late sixties. The largest gap in favor of financial success over meaning occurred in 2014, when iGeners first entered college.[2] iGeners are the generation who have lived their whole lives with computer technology and their adolescence with the popular social networking sites. As we shall see, this group provides special insights into the future of meaning in America.

However, it is not merely a dramatic decline of interest in meaning that distinguishes today's college students from their grandparents. It is the manner in which many of those who hope to find meaning plan to go about it. An older generation whose search for meaning led to an ashram or the communes will find few kindred spirits among today's youth. Young people who claim to value meaning today are likely to regard it as the by-product of a life devoted to wealth. For them, the model is not the religious seeker, but the multibillionaire, who, having accumulated more

---

1. Deresiewicz, *Excellent Sheep*, 78–79; E. Smith, *Power of Meaning*, 6.
2. Twenge, *iGen*, 168.

wealth than she can possibly enjoy, may devote herself to those social problems deemed worthy of her money and attention.

While we may not wish to discourage these ambitions, we cannot help but note the difficulty inherent in such goals. We may be reminded of the old *Peanuts* cartoon in which Linus confides his dreams to Charlie Brown in this way: "I've decided to be a very rich and famous person who doesn't really care about money, and who is very humble but who still makes a lot of money and is very famous, but is very humble and rich and famous." To which Charlie Brown wisely responds: "Good luck!"[3]

Some would criticize the young for these failings. However, the young are simply the product of the world they have inherited from their elders. We need look no further than our universities for proof of this.

From the end of World War II through the late sixties American colleges and universities were at the cultural epicenter of meaning as storehouses where the words, images, and sounds of meaning were not only housed, but made accessible to young people through general education requirements and the various humanities offerings. During the period, philosophy courses examined the Big Questions, inspired, in part, by the postwar popularity of existentialism. Psychology departments still engaged with humanistic psychology then, while Freudians and Jungians (both here and elsewhere in the humanities) explored those depths of the mind where dramas of meaning unfold. Religious Studies departments of the day led the way in the sort of interdisciplinary courses where issues of meaning were often front and center. Phenomenological studies of religion—alongside, or in conjunction with, philosophy and psychology of religion courses—posited universal modes of religious experience and expression. Elsewhere, religious studies courses examined the links between religion and art or literature, according to the notion that such creative works were often either informed by religion or explored matters of ultimate concern.

Of the various humanities departments, English was the most popular for engaging with issues of meaning which spoke to the heart and mind. Here, the various literary forms—the drama, novel, diary, and poetry—attracted large numbers of undergraduate majors. English departments also brought issues of meaning to the forefront in required English courses, according to the notion that the great works of English literature (by Shakespeare, Milton, the Romantics, etc.) were capable of

---

3. Schulz, *Big Book of Peanuts*, 167.

transcending time, race, or gender, to articulate universal truths. At the time all students were expected to devote much of their first two years to thoughtful reflection through analysis of works of literature and in essays or creative writing.

The general education ideal had first taken form in 1930, at the University of Chicago, where President Robert Hutchins sought to revive classical liberal arts education through what was termed the Great Books curriculum. Henceforth the heart of general education at Chicago would be a study of the greatest works of the Western canon through a series of one year, interdisciplinary survey courses. While Hutchins's notion found its adherents, it was not until after the war that the idea of reviving classical liberal arts education really took hold. Now the chief impetus came from a 1945 Harvard faculty committee report entitled *General Education in a Free Society*. The Harvard report argued for the broad education of students in "those common spheres which, as citizens and heirs of a joint culture, they will share with others."[4] Within a few years, the ideal had not only taken hold at Harvard, but had helped to spawn the many "Western civ" courses that became a staple of undergraduate education during the postwar years. Here, students were expected to acquire a rudimentary knowledge of the great achievements of Western civilization from the Greeks onward, and to grasp the ideas that had formed, and continued to inform, the culture in which they lived.

The impact of the "Western civ" ideal extended far beyond a few required courses. The notion of a core of ideas against which to weigh and measure what was learned informed instruction throughout the humanities, where breadth of knowledge and a willingness to engage with students were valued in university faculty as much as specialized research. And not only teaching was affected. The postwar years saw the flourishing of thinkers in an array of fields whose scholarship was formed with an eye toward a broader understanding of human nature and the search for meaning.

Notable here were the many authors associated with the Bollingen Foundation, which had been established during the war years by Paul and Mary Mellon. The primary impetus for the foundation was publication of the works of C. G. Jung, whose writings ranged broadly over religion, the arts and psychology. Along with Jung, the Mellons sought out authors who, in Mary's words, "can contribute real, scholarly and

---

4. Lucas, *American Higher Education*, 270.

imaginative books about Man, and the history of his soul."[5] For more than two decades, Bollingen published works in philosophy, psychology, poetry, art, anthropology and world religions by a "who's who" of the intellects of the day, including: Joseph Campbell, D. T. Suzuki, Mircea Eliade, Erich Neumann, Erwin Panofsky, Kenneth Clark, E. H. Gombrich, Jacques Maritain, André Malraux, Heinrich Zimmer, Herbert Read, and Gershom Scholem. When the foundation became inactive, in 1968, fewer thinkers of such breadth and substance were being generated by academia. Looking back, in 1982, Paul Mellon questioned whether books like those Bollingen produced could still find a publisher.[6]

As early as 1971, the chair of the Commission on Liberal Learning of the American Association of American Colleges asserted that the humanities are "moribund" and that "narrow vocational education has captured the larger portion of political interest."[7] Six years later, the Carnegie Council on Policy Studies in Higher Education proclaimed general education "a disaster area." Christopher J. Lucas has summarized the findings on higher education from a number of additional studies of the period in this way: "Bereft of any guiding intellectual vision, most institutions of higher learning had settled for hodgepodge curricula, which thinking students rightly disdained as 'required irrelevance.' Corrupted by populism, professionalism, and assembly-line scholarship, universities had allegedly given themselves over to turning students to specialized professional careers as quickly as possible. Having abandoned their integrity to market-place flux and flow, such institutions had lost the will to insist upon any intellectual coherence or unity in their vast offerings."[8]

The rise of "multiculturalism" dealt the final blow to the old general education ideal. The last stages of the battle unfolded on a national stage in a controversy that erupted at Stanford University, where, in 1987, the Reverend Jesse Jackson led students (chanting, "Hey hey, ho ho, Western civ has got to go!") in protest of the school's Western civilization requirement. In 1964, Stanford had been one of the top fifteen American universities to require such a course. At forty-one of the top fifty American universities, these courses then satisfied a basic general education requirement. In 1988 Stanford bowed to pressure by dropping its Western civilization requirement. By 2010, none of the top fifty

5. McGuire, *Bollingen*, 49.
6. Bruckner, "Bollingen Adventure," para. 21.
7. Lucas, *American Higher Education*, 288.
8. Lucas, *American Higher Education*, 289.

American universities required the Western civilization course. By then, only sixteen even had such a course in the curriculum.[9]

"What's left at most schools . . . ," William Deresiewicz has pointed out, "are distribution requirements, a Chinese menu of columns A through C or D or F ('quantitative reasoning,' 'languages and literatures,' 'world cultures' and such-like blandeurs) that offers students no coherence."[10] The large number and varying quality of these courses is often staggering. Under its required "Humanities, Literature, and the Arts" offerings, one university recently listed 550 possibilities.[11] By offering such diversity, schools are able to satisfy faculty whims and provide students with "easy As" in courses that lack breadth and often have little or no real substance.

In defense of today's disorderly abundance, the argument is sometimes made that such courses teach young people to think. But think *about* and *with what*? The only way to think productively about meaning in life is to engage with what the best minds of the past have to say on (and in relation to) the subject through course work in fields like literature, classics, history, philosophy, and religion. By today's logic, we might as well train medical doctors by teaching methods that make no reference to the human body or have basketball players perfect their skills by maneuvers on the court without the benefit of a ball.

Some, like Deresiewicz, chiefly decry the low quality of so many of these courses, arguing that the essential point is that students read *great* books, regardless of when or where they were written. There is much to say for this. However, unless students have a core of ideas against which to weigh and measure what they learn (a core that K–12 education is also increasingly unwilling or unable to provide) even the best selections from the world's cultures will be like so many beautiful butterflies with nowhere to land. Meaning is not like a food court, where one may have a "taste" of Indian, Middle Eastern, or Mexican food. Meaning is a well from which one must drink long and deeply. And while a life of meaning is not inconsistent with breadth of knowledge—while it may, indeed, benefit enormously from exposure to different cultures and ideas—it ultimately requires focus and a commitment to one of the great traditions. This commitment must be not only intellectual but, at some point, deeply personal.

9. Thorne, "Drive to Put."
10. Deresiewicz, *Excellent Sheep*, 62.
11. ACTA, *What Will They Learn*, 24.

Remarkably enough, the call for diversity on America's campuses comes at a time when increasing numbers of the world's population are learning the English language, adopting capitalist economies, employing Western legal systems, engaging in Western science, and seeking to build Western-style democracies. In other words, we live in a world increasingly defined by Western values at the very time higher education is abandoning the study of the underlying ideas regarding human nature and the purposes of life upon which these values and the institutions that promote and support them are based. The result is a vacuum that has left the humanities vulnerable not only to gross politicization but to a growing scientism determined not merely to marginalize them, but to eradicate the notion of the human being altogether.

Having lost its faith in a common language of the human spirit, English departments by the late seventies were foundering under the assault of the deconstructionists, who reduced all literature to political utterance. Little wonder that the once-popular English major, which attracted 7.6 per cent of undergraduates in 1971, was attracting about a third as many by 2015. Today, English departments attract students by emphasizing writing (especially composition, rhetoric, and professional) in place of literature. The essential message: forget about meaning and focus on your career.[12]

Meanwhile, Religious Studies departments, once known for the breadth of their course offerings, have adopted a narrow scholarly approach that has no place for interdisciplinary studies geared to broader issues of meaning. As one recent scholar in the field describes the current situation: "Gone are the days of encompassing theories and of daring comparative studies. The more one invokes interdisciplinary studies, the less one seems to practice that dangerous sport. Safe scholarship, with clearly defined boundaries, not to be trespassed, and with no threat of unexpected results, has become the name of the game."[13]

Most disturbing has been the shift in philosophy and psychology from the notion of a coherent self that had been so central to the existentialists, phenomenologists, analytical philosophers, depth psychologists, and ego psychologists of earlier generations. According to the new ways of thinking, the self is an illusion rooted in the social dynamics of infancy, maintained by the phantoms of language, and continually manipulated

---

12. Flaherty, "Evolving English Major."
13. Stroumsa, *New Science*, viii.

by the need for political control. The purpose of recent thought (in deconstructionism, feminism and gender studies, neurophysiology, and elsewhere) is to puncture this illusion and liberate those who have been constrained by Western traditions while eliminating the notion of an autonomous self altogether. Many believe that the "healthy pluralism"[14] of a fragmented self will free us from religious dogma and enable us to take our rightful place within the animal kingdom (even as it prepares the way for those emerging technologies which point to the merger of human beings and machines).

Thus the self, like the soul before it, is destined to the dustbin of history.

In today's universities serious inquiry has taken refuge in the arena of social justice. So preeminent is this issue that it not only dominates the social sciences, but often swallows up offerings in fields like English and American History, where the subject is viewed through the lens of this or that social group (gays, lesbians, African Americans, Native Americans, Hispanic Americans, and the like) rather than with regard to common beliefs and values. Now social justice is terribly important. But politics draws strength from the very divisions that meaning attempts to overcome, and glorifies equality at the expense of those higher strivings that are essential to the attainment of meaning in life. Humanities education, as centered in the traditional general education curriculum, aimed to provide students with the basic tools necessary for crafting a meaningful life. The role of social justice was to ensure that everyone had access to these tools. From the perspective of meaning, the real value of equality is to ensure a fair beginning in a life devoted to the continuing quest for meaning. To make equality the focus of higher inquiry is to mistake proximate for ultimate goals—with disastrous consequences for meaning.

The extraordinary decline of the humanities is dramatized by the embarrassed, apologetic stance of its contemporary defenders. Some still remember when this was not the case. As late as 1973, the British economist E. F. Schumacher could argue for the superior value of the humanities over the sciences in higher education. In his little counterculture classic, *Small Is Beautiful*, Schumacher revisited C. P. Snow's famous "two cultures" debate by arguing that a familiarity with Shakespeare is intrinsically more valuable than a knowledge of such basic scientific principles as the Second Law of Thermodynamics:

---

14. Raymond Martin and Barresi, *Rise and Fall*.

The Second Law of Thermodynamics is nothing more than a working hypothesis suitable for various types of scientific research. On the other hand—a work by Shakespeare: teeming with the most vital ideas about the *inner* development of man, showing the whole grandeur and misery of human existence. How could these two things be equivalent? What do I miss, as a human being, if I have never heard of the Second Law of Thermodynamics? The answer is: Nothing. And what do I miss by not knowing Shakespeare? Unless I get my understanding from another source, I simply miss my life.[15]

Today such "elitist" views have been cast aside in favor of a preoccupation with the sciences and vocational training—to which a large dose of political ideology is added to give the illusion of deeper thought. Today, their few remaining defenders freely acknowledge that the humanities have little intrinsic value. Now the argument is made that their primary virtue lies in training young minds for good paying jobs in science and industry. This is indeed damning with faint praise.

The slow death of the humanities is evident in the enormous increase in students majoring in STEM subjects and related fields and the continuing decline in humanities majors. Between 2005 and 2015, BAs in American universities increased 29 percent. Yet English majors declined 22 percent during these years, while philosophy and religion majors dropped 15 percent. Majors in the health fields, on the other hand, doubled. The STEM subjects also experienced major growth, with engineering up 60 percent, mathematics up 54 percent, and the physical sciences rising 49 percent.[16]

From a purely institutional perspective, the loss of the many possibilities of meaning once available in higher education is the most telling sign of the end of meaning in America.

If our universities are excellent places to observe the loss of meaning, they are also a good starting point for understanding the consequences of that loss. This is evident in what amounts to an epidemic of anxiety and depression on our university campuses.

Between 2009 and 2015, the number of American college students seeking counseling grew about 30 percent. By the spring of 2017, almost

15. Schumacher, *Small Is Beautiful*, 79–80.
16. Nietzel, "Whither the Humanities."

40 percent of college students said they had experienced depression severe enough that they had difficulty functioning, while 61 percent reported experiencing "overwhelming anxiety" in the last year.[17] Today, the same issues affect these students' younger siblings. After years of stability, teenage rates of anxiety and depression saw a sharp increase between 2012 and 2016.[18] More recently, a study of some six hundred thousand adolescents and adults by the American Psychological Association's *Journal of Abnormal Psychology* (2019) demonstrated a continuing rise in depression and suicidal thoughts.[19] Such numbers may mask the extent of the problem since many young people (especially those with eating disorders or substance abuse) are reluctant to seek help for psychiatric difficulties. However, if the precise number of those who suffer is difficult to determine, the social ills that accompany these states are visible enough. In contemporary America this is evident in the various forms of addiction affecting people of all ages, but especially prevalent among the young. These include, in addition to the old standbys (e.g., narcotics, alcohol, gambling) many that are largely distinctive of the postmodern era, e.g., prescription drugs, video games, cutting and other forms of personal abuse, online pornography, and food imbalance—the last of which now comes in two varieties, viz., too much food (obesity) and too little (anorexia).

Today, these psychological disturbances are also beginning to take shape in unprecedented acts of violence among the young. Thus in addition to the age-old problem of gang violence, the dawn of the twenty-first century saw the young gravitating toward individual acts of mass violence, the most notable of which were the many school shootings. So numerous had these become that 2018 saw an unprecedented national movement among high school students trying to insure the safety of public education. Suicide rates among the young also rose during the period, with an alarming jump of 56 percent between 2007 and 2016.[20] Nor are students at our elite colleges and universities immune. Between 2013 and 2017, fourteen students at the University of Pennsylvania committed suicide, resulting in a "Campaign for Wellness" initiative that included the addition of four new therapists, the extension of hours at the school's

17. Reilly, "Depression on Campus."
18. Schrobsdorff, "Kids Are Not."
19. Bahrampour, "Depression Rising for Young."
20. Heid, "Depression and Suicide Rates."

counseling services, and the emergence of student groups determined to make a positive impact on campus life.[21]

At the heart of all this despair is what former U.S. Surgeon General Vivek Murthy has called a "loneliness epidemic."[22] A 2018 study found that 22 percent of American adults always or often feel lonely. A survey taken the next year found that 61 percent of Americans report feelings of loneliness. And loneliness is more than the experience of a loss of connection to others. Researchers speak of an "existential" loneliness that comes from the absence of any clear sense of order and purpose in our lives.[23] This is loneliness that arises from a lack of strong social and moral guidelines regarding how to behave and what is to be expected at each stage of life. Loneliness like this especially afflicts the young, who are about to enter a world of seemingly unlimited freedom without any countervailing sense of order, purpose and personal responsibility that should come with it. Thus, by 2021 eighteen- to twenty-four-year-olds had come to be the loneliest group in America.[24]

While both genders suffer from a lack of values and guidance, women seem to bear an inordinate share of the consequences. Indeed, having achieved social and economic opportunities so long denied them, American women today suffer depression rates much higher than women in poorer countries—even as their daughters lead the way in the rising rates of depression among the young. This is also why the number of young Americans of both genders receiving a "psychopathologic score" on tests for clinical depression is not merely higher today than in recent generations. It is six to eight times higher than the rate for young people who grew up in 1938—that is, during the Great Depression, when personal autonomy was sorely limited by poverty, small towns, and conservative moral principles, but life unfolded according to an orderly plan and in proximity to family and friends, church and community.[25]

That our ills are rooted in the conditions of postmodernism is suggested by a variety of studies. For example, there is research showing that Mexican Americans who are born in the United States, while wealthier than their Mexican counterparts, are more likely to suffer from

---

21. Zeitlin, "Wellness Warriors."
22. Sweet, "Loneliness Pandemic."
23. Sweet, "Loneliness Pandemic," 33.
24. Sweet, "Loneliness Pandemic."
25. Hidaka, "Depression as a Disease," 3.

depression.[26] Evidence also indicates that urban dwellers suffer from psychiatric disorders more often than inhabitants of rural communities, and that churchgoing households have lower rates of psychiatric disorders than their secular counterparts.[27] Increasing urbanization and secularization are, of course, two of the dominant features of a world that has lost touch with the basic avenues of meaning—avenues that have sustained human beings for millennia. Where such avenues of meaning remain intact, psychiatric problems are rare. In this context, it is worth noting research on the American Amish. These people have been able to maintain a culture of strong families and communities, common (largely agricultural) labor, and a vibrant religious life. All this contributes to a remarkably low MDD (major depressive disorder) level of about 1 percent.[28]

Studies designed to focus more narrowly on the issue of "meaning in life" further support the relation between meaning loss and the postmodern condition. This is apparent from a survey of 132 nations based upon data gathered by the 2007 Gallup World poll.[29] In the study social scientists observed that, when questioned whether or not their life had "purpose or meaning," residents of poor countries fared better than citizens in wealthy nations. Although meaning was not clearly defined here, the results are consistent with all that we have said regarding the major sources of meaning in life. Thus researchers observed a particularly strong relation between meaning and religious belief. Strong family ties also strongly correlated with a sense that life has meaning.

While the conditions that threaten meaning are certainly not unique to America, the United States appears to be leading the other wealthy nations in suffering the effects of meaning loss.[30] For example, life expectancy continued to rise in Europe, Canada, and Japan from 2000 to 2019. Not so in the U.S. where it leveled off in 2013 and then began to decline. Opioid use is another area where we lead the developed world, with rates in the U.S. being 2.6 times those of other wealthy societies. Our rising suicide rates also distinguish us from other postmodern societies, while our murder rates remain double or triple those of other high income nations (and have continued to rise in the COVID years, with a jump of 30

26. Junger, *Tribe*, 22.
27. Hidaka, "Depression as a Disease," 4.
28. Hidaka, "Depression as a Disease," 4.
29. Nation, "Residents of Poor Countries."
30. Rubenstein, "Life Expectancy."

percent between 2019 and 2020—the largest yearly increase in more than a century).[31] Where meaning loss is concerned, it may be that we are not simply another example of postmodern society, but the poster child for its many failings and dangers.

As debilitating as they are, the anxiety and depression that now afflict so many in America may not be the worst of fates. According to philosopher Søren Kierkegaard, despair, while a terrible malady, is still preferable to a life lived in ignorance of the fact that we are spiritual beings with longings that can be satisfied only by God.[32] We need not believe in God, however, to recognize that we are creatures of meaning, in need of connecting to something of greater and more lasting value than ourselves. If this longing is ultimately religious in nature, it is nonetheless a fundamental feature of our humanity.

Irving Singer points this out, noting that the drive for meaning is the expression of a type of curiosity "distinctive of our species." To lose this drive, says Singer, is "to revert to a lower form of consciousness."[33] In the following pages we will come to better understand this "lower form of consciousness," and observe how it is rapidly emerging within and among us.

---

31. Gramlich, "What We Know," para. 1.
32. Kierkegaard, *Sickness unto Death*.
33. Singer, *Meaning in Life*, 4.

PART TWO

Small Is Meaningful

3

Everyday Objects and Experiences

IN ITS SIMPLEST AND most straightforward forms, meaning arises unexpectedly from the everyday occurrences of life. Even a simple exchange with someone we've never met may prove meaningful, connecting us, if only briefly, to the larger human community. A chance meeting with an old friend or relative may take on a greater depth of meaning, especially when the encounter evolves beyond the simple exchange of pleasantries and proceeds to a deeper level, triggering memories and emotions that connect us to others and to the past. Meanings of this sort may be accompanied by a nostalgia that results from a renewed awareness of the passage of time and of the difficulties in maintaining such connections. Conflicting emotions like these are indicative of the depth of feeling triggered, and of the difficulty in finding an appropriate response amid the emotions of joy, regret, and sadness.

Sometimes a specific object, like an old letter, will prove to be meaningful in much the same way. While letters date to antiquity, the form really began to flourish in the eighteenth century. The value of letters became abundantly clear by the time of the Civil War, and continues to be obvious to historians today. A major source of the enormous success some years ago of Ken Burns's documentary film *The Civil War* lies in its effective use of personal letters and diaries to illuminate the experiences of politicians, soldiers, and civilians during this critical period in the nation's history. Though Burns has continued to make successful documentaries, the presence, in *The Civil War*, of such deeply felt and, on occasion, poetic ponderings, add a depth of meaning to the story that is difficult otherwise to duplicate.

Despite inroads made by the telegraph and telephone, letters remained the most valued form of communication through most of the twentieth century. The reasons for this are not hard to understand. The letter is not only ideally suited for organizing thought and expressing emotion in a meaningful way; the slow process of letter writing allows and encourages a deeper probing than the faster and more immediate communication forms. No wonder letters continue to be prized by soldiers, who value them as substantive communications in a form that lasts. Nor should we be surprised that contemporary historians despair over the decline of letter writing, recognizing that our current welter of brief and eminently disposable communications will impose severe limitations on future generations seeking to understand the present. The handwritten letter has also been valued as an exercise in hand-eye coordination that has far-reaching potential for meaning. Anyone familiar with old letters will observe how writers so often valued a pleasing hand both for its beauty and as an exercise in self-expression and control. Artists knew that handwriting developed a skill that carried over into their work.

Most remarkable in this context are the letters of Van Gogh, which often include sketches of his paintings amid wide-ranging observations on art and life. Van Gogh's letters also illustrate how the form could prove useful in recalling and recording daily experience and the surrounding world in such detail that they became not only vivid to others but inscribed in the writer's own mind. One such letter from Arles, dated July 16, 1888, describes the artist's trip to Mont Majour in the company of a friend:

> We explored the old garden together, and stole some excellent figs. If it had been bigger, it would have made me think of Zola's Paradou, high reeds, and vines, ivy, fig trees, olives, pomegranates with lusty flowers of the brightest orange, hundred-year-old cypresses, ash trees, and willows, rock oaks, half-broken flights of steps, ogive windows in ruins, blocks of white rock covered with lichen, and scattered fragments of crumbling walls here and there among the green.[1]

The letter proceeds to describe the many summer insects of the region, such as Spanish flies "gold and green in swarms on the olives" and the cicadas, "loud as frogs"—one of whom makes an appearance amid the account.

---

1. Van Gogh, *Self Portrait*, 296.

EVERYDAY OBJECTS AND EXPERIENCES 45

Letter from Vincent van Gogh to Theo van Gogh with sketch of insect
9 or 10 July 1888, pen and ink on paper. Van Gogh Museum, Amsterdam
(Vincent van Gogh Foundation).

Creative penmanship and drawing took a turn for the worse with the death of the quill pen in the nineteenth century. However, flexible steel nibs were better than the fountain pens that had taken over by century's end, or the ball points that became popular during the fifties. Today, the variety of pen is the least of the problems for self-expression in ink.[2] Now the development of handwriting and drawing is threatened by educational methods that ignore cursive altogether and limit the teaching of handwriting to kindergarten and first grade. The idea is to turn children over to the computer keyboard as quickly as possible. This despite the fact that better handwriting skills correlate with better compositions, improved reading comprehension, and stronger mental functioning generally. Never mind what their loss means for the further decline of handwriting and drawing.

Much that has been said of the letter applies to the diary. Like the letter, the diary may be a way of giving greater significance to everyday objects and events. (As novelist and diarist Virginia Woolf once observed: "I think it is true that one gains a certain hold on sausage and haddock by writing them down."[3]) However, the inward-looking character of the diary also makes it ideally suited for introspection. Indeed, the diary in America has such roots. As Tristine Rainer recounts the process:

> In seventeenth-century England Samuel Pepys and other Protestant gentlemen developed the diary as a place to confess and account for one's life to a watchful God. The American tradition of the diary came over on the *Mayflower* with the Puritans, who furthered the association of diary writing with self-discipline and self-judgment. Puritan ministers in the New World taught children to use it to keep tabs on their consciences.[4]

By the twentieth century, the diary was associated with women, and with women writers especially. Woolf and poet Sylvia Plath are notable diarists, as was aspiring writer Anne Frank, whose popular account of her long months in hiding from the Nazis has spoken to millions. The depth psychologists of the middle decades of the twentieth century also knew the value of diaries and notebooks, which were often used for recording dreams and other manifestations of the unconscious. However, by now the diary as a popular means of self reflection was losing out to the faster pace of life. The beginning of the end came in the fifties. As Rainer recalls:

> There was a widespread merchandising of one-year diaries with toy locks and keys designed for young girls. These diaries

---

2. Berger, "What We Lose."
3. Rainer, *New Diary*, 154.
4. Rainer, *New Diary*, 20.

parodied the long tradition of women's secret diaries. They also represented the tail end of the Puritan tradition of diary keeping as a self-watching, daily discipline.[5]

While recent years have seen efforts to adapt the diary form to the computer, the new technology more readily lends itself to the blog, where individuals typically record the most superficial events of daily life for public consumption. Meanwhile, shifts in the fields of psychology and psychotherapy have rendered the diary as a method of self-exploration virtually extinct. In today's psychiatric care, dream logs have given way to food diaries and sleep diaries—the former designed as a record of calorie consumption, the latter, a log of sleep disorders. Thus the diary, like many little sources of meaning once so popular, finds itself squeezed between the perils of technology and a diminished and ever-diminishing vision of human nature.

Daily encounters with nature is another simple activity that may be rife with possibilities of meaning. This is most obvious for those who work the land, from gardeners to farmers. But farms are meaningful not only for those who work them; farms provide valuable life lessons for those who live near them. If national parks and nature preserves are nature untrammeled, and cities are nature constrained, farms (at their best) are nature and humanity in balance, the farmer putting his imprint upon the natural world while respecting and maintaining it. In farms, a harmony of land, water, trees, animals, humans, machines, and buildings is visibly apparent. Here, topography is laid bare in fields in whose colors—from yellows to greens to golds and browns—the passage of the seasons are on vibrant display.

Farmer, poet, novelist, and essayist Wendell Berry has touched upon the meanings in farming in words that align perfectly with our own notion of meaning in life. Berry recognizes that "connection" is the foundation of meaning and the source of health in individual, society, and nation. "We are working well," he says of farming, "when we use ourselves as the fellow creature of plants, animals, materials, and other people we are working with. Such work is unifying, healing."[6] Berry rightly sees the decline of farming as nothing less than a harbinger of the loss of our humanity. He writes of a coming "postagricultural" world—that is, one in

---

5. Rainer, *New Diary*, 21.
6. Berry, *Recollected Essays*, 326.

which there is no place for cultures that preserve nature and rural life. His conclusion is a chilling reminder of how the end of farming is yet another harbinger of the end of the human being as we know him: "You cannot have a postagricultural world that is not also postdemocratic, postreligious, postnatural—in other words, it will be posthuman, contrary to the best that we have meant by 'humanity.'"[7]

As Berry has suggested here, the loss of meaning we are witnessing in the loss of family farms today is not limited to one aspect of culture. It affects all. Nor are Berry's fears exaggerated. Between 1948 and 2015, four million American farms disappeared.[8] And today small farms are threatened as never before by the impact of technology and globalization—trends that help agribusiness but too often destroy family farms.

While the post–World War II years saw the beginning of the great decline of the family farm, there were still plenty of woods and open spaces (not to mention freedom and time) for children in small towns and suburbs to pursue any number of backyard and neighborhood activities that brought nature to the forefront. A partial list of these would include: exploring woods, creeks, fields, and vacant lots; hunting for small animals, fish, and amphibians; watching the clouds or the stars; blowing on dandelions and making daisy chains; building forts and tree houses; making mud pies and skipping stones; damming streams and sailing little boats of leaves or twigs; searching for four-leaf clovers, birds' nests, and butterflies; catching lightning bugs and collecting rocks, leaves, and arrowheads. These and similar activities could often be pursued while going barefoot or sitting in the grass. In this way, toes and fingers came into direct contact with the physical world in a deeply meaningful way.

In his book *Last Child in the Woods*, Richard Louv has described the outdoor activities of children who grew up in the postwar era. For our purposes, the real value of his book is in revealing how nature was for postwar children a very real and enveloping presence. Afternoons and free days then were often planned according to the availability of falling leaves, swirling snow, fields of honeysuckle and clover. In Louv's book, one woman recalls the smells of a summer rain and the various opportunities it provided. Young people then, she points out, knew nothing of "bad" weather.[9] Summer storms were an opportunity for bathing suits, mud pies, and children huddling on the front porch to enjoy nature's

---

7. Berry, *Another Turn*, 13.
8. Semuels, "They're Trying," para. 9.
9. Louv, *Last Child*, 75.

pyrotechnics. It was simply by immersing themselves in nature in this way that children were led to something larger than themselves that was immensely meaningful. As Louv puts the matter:

> Nature presents the young with something so much greater than they are; it offers an environment where they can easily contemplate infinity and eternity. A child can, on a rare clear night, see the stars and perceive the infinite from a rooftop in Brooklyn. Immersion in the natural environment cuts to the chase, exposes the young directly and immediately to the very elements from which humans evolved: earth, water, air, and other living kin, large and small.[10]

Today's housing developments offer less space for nature play while community associations often have strict rules prohibiting much traditional outdoor childhood activity. Even the prototypical neighborhood vehicle, the bicycle, is on the decline—this according to a Sports and Fitness Association survey that indicated that the number of children aged six to seventeen who rode a bike regularly (more than twenty-five times a year) decreased by more than a million between 2014 and 2018.[11] Parents and grandparents who enjoyed the freedom of the outdoors themselves are now fearful that their children and grandchildren will come to harm. An increasing concern for childhood safety is even apparent in scouting, where attention is shifting from the outdoor world that Scouts originally proclaimed as their own. As one Scout leader characterized the issue some years ago: "When I was a kid, you fell down, you got up, so what. . . . Today, if a parent sends a kid to you without a scratch, they better come back that way."[12]

There is yet another danger to the meanings found in nature, and it comes from many who might otherwise be regarded as her champions. I am thinking of those (including mountain climbers, bungee jumpers, mountain bike riders, and the like) for whom nature is not a vast, all-knowing companion, but a test of individual mettle and a challenge to be overcome. In fact, the return to nature that signified a high point of the counterculture in the late sixties and seventies soon gave way to a competitive spirit that typifies so much outdoor activity today.

---

10. Louv, *Last Child*, 98.
11. Gay, "America Needs," para. 1.
12. Louv, *Last Child*, 154.

Outward Bound is one example, and it is worth noting that participants in the program have reported that just being in nature is more restorative than the more strenuous activities for which Outward Bound is famous.[13] Nor is hiking immune to the competitive impulse. Now many hikers go to the sport less for communion with nature than as a test of endurance. Notable here is the American Long-Distance Hiking Association West, whose triple crown requires thru-hikes (from start to finish) of the Appalachian Trail, Pacific Crest Trail, and the Continental Divide Trail—a total of almost eight thousand miles of terrain through parts of twenty-two states.

In all this we seem to be very far from John Muir, the great naturalist and conservationist best known as the champion of Yosemite National Park and cofounder of the Sierra Club. Muir was a self-proclaimed "tramp" who journeyed into the wilderness with no clear itinerary and with nothing more than some bread and tea for provisions. Muir's letters, essays and journals have a strong spiritual tone. In them he spoke of his need for the great outdoors as "soul hunger." The realm of plains and mountains, rivers and woods was for him not an arena of "mere sport" or "plaything excursion." It was a place of *meaning*—a place where he came to know "the Law that governs the relations subsisting between human beings and Nature."[14]

If letters were once an important means of conveying our most basic experiences, they were even more vital to romance. Edward Heyman's popular song "Love Letters," written when letters were still the standard form of communication, captures something of the potential meanings to be found in such objects.[15] "Love Letters" nicely spans the postwar period—from Dick Haymes's silky, violin-enhanced rendering (1945) to Ketty Lester's soulful, bluesy version (1962). The song reminds us that letters were then not merely a form of communication but often keepsakes, to be treasured and pondered over. The individual handwriting gave the reader a tangible sense of the writer. Women often heightened this identity by adding a fragrance to the letter. Such letters were so familiar and so personal that the act of kissing the signature, which is mentioned in the song, undoubtedly gave additional meaning to the reader.

---

13. Louv, *Last Child*, 103.
14. L. Wolfe, *Son of the Wilderness*, 88–89.
15. See "Love Letters (Song)."

Classic cinema tells us that women often kept their love letters in a special box tied with ribbons. Love letters might also appear briefly on the screen in beautiful handwriting, with stirring music playing in the background. The letter might begin "My Dearest Jack" or "My Darling Katherine" before proceeding to what today may seem to be saccharine sentiments. Such greetings were once common in love letters. By including them along with other poetic language in their films, the old writers and directors acknowledged that the words were appropriate to love, adding meanings that ordinary prose could never convey.

The capacity of letters to powerfully convey the meanings of romance is beautifully captured in Ernst Lubitch's romantic comedy, *The Shop around the Corner* (1940), which revolves around the petty conflicts of coworkers Alfred (James Stewart) and Klara (Margaret Sullavan)—each of whom is initially unaware that the other is the beloved "Dear Friend" with whom they correspond by mail. Lubitch's film was the inspiration for Nora Ephron's *You've Got Mail* (1998), which is set at the end of the twentieth century. The implications of cultural change for the meanings of romance becomes clear by comparing the films.

Lubitch's anonymous epistolists exchange references to Tolstoy's tragic love story of Anna Karenina and to the love poetry of Victor Hugo. Ephron's email friends, Kathleen (Meg Ryan) and Joe (Tom Hanks), speak of Brinkley the dog and of business concerns—the latter by reference to the less-than-romantic ancient Chinese military treatise, *The Art of War*. Not surprisingly, *You've Got Mail's* romantic climax (Kathleen's "I wanted it to be you. I wanted it to be you so badly"[16]) doesn't hold a candle to Alfred's revelation to Klara: "Klara, darling! Oh dearest sweetheart, Klara, I can't stand it any longer! Please take your key and open Post Office Box 237 and take me out of my envelope and kiss me!"[17] But then, in a culture where poetry is no longer vital, romance must necessarily lose its luster.

The same dearth of poetry where romance is the theme is evident in the language of today's popular music compared to the words of the old songs. Anyone familiar with fifties melodies is aware of how often lyricists looked to the heavens to proclaim the glories of romance. One notable example is "Stranger in Paradise," which enjoyed extraordinary success in both America and the UK in a number of versions between 1953 and 1955.[18] "Stranger in Paradise" speaks of a feeling of ascension brought on

16. Ephron, *You've Got Mail*, 1:54:15.
17. Lubitch, *Shop around the Corner*, 1:36:16.
18. Forest and Wright, "Stranger in Paradise."

by love that recalls the poet Dante's heavenward journey accompanied by his beloved Beatrice. Such sentiments were everywhere in love songs of the day—from the crooners to the doo-wop groups, country stars to teen idols. We get a sense of this simply from the titles of popular hits of the fifties and early sixties—"My Prayer," "Heaven and Paradise," "Stairway to Heaven," "Trouble in Paradise," "Venus," "Venus in Blue Jeans," "Cupid," and "The Ten Commandments of Love." To this could be added the numerous "angel" songs, including: "Johnny Angel," "Angel Baby," "Earth Angel," "Pretty Little Angel," "Pretty Little Angel Eyes," "Devil or Angel," "The Angels Listened In," "My Special Angel," "Next Door to an Angel," and "Teen Angel."

Among such songs was Cole Porter's last big hit, "True Love," which appeared in the 1956 film *High Society*. Porter is often remembered for his sophisticated lyrics, which find their poetry in understated sentiments and simple phrases. But he could also look to the heavens to try to understand love, or to thank the gods for sending him someone to adore. His last big hit, "True Love," has a soft, romantic quality in keeping with the preferences of the fifties. The lyrics, sung to a young Grace Kelley in the mellow tones of crooner Bing Crosby, go like this:

> For you and I have a guardian angel,
> On high with nothing to do,
> But to give to you
> As you give to me
> Love forever true.[19]

An internet search for the song "True Love" today will likely turn up a 2013 hit of that title by Pink.[20] Today, Pink is one of the most acclaimed performers in the world. Clearly, she speaks to today's young. And the language in her version of "True Love" is very much down to earth in its description of the anger and frustrations of young lovers. But then "true love" today is unlikely to be "forever true."

For earlier generations of Americans, photographs often had much the same significance as letters. People once kept a photograph of a loved one for years in their wallet or purse, while a single photograph of a beloved spouse or family member often appeared at one's work desk, or above the beds of soldiers, prisoners, or students away at school, stirring the imagination with the deepest longings. Locks of hair, ribbons, and

---

19. Porter, "True Love."
20. Moore et al., "True Love."

other keepsakes were similarly cherished at a time when communication was limited. Here again, the tangible features of the object, and its proximity to the loved one, provided a source of meaning that is now difficult for many to imagine.

Today photography has become easier than ever with the use of cell phones and computers. Now we have countless photos of our loved ones—as well as images of cute kitties and reminders of a recent dinner out. In fact, we have so many photographs that the images become a blur and their significance obscured. Where meaning is concerned, more is not better. A single photograph, or a few images, are able to communicate more deeply and more directly. Such images were once kept in an album to be taken out and pondered over on special occasions. Holding them gave them an intimacy that their location today, somewhere amid the millions of megabytes, fails to achieve.

One disturbing consequence of today's proliferation of images is the destruction of that immediate involvement with the world upon which meaning so often depends. Thus the popularity of photography has bred the jaded subject, whose experienced smile is indicative of the loss of that spontaneity that provides deeper insight into character. Anyone familiar with old photographs will have observed that this was not often the case. In these images we often observe the serious subject, who seems to be aware that the image is a lasting record. Sometimes we note a scowl, as if the subject (like some tribal peoples) believed that the camera was a tool for capturing their soul. In this they may not have been altogether wrong.

Today's technology has also produced the popular "selfies," which place the subject alongside friends or against the backdrop of some painting, natural wonder, or great cathedral. Planning such photographs, or staging them, often becomes an immediate preoccupation of the traveler upon arriving at a sight. In many cases, the photographs take the place of the experience itself, eliminating the sense of quiet presence that is necessary if meaning is to unfold. Such distancing from experience even has tangible dangers. This is evident from the number of photographers who are injured or killed each year by unwittingly stepping backwards off a ledge, into oncoming traffic or the like.

A diary of one's travels, or a letter or postcard—anything that requires us to thoughtfully recall events and put them into words—is more likely to bring them to mind as a treasured memory.

To say that objects like old letters or photographs are meaningful in themselves, and apart from the particular associations that give them value, would seem to be absurd. We should observe, however, that objects apparently lacking all personal relevance are capable of having meaning when perceived in a particular context or framed in a certain way.

The common fascination with historical artifacts is one good example. In museums, we may marvel at the simple craftsmanship of an early tool, or a handwritten note from centuries past, whose basic human sentiments lead us to contemplate both our common humanity and the distance that separates us from earlier human beings. Objects like these are heightened by the presence of an individual sensibility indicated by the skills of the toolmaker and the distinctive handwriting in the letter. These human touches are often valued as sources of meaning in the contemporary world. As the most tangible expressions of an individual sensibility they seem uniquely suited to engage our minds and trigger our emotions.

An appreciation of the individual character of handmade objects inspires many a lover of antique furniture. In America, regard for antique furniture is a fairly recent phenomenon, and one whose history deserves our attention. Not only is the antique a perfect example of how simple, everyday objects may attain meaning: the story of antiques is a cautionary tale about how meaning may be lost in a society that no longer has any wish to maintain ties with the past.

At the dawn of the twentieth century, the notion of the antique referred broadly to everyday objects of historical interest but little monetary worth. However, interest soon began shifting to old furniture, which was valued not merely for its historic significance, but according to the quality of workmanship and aesthetic merit. As America's fortunes in the world rose, antique furniture came to be seen as a source of national pride. By the twenties, it had assumed a prominent place in upper-end stores and museums. The latter included the American Wing of New York's Metropolitan Museum of Art, whose opening, in 1924, revealed no less than twenty period-room tableaux, each including an array of fine antique American furniture.

Briann Greenfield characterizes the American notion of the antique as referring to objects of great aesthetic and monetary value as a twentieth-century "invention."[21] Antiques were now a visible record of American history and its values, as well as an expression of the nation's aspirations toward "culture" along the lines of the European powers.

---

21. Greenfield, *Out of the Attic*.

This ambition gained additional force in the late forties and fifties when collectors began to turn from the northeastern US to fine old southern furniture. By now, antiques were no longer merely the province of the wealthy, but objects valued by middle-class Americans who searched the various venues for modestly priced pieces to help furnish their homes. These were generally placed alongside the reproductions of older furniture that were also popular at the time.

The growing interest in antique furniture went hand in hand with efforts to preserve and recreate America's past for future generations. The antique furniture collections of the Welles family, in western Massachusetts, would lead to the opening, in 1946, of Old Sturbridge Village, a complex of more than forty restored or relocated historic structures and authentic reconstructions. At the same time, in eastern Virginia, a restoration and reconstruction of the colonial capital of Williamsburg proceeded, thanks to support from John Rockefeller. The more than two hundred restored or reconstructed rooms there today house an array of valuable antiques, while the museums contain an outstanding collection of antique furniture.

The antique craze culminated in the Kennedy years, when First Lady Jacqueline Kennedy set about restoring the White House, acquiring valuable antiques to replace the undistinguished furniture that had accumulated over the years.[22] In this effort she was greatly aided by Henry du Pont, America's foremost expert on antique furniture and a man whose establishment of the Winterthur Museum, in 1951, was a further indication of the value of these objects in postwar America. The restoration of the White House, like the cultivation of the arts generally by the president and his wife, was meant to instill an appreciation of such things in ordinary Americans and give them a sense of pride in their country and their cultural inheritance.

On Valentine's Day, 1962, Ms. Kennedy joined with journalist Charles Collingswood in giving some eighty million American TV viewers a tour of the refurbished White House, pointing out many of the newly acquired furnishings and paintings. The popular and critical response was highly favorable, with Ms. Kennedy receiving an honorary Emmy for her efforts.

Today the meanings to be derived from antique furniture are clearly on the wane. While the high-end market for fine American furniture

---

22. Esposito, *Dinner in Camelot*, 32–37.

remains strong, the demand for "middle-market" furniture of the sort that once inspired middle-class Americans on weekend excursions to flea markets, estate sales, and antique stores, has grown soft. Young people now place little value on symbols of early American history and culture. Today, the comfort of over-stuffed chairs and the coolness of high-tech style (reflecting the dominance of entertainment generally in our homes) is preferable to the warmth, craftsmanship, and sense of connection to country and culture that comes from fine old furniture. Even the wealthy don't value antiques as they once did. Greenfield points out that those who once would have taken pride in a collection of fine antiques are now inclined toward "a culture of carefully crafted eccentricity and personal expression."[23] History and tradition, that meaningfully connect us to the past, are now losing out to individuality and an embrace of the new for its own sake. As we shall see, this has become a commonplace tale.

Old toys are another item that often appears in museums. One popular example is the "teddy bear," which became fashionable in Europe and America in 1906 as cuddly companions for young children. A major virtue of the teddy bears, who took their name from a popular president, was their combination of potential strength and cuteness, which made them appropriate for both boys and girls. Items for either gender have had a place in children's toy boxes since toys really came into their own in the Civil War era. Other toys are gender specific. The primary purpose of these toys has been to prepare the young for meaningful lives in accordance with the roles they are expected to play in society. In regard to meaning in life, this is a vital point. For, in addition to engaging the imagination, the teaching of attitudes and skills necessary for adulthood was once vital to the place of toys in our culture. In *Kids' Stuff: Toys and the Changing World of American Childhood*, Gary Cross has shown how today's toys fail in this vital role while planting the seeds of consumerism and dissatisfaction in young and pliable minds. In the following pages we will look to Cross, much as we looked to Louv and Greenfield, to better understand this aspect of the loss of meaning in America.

The prosperity of the postwar era in America spurred an enormous increase in wholesale value of toys, which grew from $86.7 million in 1939 to $608.2 million in 1953.[24] Still, parents demonstrated a notable conservatism in their attitude toward toys. Popular toys of the day tended

---

23. Greenfield, *Out of the Attic*, 209.
24. G. Cross, *Kids' Stuff*, 153.

to be multigenerational, the toys of the child being very much like those of the parent, thereby bonding the two in important ways. As in the past, toy manufacturers made their pitch chiefly to parents rather than children, highlighting the capacity of their wares to aid the child's development. Spending on toys was then largely limited to Christmas. The result was that new toys were associated with home and hearth—as well as with good behavior, since a popular song reminded children that Santa punished those who shouted, pouted, or cried.

An ad for Playskool from a 1946 *Parents Magazine* gives insight into the thinking of the times. The ad pictures a delighted little girl enjoying her educational toys alongside the caption, "A child at play today . . . a responsible citizen tomorrow."[25] In fact, preparation for adulthood through play was the overriding theme of the era. In addition to the requisite nesting blocks, pull toys and peg boards for tots, boys and girls were introduced to music through plastic guitars, ukuleles, and toy pianos; to art through paint sets, coloring books, modeling clay, Play Doh (1955), and Etch-a-Sketch (1960); and to the virtues of saving through piggy banks and mechanical savings banks.

Cross has noted that toys for playing grown-up roles in society were especially popular in the era.[26] Along with Lionel trains and Tonka trucks, boys had access to chemistry sets and to doctor, dentist, and detective kits. Boys were introduced to building activities through Tinkertoys, Lincoln Logs, and erector sets.

Girls were also prepared for adulthood though, sadly, their pictured future was almost exclusively domestic. Little girls of the period were given doll houses, tea sets, toy sewing machines, and bake sets—along with those few toys (games, musical instruments, and the like) that were unisex. The centerpiece of girls' toys was the baby doll. Lifelike dolls were a fairly recent phenomenon, having begun with the Patsy dolls of the twenties. Mothers who grew up with dolls like Patsy gave companion dolls (e.g., Betsy Wetsy, Tiny Tears) to their daughters in the forties and fifties.

The revolution in girls' toys came with the appearance of Barbie in 1959. Not that fashion dolls like Barbie were altogether new. Paper fashion dolls were a part of little girls' toy boxes long before Barbie. Plastic dolls of adolescent girls had also enjoyed modest popularity, though these had little girl faces and figures. Barbie was different. Barbie was

25. See illustration in G. Cross, *Kids' Stuff*, n.p.
26. G. Cross, *Kids' Stuff*, 155.

taller, with a young woman's face and a voluptuous figure. No wonder a Mattel market survey showed that mothers were not altogether receptive to the new dolls. But Barbie was the future. By 1975, baby dolls accounted for only 38 percent of the doll market—down from 80 percent in 1959. During the period the number of American doll makers declined from over two hundred to sixty.[27]

The shift from the baby doll to the babe doll had the virtue of breaking the iron hold of domesticity on little girls' toys. However, the change came at an enormous cost. Though Barbie had numerous incarnations (e.g., as rock star, nurse, and astronaut), the doll was less the liberated lady than the poster child for the self-absorption and consumerism that took hold in the seventies and eighties. Baby dolls may have been confining, but they had the great virtue of inculcating the loving, responsible behavior that is vital not only to motherhood, but to any meaningful relationship. Barbie's world ended at the altar with the wedding dress—which came along with the suburban shopper and Barbie-Q outfits in the early Barbie clothing ensembles. Little wonder that Barbie eventually became the focus of issues of sexuality. For some preadolescent girls, date rape would become a common playtime motif, with boyfriend Ken the perpetrator. Themes of pregnancy, incest, and abuse have also been commonly enacted in the Barbie play of young girls.[28]

For boys, the shift from toys designed as preparation for adulthood began with the introduction of G. I. Joe in 1964. G. I. Joe became the template for the various sci-fi action figures that would begin to dominate the boys' playbox in the late seventies and have dominated their imaginations ever since. In this shift, whatever bond existed between the boys' action toy and the world of fathers, uncles, and older brothers tended to evaporate. More importantly, the new action figures signified a world of play far removed from family and social responsibility.

By the seventies, toys were no longer seasonal items. Now Santa and his elves shared billing with the workers at the local fast-food chain, who served up toys alongside burgers and fries. Toy makers now made their pitch directly to children, bypassing their parents and overriding their concerns. Soon, erector sets, Tinkertoys, and Lincoln Logs became relegated to preschoolers, while manufacturers began to introduce sci-fi themes into their educational toys.

---

27. G. Cross, *Kids' Stuff*, 174.
28. Sugarman, "Playing the Game," 134–35.

Like the change to Barbie, the shift to G. I. Joe was not altogether unprecedented. Buck Rogers costumes, play sets, and disintegrator pistols had proven popular in the thirties. However, the postwar period had little regard for sci-fi strongmen or toy soldiers and their armaments. The primary idols for little boys came from American history and the Wild West, thus serving to create a meaningful bond between child and country. Foremost among the historical figures was Davy Crockett, who came with a coonskin cap and the motto: "Be sure you're right, then go ahead." Of course, the centerpiece in boys' fantasy play was the Western hero of film and, increasingly, television. It is important to note, however, that the requisite gunplay always came with moral strictures. Cowboy great Roy Rogers put it best in a song that proclaimed: "We taught you how to shoot straight—Hoppy, Gene, and Me."[29] Little buckaroos knew that Roy was referring not to marksmanship, but to the sense of honesty and fair play instilled by figures like Rogers, Gene Autry, and Hopalong Cassidy.

Today, Barbie remains the most popular toy ever sold, while sci-fi action figures, in their many incarnations, continue to dominate the boys' market. However, the twenty-first century has seen a notable effort to break the stereotyping of the past by popular efforts to eliminate the labeling of toys by gender. Many parents have gone even further, giving traditional boys' toys to girls and vice versa.

While a greater flexibility in toys may certainly be useful, the move to genderless toys seems not only to run counter to human nature but to exacerbate a larger social concern. As we have seen, the meaning of toys has traditionally been rooted in their capacity to develop those values and skills needed for adulthood. This is important inasmuch as meaning in life largely depends upon finding one's place in society and adopting the rituals and forms through which that role is defined. These roles and rituals are not ironclad—nor should they be, especially in a society where gender uncertainty is for some a very real issue. However, their complete obliteration further complicates a meaningful transition to adult life that is already floundering from a lack of guidelines for young men and women.

Simply put, genderless toys for all may not be the best idea in a society where young people lack direction and constraints and adolescence already extends into what was once maturity and well beyond. I will have more to say of this later.

29. Merlock, "Growing Up with Westerns," 249.

Old handmade clothes are a final example of meaningful everyday items frequently encountered in museums. For the individual, the meanings to be found in clothes would seem to be modest enough. Even the discerning dresser will likely recognize that clothes generally have less to do with personal expression than with basic social distinctions. I am referring here not simply to the clothing differences between preacher and police officer, banker and butcher, though these are part of the story. I am speaking of clothes as a way of delineating male and female, sacred and secular, adult and child, as these relate to the meanings associated with childhood and adulthood, manhood and womanhood, religion and everyday life. It is here, in the little rituals of meaning governing society, that clothes chiefly find their value—a value often greater than that of more expensive items such as cars and appliances. And it is in the loss of these little rituals, and a broader leveling of society that goes along with it, that we find a perfect microcosm of the end of meaning in America.

Handmade clothes were commonplace in the US until the twenties, when women began to buy manufactured apparel for themselves and their families. Even amid the prosperity of the postwar years, mothers often made simple outfits for girls while repairing clothes for all family members. Such items may have had special significance for the maker and the recipient. However, "store bought" was generally preferred for obvious reasons. Clothes of a certain style and brand name have for generations taken on value as manifestations of social status and continue to do so to this day.

But clothes in postwar America had other meanings apart from social status. Apparel played a vital role in enhancing the little rituals of meaning in daily life. The most obvious example of this came on Sunday mornings, when nearly half the nation's population could be found in church. At the time, the term "Sunday best" meant just what it said. In fact, many Americans had outfits that were worn only on Sundays, or on other truly special occasions. Clothes then were a very tangible expression of the central place of religion in life—a situation elsewhere evident in the purchase of special Easter attire. During the period, clothes were also an important indication of one's labor, as well as a reminder of the differences between work and leisure, home life and social activity, morning and night, young and old. Most importantly, they distinguished the sexes in ways that most at the time felt to be essential to the meanings of romantic love.

Women's fashion in the fifties stressed romance and femininity, as well as a certain extravagance in color and material that signaled the end of wartime austerity. Most influential was Dior's New Look, which had an impact on fashion throughout the decade. Popular dress styles of the era featured unpadded shoulders, nipped waists, and billowy skirts. Romantic and even extravagant cocktail dresses and formal wear were also in vogue as many Americans celebrated a return to consumerism. Color in women's clothing was rich and varied, with pinks and lavenders, apricot and orange, as well as sophisticated blues and greens inspired by Asia. Most significant of all was the variety of clothing designed to heighten the little meanings found in daily activities. As Emmanuella Daix explains:

> Different looks and garments were worn at different times of day with postwar polite society seeing a close return to nineteenth-century etiquette rules about correct behavior and good taste, which dictated the appropriateness of garments, fabrics and accessories based on occasion and place. So a Chanel tweed suit was appropriate for afternoon city excursions but would be considered too underdressed for a formal evening dinner or ball at which a Dior, Balenciaga, Fath, or James ball gown would be expected.[30]

Needless to say, not all women needed ball gowns, though men and women did their best to capture something of the romance seen on TV and the silver screen. Middle-class women also had different apparel for working at home, lunching with friends, running errands, or lounging around the house. And while high fashion may have been out of reach for most, nearly all women could accessorize, displaying their sense of taste in choice of hats, gloves, shoes, and handbags, all of which gave added significance to the little occasions of life.

Many regard the fifties as a time of stifling conformity in men, best exemplified by the ubiquitous grey flannel suit referenced in Sloan Wilson's best-selling novel of 1955.[31] But what *Esquire* had termed the Bold Look insured a surprising amount of freedom for men in the choice of many items of apparel. The Bold Look was most apparent in the wide array of colorful sport shirts in bold patterns that proved so popular throughout the fifties. But it could also be seen in ties, belts, vests, and cuff links. Even the requisite hat could be enlivened in the summer by a

---

30. Dirix, *Dressing the Decades*, 122.
31. Wilson, *Man in Grey Flannel*.

brightly colored hat band. Working men naturally required less variety in clothing than stay-at-home moms. While after-work shirts and slacks were preferred by some, many a father appeared at dinner dressed much as he had for work. Relaxation was signaled by the removal of the coat and tie or, later in the evening, by donning pajamas, robe, and slippers. The omnipresent sweat suit of today was notably absent in an era when few men exercised regularly. In any case, like rubber-soled shoes, athletic wear had its specific (and very limited) time and place.

In the fifties, genders were sharply defined by clothes, with the young generally aspiring to dress much like their parents. Though little girls (and their older sisters) occasionally wore jeans, dresses or skirts were standard in school and at social gatherings. Older girls and coeds were expected to look wholesome. Among the most popular looks on campus were Peter Pan–collared blouses, skirts, and sweaters. Girls of all ages enjoyed circle skirts, which were often paired with ballet shoes. College men sometimes wore jackets with ties, though the tendency was toward sweaters (with or without ties) and slacks. Like their parents, young people generally shunned athletic wear and knew the importance of the right clothes at the right time and place.

The sixties saw a relaxation of standards regarding proper clothing and a growing confluence of men's and women's attire. Over the decade, those little accessories that had possessed significance for men and women disappeared amid a general collapse of standards distinguishing sacred and secular, night and day, the formal and the casual. Even sleepwear was a casualty, as men began to abandon pajamas and started sleeping in their underwear. By the late sixties, denim was omnipresent among the young as a fabric that could be worn summer and winter, night and day, in casual settings and even on special occasions. As the seventies wore on, the natural fabrics and bright colors favored by the counterculture lost ground to man-made fabrics and athletic wear. Soon, the latter even began appearing at airports and restaurants—despite the protests of designers like Karl Lagerfeld, who once proclaimed sweatpants "a sign of defeat."[32]

By the nineties, the move to casual clothing was even becoming apparent in corporate offices and big law firms with the appearance of "casual Friday" and "business casual." Both movements began on the West Coast before eventually taking hold in the Eastern bastions of conservatism. In

---

32. Gay, "Sweetest Kind of Surrender," para. 17.

2016, venerable investment banker J. P. Morgan circulated an internal memo stating that casual shirts and pants might be acceptable attire. In 2019, Goldman Sachs followed suit by announcing a firm-wide flexible dress code. By now informality was also obvious in houses of worship, as suits and ties began to disappear in many mainline sanctuaries and shorts and jeans took over in the new megachurches. The same informality is apparent today in symphony halls, museums, and restaurants. In the last, patrons at least respect the notion of "no shirt, no shoes, no service," although T-shirts and flip-flops are commonplace.

Where clothing is concerned, the chief issue since 2015 has been gender distinctions.[33] In that year, a survey indicated that half of millennials viewed gender on a spectrum. Accordingly, by 2019, one newer bicoastal brand was showcasing balloon-sleeved jackets for men and boxy blazers for women. Los Angeles designers at the time were featuring clothing that was essentially genderless.

"Unisex" has grown alongside a tendency toward "unicolor" that gives additional evidence not only of the end of clothing as a modest vehicle of meaning but of the remarkable confluence of technology and visual drabness across a range of American culture. The fifties was not only the era of the grey flannel suit but a time of bright sportswear and accessories, colorful cars, and homes with brightly papered walls and upholstery. The twenty-first century is proving to be the era of the grey everything. Today, young people clad mostly in grey leave their grey offices and hop in their grey cars (having first checked their grey cell phones) and drive along grey highways to their grey homes with their grey walls. Here, they exercise on grey machines before changing to grey casual wear to relax in their grey furniture while staring blankly at their grey TVs, phones, or computers.

This explosion of grey eventually led to the fad of grey hair for women of all ages. Between 2017 and 2018, Pinterest reported a jump of 879 percent in use of the search term "going grey" by many Americans eager to follow the example of celebrities like Kim Kardashian and Lady Gaga.[34]

So ubiquitous had grey become by 2018 that a popular iPhone commercial appeared featuring young men running and jumping in brightly colored uniforms to a tune encouraging the listener to flee from the "humdrum."[35] But brightly colored phones will not eliminate the grey.

33. Gallagher, "Cut from the Same."
34. Satran, "Seize the Gray."
35. GoWireless, "iPhone XR."

Grey is the color of the postmodern world for two reasons. One is that it is the color of technology, which increasingly shuts out the glories of nature and begins to function as not only our trusted aide, but our closest companion. The second is that it signifies the union of opposites, in this case, black and white. This union is not the creative tension of yin and yang—not the harmony of "ebony and ivory" in the old Paul McCartney and Stevie Wonder song.[36] It is a *blending* in which the many distinctions that once gave so much intensity to experience and so much depth to meaning are being sloughed over and lost. Today's culture frowns upon any act of discernment—to say, for example, that this music is better than that or that one idea is more nourishing to the spirit than another. Clothes play a small part in this grey uniformity through the loss of those distinctions (e.g., night and day, formal and informal, sacred and profane, men and women, child and adult) that once met us on a daily basis and gave greater meaning to our lives.

---

36. McCartney and Wonder, "Ebony and Ivory."

4

Poetry and Art

WHILE MANY WILL GLEAN meaning from old letters or antiques, art and poetry are able to give meaning to any object by giving it a form that awakens us to its presence and integrates it into a larger world of value. The short poem "The Red Wheelbarrow," by William Carlos Williams, succeeds in giving meaning in precisely this way by illuminating a little barnyard scene in a few carefully chosen words:

> so much depends
> upon
>
> a red wheel
> barrow
>
> glazed with rain
> water
>
> beside the white
> chickens[1]

The opening words, "so much depends," generate a sense of heightened expectation that becomes meaningful through contrast to the simple wheelbarrow, whose appearance surprises us and leads us to see it as if for the first time. The wheelbarrow briefly stands alone, isolated by a few simple syllables, only to be immediately linked in a single image to the water and the chickens. The three objects are united by the symmetry of

1. William Carlos Williams, quoted in Pratt, *Imagist Poem*, 79.

the syllables in the lines (four, two, three, two, three, two, four, two) and by the location of the objects (barrow, water, chickens) at the end of the last three lines. In effect, Williams has painted a picture of a little world in which each thing attains value through its essential relation to the things around it.

Williams is associated with the Imagist movement, which began in London among British and American poets in the years just before World War I. Imagism is said to mark the beginning of modern verse. As defined by its cofounder and most famous proponent, Ezra Pound, the image "presents an intellectual and emotional complex in an instant of time."[2] We may note the union of the cognitive and the emotional, which is essential to meaning. In fact, Imagism was a reaction against the rhetorical excesses of the times (Pound proclaimed rhetoric at the furthest remove from the image) in an effort to reaffirm the immediate world of the poet's experience and to convey something of that immediacy to the reader. In this emphasis upon the immediate, Imagism was linked to French Symbolist poetry and to Wordsworth's glorious field of daffodils. It was also close (if not closer) to Japanese *haiku*, which served as an important influence upon the poets.

Pound and his contemporaries consistently maintained the primacy of the image in all poetry—Eastern and Western, ancient and modern. What was new here was a concreteness that gave enormous weight to ordinary objects and experiences and a concision that not only heightened the emotional impact of the poem but made certain demands upon the reader. As William Pratt has pointed out, Imagism relies upon some implicit notion of an "ideal world" lying within or beyond everyday experience.[3] This spiritual reality was widely accepted in Wordsworth's time and by the Buddhist culture that framed the *haiku*. Symbolism, too, had embraced the notion of a greater truth, and Pound had it in mind when he referred to "absolute rhythm" and "permanent metaphor" in his writings on verse.[4] Pound's contemporary, T. S. Eliot, found his truth in Christianity, while the great Irish poet, William Butler Yeats, located it in mysticism and the occult. When Yeats once observed that he did not think he could "live" without religion he might just as well have been speaking of his poetry.[5]

2. Pratt, *Imagist Poem*, 18.
3. Pratt, *Imagist Poem*, 34.
4. Pratt, *Imagist Poem*, 34.
5. Yeats, *Autobiography*, 15.

It is precisely this sense of something "higher"—something that gives greater and more lasting value to the momentary—that began to be lost in the last half of the twentieth century. The most prominent poet of the postwar years, Wallace Stevens, acknowledged this loss while placing his faith in a "supreme fiction" that might take the place of organized religion. However, to prove truly meaningful, poetry must be rooted in a metaphysics rather than try to be a substitute for it. By the fifties, many American poets were following the lead of many other Americans, looking within and adopting a variety of psychologies in their search for a sustaining truth. Sadly, the inner world proved to have its own limitations. The best of a later generation of poets, John Ashbery, labored under the death of all certainties, including a coherent self. I will have more to say of this shortly.

Imagism has a storied history in modern literature, with important links to prose as well as poetry. The "privileged moment" of the Imagist poet is akin to those "epiphanies" that are widely associated with major modern novelists like William Faulkner, James Joyce (who wrote Imagist verse), and Virginia Woolf—that is, moments in which the "trivialities" of everyday life acquire the character of a revelation. The Imagist method is apparent in the longer verse of Eliot, Stevens, and the later Pound, while the Imagist influence extended into the fifties and sixties through the work of an array of poets, as well as groups like the Beats, the Black Mountain poets, and the "deep-image" poets. The last, who rose with the counterculture, also turned to depth psychology and Symbolist aesthetics to provide a meaningful foundation for their work. Other major poets who came of age in the postwar years (e.g., Theodore Roethke, Alan Ginsberg, Gary Snyder) looked to Buddhism or to the mystics for inspiration and meaning.

While the major modern poets typically perfected their craft working in relative isolation and while toiling, for example, as bankers (Eliot), insurance executives (Stevens), or physicians (Williams), the postmodern poet is usually cloistered in the university, thanks to the continued popularity of creative writing programs that began in the sixties. Today, such programs (which, by 2012, were turning out some twenty thousand poets a decade[6]) are virtually essential to a poet's career. This hot-house environment isolates poets from human affairs and encourages both a writing "on demand" mentality and a similarity in style that has been

---

6. Chasar, *Everyday Reading*, 217.

widely observed.[7] It may be that the need to move outside the academic world to earn one's bread provides an independence vital to the flowering of imagination. Dana Gioia suggests this in looking at Eliot and Stevens as poets who allowed their work to flow from within, following its own, sometimes slow path of development. Gioia points to poets Paul Valéry and Rainer Maria Rilke, who endured years of silence—silence that provided fertile soil for their greatest creations.[8]

But this is only part of the story. The broader collapse of humanities education has deprived generations of young writers of that larger realm of ideas that was so vital to the work of poets like Eliot, Pound, and Stevens. Wordsworth's notion that the poet should not only "feel" but think long and deeply is now rarely taken to heart. Today, too many American poets believe that all that really matters is that the poem be "sincere." Thus the countless poems that, though written well enough, move along the surface without the depth that is achieved when thought and feeling come together in a powerful image or phrase. Today's writing programs turn out too many poets for whom feeling is all.

Meanwhile, the "image" has been discredited. This began in earnest in the seventies with poet (and eventual US poet laureate) Robert Pinsky, whose book-length essay, *The Situation of Poetry* (1976), proved enormously influential. In his book, Pinsky argued that poets needed to adopt "prose virtues," and he reacted to the drift toward abstract language in recent verse by urging "discursiveness"—an approach that was at odds with the Imagist call for conciseness. By the eighties, a distrust of Imagist values was apparent in most American poets. In his introduction to *The Vintage Book of Contemporary American Poetry* (1990), editor J. D. McClatchy pointed out that poets were now wary of the "Privileged Moment." McClatchy added that this is especially evident in Ashbery. "In John Ashbery's work such epiphanies are deflected or forgone," notes McClatchy, "his poems slide among possibilities, distrustful of intensity or flourishes."[9]

Ashbery is important to us for a number of reasons. For one thing, he is a poet who originally adopted the Imagist aesthetic before turning from it in his mature work and achieving what Harold Bloom has called a "triumphant centrality" of style.[10] For another, his work developed outside the university, allowing it to evolve at its own pace. Ashbery spent

---

7. Bawer, "Poetry and the University."
8. D. Gioia, "Business and Poetry."
9. McClatchy, *Vintage Book*, xxvii.
10. Lehman, *Beyond Amazement*, 22–23.

more than twenty-five years working as a copywriter, translator, art critic, and art editor before achieving fame, in 1976, when his *Self-Portrait in a Convex Mirror* won all three of America's most prestigious literary awards. It is difficult to imagine his verse absent such a background. And this leads to the third reason for looking at Ashbery, which concerns his engagement with the larger intellectual currents of his day. A perfect example of this engagement can be found in his poem "Syringa," where Ashbery questions the poet's ability to find meaning in a world where belief in anything enduring has lost its hold.

The subject of "Syringa" is Orpheus, the hero of Greek mythology, who is remembered chiefly for two things: one is his ability to charm all of nature with his song, so that even rocks and trees would dance; the second is his failure to retrieve his beloved Eurydice from the shadowy underworld when he disobeyed the command of the gods and turned to look for her as they were about to emerge into the light. In "Syringa" Ashbery weaves these two themes together to illuminate the contemporary poet's plight.

> Orpheus liked the glad personal quality
> Of the things beneath the sky. Of course, Eurydice was a part
> Of this. Then one day, everything changed. He rends
> Rocks into fissures with lament. Gullies, hummocks
> Can't withstand it. The sky shudders from one horizon
> To the other, almost ready to give up wholeness.
> Then Apollo quietly told him.: "Leave it all on earth.
> Your lute, what point? Why pick at a dull pavan few care to
> Follow, except a few birds of dusty feather,
> Not vivid performances of the past." But why not?
> All other things must change too.
> The seasons are no longer what they once were,
> But it is the nature of things to be seen only once,
> As they happen along, bumping into other things, getting
>   along
> Somehow. That's where Orpheus made his mistake.
> Of course Eurydice vanished into the shade;
> She would have even if he hadn't turned around.
> No use standing there like a grey stone toga as the whole
>   wheel
> Of recorded history flashes past, struck dumb, unable to
>   utter an intelligent
> Comment on the most thought-provoking element in its
>   train.

Only love stays on the brain, and something these people,
These other ones, call life. Singing accurately
So that the notes mount straight up out of the well of
Dim noon and rival the tiny, sparkling yellow flowers
Growing around the brink of the quarry, encapsulizes
The different weights of the things.
                                    But it isn't enough
To just go on singing. Orpheus realized this
And didn't mind so much about his reward being in heaven
After the Bacchantes had torn him apart, driven
Half out of their minds by his music, what it was doing to
    them.
Some say it was for his treatment of Eurydice.
But probably the music had more to do with it, and
The way music passes, emblematic
Of life and how you cannot isolate a note of it
And say it is good or bad. You must
Wait till it's over. "The end crowns all,"
Meaning also that the "tableau"
Is wrong. For although memories, of a season, for example,
Melt into a single snapshot, one cannot guard, treasure
That stalled moment. It too is flowing, fleeting;
It is a picture of flowing, scenery, though living, mortal,
Over which an abstract action is laid out in blunt,
Harsh strokes. And to ask more than this
Is to become the tossing reeds of that slow,
Powerful stream, the trailing grasses
Playfully tugged at, but to participate in the action
No more than this. Then in the lowering gentian sky
Electric twitches are faintly apparent first, then burst forth
Into a shower of fixed, cream-colored flares. The horses
Have each seen a share of the truth, though each thinks,
"I'm a maverick. Nothing of this is happening to me,
Though I can understand the language of birds, and
The itinerary of the lights caught in the storm is fully
    apparent to me.
Their jousting ends in music much
As trees move more easily in the wind after a summer storm
And is happening in lacy shadows of shore-trees, now, day
    after day."

But how late to be regretting all this, even
Bearing in mind that regrets are always late, too late!
To which Orpheus, a bluish cloud with white contours,

Replies that these are of course not regrets at all,
Merely a careful, scholarly setting down of
Unquestioned facts, a record of pebbles along the way.
And no matter how all this disappeared,
Or got where it was going, it is no longer
Material for a poem. Its subject
Matters too much, and not enough, standing there helplessly
While the poem streaked by, its tail afire, a bad
Comet screaming hate and disaster, but so turned inward
That the meaning, good or other, can never
Become known. The singer thinks
Constructively, builds up his chant in progressive stages
Like a skyscraper, but at the last minute turns away.
The song is engulphed in an instant in blackness
Which must in turn flood the whole continent
With blackness, for it cannot see. The singer
Must then pass out of sight, not even relieved
Of the evil burthen of the words. Stellification
Is for the few, and comes about much later
When all record of these people and their lives
Has disappeared into libraries, onto microfilm.
A few are still interested in them. "But what about
So-and-so?" is still asked on occasion. But they lie
Frozen and out of touch until an arbitrary chorus
Speaks of a totally different incident with a similar name
In whose tale are hidden syllables
Of what happened so long before that
In some small town, one indifferent summer.[11]

    At the poem's beginning, Orpheus is characterized as a poet who rejoices in "the glad personal quality / Of the things beneath the sky." By these words Ashbery is telling the reader that the poet happily assumes that nature speaks to him in intelligible ways. It is precisely this assumption that the poem calls into question. Orpheus first recognizes his dilemma when he turns to look for Eurydice, only to discover she is not there. In fact, she would have been absent whether he turned to look for her or not. The poet has forgotten that the things of this world appear only once. Much as syringa has the ability to destroy stone, so does life move as a vital force bringing ruin to all constructions, whether of stone, bone, or words. Hence Orpheus's lament, which pulverizes stone—just

---

11. Ashbery, *Houseboat Days*, 69–71.

like the little yellow flowers of the poem's title, whose lovely blooms spring from their roots in broken rock.

Although Orpheus's song is the song of ever-changing nature, he is a poet for whom change is not enough. Orpheus searches for a point where things come together, only to see his carefully crafted forms fall apart:

> The singer thinks
> Constructively, builds up his chant in progressive stages
> Like a skyscraper, but at the last minute turns away.
> The song is engulfed in an instant in blackness

Orpheus turns away, losing the poem in blackness just as Eurydice disappeared into the dark shadows of the underworld when he imagined her as something solid and unchanging. Even Orpheus shifts form. This is made clear in the poem when the poet reappears as the most evanescent of shapes—"a bluish cloud with white contours." However, the poet is not like the horses mentioned in the poem, who recognize the music of sky and trees in a summer storm but think themselves immune to mutability. The poet *knows* that his is the task of grasping a world of incessant movement by means of a consciousness that is itself ever changing. Ashbery renders this difficulty by personifying both the poem and its subject (and distancing one from the other) in this way:

> Its subject
> Matters too much, and not enough, standing there helplessly
> While the poem streaked by, its tail afire, a bad
> Comet screaming hate and disaster, but so turned inward
> That the meaning, good or other, can never
> Become known

Orpheus's change in appearance also marks his transformation from poet to historian. Thus even as he is transformed into a "bluish cloud," his words are changing from a poet's regrets to the historian's record of events:

> these are of course not regrets at all,
> Merely a careful, scholarly setting down of
> Unquestioned facts, a record of pebbles along the way

This link had been hinted at earlier in the poem, when history is characterized in language ("the whole / wheel/ Of recorded history flashes past, struck dumb, unable to utter an / intelligent / Comment on the most thought-provoking element in its train") much like that used above to characterize the poem.

The association of poet and historian is natural enough. Poet Robert Penn Warren once declared that "historical sense and poetic sense should not, in the end, be contradictory." Warren regarded poetry and history as alike as ways of giving meaning to our world, the chief difference being that poetry is "the little myth we make," while history is "the big myth we live, and in our living, constantly remake."[12] Ashbery sees the matter differently. For Ashbery, poetry and history are alike in their failure to meaningfully grasp a reality that is always retreating into the past. The poet dramatizes this by concluding with reference to the fate of any historical record of the departed and their world:

> they lie
> Frozen and out of touch until an arbitrary chorus
> Speaks of a totally different incident with a similar name
> In whose tale are hidden syllables
> Of what happened so long before that
> In some small town, one indifferent summer.

For us, the real issue here is the one raised by David Lehman: "Does Ashbery's poetry yield meanings, or does it militate against the very possibility of articulating them?"[13] Ashbery's poetry is certainly cognitively and emotionally engaging. Yet the world of "Syringa" is one where belief in something higher and more permanent has lost its hold. It is a postmodern realm of flux where the poet is no longer able to realize something of "lasting value."

The beginning of the twenty-first century saw the popularization of poetry in poetry "slams," cowboy poetry, and rap. The continuing growth of technology has led to an explosion of verse. Writing in 2012, Mike Chasar could observe:

> My recent "poetry" search on eBay netted over 105,000 results (over 464,000 when I checked the "include description box); my search on Google produced 142 million results; Poetry Daily receives a million hits per month; and David Alpaugh estimates that one hundred thousand poems are printed in print and online literary magazines each year."[14]

Like the surfeit of information generally, this excess of poetry has come at a cost. We have already noted the effect of the institutionalization

---

12. McClatchy, *Vintage Book*, xxiv.
13. Lehman, *Beyond Amazement*, 18.
14. Chasar, *Everyday Reading*, 218.

of poetry on the quality of verse. To this we may add the problem of superabundance, which has made it almost impossible for readers to distinguish the bad from the mediocre, the exceptional from the merely good. In 2014, the monthly magazine *Poetry* received one hundred thousand submissions for the three hundred poems they chose to publish.[15] The situation is so bad that some poets and critics have argued that, to save poetry, we must return it to the state of secrecy and seclusion that it possessed before the advent of creative writing programs and the internet. James Longenbach has noted that the recent audience for poetry "has been purchased at the cost of poetry's inwardness: its strangeness."[16] Like many others, Longenbach fondly recalls poets like Dickinson, who embraced isolation while welcoming the idiosyncrasies of her verse.

In recent years, poetry has taken a notable turn for the worse with the rise of those "instapoets" who employ social media to promote their work. Successful instapoets include the reclusive Canadian writer known as Atticus, and the Punjabi-Canadian versifier Rupi Kaur, who relishes her celebrity. Atticus's poems are of the sort one expects to find on T-shirts—which is not surprising given that they adorn a line of caps, tote bags, and jewelry available online under the writer's imprimatur. Kaur's verse is a little less Imagistic and comes closer to prose. Neither writes the kind of verse capable of engaging the mind and senses so as to gently awaken us to the surrounding world (like Williams) or startle us with the power of a revelation (as Ashbery so often does). Both have achieved fame and fortune better poets can only dream of.

Critical comments like these have themselves often been criticized. Indeed, in today's fervent embrace of a vapid equality in all things, even Harvard professors believe there's plenty of room for bad verse. This is the view of Harvard English professor Stephanie Burt, who tells us that providing meaning is only one of a large number of things that a poem may succeed in doing. According to Burt, poetry can also "help you quit your job or find a new one, give you pleasures like those you might get from crosswords or sewing or playing basketball or contemplating a mathematical proof, and (maybe most of all) show you that you are not alone."[17]

As we shall see, Burt's view is similar in some ways to that of contemporary art critics, for whom merely describing works of art and

15. Simon, "Writers Love to Hate," para. 43.
16. Longenbach, *Resistance to Poetry*, 6.
17. Burt, "There Is a Poem," para. 12.

locating them within the current art scene is preferable to probing for a deeper purpose. We are very far indeed from Stevens's ambition for a "supreme fiction" or Shelley's notion that the poets are "the unacknowledged legislators of the world." And if this is the future of poetry, as some now believe, we may wish to ponder the words of a true poet:

> Meanwhile, it seems to me often,
> Better to slumber than live without companions, like this,
> So to linger, and know not what to begin or to utter,
> Or, in such spiritless times, why to be poet at all?[18]

In Western painting, attempts to capture the potential meaning of everyday objects is most often associated with the still life, whose emergence to serious status is associated with the work of the eighteenth-century French artist Jean-Baptiste Simeon Chardin. In Chardin's day, French painters tended to render assembled objects with cool precision, arranging them so that they bore little relation to one another. Chardin saw them differently. "When we look at the objects around us," noted Chardin, "we observe a sort of *liaison* between them, produced by the atmosphere that envelops them and by all kinds of reflections which somehow make each of them partake of a general harmony."[19] Such close observation was joined in Chardin's work to that "feeling" which the artist once cited as the one truly indispensable tool of the painter. This union is apparent in the still lives, where Chardin adopted the approach of the esteemed "history" painters of the day, carefully arranging everyday forms to indicate a relation between them and rendering them with feeling generally reserved for human subjects.

Still Life of Kitchen Utensils is a good example of Chardin's mature style, which so often delights in the objects one might expect to find in the typical bourgeois kitchen. As Williams has done in the poem of the wheelbarrow, Chardin has drawn our attention to items joined by a common purpose, which here has to do with the preparation of food. Once again, the link is not merely logical, but formal. We will note that the composition is organized as a series of curves, beginning with the pitcher to the left and embracing the eggs, bowl, fish and pot before ending with the pitcher at the right. Touches of radiant light further unite the work,

18. Friedrich Hölderlin (d. 1843), as cited in E. Heller, *Disinherited Mind*, 50.
19. Rosenberg, *Chardin*, 68.

as does a frame suggested by the wall and ledge. Through such means, Chardin, like Williams, has evoked a little world of the everyday in which objects take on a timeless, universal significance.

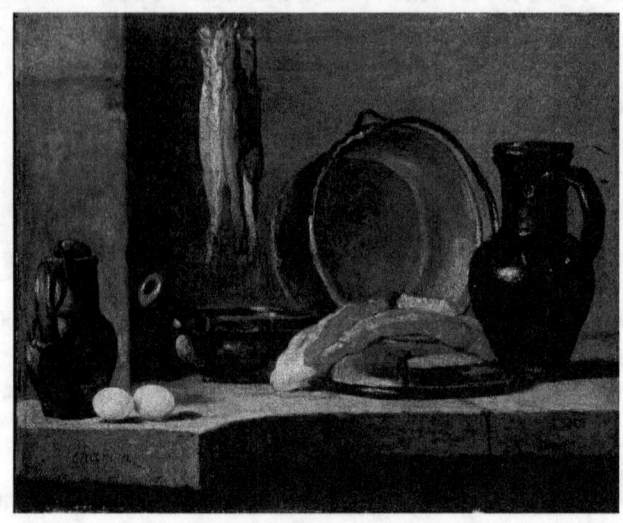

Jean-Siméon Chardin, *Still Life of Kitchen Utensils*, c. 1733–34, oil on canvas. Ashmolean Museum, Oxford, WA1927.3.

Chardin's compositions anticipated Cézanne's still life's, while his brushstrokes inspired Van Gogh, who occasionally treated everyday objects symbolically to give them deeper meaning. The symbolism of everyday objects was even more pronounced in the works of the surrealists, and in the surrealist-inspired boxes of American artist Joseph Cornell (d. 1972). Cornell was among the foremost artists of postwar America, and a man responsible for creating his own art form. He was also a poet, who traced his lineage to the Symbolists—and an alchemist, capable of instilling objects of everyday life with enormous meaning.

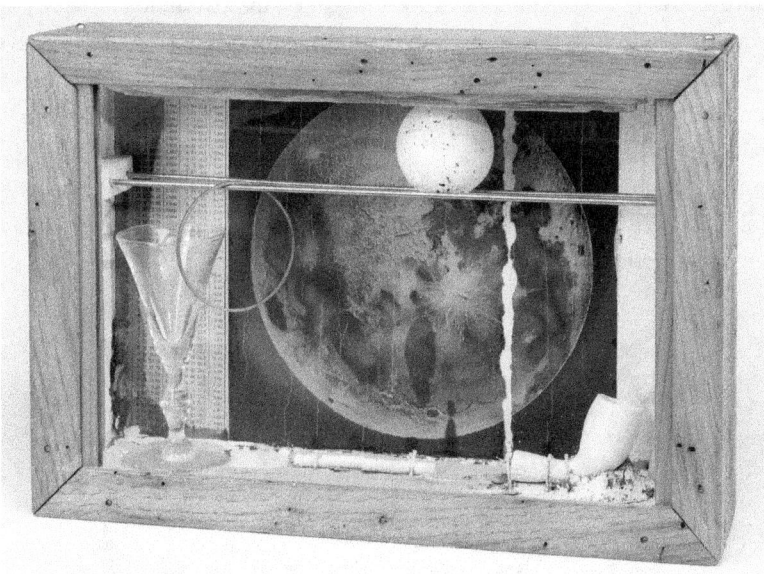

Joseph Cornell, *Soap Bubble Set*, ca. 1959, mixed media. Amon Carter Museum of American Art, Fort Worth, Texas 2009.3 ©The Joseph and Robert Cornell Memorial Foundation/licensed by VAGA at Artists Rights Society (ARS), New York.

Soap Bubble Set from Cornell's *Lunar Space Object* series may remind us of Chardin in its repetition of forms and its clear system of horizontals and verticals. But while Cornell has organized his objects to join them in a harmony of color and shape, their primary purpose here is to evoke a range of associations revolving around space, flight, orbits, and luminescence. Chardin, we may say, arranged his forms to reveal their underlying essence, as rooted in everyday life. Cornell recognizes in the everyday a power to evoke other realms of being. Hence the twofold significance of his glass-covered box, which gives the viewer a sense of peering into a private little world even as she seems to look out through a window into the beyond.

Cornell was one of a number of outstanding American artists capable of producing works of great meaning in the forties and fifties. As we noted earlier, older artists like Burchfield, O'Keeffe, and Marin were still producing remarkable works of art in the period. Outstanding paintings were also being produced by the more abstract painters, like Willem de Kooning, Mark Rothko, Robert Motherwell, Arnold Gottlieb, and Jackson Pollock. Some of these younger artists found inspiration in Native American culture. Many also looked to existentialism or the psychology of the collective unconscious and its archetypes for meaningful forms and imagery. The important place of the latter is most apparent in de Kooning's famous renderings of the archetypal female—or what the artist called "the female painted through all the ages, all those idols."[20] Archaic forms were also present in the work of Rothko and Gottleib, and appear in the totems in Pollock's early painting, while persisting as an undercurrent in the artists' later abstractions.

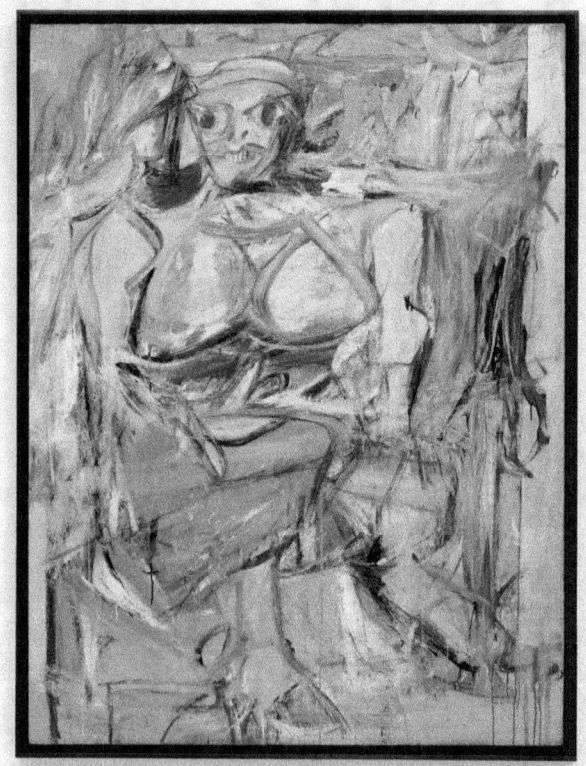

Willem de Kooning, *Woman, I*, 1950–52, oil on canvas.
The Museum of Modern Art, New York.

However, by the late forties, the meaning of such forms was becoming secondary to the meanings derived from the act of painting itself. Now the Abstract Expressionists were working much like the popular bebop performers, for whom melody was primarily a springboard for spontaneous

20. Sandler, *Triumph of American Painting*, 133.

creative forms. In describing his own compulsion to "act" upon the canvas, Pollock likened the creative process to that of nature itself.[21] Motherwell, who had studied philosophy (and who, like Pollock and the others, had been influenced by the ideas of the artist, Theosophist, and European expatriate Piet Mondrian) employed the language of the spirit to express much the same thing. At a symposium on abstract American art held in 1951, Motherwell acknowledged that some may reasonably think that the new artists cared for nothing but the act of painting itself. But this was not entirely true. In a world of alienation, artists had discovered, in abstraction, "a form of mysticism" capable of wedding themselves to the universe and healing the divisions within. Abstract art is a true mysticism, Motherwell concluded, or, rather, "a series of mysticisms that grew up in the historical circumstance that all mysticisms do, from a primary sense of gulf, an abyss, a void between one's lonely self and the world. Abstract art is an effort to close the void that modern men may feel. Its abstraction is its emphasis."[22]

While Abstract Expressionism was at its height and Cornell was still fashioning his boxes in his Flushing, New York, home, Robert Rauschenberg was scouring the New York shops in search of objects for his "combines"—so named because they typically include a frame with (or without) canvas in an art work combining painting, collage and assemblage. Cornell organized his boxes from the perspective of a poet; Rauschenberg saw his combines with a materialist's eye. When friend and critic Barbara Rose once suggested to the artist that the images in his works were "allusive, like poetry," he corrected her by pointing out that they were merely "facts."[23] The visual glue that holds these facts together is the brushstroke of the Abstract Expressionists, for whom drips and smears had meaning as direct manifestations of the unconscious depths or as efforts to bridge the gap between self and world. In Rauschenberg's hands, they are merely style.

As if to make this clear, in 1953 Rauschenberg obtained a drawing from de Kooning, which he proceeded to erase. At the time, de Kooning was in the middle of the series of monumental female figures. However, the notion that art could convey such timeless and deeply felt truths was alien to Rauschenberg's way of thinking. Although the younger artist proclaimed his erasure of the de Kooning an act of homage, this was true only with regard to the Abstract Expressionist *style*. From the perspective of Abstract Expressionist *meaning*, it was an act of pure obliteration.

21. Solomon, *Jackson Pollock*, 116.
22. Chipp et al., *Theories of Modern Art*, 564.
23. Barbara Rose, *Rauschenberg*, 114.

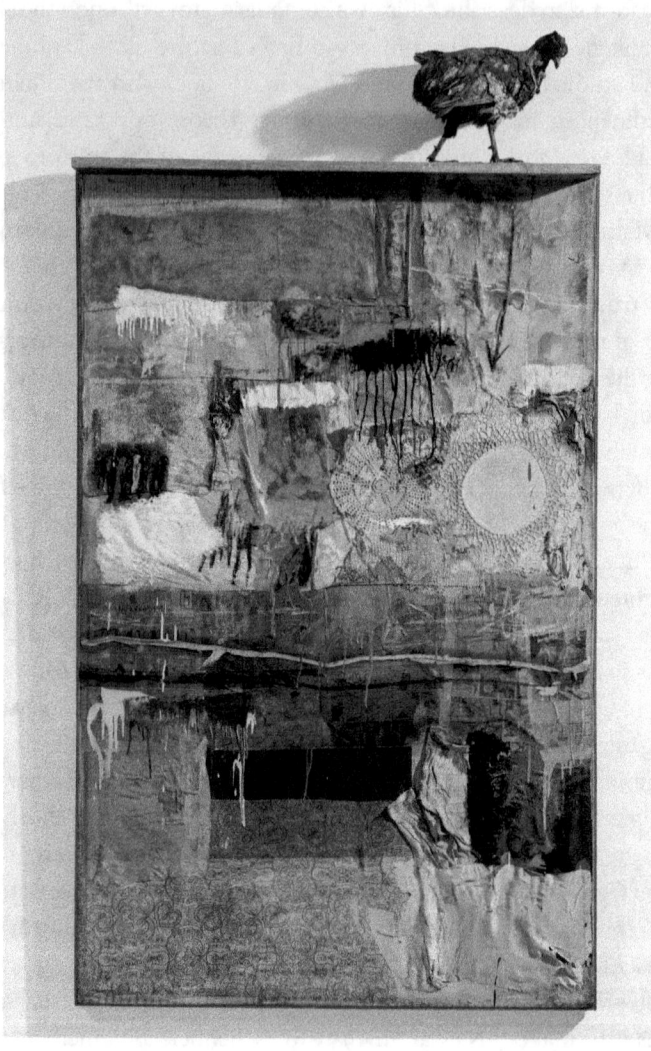

Robert Rauschenberg, *Satellite*, 1955, oil, fabric, paper, and wood on canvas with stuffed pheasant. Gift of Claire B. Zeisler and purchased with funds from the Mrs. Percy Uris Purchase Fund. Inv. N.: 91.85. Whitney Museum of American Art, New York.

A notable example of Rauschenberg's technique can be seen in the work *Satellite* from 1955. *Satellite* consists of a long vertical canvas covered with fabric and newspaper clippings and painted with bright bands of color rendered in Abstract Expressionist-style brushstrokes. Atop the frame, to the right, is a stuffed pheasant. Although the canvas is beautifully balanced between horizontal and vertical elements, bright and subdued color masses, close detail and dripping paint lines, the pheasant is really the vital visual ingredient here—a fact that is accentuated by a downward pointing arrow painted in the upper right corner of the canvas, just below the bird. Rauschenberg once said that he thought the insertion of objects like the pheasant ennobled them.[24] However, in *Satellite* we are very far from the poetry of Cornell's *Soap Bubble Set*, with its heavenly colors and forms. Deprived of its tail feathers and yanked into the composition by the arrow, Rauschenberg's bird is incapable of generating either physical or metaphysical flight.

If Rauschenberg was an ironist in his relation to Abstract Expressionism, Andy Warhol was a nihilist who launched a frontal assault upon the fundamentals of meaning in art. Warhol's method was simplicity itself. Western artists had traditionally endowed art with meaning in two ways: by choosing subjects that were inherently meaningful (i.e., "history" painting) or gained meaning by relation to other conceptions (i.e., the symbol); by the unique style of the artist, whereby form itself became a means of integrating objects and joining them to larger philosophical or psychological themes. Beginning in the late fifties, Warhol sought to eliminate meaning at its roots by painting meaningless objects in a totally meaningless style.

Lacking real imagination, Warhol initially asked friends for suggestions as to what to paint before hitting upon his method. He began by paintings of funny paper characters (e.g., Popeye, Nancy) to which a few Abstract Expressionist-style brushstrokes were added. However, this was too much meaning. Warhol then produced thirty-two separate paintings of Campbell's soup cans without any gestural embellishment—which still seemed like too much meaning. Finally, at the suggestion of a Los Angeles gallery owner, Warhol reconfigured the soup can paintings as a single work, showing them as they may appear in a soup factory or grocery shelf, to all intents and purposes depriving them of their uniqueness or any value by association.[25] The appearance of Warhol's thirty two *Campbell's Soup Cans* in the Ferus Gallery in July 1962 signaled the emergence of Warhol and the broader acceptance of pop art.

24. Barbara Rose, *Rauschenberg*, 59.

25. Gompertz says that the paintings actually have subtle differences in brushwork and label design (*What Are You Looking At*, 304–5). The viewer will decide whether this sufficiently counters the assembly-line character of the canvases.

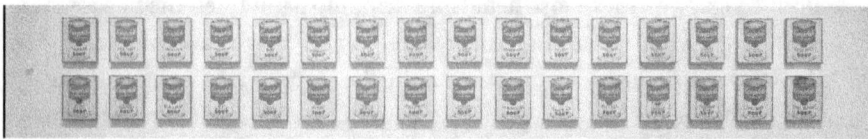

Andy Warhol, *Campbell's Soup Cans*, 1962, synthetic polymer paint on thirty-two canvases, each 20x16. Gift of Irving Blum; Nelson A. Rockefeller Bequest, gift of Mr. and Mrs. William A. M. Burden, Abby Aldrich Rockefeller Fund, gift of Nina and Gordon Bunshaft in honor of Henry Moore, Lillie P. Bliss Bequest, Philip Johnson Fund, Frances Keech Bequest, gift of Mrs. Bliss Parkinson, and Florence B. Wesley Bequest (all by exchange). The Museum of Modern Art, New York.

At this point, Warhol's evolution was still incomplete. Soon images of mass production were being supplemented by mass produced art, as Warhol turned from painting to silk screen. Warhol now referred to his studio as "the factory," and he hired a staff to fashion his paintings. On one occasion, Warhol is said to have acknowledged, "I am a machine." This cheerful admittance said it all regarding the changing character of American art. Some twenty years earlier, the Abstract Expressionist star, Jackson Pollock, had proclaimed that he was nature.

Although Warhol's work signaled the most direct assault upon meaning in art, it did not stand alone. By the sixties, a number of artists were jettisoning meaning like so much excess baggage. Many of these artists were influenced by critic Clement Greenberg, who emerged to prominence in the postwar years. Greenberg was philosophically a materialist and critically a formalist. He was also an early advocate of Abstract Expressionism, whose spiritual ambitions he completely ignored. In Greenberg's view, Abstract Expressionism was important for having abandoned "illegitimate content"—by which he especially had in mind religion, mysticism, and political certainties.[26] The history of painting, as Greenberg understood it, was an ongoing quest to uncover those physical features (e.g., purity, flatness) that he regarded as essential to its nature. The result was paintings whose significance extended no further than the physical form before the eye.

Greenberg's ideas proved popular among a number of major artists of the sixties, including Frank Stella and Kenneth Noland. In 1959 a young Stella showcased his early style in a series of pin-striped paintings on shaped canvases exhibited at MOMA. In a famous artist's statement, in

---

26. Doss, *Twentieth-Century American Art*, 126.

1964, Stella defined his views in Greenbergian terms: "My painting is based on the fact that only what can be seen there *is* there. It really is an object."[27]

Noland's paintings at the time bore a general similarity to Stella's, the chief difference being that Noland preferred bands of color to pinstripes.

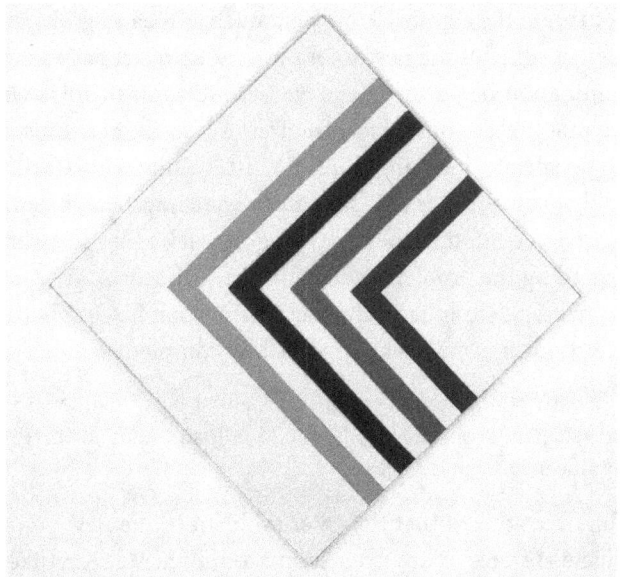

Kenneth Noland, *Drive*, 1964, acrylic on canvas, 69 ½ x 69 ½ inches; Saint Louis Art Museum, Museum Purchase 149:1966; ©2023 The Kenneth Noland Foundation/ licensed by VAGA at Artists Rights Society (ARS), New York.

In a review of Noland's work, in 1964, *New York Times* art critic John Canaday made the vital point regarding art of this sort:

> The trouble with an art of color decision is that color decision has always been a concern of the artist along with line decision, form decision, relationships decision, space decision, iconographical decision, and a dozen other decisions taken for granted as preliminaries in the creation of paintings summarizing some philosophical statement of consequence pegged to a dictated subject. That the contemporary artist can be content, or reconciled, to fencing himself off into so small an area of what was once a limitless field, is incomprehensible to me.[28]

27. Doss, *Twentieth-Century American Art*, 164.
28. Canaday, *Culture Gulch*, 20.

Canaday noted (with an eye toward Greenberg) that this reduction of art to pure theory was not a reduction to essentials but to "incidentals." He added that all this was a clear admission that the contemporary world offered "no meaningful goal for the painter's endeavors."[29]

Some looked to the return of meaning with the reemergence of expressionism in the eighties. However, much as meaning was now proving illusive in some of the best recent poetry, so did it evaporate upon a close examination of the art of the Neo-Expressionists. Elizabeth Baker suggested that the iconographical features of Neo-Expressionist painting often had no specific meanings for the artist,[30] while critic Carter Ratcliff observed that conventions of iconography were now bearable only if artists were free to confound them, inviting the viewer "to see what he can see."[31] Regarding the problem of meaning in such work, Suzi Gablik said it best. In reference to Julian Schnabel's claims that his art alluded to the power of primordial, magical things, Gablik commented:

> You can't attach some broken plates and a pair of antlers to a canvas, pass it on to Mary Boone to sell, and hope for mythic significance.[32]

Gablik recognized that the chief problem in the new painting was the complete absence of any connection to the sacred. Art (like poetry) had lost that "transcendental realm of being,"—a realm that provided its "meaning-giving" function, and prevented it from "lapsing into mere self-expression."[33] In fact, this separation from the sacred had long been a problem for artists whose abstractions, though rooted in various spiritual traditions, had been inaccessible to large numbers of the public. As long as mysticism, myth, metaphysics, and depth psychology had at least been part of the language of artists and intellectuals, painting and sculpture had a common background against which abstract forms attained meaning. However, by the end of World War II, modern art was on its last legs. The situation finally reached a point of crisis with the Abstract Expressionists, whose paintings provided fodder for critics like Greenberg, and for a culture inclined to look for dollars where others had found "sense."

---

29. Canaday, *Culture Gulch*, 21.
30. Gablik, *Has Modernism Failed*, 92.
31. Gablik, *Has Modernism Failed*, 91.
32. Gablik, *Has Modernism Failed*, 92.
33. Gablik, *Has Modernism Failed*, 80.

By the eighties, many were aware of what had been lost in recent years. Among these was the aging Motherwell. Surveying the New York art scene during the period, Motherwell dolefully recalled: "When we started out, there were people like Mondrian, who regarded art as a calling, something that expressed the world of the spirit. People now are quite cynical about that. They have forgotten what art is all about..."[34]

Motherwell's comments remind us of the words of Hölderlin with which we concluded our discussion of verse. Of course, art and poetry have historically endured fallow times. But postmodernism is different. Never has there been such a thoroughgoing attack on the possibilities of meaning nor one that has lasted so long. Never has a culture shown itself so utterly unable to give birth to those ideas which are essential to meaning in the arts—or in life. The older and wiser of today's successful artists know this. One of these is Gerhard Richter, who, speaking in 2012, put the matter this way: "It seems we don't need painting anymore. Culture is more interested in entertaining people. Every museum is full of nice things. That's the opposite of before. It was important things or serious things. Now we have interesting things."[35]

Despite (if not because of) this lack of substance, art, like poetry, has seen an explosion in popularity in recent decades. Like the poet, the artist of the twenty-first century tends to have a graduate degree from a respected institution where he has perfected his brand while remaining blissfully unaware of the larger realm of ideas which had inspired earlier generations of artists. Art, like poetry, even has its own arcane language—one with political inflections but otherwise little content. The same language is spoken by critics, whose purpose is to keep the art world spinning on its own little axis without raising issues of substance or meaning.

A survey conducted by the Columbia University National Arts Journalism Program in 2002 found that judging art works and theorizing about their "meaning" were the least popular goals of American art critics. Simply describing art was most popular.[36] (James Elkins, who has cited the survey, rightly finds this reversal of expectations "as astonishing as if physicists had declared that they would no longer attempt to understand the universe, but just appreciate it."[37]) More recently, Sarah Thornton observed much the same thing in her visits to America's top art publications. On more than one occasion, officials deflected her criticism that their periodical hesitated

34. Thompson, *American Culture in 1980s*, 67.
35. Luscomb, "10 Questions."
36. Elkins, *What Happened*, 12 and 49.
37. Elkins, *What Happened*, 12.

to publish negative reviews. One critic suggested that the function of art criticism now was simply "to give people something to read" and likened his function to that of "a stand-up comic."[38] Another writer characterized the changing role of criticism in this way: "Now, instead of moving culture ahead, it's about finding a group of people you can promote."[39]

Little wonder that, while art criticism continues to flourish (as does poetry), it now exists largely outside the realm of contemporary intellectual discourse (also like poetry).

Where postmodern art chiefly differs from postmodern poetry is in its enormous economic potential. Following the lead of Warhol, successful artists in recent years (e.g., Jeff Koons, Takashi Murakami, Damien Hirst) serve as CEOs of enterprises where works are manufactured by a staff of assistants. Like big business, big art is always on the lookout for the next big thing—with the emphasis on "big," since today's artists realize that size will invariably be mistaken for significance. Where "big" is concerned, no one outshines Koons. Among this artist's best known works is a forty-three-foot-tall sculpture of a puppy dog, which consists of thousands of flowering plants. In a world where originality was once vital, Koons finds inspiration in the cliché. Koons believes that anything can be art and that art can be anything anyone wants it to be. The big philosophical issue here is whether such a view is the ultimate expression of our nihilism, our narcissism, or both.

Given all this, it should not surprise us that art today has abandoned any notion that the work should harbor "timeless" truths or values. In the contemporary art world metaphysics has given way to fashion. Thornton observed this, too, in her journey through the contemporary art world, and it is perhaps the most chilling of her many revelations:

> Art used to embody something meaningful enough to be relevant beyond the time in which it was made, but collectors today are attracted to art that "holds up a mirror to our times" and are too impatient to hang on to the work long enough to see if it contains any "timeless" rewards. Experts say that the art that sells most easily at auction has a "kind of immediate appeal" or "wow factor."[40]

---

38. Thornton, *Seven Days*, 157.
39. Thornton, *Seven Days*, 170.
40. Thornton, *Seven Days*, 35.

5

Peak Experiences

WE HAVE SEEN HOW poets and artists are sometimes able to fashion works in which something of greater and more lasting value seems to become tangible in simple, everyday forms. Moments like these are not confined to poetry and painting. On rare occasions, meaning may appear in daily life so suddenly and with such intensity that we may feel as if we had discovered a deep and vital truth regarding ourselves and the world around us. At such times, the world appears in a new light—richer, more intense and more alive. Now the distance separating us from our surroundings seems to diminish and time to stand still. Experiences of this sort are both richly cognitive and emotional. For one thing, they make us aware of an inherent order and purpose in life—an insight that carries enormous conviction although we may have difficulty in fully articulating it. They also allow us to see objects and living beings as if for the first time, accepting them as full and complete in themselves and joining us to them in a deeply emotional way. Not surprisingly, events like these are among the simplest and most profound examples of the experience of meaning in life.

In the early sixties, psychologist Abraham Maslow coined the term *peak-experience* to describe moments of this sort. Maslow noted that accounts of peak experiences had been described to him by colleagues, friends and students, and he believed that, while they were rare in an individual's life, they were a common feature of human experience. In addition to the sorts of everyday events that inspire artists and poets, Maslow found peak experiences in athletics, in sexual love, and in moments of insight in science, philosophy, and the like. Maslow made a distinction between individuals who tended to have these experiences ("peakers") and those who did not ("non-peakers"). He argued that, while traditional psychology tended to view such experiences as pathological, they are really indicative of mental health.

Maslow further suggested that peak experiences were associated with a tendency toward self-actualization. By this term he had in mind the ultimate level of personal development in which an individual strives to achieve his or her full potential as an expression of their uniqueness. However, self-actualizers not only *had* peak experiences; they seemed to view all of life from the perspective of a broader, deeper reality lying beyond the surface of things. Accordingly, they tended to be independent thinkers and doers—people who had a sense of mission that they associated with the highest human good rather than with narrow self-interest or ordinary measures of success. In Maslow's view, self-actualization is a rare phenomenon, and one most widely associated with historical figures like Einstein, Thoreau, and Schweitzer.

In his book, *Religions, Values, and Peak-Experiences* (1964), Maslow was particularly concerned to develop the analogies between religion and peak experiences. In this context he provided a list of those characteristics of peak experiences that were essentially religious in character. For us, the most important of these is the fact that peak experiences typically convey a strong and often unshakable sense that life has meaning. As Maslow put it:

> [A peak-experience] proves to the experiencer that there are ends in the world, that there are things or objects or experiences to yearn for which are worthwhile in themselves. This in itself is a refutation of the proposition that life and living is meaningless. In other words, peak-experiencers are one part of the operational statement that "life is worthwhile" or "life is meaningful."[1]

Maslow added that a peak experience may leave individuals with a profound feeling of gratitude—a sense of what Christians refer to as grace. The awareness of an underlying unity in life that accompanies moments like these may also lead individuals to recognize the essential role of evil and death in the scheme of things. Maslow noted that a peak experience may give one the sense that they are dying while simultaneously conveying the insight that death is inherently good. In the short run, a peak experience may provide an anecdote to anxiety and despair. In the long

---

1. Maslow, *Religions, Values*, 62–63.

run, it is capable of enlarging and transforming our understanding of ourselves and our world.

Although peak experiences generally occur outside organized religion, Maslow believed that they are at the core of religion, and that the insights of the great mystics came in moments like these. Much of *Religions, Values, and Peak-Experiences* is devoted to attempting to show how peak experiences constitute a "secularized religion," and to demonstrating the need to remove religion from the narrow context of orthodox faith and belief and see it as a feature of everyday existence. And, indeed, mysticism often has its roots in everyday occurrences of this sort. The German cobbler Jacob Boehme came to understand the nature of God, man, and the universe when he gazed at the reflection of a beam of light in a pewter dish. The French mystic Brother Lawrence was similarly awakened to the power of God when witnessing a bare tree in the winter and perceiving how, through God's power, it would soon flower and bear fruit.

However, Maslow is wrong in believing that there is value in separating peak experiences from their original sacred context. One great virtue of religion lies in its capacity to clothe our deepest feelings and intuitions in forms that give them heightened importance. Understood in this way, the very tendency to view peak experiences apart from their original religious context is indicative of a broader decline that is characteristic of postmodern society generally. For us the major lesson to be drawn from peak experiences is the vital role of culture in fleshing out these events and giving them the greatest possible meaning.

In fact, Maslow's notion of the peak experience is inseparable from an era in America that valued unitary consciousness, seeking to encourage and nurture it through meditation, a return to nature, Eastern metaphysics, and the like. And while psychologists today assure us that peak experiences still occur, we should be no more surprised that they now have a different character than they once did than to observe that the popularity of bell bottoms and tie-dyed T-shirts is on the wane. The later development of Maslow's ideas both within humanistic psychology and in rival schools of psychological thought serves as a clear example of this. By briefly looking at changes in the last half century or so we are reminded of how culture shapes experience and helps give our world whatever lasting significance it may possess.

From its origins in 1941 through the sixties, humanistic psychology occupied a respected position in the academic world. The rapid growth and enormous popularity of the movement even led many to believe that it might succeed in bridging the growing chasm separating the sciences and the humanities. As we have seen, this chasm is today wider than ever. This is in some measure a consequence of dissension within humanistic psychology itself. This dissention began just prior to Maslow's death and continues today.[2]

By 1967, Maslow had come to believe that peak experiences signified nothing less than a new frontier in psychology—a "fourth force" regarding states of unitive awareness that led beyond humanistic psychology itself. In response to what was perceived as an undervaluation of such spiritual dimensions, Maslow and a close associate, Anthony Sutich, left their leadership positions in 1969 to establish the Association for Transpersonal Psychology. Not surprisingly, most of the leading figures in humanistic psychology followed them. Maslow's death, that same year, proved to be a harbinger of what was to come. During the seventies, humanistic psychology came to be seen by many as having abandoned the rigors of the academic world for the dubious spiritualities of the counterculture. In the eighties and nineties, the movement was notable mostly for divisions within and declining influence without. By the end of the twentieth century, many mainstream psychologists were ignoring the humanistic movement altogether or criticizing it for being unscientific and guilty of promoting the cult of narcissism.

In the twenty-first century, Maslow's ideas have been picked apart by proponents of "positive psychology"—a movement widely associated with University of Pennsylvania professor Martin Seligman.[3] The term "positive psychology" derives from Maslow's work, and many positive psychologists readily acknowledge their debt to Maslow. Still, the leaders of the new movement have often been critical of Maslow and his contemporaries. The new ideas certainly reflect a different point in a view. For one thing, positive psychology has a different notion of the highest level of psychological functioning. Where Maslow had referred to self-actualization, recent psychologists have looked to "happiness" as the highest human good. Indeed, the psychology of happiness has proven wildly popular in the early twenty-first century. In the eighties and nineties, only some fifty books on happiness were published. In 2008 alone the number

---

2. Taylor and Martin, "Humanistic Psychology."
3. Seligman and Csikszentmihalyi, "Positive Psychology," 5–14.

was four thousand. Meanwhile, the number of studies on happiness grew from a few hundred a year to more than ten thousand in 2014.[4]

This shift from Maslow may seem reasonable enough. The criticisms that Maslow's work too often lacked a strong empirical foundation and that his notion of self-actualization had encouraged a shallow, narcissistic view of personal development have legitimacy. In fact, toward the end of his life Maslow seemed to be moving from self-actualization toward some notion of self-transcendence as the highest in the hierarchy of needs.[5] This is a natural change, and one that accords with the notion that religion is the final point in any genuine search for meaning. In the following pages I want to suggest that this is the case, and that self-transcendence, achieved within the context of a basic religious or metaphysical point of view, represents both the most profound experience of meaning in life and the high point in personal development.

Of course, the embrace of the happiness ideal also appears justifiable for a more obvious reason. After all, what's wrong with being happy? The problem is that, while happiness is a positive good, it lacks that dimension of depth we associate with the profounder manifestations of meaning—depths that come not only from encountering the pleasant things in life, but of knowing deprivation and despair. The poet Rainer Marie Rilke once hinted at this link when, in reference to his hesitancy to seek psychiatric care, he observed that, if his devils were driven out, his angels might also depart.[6] Where meaning is concerned, a better concept is joy, which is rooted in the deeper movements of the human spirit. Maslow's contemporary, the great humanist psychologist Rollo May, once drew the distinction in this way:

> Happiness depends generally on one's outer state; joy is an overflowing of inner energies and leads to awe and wonderment. ... Happiness is the absence of discord; joy is the welcoming of discord as the basis of higher harmonies. Happiness is finding a system of rules which solve our problems; joy is taking the risk that is necessary to break new frontiers.[7]

---

4. E. Smith, *Power of Meaning*, 9–10.
5. Kolto-Rivera, "Rediscovering the Late Version," 302–17.
6. See Leppmann, *Rilke: A Life*, 269.
7. Schneider, *"Towards a Humanistic,"* 32–38.

In fact, a number of recent psychological studies have indicated a negative correlation between happiness and a sense of meaning in life.[8] The reason for this, it appears, is that, while meaning and happiness overlap and tend to "feed off each other," they have very different roots. Happiness is typically associated with a relatively stress-free life and the satisfaction of basic needs. To the extent that the pursuit of happiness becomes the primary goal of life, it often leads to shallow, ego-driven behavior. Meaning is different. Meaning requires engagement in something larger than ourselves, thereby opening us to the anxieties and stresses that come from a thoughtful and emotional engagement with the world. While the experience of meaning is not always a happy one, research indicates that it is deeper and longer lasting than happiness.

The relative shallowness of so much positive psychology is evident not only in the virtual abandonment of the dimension of depth in its embrace of happiness as the highest good; it is apparent in the psychologists' treatment of peak experiences, which today have been divided into two distinctive forms, each of which has been thoroughly analyzed and, wherever possible, placed upon a firm experimental foundation. In the process, both the characteristics of the experiences and their significance for our lives have changed in ways consistent with the ongoing loss of meaning in America.

The first of these forms is *flow*, which is widely associated with the work of Mihaly Csikszentmihalyi, who coined the term in 1975. Flow involves those peak experiences having to do with concerted mental and physical effort. It is manifest as a sense of almost effortless action that may occur when we are deeply involved in activities that have clear goals and obvious markers of success—activities that tax our skills to the limit, but not beyond. When we are in a state of flow we are so focused on our task that we temporarily identify with the activity and lose all awareness of time. Here, things seem to develop of their own accord, without conscious effort or control. The flow experience is intrinsically rewarding—a feeling the psychologists refer to as "autotelic." Ideally, this sense of gratification carries over from work or play into everyday life, giving it heightened value and meaning.

Maslow chiefly found flow in athletics. Csikszentmihalyi finds it in a much wider variety of activities. As he explains: "Flow is generally reported when a person is doing his or her favorite activity—gardening,

---

8. E. Smith, *Power of Meaning*, 14–18. Although meaning is not specifically defined here, it clearly refers to the sorts of "connections" we have in mind.

listening to music, bowling, cooking a good meal. It also occurs when driving, when talking to friends, and surprisingly often at work."[9]

Csikszentmihalyi even wrote a book on the role of flow in business, noting how workplaces may be adapted to facilitate flow as a way of increasing productivity and raising the happiness quotient of employees. While this may be all to the good, we cannot help wondering if this turn from the metaphysical ambitions of the counterculture toward those economic values so prized in recent years isn't indicative of a major diminishment of the concept.

However, there is another, more serious problem with the notion of flow—and one that leads back to Maslow, and to the lack of a religious or metaphysical grounding for peak experiences whose implications Maslow failed to recognize. While flow is often experienced in sports, it is also widely felt in games like chess, poker, and, most especially, video games (one student of flow even developed a video game based upon his research). In essence, flow may lead not only to potentially meaningful relationships, but to activities that have no lasting value and may be addictive in nature. Such activities tend not only to separate us from reality, but to alienate us from it. As Csikszentmihalyi himself acknowledges, the experience of flow is neither good nor bad.

And this raises a vital issue, which has to do with the fact that, if the meanings found in flow are to have real and lasting value, they must ultimately take their significance from a broader cultural awareness of human nature and the Good. How else are we to distinguish the video game addict from the productive worker? The productive worker from the workaholic? And what about athletics? Is flow simply one fleeting dimension of skills whose real value lies in the attainment of competitive excellence? Is flow in sports merely a side effect of a drive for fame and fortune?

In fact, flow has been an important theme in Far Eastern cultures for millennia, where it has found extraordinary meaning through metaphysical principles that lead to a much broader sense of self and a deeper, richer notion of relation to the world. Possibly the earliest literary expression of the notion appeared over two thousand years ago in the ancient Chinese text the *Chuang Tzu*. By looking at it briefly, we get a sense of how the same experience may take on much greater meaning (and contribute to the greater social good) when defined within a culture that understands and interprets it in a larger religious or metaphysical context.

9. M. Csikszentmihalyi, *Finding Flow*, 33–34.

The *Chuang Tzu* tells the tale of Cook Ting, whose skill is such that he is said to cut up an ox "as though he were performing the dance of the Mulberry Grove." When Lord Wen-hui expresses his admiration of such skills, Ting replies, "What I care about is the Way, which goes beyond skill."[10] Ting proceeds to explain that he moves by spirit, which goes where it wants, following the makeup of the ox and moving so effortlessly that his knife never needs sharpening. As Ting puts it:

> There are spaces between the joints, and the blade of the knife has really no thickness. If you insert what has no thickness into such spaces, then there's plenty of room—more than enough for the blade to play about it. That's why, after nineteen years the blade of my knife is still as good as when it first came from the grindstone.[11]

When he does come to a difficult place, says Ting, he sizes up the difficulties, keeps his mind on what he's doing, reminds himself to be careful and moves with subtlety "until—flop! the whole thing comes apart like a clod of earth crumbling to the ground." To this, Lord Wen-hui responds: "Excellent! I have heard the words of Cook Ting and learned how to care for life!"[12]

In speaking of "the Way," Ting is referring to the Tao, which is the foremost metaphysical principle of ancient China. The Tao is manifest throughout nature as a creative energy whereby all things come into being, thrive and eventually perish. As both Ting and Lord Wen-hui make clear, it is the Tao, rather than mere skill, that is the true aim of life. To act according to the Tao is to abandon narrow self-interest and self-control and, like Ting, to rely upon intuition and a feel for things. But the Tao is not only a way of *acting*. As Lord Wen-hui indicates, it is a way of *living*, in which we disavow egoism and aggression and behave with modesty and dispassion. Here, ethics follows naturally from experience, the sense of being in touch with something beyond the self leading the individual to recognize the limits of selfish, ego-driven behavior. In this, Taoism has a general kinship with Christianity, where the experience of a loving God compels a realization that love is never a matter of narrow self-interest.

Taoist metaphysics was synthesized with Buddhism in China to create a school know as Ch'an, which came to Japan as Zen Buddhism. In the

---

10. Tzu, *Complete Works*, 51.
11. Tzu, *Complete Works*, 51.
12. Tzu, *Complete Works*, 51.

postwar years, Zen proved popular among Americans who were already attuned to existentialism and to the notion of the creative unconscious. By the fifties, echoes of Zen were everywhere, from painters to poets, jazz musicians to method actors. Looking back at the arts at the decade's end, poet Frank O'Hara described the creative process as understood by so many at the time in this way:

> This is not a mystical state but the accumulation of decisions along the way and the eradication of conflicting beliefs toward the total engagement of the spirit in the expression of meaning. So difficult is the attainment that, when the state has finally been reached, it seems that the artist has reached a limitless space of air and light in which the spirit can act freely and with unpremeditated knowledge. His action is immediately art, not through will, not through esthetic posture, but through a singleness of purpose.[13]

The echoes of Cook Ting are obvious. Indeed, it is clear from O'Hara that flow is regarded here as a state that, although apparently effortless on the surface, is achieved only with great difficulty and is intrinsically spiritual in character. It is true, of course, that the postwar era was unable to supply the deeper meanings available in Taoist metaphysics. However, it was still able to draw from philosophy and psychology ideas that grounded these experiences in something "greater" and of "more lasting value" than the individual ego. It is this something larger and more lasting for which the counterculture continued to search and that humanistic psychology attempted to understand and to foster. And if the movement from Taoism to postwar America is one large step away from meaning, it is another large step from the fifties and sixties to today.

The other variety of peak experience extensively studied by positive psychology is *awe*. Awe can reasonably be related to a wide number of Maslow's peak experiences, including moments with loved ones, looking at great art or listening to great music. However, it is especially associated with encounters with natural phenomena like imposing mountains, vast oceans, violent storms and the like. The positive psychologists rightly observe that, understood in this way, awe may be not only an uplifting experience but a fearful one. Much of their work has emphasized the capacity of awe (as experienced in scenes of natural power and majesty) to increase selfless behavior and lead to socially useful actions (e.g., generosity). This

---

13. Frank O'Hara, quoted in Lhamon, *Deliberate Speed*, 185.

is achieved, they reason, by the capacity of awe to induce a sense of the "small self" in those who experience it.[14]

By the latter notion the psychologists may have in mind what Rudolf Otto, in his classic on religious experience, *The Idea of the Holy*, referred to as "creature consciousness." Or maybe not. Otto meant by his term a creature's sense of being "submerged and overwhelmed by its own nothingness to that which is supreme above all creatures."[15] Dramatic examples of "creature consciousness" occur in major religious texts like the Bible and the *Bhagavad Gita*. Among the many examples in the former is the famous revelation to Job, when God reminds Job that it is God who laid the foundations of the earth, and to whom all creatures pay obeisance—from the birds in their nests to the great Leviathan of the sea. To God's revelation of his supreme majesty, Job can only respond:

> I have heard of thee by the hearing of the ear: but now mine eyes seeth thee.
> Wherefore I abhor *myself*, and repent in dust and ashes.
> (Job 42:5–6 RSV; emphasis original)

A similar scene occurs in the *Bhagavad Gita*, where Vishnu consents to reveal himself to Arjuna in all his fearsome glory. This leads Arjuna to exclaim:

> Like the fire at the end of Time which burns all in the last day, I see thy vast mouths and thy terrible teeth. Where am I? Where is my shelter? Have mercy on me, God of gods, Refuge Supreme of the world![16]

The religious experience of awe, in other words, is not simply one of "absence" (i.e., the "small self"). It is one of "presence" since it implies the revelation of an eternal power that lies far beyond the individual.

Examples like the above are simply the most dramatic instances of a theme that runs throughout imaginative literature and is especially apparent in accounts of profound religious experiences. Otto wrote of them, as did William James in his classic *The Varieties of Religious Experience*. Maslow probably encountered a few in his research, and they can certainly be found in hymns. Among the latter is "How Great Thou Art," an enormously popular Christian hymn based upon a work by the

---

14. Piff, "Awe, the Small Self."
15. Otto, *Idea of the Holy*, 10.
16. Mascaro, *Bhagavad Gita*, 91.

Swiss poet Carl Boberg. Boberg's poem was inspired by a series of natural manifestations of God's majesty, beginning with a violent thunderstorm encountered upon returning home from church. The English hymn was written by Stuart K. Hine, after his own personal experiences in the Carpathian Mountains. As rendered in George Beverly Shea's wonderful bass-baritone, "How Great Thou Art" inspired millions in the Billy Graham Crusades throughout the last half of the twentieth century. Its opening words go as follows:

> O Lord my God, When I in awesome wonder,
> Consider all the worlds Thy hands have made;
> I see the stars, I hear the rolling thunder,
> Thy power throughout the universe displayed.
> Then sings my soul, My Savior God, to Thee
> How great Thou art, How great Thou art.[17]

In a religious context, the experience of awe is capable of instilling a deeper meaning by its capacity not merely to overwhelm, but to *connect* us to something of infinitely greater and more lasting value. Such experiences encourage selfless social behavior not only for a time; in a religious context, they may have life-changing consequences.

There are a few thinkers in recent years who still recognize the vital role of religion in fleshing out peak experiences in a way that gives them deeper meaning. These include philosophers Hubert Dreyfus and Sean Dorrance Kelly, who deal with the issue in *All Things Shining: Reading the Western Classics to Find Meaning in a Secular Age*. I want to conclude by briefly looking at this book. As we shall see, it also relates to the changing character of peak experiences and to the ongoing decline of meaning in America.

All Things Shining begins by acknowledging the nihilism of the present age.[18] Nor do the authors think we should place much stock in the many and varied "spiritualities" of our day. Indeed, as they point out, our view that all these are equally valid as answers to the most vital questions is the essence of nihilism.

The book proceeds to discuss the remedy to our plight proposed by David Foster Wallace, the great writer whose life was cut short by suicide at age forty-six, in 2008. Wallace often wrote of the "lostness" of Americans at the end of the twentieth century. He was especially concerned

17. Hine, "How Great Thou Art," lines 1–6.
18. Dreyfus and Kelly, *All Things Shining*, 1–21.

about his generation, who, as he put it, "has an inheritance of absolutely nothing as far as meaningful moral values."[19] Wallace's unfinished novel *The Pale King* was an attempt to provide a solution by urging us to find meaning in the most banal and irritating experiences. This involves complete mastery of our thoughts—a capacity to dig deep within in order to transform, for example, a postmodern "consumer-hell type situation" into something meaningful, even sacred. As Dreyfus and Kelly put it: "The sole possibility of meaning, according to Wallace, is found in the strength of the individual's will."[20]

In this matter of personal thought control, the reader may be reminded of J. D. Salinger, who spoke to an earlier generation more receptive to spiritual instruction. In *Franny and Zooey*, Salinger chronicled the experience of young Franny Glass, who attempts to pray without ceasing—that is, to say the Jesus Prayer ("Lord Jesus Christ, have mercy upon me") until it becomes an unconscious part of her being. Franny's efforts result in an emotional breakdown that is allayed only through the guidance of brother Zooey. In fact, there is no denying the great emotional demands placed upon Franny by her religious quest, nor those imposed by Wallace's ideal. Little wonder that Dreyfus and Kelly regard such notions as asking too much of contemporary Westerners.

Unlike Salinger, who so often looked to the Eastern religions for inspiration, Dreyfus and Kelly dismiss traditions like Zen Buddhism or Vedanta as holding out possibilities of meaning in an increasingly secular world. Neither do they see an answer in Christianity, whose emphasis on inner states of awareness the authors regard as having set the stage for our current malady. Instead, they propose the religion of the ancient Greeks, who posited no ultimate reality, but recognized a pantheon of deities to whom they expressed gratitude for all the wonders of life—from good fortune and everyday joys to feats of human excellence. In noting the necessity of some sense of the sacred in giving meaning to experience, Dreyfus and Kelly take us a major step beyond the positive psychologists. It is chiefly through expressions of gratitude and joy that we enter into relation with the universe in a deep and abiding way. Poetry is a characteristic means of doing this. And it is no accident that, from the Vedas through the Psalms, the poetry of praise and thanksgiving have had a vital place in religion. Religion is not a betrayal of our humanity, as many believe. It

---

19. Dreyfus and Kelly, *All Things Shining*, 25.
20. Dreyfus and Kelley, *All Things Shining*, 45.

is a means, through external forms, of knowing ourselves and expressing ourselves at a higher, more deeply meaningful, plane of experience.

Unfortunately, the polytheistic view advocated by the authors is able to join us only to the transitory joys of the natural and physical worlds. It is silent regarding a higher, unchanging Essence that may speak to us in the depths of our being and the entirety of our lives. And if the biblical faiths fall short in their view, the authors would still be better served by turning to the Tao, which is capable of providing some guidance in human behavior and enabling us to separate the gold from the dross. Absent some such notion of the Absolute, the elements Dreyfus and Kelly seek to join together fall apart—as we see in the concluding sections of the book.

In the middle chapters, the authors trace their theme through Western philosophy and literature before arriving at a position much like that of the positive psychologists. Here, too, the experience of "flow" is critical, and the athlete who demonstrates it (like basketball great Bill Bradley and tennis star Roger Federer) is an ongoing theme in the book. But flow is understood by the authors not only as something an athlete *feels*; it is something a knowing spectator *sees* and *experiences*. Such experiences typically occur in arenas where our senses are heightened by the bright symmetries of the playing field and by feelings of anticipation and camaraderie in the crowd. *All Things Shining* quotes Albert Borgmann, who puts the matter like this: "When reality and community conspire in this way, divinity descends on the game, divinity of an impersonal and yet potent kind."[21] Little wonder that the supreme tennis fan Wallace could write an essay with the provocative title "Federer as Religious Experience."[22]

The extraordinary potential for meaning in such moments is evident from the fact that the sense of flow may be joined here to the sense of awe. This is evident in what Dreyfus and Kelly refer to as a "powerful wave" that carries along spectators at sports events and temporarily gives meaning to life. As Borgmann describes the experience:

> At the beginning of a real game, there is no way of predicting or controlling what will happen. No one can produce or guarantee the flow of a game. It unfolds and reveals itself in the playing. It inspires grace and despair, it provokes heroics and failure, it infuses enthusiasm and inflicts misery. It is always greater than the individuals it unites.[23]

21. Dreyfus and Kelly, *All Things Shining*, 194.
22. Dreyfus and Kelly, *All Things Shining*, 145.
23. Dreyfus and Kelly, *All Things Shining*, 199.

Dreyfus and Kelly liken this feeling to Homer's notion of *physic*, which they translate as "whooshing up." Regarding the limitations of such experiences as sources of meaning, we will have more to say later on, when we look at sports in more detail. For the moment we simply want to note that, although the authors also acknowledge the limitations of experiences like these (and caution against their potential dangers), they remain the book's most compelling instances of meaning in our contemporary world. In itself this is a clear indication of the depth of our plight and one that should give us pause regarding facile remedies.

In the concluding section, the authors urge the reader to attend to the sacred things in the world and to cultivate meaning by mindfully enacting the little rituals of life, like enjoying a good cup of coffee. They further point out that, while we cannot (and would not wish to) return to the Homeric world, "we can become receptive to a modern pantheon of gods—to the ways in which Gehrig and Federer shine, the ways in which Marilyn Monroe or Albert Einstein changed how we see the world in which we live."[24] This is certainly a tepid finale, and one that may lead us to conclude that even the faintest shadow of the old gods is preferable to the glitter of the new.

In fact, the primary virtue of *All Things Shining* is that, like the work of the positive psychologists, it reminds us how very far we have come in our abandonment of meaning. Ours is indeed a society with strong nihilistic tendencies, and one no mere urging to private action will alone revive. Terms like "whooshing up" and "flow" are tangible indications of a meaning impoverished culture. So, too, for that matter, is the paltry nomenclature of "the big bang"—as Calvin wisely pointed out to his pal Hobbes in a classic comic strip.

---

24. Dreyfus and Kelly, *All Things Shining*, 222.

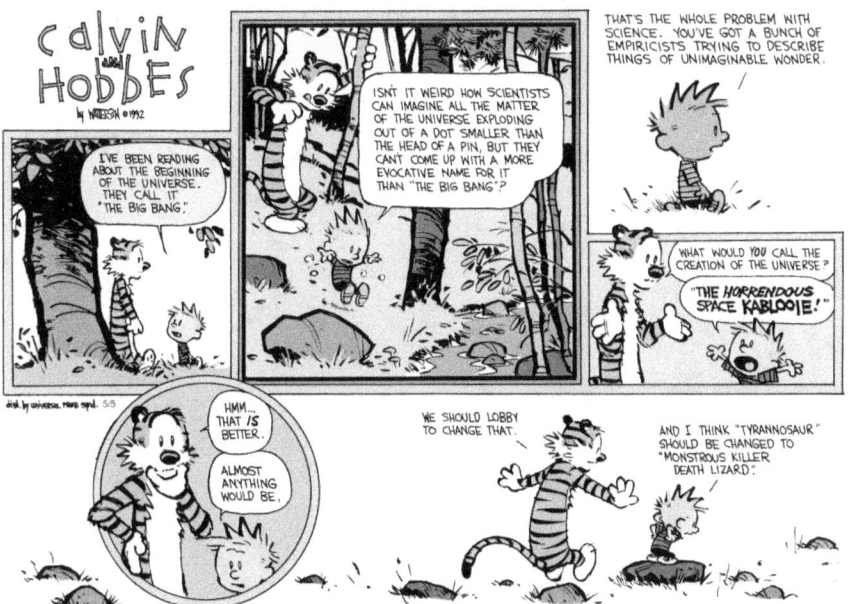

Calvin and Hobbes ©1992 Watterson. Reprinted with permission of Andrews McMeel Syndication. All rights reserved.

This verbal poverty is a consequence of a decline in myth, religion, and poetry, and of an educational system that today has little or no place for subjects where the spiritual may gain a foothold. Most regard this loss as of no great importance. But without language adequate to the majesty and mystery of existence, the universe ceases to possess these in any fundamental way. The result is that we move from one "high" to another without latching onto something that gives our life order and a deeper purpose. This reminds us once more that it is culture that ultimately determines whether meaning will saturate our world or disappear from it altogether. In other words, meaning is basically a matter of choice—specifically, a choice of how we describe and interpret our world. As Erich Heller has wisely observed:

> It is indeed amazing how malleable the world is and how easily it models and remodels itself according to the inner vision of man, how readily it responds to his theorizing! Thus the most important advice which an educator might give to his pupils may easily be: Be careful how you interpret the world; it *is* like that.[25]

25. E. Heller, *Disinherited Mind*, 26–27; emphasis original.

PART THREE

Meaning Writ Large

6

Family and Community

FOR MOST AMERICANS, FAMILY is the most basic source of meaning available. Family relationships form bonds that last, linking us across the years and, increasingly, the miles. However, the importance of the family for meaning extends far beyond the immediate contact of family members. A stable, loving family is also vital in producing children with the capacity to function outside the family in ways that will give their lives meaning. The family has traditionally been the primary means whereby children learn those values (e.g., honesty, kindness, cooperation, trust, responsibility) that enable them to live as productive citizens and engage with the larger society. It follows that the problematic nature of the family in recent decades has widely been regarded as a harbinger of the breakdown of society generally.

That the postwar years were extraordinary ones for American families is apparent even to critics like Stephanie Coontz. In her book on the fifties family (tellingly entitled *The Way We Never Were*) Coontz makes the following observations:

> The 1950s was a profamily period if there ever was one. Rates of divorce and illegitimacy were half what they are today; marriage was almost universally praised; the family was everywhere hailed as the most basic institution in society; and a massive baby boom, among all classes and ethnic groups, made America a "child-centered" society. Births rose from a low of 18.4 per 1,000 women during the Depression to a high of 25.3 per 1,000

in 1957. "The birth rate for third children doubled between 1940 and 1960, and that for fourth children tripled."[1]

In the fifties, the age of first marriage was twenty-three for men and twenty for women. Today, the numbers are twenty-nine and twenty-seven respectively. In 1960, the proportion of an average adult life spent with a spouse and children stood at an all-time high of 62 percent. By the end of the century, it was at an all-time low of 43 percent.[2] In 1960, 73 percent of babies in America were born into a traditional family—that is, to a couple in their first marriage. By 2014, that number was down to 46 percent.[3]

Perhaps most telling in regard to families today is the number of Americans who do not intend to have children. While fifties birthrates were exceptionally high, the birthrate in America reached an historic low in 2019, and the "replacement" fertility rate was also a record low at 1.72. In the same year, a *Wall Street Journal*/NBC poll showed that only 43 percent of Americans considered having children "very important."[4] As we noted in our first chapter, that number had dropped to 30 percent by 2023.

Both declining birth rates and the instability of the family take a special toll on young children. And this is really the vital issue. For the situation of children is important to them not only as individuals, but to the larger society, and to the possible meanings that society will be capable of providing. Too often, debate over the family has focused on the welfare of men and women, with children added almost as an afterthought. This is a serious mistake. As David Popenoe has made the point:

> People today, most of all children, dearly want families in their lives. They long for that special, and hopefully life-long, social and emotional bond that family membership brings. Adults can perhaps live much of their lives, with some success, apart from families. The problem is that children, if we wish them to become successful adults, cannot. (In fact, most young children, other things being equal, would probably prefer to live in the large, complex families of old.) Adults for their own good purposes, most recently self-fulfillment, have stripped the family down to its nucleus. But any further reduction—either in functions or in

---

1. Coontz, *Way We Never Were*, 24.
2. Popenoe, *War over the Family*, 6.
3. Pew Research Center, "Parenting in America," sect. 1, "The American Family Today," para. 2.
4. Day, "Americans Have Shifted," para. 4.

number of members—will likely have adverse consequences for children, and thus for generations to come.[5]

Little wonder that, since the eighties, cries for a rebirth of the family along the fifties model have been raised by many conservatives. This notion has in turn been widely criticized by progressive scholars like Coontz. The latter point out that certain social groups had no real place in the fifties ideal. They further note that the fifties family was an historical anomaly, engendered by a combination of postwar prosperity, an unprecedented desire for the security of hearth and home, sympathetic family laws, and a socially sanctioned division of labor based upon gender. In effect, the argument seems to be that the specialness of the postwar family wasn't really special because it was a result of special circumstances and because it wasn't special for everyone.

That the fifties family wasn't perfect should go without saying. However, it is important to note that the vast majority of men and women of the era found happiness in the home. Coontz cites one survey from the fifties that showed that only 20 percent of couples regarded their marriages as unhappy. Another survey of middle-class husbands and wives from the era found that a remarkable two-thirds regarded their marriage as "decidedly happier than average."[6]

The key to the success of the postwar family lay in the "companionate marriage." In 1954, *McCall's* magazine coined the term "togetherness" to describe the arrangement, which it characterized as "this new and warmer way of life, not as women *alone* or men *alone*, isolated from one another, but as a *family*, sharing a common experience."[7] While family law still gave fathers substantial authority at home, the new ideal undermined the notion that mothers should defer to their husbands in all family matters. Parents were now expected to work together, drawing upon each other's strengths and supporting each other in dealing with any issue that arose. And this is the way the ideal played out in the popular family TV shows of the period—and, in most American homes, where, as on TV, father may "know best," but it was just as often *The Donna Reed Show*.

But "togetherness" went far beyond the family itself. Families then were supported by tight-knit communities with modest middle-class homes, neighborhood schools, strong community organizations, and,

---

5. Popenoe, *War over the Family*, 37–38.
6. Coontz, *Way We Never Were*, 36.
7. Cherlin, *Marriage-Go-Round*, 84.

especially, strong religious institutions. Home and church went hand and hand in postwar America, with homes and congregations assisting one another in the raising of children. During the fifties, churches and synagogues spread rapidly in the suburbs, providing a wide range of activities that extended far beyond the weekly services. There were special weekday groups for boys and girls, teens, women and men. In addition to the extensive Sabbath or Sunday activities, many congregations had church dinners and an additional mid-week "prayer meeting."

In an era when children significantly outnumbered parents, the combination of the "companionate marriage" and strong supporting groups and organizations clearly worked well for the majority of family members. For children, home life then typically comprised two family meals a day, homework, yard or neighborhood play, simple chores, babysitting or a paper route, an hour or two for family TV watching and bedtime stories. Outside the home, they were generally on their own, riding bikes, playing outside, visiting friends, walking to (and/or from) school, and engaging in community activities at YMCAs, Boys Clubs, 4-H, churches, and Scouts. The result was a balance of parental support and individual freedom and initiative that was difficult before and unthinkable today.

A central responsibility for fifties housewives was the family dinner. Although many families skimped on breakfast, dinner (or supper as it was as often called) was an important family event where all were expected to be in attendance and news of the day was typically shared. The responsibility of a meal with an entrée, vegetables, bread, beverages, and (often) homemade desserts may seem daunting to many young women today (just as the work and exercise routine of many young women today would seem formidable to their fifties forbearers). But home-cooked meals were not only natural at a time of stay-at-home mothers but inevitable, given the cost of an alternative and the relative lack of fast-food options. Besides, many housewives of the era had grown up on farms and had learned cooking from their mothers or from the home economics courses that were commonplace in the schools.

Some older Americans today may still remember when supper was almost always prepared at home, with the menu varying according to items available from one's garden, the neighbor's garden, produce stands and farmers' markets, canned and frozen summer produce, or the local A&P. Since fruits and vegetables were seasonal, so were desserts, which consisted largely of simple cakes or fruit pies—the latter varying with the time of year. While the family meal was an act of love chiefly for the cook, at its best it was a modest ritual of meaning in which other family members participated by setting the table, preparing beverages, washing dishes, and the like. At the center of all this was usually a simple blessing. This little ritual was a tangible expression of the linking of family members to each other, to their food, and to its Provider.

The status of the family meal as a source of meaning today scarcely needs comment. Indeed, the divorce of produce from season, food preparation from home, and the family members from one another and their God is a perfect little emblem of the breakdown of the many "connections" that are so vital to a meaningful society. But the social revolutions of the late sixties not only put a strain on the old family ties; they changed our understanding of what the family was all about.

By 1980, the fifties notion of "togetherness" as a family ideal was giving way to what Andrew Cherlin refers to as "expressive individualism."[8] Once again, the new ideal was spelled out in popular magazines like *McCall's*. The title of one 1980 article posed the following question to its (mostly) women readers: "Time for Yourself: Must It Hurt Your Marriage?"[9] By 1990, the notion of marriage as a joining of distinct individuals was so widely accepted that an article from the magazine could aver: "What Every Woman Needs: A Place to Call Her Own."[10] In fact, the need to develop one's own identity separate from one's spouse was the first and primary value in the new marriage ideal. Others were that traditional marriage roles like breadwinner and homemaker should now be more flexible and that honest and open communication between spouses on all matters was essential.

At the bottom of "expressive individualism" was the belief that individual growth and personal satisfaction were paramount in all things. Marriage was not so much an obligation to one's spouse, one's children and to society, as it was one among the many avenues to fulfillment that were now being touted on TV and film, in periodicals and books. The transformation in society at large—and the implications for marriage, in particular—was extraordinary. The emergence of the erotic as a vital element of personal well-being was especially notable. Along with guides to personal growth, the seventies and eighties saw an avalanche of popular manuals on finding sexual fulfillment. Here, too, it was assumed that

---

8. Cherlin, *Marriage-Go-Round*, 87–115.
9 Cherlin, *Marriage-Go-Round*, 87.
10. Cherlin, *Marriage-Go-Round*, 87–88.

individuals could reasonably be expected to look elsewhere if satisfaction was not available in the home.

The new individualism within the family was widely supported by changes in family law. In some cases, the courts were simply catching up with the notion of the "companionable marriage," revisiting badly outdated laws and establishing equality within the home. However, the American family would be forever changed with the California "no-fault" divorce law of 1969. Previously, divorces had been granted only if a husband or wife could demonstrate that their spouse had committed a specific act, such as infidelity, desertion, mental cruelty, or physical abuse. Divorce could now be granted if one party felt that the couple had grown apart, that the lines of communication had broken down, or if they didn't love each other sufficiently. Now the presence of children in the family was no longer a major obstacle. In 1962, about half of Americans disagreed with the statement that "where there are children in the family, parents should stay together even if they don't get along." By 1985, that number had jumped to 82 percent.[11]

The new law fitted perfectly with the idea of "expressive individualism." Now the notion of personal fulfillment was leaving the institution of the family in the dust. By 1980, a new marriage had about a 50 percent chance of ending in divorce. In that same year, conservative Christians calling for a return to "family values" formed an alliance with the Republican Party that began with the election of Ronald Reagan and would continue into the George W. Bush years (2001–2008).

One notable incident from the era that illuminates the divide in America came during the 1994 presidential campaign. At the time, the popular TV sitcom *Murphy Brown* had a plotline in which the title character decides to bear a child on her own. Speaking at the Commonwealth Club of California, Republican vice presidential candidate Dan Quayle criticized the TV series. Said Quayle:

> Bearing babies irresponsibly is simply wrong. Failing to support children one has fathered is wrong. We must be unequivocal about this. It doesn't help matters when prime-time TV has Murphy Brown—a character who supposedly epitomizes today's intelligent, highly paid, professional woman—mocking the importance of fathers by bearing a child alone, and calling it just another "lifestyle choice."[12]

11. Popenoe, *War over the Family*, 25.
12. Sawhill, "20 Years Later," para. 2.

Quayle's comments drew support from those who saw marriage as the unwavering foundation of society and widespread criticism from others who felt the institution needed to change to accommodate any number of personal needs and purposes. Beneath all the furor lay an enormous social shift. By the nineties, single-parent households were the fastest growing family type in America. Almost 90 percent of these households were headed by women.[13]

From the "go-it-alone" approach of Murphy Brown, the American conception of family in the new millennium has moved to a "do-it-yourself" model. This is evident in everything from the "separate but equal" lifestyles of so many young couples to the many sorts of "blended" families that exist today. In 2019, the average number of people in the US household increased for the first time in over 160 years due to the "doubling up" of generations and the increase in "extra adults" in the household.[14] Indeed, the notion of family is not what it once was. Younger generations raised on popular TV sitcoms like *Friends* and *The Big Bang Theory* are often more likely to associate family with close friendships rather than biological kin. Meanwhile, Fido has traded in his backyard domicile for the comfort and companionship of the home. This, according to a 2022 article in *Frontiers in Veterinary Medicine* that notes that 90 percent of pet owners regard their animal companions as family members.[15] Today, many pet owners not only sleep with their pets but cook for them, buy them presents, and regard them as their children. Some go even further. A 2015 article highlighted a website where people can marry their pets.[16] The woman who created the website (who claimed to have performed about one hundred such marriages) acknowledged that the ceremonies are not legally binding, though she had become an ordained priest to give them weight.

This humanization of animals is one of the most remarkable changes in American culture in recent decades, and while it is valuable in ensuring humane treatment of the creatures, it also points to a new understanding of ourselves that is telling. We have already noted one example of this in Irving Singer's inclusion of all species in his understanding of "meaning"—a view that temporarily blinds him to those strivings distinctive of human beings. More recently, we see it in philosopher John Gray's book *Feline Philosophy: Cats and the Meaning of Life* (2020), which

13. Popenoe, *War over the Family*, 24.
14. Fry, "Number of People," para. 8.
15. Nugent and Daugherty, "Measurement Equivalence Study," para. 1.
16. Dogster, "Want to Marry."

advises us to look to our pets to avoid the sort of self-awareness that is typical of human beings and too often brings on guilt and angst. All this, of course, is in full accord with the "happiness" ideal of the positive psychologists, who also aim to cheer us up by bringing us down to earth. In regard to the need for meaning that is distinctive of human beings, such tendencies are indeed telling.

In addition to rotating spouses and pets who teach us how to live, computers will undoubtedly soon be welcomed into the clan. After all, we already converse with them, and studies show that little children confuse computers that talk with people.[17] In fact, any number of new forms may one day replace the nuclear family. If meaning comes from a sense of connection, there is no reason why strong relationships forged outside the old framework cannot prove valuable up to a point. However, it's hard to imagine any arrangement better suited to serving the needs of children than the family of old—nor any ties capable of conveying connection to something of "greater and more lasting value" than biological kinship.

The best news regarding the family in recent years is the decline in divorce. An article from 2020 pointed out that, for every thousand marriages in the last year, only 14.9 ended in divorce.[18] While this is still much higher than 1960, when statistics began to be kept, it represents the modest reversal of a trend that alarmed many sociologists in the eighties and nineties. Of course, the decline in divorce must be understood in the context of other changes since 1960. The same article observed that marriage rates today are at an all-time low, with only thirty-three newlyweds a year getting married for every thousand Americans—compared to eighty per thousand in 1960. There are also the huge numbers of young people who may cohabitate a number of times before marrying, the rising ages of first marriages, and the historically low birth rate.

Nor are today's stable families otherwise identical to those of the postwar period. Today, both parents must often work, leaving much of the child-rearing to others. Meantime, the length of the workweek continues to grow. In postwar America, the forty-hour workweek was more or less standard. In 2014, Americans worked an average of forty-seven hours a week—or 1.4 extra hours a work day.[19] Growing, too, are commuting times. In 2018, average commute times in America reached a

17. Turkle, "Attack of Friendly Robots."
18. Wang, "U.S. Divorce Rate," paras. 1, 5.
19. Ward, "Brief History," para. 2.

record fifty-four minutes on average—nearly another potential family hour lost each day.[20] Of course, the COVID pandemic has changed this by encouraging many more couples to work from home. How this and any other prospective diseases will affect other ties of meaning, such as those in the workplace and in school, remains to be seen.

What we do know is that time spent daily with children—especially time when experiences may be shared and lessons learned—is vitally important in creating close bonds between family members and instilling those values essential to finding meaning in the larger society. Here again, the postwar era provides guidance. We have already mentioned the family supper. Now we want to draw attention to the daily ritual of TV watching.

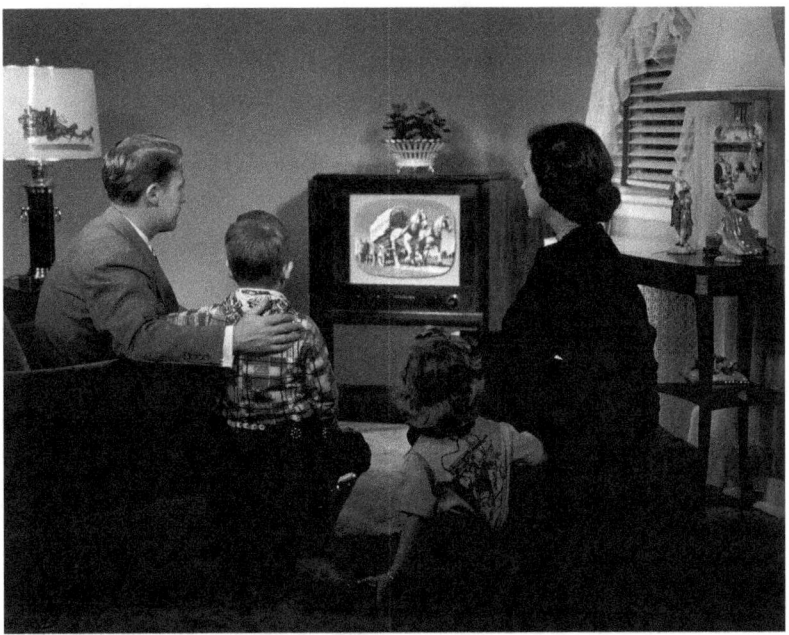

Television Influence. Photo by Harold M. Lambert/Getty Images.

Television watching in America began to take hold early in the fifties, when TV replaced the radio as the focal point of family gatherings in the evening. Programs then were often intended for multiple generations of viewers and had no questionable language or content.[21] Many conveyed simple moral lessons involving sharing, honesty, and respect

20. Ingraham, "Nine Days."
21. Wallace, "Watch TV."

for others. This was true especially of the popular family sitcoms, like *Ozzie and Harriet*, *Father Knows Best*, *The Donna Reed Show*, and *Leave it to Beaver*. The world of the American family, as depicted on TV, was one of firm rules enforced by parents who supported one another and who could be counted on to try to do the best for their children. This is very different from today's TV world of dysfunctional families with clueless fathers, indifferent mothers, and children who must often fend for themselves.

In the fifties and early sixties, there was generally only one television set in the home. At that time, the notion that individual family members may have their own sets, allowing them to withdraw into their own private entertainment universes, was both economically unviable and socially unacceptable. In its singularity, the television was like the telephone. And while this might have proven inconvenient (especially if there were teenagers in the house) such technological poverty served to draw family members into a common communication network in which each TV program (like each phone call) was a matter of general interest and concern.

In their capacity for shared experience, TV viewers of the period differed from family members in the contemporary household, where TV watching is often an individual experience, and as many as 90 percent of television viewers are busy multitasking during shows.[22] Perhaps this is just as well. While recent studies have shown that family-centric entertainment is effective in improving children's social and emotional skills, few TV shows today are suited to the purpose. This is evident from a 2013 study of twenty-one family shows, which revealed that 99 percent of TV episodes contained adult content in the form of sex, violence, or profanity.[23] And this does not count the many condom and "bent carrot" commercials that have sprung up on TV in recent years.

In an effort to compensate for the breakdown of the old rituals of meal time and TV viewing, most families today have turned to youth sports as a means of bonding. Given the number of sports available, the lengthening of the sports year, and the extension of competitive sports to the youngest children, some families now find themselves on a sports merry-go-round that consumes nearly all the family time through the high school years. As a means of establishing meaningful family

---

22. Wallace, "Watch TV," para. 2.
23. Wallace, "Watch TV," para. 5.

relationships and inculcating the young with the character traits needed for meaningful lives as citizens, this is deeply problematic. In fact, youth sports function less as a family activity than as an arena in which one family member performs for the others, with children attempting to win parental approval and adulation from their peers. Sports thus encourage that ego-driven personality that is now so prevalent among athletes—a trait that poses a major obstacle to forging meaningful social bonds.

Of course, sports are also capable of reinforcing links between team members and encouraging cooperation. But sports thrive on competition, which develops not only on the field but off it, pitting children against parents, parents against coaches, the entire family against umpires, referees, and opponents. The extraordinary growth in organized sports for children has thus spread alongside an enormous increase in acts of anger and even violence at competitions. In 2018, the abuse of referees and umpires in youth sports was so bad that, throughout America, games were being postponed or cancelled due to an unwillingness of officials to assume the thankless task.[24] Things were no better as of late 2021. At that time a CBS news telecast reported that the toxic combination of parental abuse and COVID had resulted in the forced cancellation of some thirty thousand youth sports events since 2018. The telecast included images of enraged parents physically assaulting referees and officials.[25]

Like self-absorption, competitiveness is a major hindrance to social integration. Indeed, it is hard to imagine traits more poorly suited to nurturing a capacity for self sacrifice and cooperation that is essential if individuals are to join with other members of society in a meaningful way. In the fifties, children's education stressed citizenship and getting along with others. Today, ambition is the chief value, with nearly 90 percent of men and women saying they were raised to believe it is important.[26] Now many husbands and wives work as a tag team to insure their children succeed in a competition that begins with getting them into the best preschool and won't end until they have successful children of their own. As one high school counselor has put it: "In this society fueled by wealth and status, the father's job is to make a lot of money so that the family can continue to live in the right neighborhood and go to the right school, while the mother's job is to make the children successful."[27] The

24. Thayer, "Youth Sports Faces Shortage."
25. Seen on CBS on Dec. 27, 2021.
26. Van Ogtrop, "Why Ambition Isn't Working," 54.
27. Glass and Tabatsky, *Overparenting Epidemic*, 72–73.

counselor went on to speak of marriages dissolving because the mother failed to assure her child's success, and of a father who committed suicide when he lost the lucrative job that paid for a fine home and school for the children. What sort of children will such marriages produce?

Today's epidemic of "overparenting" comes in a variety of forms, including "the hyper-protector," "type As," "buddies," and the rest. The common thread in each case is a loss of that balance between solicitude and benign neglect that typified parents of the fifties. The result is children with emotional problems running the gamut from a lack of self-confidence to a sense of entitlement. Overparenting may also lead to children who have no sense of self. These are children who have learned that their value derives from following their parents' lead rather than exploring their own path. Though a number of these children may find wealth and status, few will attain the depth of meaning that comes from having a secure and stable sense of identity.

While scholars have analyzed the various forms of overparenting and their consequences, few seem to have a firm grasp on the causes. Parents typically explain their behavior as children may, professing that they act the way they do because others do it. In fact, there are many causes of overparenting, ranging from the prevalence of communications that preclude independent children to a cacophony of commercial messages urging us to "Be all that you can be!" Behind and beyond all this is the fact that ours is a meaning impoverished culture that has bred generations of parents who don't know where to find it in their own lives or nurture it in their children. In the fifties, relatively few adults idolized celebrity, athletic prowess, or financial success. Most were content to find meaning in the home, among extended family, and in community, country, and church. Being content themselves, they raised children with the freedom to follow their own impulses without their parents looking on. Parents today need to spend more time with their children and less time watching them perform—more time alongside them and less time hovering overhead.

Meanwhile, young people seem to be fleeing parenthood in droves. Nor are those who accept the enormous responsibility as content as their grandparents had been. Since the appearance of therapist Roszina Parkers's *Torn in Two: the Experience of Maternal Ambivalence* (1995), Americans have been aware that growing numbers of young mothers have mixed feelings about parenthood.[28] These feelings are typically manifest in lukewarm attitudes toward offspring and periodic urges to abandon the family altogether. More recently, therapists have observed the same dissatisfaction in fathers, who normally express their feelings by being overly critical of children and pressuring them to excel. The primarily underlying cause of dissatisfaction, in each case, is the sense of identity loss that comes with the enormous personal investment required by child rearing. Coming on the heels of the sacrifices of marriage, this is often more than young people today can bear.

At best parenthood seems to be a mixed bag—some studies suggesting that parenthood is associated with increased happiness; others, that it leads to greater dissatisfaction. But we are dealing here with happiness. What happens when meaning is added to the equation?

In 2012, a group of psychologists published the results of a series of experiments designed to understand not only the satisfactions and dissatisfactions of parenthood, but its potential for meaning.[29] Researchers found that the way people experience parenthood depends largely upon age and gender, with older parents tending to be happier than younger, and men happier than women. Yet *all* parents—regardless of age or gender—found higher levels of meaning than nonparents. This seems to be consistent with what we said in an earlier chapter about the relation between happiness and meaning. Parenthood opens us to the miracle of life and ties us to the future in an immediate and intensely personal way. The potential for meaning is extraordinary, and the price in terms of short-term, everyday contentment may accordingly be great. Little wonder that many young Americans trained to focus on themselves and their own success are increasingly unable or unwilling to make the sacrifices that the meanings of parenthood demand. Others look for a quick return on their investment in the way of a child's success, while still others look to the birth of grandchildren who can provide meanings with relatively few of the costs. Increasing numbers simply forgo the experience altogether in exchange for the greater personal or financial rewards of childlessness.

To parent or not to parent is the central issue for the family in the twenty-first century. At its base, the question concerns how we understand ourselves and the values we embrace. How we decide greatly effects the fate of meaning generally in our society.

28. Drexler, "It's OK for Parents."
29. Nelson et al., "In Defense of Parenthood."

Anyone observing early postwar American neighborhoods today will likely note physical reminders of the importance of community. In suburbs and small towns, houses and lots seem claustrophobic by today's standards. Then, it was possible to step out your front door and see your neighbor's front door or look into their yard—not to mention hearing their arguments, loud TVs, and more. Houses often had front porches for socializing and were joined by sidewalks that served both as thoroughfares for biking and walking and as playgrounds for hopscotch, jacks, jump rope, rock or chalk drawing, and other activities. Distinctive physical or geographical features of the neighborhood (if such existed) were generally well known to children, if not to adults. One neighbor's yard might have been ideally suited to hide-and-seek, another's to rolly bat, a third to tree climbing, and so on. The vacant lots and woods that were then so prevalent were also valued as places for exploration and play.

Postwar towns and small cities were still arranged in a way that harkened back to an era before the automobile began to dominate daily life. Churches, schools and municipal buildings were clustered near the town center, where pedestrian traffic might have continued well after dark—especially if a popular film were showing. Nearly all towns had a hotel located near the center of the business district, where it served as a hub of activity. Socializing was also encouraged by little restaurants, sandwich or doughnut shops, and newsstands. School children often had drug stores or soda shops where they could congregate after school. Teens with cars had access to burger joints and drive-ins. Most children still walked to and/or from school and to many after-school activities. Though wealthy adults often socialized with the other well-to-do, their children were usually not so discriminating in their friendships. Segregation by race, on the other hand, was everywhere—especially in southern towns, where the black neighborhood was not only separate from white neighborhoods but often carried a different name.

Although conditions were changing in the postwar years, communities in the American metropolises continued to thrive into the sixties. Businesses still bustled, corporate offices were filled, and movie theaters, restaurants, and nightclubs attracted patrons who felt relatively safe on the sidewalks, or in buses, trolleys, and subways. Industries, warehouses, and harbors surrounded many city centers, providing jobs for blue-collar workers who lived in friendly, vibrant communities. Here, small businesses prospered, and people could be found congregating on the stoops and sidewalks well into the night—especially if it were a warm evening. Each community had its own identity—Italian, Irish, Chinese, and so on. Ethnicity was the glue that held these communities together, reminding newer residents of the small towns they had left behind. Communities were still of a modest size and fairly stable, while the presence of a wide variety of ethnic groups nearby usually assured a degree of tolerance.

The communal atmosphere of American cities and towns was dealt a fatal blow by the emergence of the automobile and the suburbanization that spread in its wake. While the nation's population grew 50 percent between 1950 and 1970, the number of cars jumped 200 percent.[30] The suburban population followed accordingly by doubling between 1950 and 1970—making suburbanites the largest segment of the population. To accommodate America's growing love affair with the car, Congress passed the Federal-Aid Highway Act in 1956. The act not only marked the beginning of interstate travel; it also provided thousands of miles of outer-belt expressways that sped up traffic to and from the cities. While home dwellers led the exodus to the suburbs, retailers, industries, and big corporations soon followed, gobbling up open land and decimating many urban areas.

The transition to the centerless world of contemporary America began with those suburban communities that sprang up (some may say "like weeds") in response to the housing crisis immediately following the war. Lakewood (in Southern California), Park Forest (south of Chicago), and the various Levittowns (New York, New Jersey, and Pennsylvania) are the best known of these. Critics of the day decried the new suburbanites as tasteless, politically apathetic (with conservative tendencies), and emotionally wanting. Most troublesome was their conformity. "All dwellings are the same shape," sniffed one critic, "all dwellers are squeezed into the same shape."[31] What the critics failed to sufficiently appreciate was that the early suburbanites tended to bring their manners and their social skills along with them in exiting the city. In our first chapter we noted the many community organizations in the new developments and the inclination of the residents to share resources. To this we may add the

---

30. K. Jackson, *Crabgrass Frontier*, 246.
31. Skolnick, *Embattled Paradise*, 60.

car pools and babysitting co-ops, the coffee klatches, bridge clubs, and book-of-the-month clubs.

The worst that could be said of the new suburbanites was that, like most Americans, they were racially intolerant. Otherwise they were generally more accepting of differences and more democratic than earlier generations—more willing to take people as they found them and judge them on their merits. William O'Neil observes that their most striking feature, as noted by most fair-minded observers, was their "niceness."[32] "They tried hard to be open, cooperative, helpful friends, concerned citizens and good parents," he adds. Their children had much the same spirit of community, leading one critic to complain that they were being "brought up in a kind of communism."[33]

Of course, the new planned communities were only a part of the story. In *The New Urban Crisis*, Richard Florida reminds us that many new suburbanites simply moved from crowded cities to smaller towns nearby.[34] Florida recalls how, while still a toddler (around 1960), the family moved from Newark, New Jersey, to the small town of North Arlington in search of better schools for the children. Though only about a fifteen-minute drive from Newark, North Arlington was in many ways a typical suburban community. "Growing up in North Arlington," recalls Florida, "I walked to school starting in the first grade, rode my ten-speed bike everywhere, played sandlot baseball and touch football, and started a rock and roll band with my brother."[35] Florida adds that, for a number of years, the family regularly returned to Newark for shopping, music lessons, and large family dinners. All this changed following the summer of 1967, when Newark, like many American cities, was roiled by race riots. Florida notes that the city never recovered.

By the mid-sixties, small-town America was also in decline. Here again, the emergence of the automobile played an important role. We see this, for example, in the growth of chain motels and fast-food restaurants. Both had been around for years. However, in 1952, in Memphis, the first motel of the famous Holiday Inn chain opened. Three years later, the first of Ray Kroc's McDonald's outlets appeared in the Chicago suburb of Des Plaines. During the sixties, both motels and fast-food restaurants made their presence felt. By 1972, an old hotel was closing somewhere

---

32. O'Neil, *American High*, 25.
33. Skolnick, *Embattled Paradise*, 60.
34. Florida, *New Urban Crisis*, xi–xii, 151–52.
35. Florida, *New Urban Crisis*, 152.

in downtown America every thirty hours.[36] Fast-food chains similarly provided competition for local dining establishments. Between 1970 and 1998 the number of full-service restaurants per one hundred thousand Americans declined by one quarter, while the number of bars and diners was cut in half. During the same period, the number of fast-food outlets doubled.[37] This development has had terrible consequences for the little meanings found in everyday exchanges. "Unlike the 'regulars' at the local bar or cafe," observes Robert Putnam, "few of the other people waiting impatiently at McDonalds are likely to know your name or even care that they don't."[38]

Both cities and small towns suffered from the emergence of shopping malls in the sixties. Though the concept was also an old one, the modern mall is often said to have begun with the Austrian-born immigrant Victor Gruen, who designed the first outdoor shopping center near Detroit in 1954. Gruen had hoped to create places for community amid the growing deserts of the suburbs. However, he would come to regret his innovation for its impact upon American life. As an expert on urban retail planning, Robert J. Gibbs, explains:

> The first generation of malls built in the mid-1950's to mid-1960s devastated small towns. They pulled out the department stores from the city centers and shifted the center of commerce from downtown to the mall . . . the effect was devastating.[39]

In the early postwar years, main street retailers had as much as 80 percent of America's retail business. By 1984, the country's twenty thousand large shopping centers accounted for almost two-thirds of the retail trade. Gibbs points out that, as of 2017, only twenty-three to thirty American cities had regained as much as 20 percent of the market share.[40] Of course, retailers were not the only victims. Restaurants and movie theaters soon flocked to where the people were, further reducing downtown traffic and turning the areas into ghost towns.

Many big cities, for their part, would seem to be undergoing a recent Renaissance, as professionals, techies, and the well-to-do seek out the excitement of an urban atmosphere. Yet as Florida points out, such

36. K. Jackson, *Crabgrass Frontier*, 254.
37. Putnam, *Bowling Alone*, 102.
38. Putnam, *Bowling Alone*, 102.
39. Glennen, "Rise and Fall," para. 10.
40. Glennen, "Rise and Fall," para. 13.

"revitalization" comes at an enormous cost.[41] As the better-off emigrate into the urban areas, the poor must flee, taking their problems (poverty, drugs, mental illness, crime, etc.) with them to the suburbs. The result is that the suburbs of our largest cities have now become poorer than the inner city itself. Meanwhile, those who remain behind to tend the new city dwellers fail to profit as much as we may imagine. When housing is factored in, the remaining blue-collar workers and service workers are actually financially worse off than they were before the recent influx. Florida laments how the middle class has been "hollowed out" of our cities, and wonders how they can survive when police officers, teachers, nurses, restaurant workers, and the like can no longer afford to live within reasonable commuting distance.

Thus far we have been primarily concerned with the physical context of community—that is, the settings within which the meanings to be found in community life unfold. Now we want to look more specifically at community activity, as especially indicated by the involvement of Americans in community organizations. Here, the vital resource is Robert Putnam's classic *Bowling Alone: The Collapse and Revival of American Community*. While Putnam's insights have been amplified and expanded upon in recent years (including by Putnam himself) the book remains the basis for any understanding of the changing character of community life in postmodern America.

Putnam's data indicates that, across the wide spectrum of social interaction, America has suffered a serious loss of social capital that began at the end of the postwar period (about 1965) when social capital was at an all-time high. From PTA's to trade unions, Kiwanis clubs to churches, political organizations to bowling leagues, Americans have, for decades, been withdrawing into a narrow network of family and friends and forsaking those larger bonds that had once given meaning. This change has been accompanied by a shift in viewpoint regarding the major institutions (e.g., church and government) that are essential to the experience of broad and lasting connections. Americans at the end of the twentieth century were especially distrustful of government. In 1960, three out of four Americans surveyed agreed that you could trust the government in Washington to do what is right "all or most of the time." By the nineties,

---

41. Florida, *New Urban Crisis*, 155.

about three out of four Americans *didn't* trust the government to do what was right most of the time.[42]

There were, of course, developments that seemed to run counter to the ongoing decline in civic engagement. However, even these are telling regarding the nature of communities in the twenty-first century and the difficulties in maintaining the old connections. Putnam observes, for example, the rise of support groups, including those that help gays, the overweight, and Americans with special needs. He points out that, despite their obvious value, such groups tend to be narrowly focused, and their members less likely to be engaged in broader community activities like organizations of the past. Large social movements, like the numerous environmental groups that have become so popular, also have serious limitations. Putnam observes that groups like these are really "tertiary" organizations whose members typically do no more than make a modest contribution in exchange for bumper stickers or return address labels.[43] Nor do the expanded use of phones and the emergence of the internet appear to be useful in strengthening community. Putnam speaks of how the former encourages a trend toward "privatization," and the latter, a move toward "cyber balkanization."[44]

The impact of such technological shifts have been of special interest to scholars working in the wake of *Bowling Alone*. Among these is Marc Dunkelman, whose *The Vanishing Neighbor: The Transformation of American Community*, argues that our new technologies have led to an erosion of the "middle rings" of social interaction. Americans, Dunkelman claims, are today investing more time and energy in close family and friends and in distant contacts—the first and third rings of social interaction, respectively. What they are losing is the middle ring relationships of the sort Putnam clearly values. Dunkelman cites evidence indicating that, unlike the old land lines, cell phone conversations generally involve our most intimate relationships.[45] Husbands and wives tend to keep in frequent contact by phone, as do "helicopter" parents and their children. And while our cell phones pull us toward our most intimate relationships, the internet leads us toward the outer bands of the communication network. This is because internet contacts are likely to be with people to whom we are only tangentially linked, such as old friends and coworkers,

42. Putnam, *Bowling Alone*, 47.
43. Putnam, *Bowling Alone*, 154–66.
44. Putnam, *Bowling Alone*, 166–80.
45. Dunkelman, *Vanishing Neighbor*, 104.

or people with whom we share a narrow interest, like a hobby or an online game. These may be people from the distant reaches of the country or other parts of the world. In any case, they are often people with whom we have little, if any, direct personal contact.

The essential point is that both communication networks take us further from the community around us—that is, from the second rings of our social network. This may seem to be of little importance, since we are likely to feel more "connected" than ever. However, it is largely the people in the second rings—e.g., the people we see walking their dogs, the friendly waiter at our favorite restaurant, the people who sit near us at church—who "humanize" our world in a way that not only gives meaning, but makes it seem to be a friendlier and more trustworthy place. People like these are important not only to our own sense of well-being but to the health of society. For without a constant and reinforcing sense of connection to a varied and diverse population, we are likely to seek out people who feel "safe" because they look like us.

The loss of the "second rings" are evident in the growing social and political polarization of America. *The Vanishing Neighbor* cites studies based upon voting data that reveal that Americans are more likely to live in communities of common interests and points of view than at any time in recent history. In the presidential elections of 1976, for example, just over a third of American counties voted overwhelmingly for either Gerald Ford or Jimmy Carter. Almost two-thirds were competitive.[46] When John Kerry ran against George W. Bush, in 2004, the percentage of noncompetitive counties had grown to nearly 60 percent. During roughly the same years, the percentage of moderates in Congress fell from 30 to 8 percent, while those with "strong" political leanings rose from 27 to 57 percent.[47] In effect, our technology is pulling us apart even as it deprives us of those countervailing contacts which suggest that our world is a warm and welcoming place.

The political implications of our changing communities has also been a vital theme in Putnam's more recent work. Several years after the appearance of *Bowling Alone*, the sociologist again created a stir with the publication of his paper "*E Pluribus Unum*: Diversity and Community in the Twenty-First Century." The essay dealt with the results of research designed to determine the impact of immigration and ethnic diversity

---

46. Dunkelman, *Vanishing Neighbor*, 47.
47. Dunkelman, *Vanishing Neighbor*, 184.

on social capital. Putnam noted that many scholars have traditionally believed that contacts between different immigrant groups and other Americans furthered understanding between them. However, the evidence did not support this assumption. In fact, Putnam's research indicated that diversity generates "anomie and social isolation."[48]

In his essay, Putnam's discomfort is palpable as he puts forth his findings and marshals evidence to support them. Putnam emphasizes that researchers made every effort to uncover alternative explanations for their conclusions. However, factors like economic inequality and generational differences within ethnic communities appear to have no significant role in the results. Ethnically diverse communities are simply low in the sort of social capital Putnam values so highly. They are communities of distrust. And it isn't that residents simply distrust other ethnic groups. They are distrustful generally, withdrawing from community life and shunning nearly all voluntary organizations. Worse yet, they are unsure of their neighbors and tend to expect the worst of their government. In Putnam's terms, they "hunker down" like turtles, isolating themselves as much as possible from the society around them.[49]

Perhaps the biggest surprise in "*E Pluribus Unum*" is the author's surprise at his findings. America's famed "melting pot" was always more of an ethnic stew whose effectiveness depended upon the right balance of mostly homogeneous ingredients and a savory seasoning made up of the inspiring stories of the nation and its founders. Our more recent immigrants tend to be groups who have too little or too much in common, while our country has begun to question the old stories. Hence the emergence in America of those "parallel" societies which have also formed in Europe—to the alarm of Europeans who, like many Americans, once found meaning from people with histories much like their own in a nation that took pride in its past.

"*E Pluribus Unum*" was followed by the 2015 bestseller *The Kids*, in which Putnam looked at more recent studies that indicated that the decline in social capital was especially apparent among the poorest, least educated Americans. Data indicated, for example, that those in the top one fifth in the socioeconomic hierarchy had 20–25 percent more close friends than those in the bottom fifth. Surprisingly, the former had more "weak" social ties as well.[50] Not surprisingly, both groups had experienced

48. Putnam, "*E Pluribus Unum*," 149.
49. Putnam, "*E Pluribus Unum*," 149.
50. Putnam, *Our Kids*, 207.

a decline in social trust in recent decades, although the decline was much more notable among poor parents and their children. Church attendance showed a similar pattern. While church attendance among middle-aged, college-educated Americans had remained flat in recent decades, it dropped by a third among non-college-educated Americans.[51] And there was evidence that these disparities in social capital were continuing to grow—much like the financial disparity between the poorer and better-off in America.

Not everyone seems to agree with Putnam's conclusion that the poor are weaker in social capital. Amy Chua has observed that poor Americans are also involved in a variety of groups that provide social support and reinforcement, though these tend to be the sorts of social groups the better-off disdain.[52] Many poor blacks and whites are proponents of the prosperity gospel as preached by celebrity pastors like Joel Osteen and televangelist Creflo Dollar. Other poorer Americans are members of NASCAR nation, or revel in the antics of World Wrestling Entertainment, Inc. Young men of all ethnicities find camaraderie in street gangs, while scores of American Latinos have become involved in the cult of Nuestra Señora de la Santa Muerte—Our Lady of the Holy Death.

While it seems to me that Chua is right to point all this out, from the perspective of meaning, Putnam's conclusion remains correct. As we have already indicated (and will again) sports and pseudo-sports like NASCAR racing and WWE are, at best, modest sources of meaning, whose effectiveness relies upon pitting one individual or group against another, and whose impact is shallow and short lived. Such activities are more like fads than like real communities—more like junk food than real nourishment. On the other hand, Santa Muerte and the gospel of prosperity are both distortions of the Christian faith. At their best, they provide a network of support at the expense of the greater depth and breadth of meaning available from a genuine theology.

None of these activities has the capacity to join diverse groups of people in a community that is truly of greater and more lasting value than themselves. All are indicative of lives lived on the edges of meaning in a society that has lost the richness available from truer and deeper sources—sources now receding into the past.

---

51. Putnam, *Our Kids*, 225.
52. Chua, *Political Tribes*, 143–61.

7

Labor

INASMUCH AS LABOR WILL typically occupy more than one third of our waking hours for most of our lives, the possibility of finding meaning in work is of obvious importance. This may explain why labor is one area where a notable effort has been made in recent years to study the issue of meaning. While these studies are certainly worth our attention, they must be approached with caution. Here, as in the psychological studies on meaning we cited earlier, meaning is treated as a subjective experience and remains essentially undefined. However, as in the earlier cases, it is clear that most people understand meaning as a sense of "connection" to something greater and longer lasting than themselves. And, as we have seen elsewhere, such connections are now generally in decline in America.

Perhaps the most important discovery in this research is that workers who view their labor as a "calling" tend to find greater meaning than those who view it as a career, or merely as a way of making ends meet.[1] This should not surprise us. The notion of work as a calling harkens back to a religious viewpoint that sees all of life as the working out of a divine plan. The meanings available from relating our lives to a divine purpose are enormous. Moreover, even when a religious framework may not be clearly defined, the idea of work as "calling" points beyond ordinary experience—to some larger dimension in ourselves, perhaps, or to some greater need in society or trend in human history. In either case, a sense of "calling" runs counter to our tendency to weigh labor today simply on the basis of status

---

1. Wrzensniewski et al., "Jobs, Careers, and Callings."

and income. In the following pages we will note one profession where the notion of "calling" has recently given way to a preoccupation with wealth and status to the enormous detriment of meaning.

Some workers derive meaning by recognizing that their work is necessary to their family. To the extent that success here may take tangible form in more money for basic needs, this view may certainly provide meaning. Others may find meaning simply by taking the right approach to their daily labor. Emily Smith cites the example of a food cart owner who gave a free taco to one patron who had forgotten his wallet, saying, "My job isn't to take your money. My job is to feed you." She also cites the example of a man whose job was to control traffic for highway repair by turning a sign that read "stop" on one side and "slow" on the other. This man saw the purpose of his work as making workers and drivers safe.[2] Again, meaning came from looking beyond immediate experience by regarding labor as serving the larger social good.

The idea that meaning comes from the belief that our labor benefits others has inspired a recent PayScale poll of over two million workers in five hundred jobs, who were asked to answer whether or not their work "makes the world a better place."[3] Not surprisingly, the clergy, educators and a variety of medical practitioners rated highest on the list. Adam Grant has rightly noted that these are jobs that prove beneficial to others. However, it does not follow, as Grant has suggested, that this bodes well for the future—especially in an economy where 80 percent of jobs are now in the service sector.[4] In fact, an analysis of the PayScale data shows that most service jobs (not only cooks, dishwashers, and bartenders, but clerks, bank tellers, parking lot attendants, and the like) rank among the lowest in meaning according to the survey. For the foreseeable future, jobs like these are likely to be in greater demand than the clergy. Meanwhile, and despite high demand for their services, young people today are rejecting careers in public school teaching in record numbers.[5] We will have more to say of this shortly.

Indeed, there are many factors contributing to a worker's sense that their labor has meaning. And the most significant of these, I would argue, is the work experience itself. After all, while framing one's labor in a meaningful way by thinking of its necessity for the family or deciding

---

2. E. Smith, *Power of Meaning*, 96.
3. PayScale, "Most and Least," para. 1.
4. A. Grant, "Three Lies," paras. 5, 7.
5. Peetz, "Status of Teaching Profession."

that it serves others may be very helpful in enhancing its meaning, it is not usually something we carry to work on a daily basis.

In this context, it is worth noting that a Gallup poll from some years back indicated that the percentage of workers who enjoyed their hours on the job more than their hours away from work had dropped from 44 percent in 1955 to a mere 16 percent by 1999.[6] Although an old poll, it is recent enough to reflect the impact upon labor of the dramatic turn toward computers that marked the last years of the twentieth century. In many cases, these have replaced hands-on labor that workers previously found meaningful (once again, there is an example to follow). The new technology has also siphoned off meaning by eliminating contact to customers. An online purchase with an emailed thank-you is simply not the same as a purchase in the local clothing store or record shop. Nor are we likely to find the little meanings available from a local diner at the nearby McDonald's where, today, even our order may be taken by computer.

Surveys have further indicated that, in addition to interaction with customers, interaction with fellow employees is meaningful—in fact, that it is often the most meaningful aspect of labor.[7] In this context, we should note the recent rise of the *gig economy*. The gig economy involves the use of contractors or on-call workers throughout the economy, from big businesses to private transportation (e.g., Uber) and home delivery (Grubhub, DoorDash). Here, laborers often work alone, seldom form ties to clients, and typically move from one job to another. It is the ultimate form of labor without meaningful attachments, and typical of the hyperindividualism that today presents one of the greatest threats to meaning in life. As Timothy Carney explains:

> The Gig Economy is a perfect capitalist microcosm of our age of individualism: no entangling alliances or permanent commitments. Easy come. Easy go. Two or three parties come together on the occasions when they can derive mutual benefit. Then they go different ways. No strings attached. It's like free love, but for groceries and a $5 dollar surcharge.[8]

This "go-it-alone" approach to work has also begun to affect forms of white-collar labor where collegiality has especially been prized. Law is one of many examples. Later on we want to note how pressure to achieve

---

6. Putnam, *Bowling Alone*, 91.
7. Putnam, *Bowling Alone*, 90.
8. Carney, *Alienated America*, 182–83.

the requisite "billable" hours has in recent years placed severe restraints on the social and professional interaction that attorneys in large firms once found so meaningful. For the moment we want to note the impact of opportunities to work from home, which here, as in many other white-collar professions, is one of the mixed blessings of a post-COVID America. Many lawyers, it is clear, prefer the stay-at-home option. But not all do. A survey conducted by the ABA in 2022 indicated that older attorneys regretted the change. The same survey found that both young and old acknowledged increased stress (23 percent) and a heightened sense of social isolation (42 percent) as consequences of working from home.[9]

On the other hand, the likelihood that labor will increasingly be unable to give meaning to life may be of less concern for today's young Americans.[10] Baby boomers (and, to a lesser extent, their Gen X successors) looked to labor as a prominent source of meaning, either by searching for work that was intrinsically engaging or by seeking to develop close relationships with other employees. Millennials were different. Millennials seemed to care less about meaning on the job, regarding labor as a necessity that, hopefully, would not unduly interfere with social activities on the job or outside it. IGeners are unlike either. Young Americans today are willing to work, but seem to care only for the financial rewards. Neither the intrinsic value of their labor nor the possibilities of meaning through on-the-job relationships motivates them. They simply expect to show up, do the necessary labor, and be fairly compensated.

In the following pages we hope to get at changes in work experience in more detail by looking at how workers describe their work and by examining the factors that have aided or hampered their search for meaning. Our evidence is based upon a combination of firsthand accounts and statistical evidence on labor and changes in the workplace. The range of this inquiry is obviously limited to a few of the wide variety of possible occupations. It is restricted to labors that span the many decades in question and to those where both statistical evidence and firsthand accounts are readily available. An effort has also been made to capture something of the variety of labor in America and to look at jobs that appeal to women, to men, or both.

We will be looking at factory work, law, and public school teaching. The first, which epitomizes blue-collar labor, has experienced significant decline in recent decades, while law, the prototypical white-collar career,

9. Merken, "As More Lawyers Return," para. 11.
10. Twenge, *iGen*, 179–201.

has seen major growth. Despite significant social changes, factory workers are still predominantly men and public school teachers women, while law has a good mix.

On September 15, 2019, forty-nine thousand GM autoworkers went on strike for higher wages, better benefits and greater job security. It was the first work stoppage in America in over a decade, and it lasted until October 25. Although workers failed in their efforts to convince GM to move car production from Mexico to a shuttered facility in Ohio, they were generally pleased with their efforts. At the strike's conclusion, lead UAW negotiator Terry Dittes not only gave credit to union solidarity, but cited the support of the whole community in helping workers achieve their goals. Said Dittes: "This is about standing up for us, the families and the communities that are affected because this is not just about our members."[11]

While the experience of the 2019 workers in some ways echoes that of earlier striking laborers, today's industrial America differs significantly from its postwar counterpart. In the twelve months following the end of World War II, one third of American unionists would strike in what has been called "the greatest wage offensive in U.S. labor history."[12] The era of massive work stoppages continued through the fifties, culminating in the great Steel Strike of 1959. On July 15 of that year, five hundred thousand steelworkers (representing nearly 1 percent of America's entire labor force) failed to show up for work. The strike continued into January, and even then was not fully resolved. During these months, the strike was big news, with the president, vice president, and the Supreme Court getting involved. The size and length of the Steel Strike of 1959 ensured that steelworkers would hesitate to strike thereafter. In any case, the major American unions had by then achieved real wage increases, paid vacations and holidays, health insurance, sickness and accident and disability insurance, pensions, and job security.[13]

It is important to understand all this to have a sense of the meanings that American blue-collar workers found in their labor during the postwar years. Then, as today, most found little meaning in the daily grind. These men (and they were almost exclusively men) were wage earners, who typically saw their job as a way to make ends meet. But unions then

11. Stelloh and Elbaum, "Tens of Thousands," para. 6.
12. Metzgar, *Striking Steel*, 28.
13. Metzgar, *Striking Steel*, 58–93.

were formidable, with one in three American households a union home. The most successful union families of the period, like the steelworkers, had a sense of real prosperity that came in the form of TV sets, refrigerators, and family cars—all of which flowed slowly but steadily from hard-fought union gains. This was new. It was only in 1953 that the average steelworker in America escaped poverty.

Most steelworkers of the fifties also derived a profound sense of satisfaction from remembering when they were at the mercy of foremen and superintendents, from whom they were forced to curry favor. Some recalled when many of their number had suffered serious injury under unsafe working conditions.

Those who remembered the past included Johnny Metzgar, whose life in the company mill town of Johnstown, Pennsylvania, is recalled in his son Jack's memoir *Striking Steel: Solidarity Remembered*. Johnny Metzgar's Uncle Will was a hunchback from carrying heavy water buckets as a child. His father had lost both arms in the mill in 1917. In the fifties, Johnny served as a griever, charged with looking out for the interests of fellow employees. While he professed to despise his work, Metzgar delighted in the union, which he saw through the eyes of a strong fundamentalist faith. The union was the worldly arena where an Old Testament–like justice was meted out. It was this conjunction of union and faith, as experienced within the context of family, that gave his life meaning.

However, the sense of being joined to something of greater and more lasting significance extended beyond the increasing power of the unions. *Striking Steel* is important for illuminating a larger working-class culture that by the fifties had taken hold in factory and mill towns across America.

In Johnstown, everyone understood then that workers' pay increases benefited "Bantley's Hardware, DeFazio's corner grocery, Glosser Brothers' department store, the church collection plate."[14] This fact, in conjunction with the integration of the workers' families and the community, led to widespread sympathy for the striking unionists. Decades later, this sense of "togetherness" was fondly recalled, and it helps to explain why so many young people were for years hesitant to forsake "the valley" for the world beyond. As Metzgar recalls the experience:

> Sticking together was one of the things that made growing up in the working class so secure and warm in those days. In contrast to the professional middle-class tendency to subject all personal

14. Metzgar, *Striking Steel*, 21.

relationships to a utilitarian calculus, a cost-benefit analysis, in working-class life there were both narrow and broad groups of people to which you belonged whether you liked it or not, and for the most part you could count on these people sticking with you.... While all these interlocking groups imposed their own obligations and responsibilities... being able to take your presence in them for granted lent a stability and a calm, perhaps an integrity, to life that seems rare today.[15]

For the steelworkers, as for most blue-collar workers, the world of the unions and the factory towns began its decline in the mid-seventies. Work stoppages were becoming rare, and negotiations with management were now conducted in a more private, professional manner. Indeed, the big unions had long since achieved their primary goals. Many Americans thought they were becoming greedy. Unions thus began a dramatic decline that, by century's end, would result in the halving of their membership. With this came the loss of the sense of solidarity in a just cause that had served as a powerful source of meaning for so many. This was evident in a new sort of worker—someone who thought "primarily of himself," as one labor economist put it in 1979. "We are experiencing the cult of the individual," he continued, "and labor is taking a beating preaching the comfort of coalition."[16]

The growing emphasis on the individual also worked against the meanings to be found in industrial labor in another way, as "industrial egoism" began to take hold among corporate leadership. Matters came to a head following the severe recessions of 1974 and 1980, which resulted in a dramatic shift to free-market policies that would make fortunes for the few while leaving the majority behind. As Paul Roberts describes the new philosophy:

> This more Darwinian view of business represented a dramatic departure from the postwar philosophy. In that era, corporations had been seen as obligated not just to shareholders, but to all "stakeholders," not least workers and their communities. But the stakeholder idea, conservative theorists now argued, was simply wrong. A corporation is not some social entity with dependent constituencies. It is merely a legal contrivance... whose sole purpose is maximizing "shareholder value."[17]

15. Metzgar, *Striking Steel*, 116–17.
16. Putnam, *Bowling Alone*, 82.
17. Roberts, *Impulse Society*, 44.

Toward this end, corporations shifted emphasis from long-term growth to fast results. The easiest way to quickly raise profits was layoffs, which were made easier by the emergence of computer technology. This was revolutionary. For while layoffs during economic downturns were nothing new, the manufacturing jobs now being lost were never coming back.

In the early eighties, an agency called Mainstream Access came to Johnstown to help displaced workers find new jobs. An essential part of this effort involved helping the workers prepare resumés. While many workers appreciated the effort, most found the notion of listing "accomplishments" and "work objectives" difficult to comprehend. Older workers were unaccustomed to thinking of themselves as having specific goals and skills apart from the factory and community where they lived. Few were ambitious or had considered the possibility of advancement. Meaning, for them, had a different source. As Metzgar succinctly puts it, "Working-class culture emphasizes being and belonging, not achieving and becoming."[18]

What was true then of Johnstown still remains largely true for factory communities today. For while much has changed since the fifties, most blue-collar workers still find meaning by looking beyond themselves to their roles in workplace, family and community. For such people, retraining presents enormous challenges. Workers who years ago rejected the educational pathway to the middle-class find programs requiring a return to school unnerving. Others suffer "identity mismatch"—as when, for example, a steelworker is encouraged to retrain as a nurse. Nearly all are reluctant to abandon the world they have known for relocation to a new community. Little wonder that a 2012 Labor Department assessment found that, four years after retraining, only 37 percent of participants worked in the targeted industries. Incomes of older retrained workers never caught up with earlier wages.[19]

People like these may be warned that the old factory jobs are never returning. But we will never understand their inability to adapt as we think they should until we understand the loss of meaning that accompanies the loss of our factories and mills.

At some remove from the typical steelworker are tool and die makers. Tool and die makers are the artisans who make many of the tools of manufacturing. These craftsmen typically work in small businesses (fifty

---

18. Metzgar, *Striking Steel*, 203.
19. Selingo, "False Promises."

workers or fewer), and their labor requires precision and a knowledge of various machines and materials. Many have college training in mathematics, engineering, and design. Like most manufacturing jobs, their work has recently suffered from foreign competition. Only here, where meaning often derives from the laborers' skills, the challenge comes directly from computers, which threaten to deprive work of its value even when it does not eliminate it altogether.

The dangers posed by computers to the meanings found in mechanical labor are the subject of Frank Burke's essay "The Tools of Man: The Decline of Traditional Manufacturing Is a Symptom of a Deeper Loss." In his essay, Burke draws heavily upon his experience working with a large manufacturer of metal cutting machine tools. However, Burke's observations are intended to cover a range of manufacturing jobs impacted by the new technologies.

Early in the essay, Burke speaks fondly of "the real treasures of manufacturing"—that is, the measuring tools that were once so vital to the individual worker. These tools were silver or grey, with finely incised gradations and numbers. Some (such as gauge blocks) were so finely finished that they tended to adhere to each other. Tools like these were objects of personal pride—as well as of meaning, since it was here that man and machine fruitfully intersected to help create forms of lasting utility and value. Burke describes how workers used to wipe their tools clean after each task and kept them in oaken chests lined with felt. A great deal of personal value was attached to these chests. Many workers placed family photos in them. And while the tools themselves would eventually be sold to coworkers, the chests were often kept as a family heirloom.

These rituals of meaning having to do with the workers' tools sometimes extended to the large machines. Burke describes how he was once called by a coworker to observe another, older worker as he prepared to leave his post just before the Thanksgiving holiday:

> The man ran a horizontal milling machine, for which he had had special handles made for the controls. After the closing bell rung—a time when most of his co-workers rushed to wash up and get home—he removed a stack of shop rags—red-orange cloths about a foot square—from a shelf and began to cover the working surfaces of his machine. I noticed a number of others watching as he proceeded to literally wrap the entire machine to protect it

over the long weekend. Although his actions were extreme, no one laughed. It was clearly a sign of respect, if not affection.[20]

Burke observes that the meaningful interaction of hand and tool has lost its vital place in manufacturing in recent years. Today, the rules, T-squares, drawing boards, and compasses once employed by designers have given way to CAD-CAM (computer-assisted design–computer-assisted manufacturing) systems. Operators in caps and aprons who once took careful measurements after each operation have been replaced by men and women in lab coats whose job is to note data on the screens of sophisticated electronic controls. All the while, traditional production processes are being supplanted by techniques that increase productivity while depriving the worker of the meanings found in labor—or eliminating them altogether.

One of Burke's most telling observations concerns the different attitudes of the young workers from those older workers whose parents had lived through the scarcity of the Depression years. Older workers were more likely to be aware of the effort that went into the production of everyday objects and were more alert to their continuing utility. These were workers who, as children, knew that old tires made marvelous swings, and that baby carriage wheels were ideal for homemade wagons or race cars. Younger workers today regard such objects as disposable, with little or no real value. Burke is well aware that such a shift in viewpoint has enormous implications for meaningful factory work: "The knowledge that a new phone, dining room chair, or anything else will require replacement in relatively short order precludes the development of a meaningful relationship with it—and thereby hollows out a critical source of pride that workers once took from producing such things. That pride has been traded for empty abundance."[21]

Today, all emphasis is upon the "tickle to the eye" of design, with the understanding that the object itself will soon be replaced. Speed is the name of the game. Workers now struggle to keep up with the newest fads and innovations without ever experiencing the deeper meaning that comes from producing something that will stand the test of time. Hence Burke's closing admonition of a few things we would do well to remember and preserve: "pride in individual craftsmanship, the bond between

---

20. Burke, "Tools of Man," 17.
21. Burke, "Tools of Man," 18.

man and machine, and a reverence for well-made objects and the tools that bring them into being."[22]

If factory workers are the embodiment of blue-collar labor, law may reasonably be said to exemplify white-collar work. Lawyers have a long and storied place in American history. Writing soon after his visit to America in 1831, the famous French observer Alexis de Tocqueville spoke of lawyers as the "aristocracy" of the republic.[23] Indeed, from the founding fathers through men like Lincoln and Franklin Roosevelt, lawyers were preeminent among America's leaders. And while this ideal of the "lawyer statesman" had been somewhat tarnished by the postwar years, it could still be observed in men like Dean Acheson, John McCloy, Robert Jackson, and Henry Stimson.[24]

Stimson's lengthy career of public service included two terms as Secretary of War. The last was notable, among many other things, for his intervention to save Kyoto from nuclear attack and his insistence on proper judicial proceedings against war criminals—a stand that eventually led to the Nuremberg Trials (whose team of American prosecutors was led by Jackson). Stimson's critically acclaimed memoirs, published in 1948, included many insightful comments on the legal profession. Stimson pointed to countries with constitutions and bills of rights like ours who had lost their liberties because their bars failed to establish and maintain those rights. Without a bar trained in "the conditions of courage and loyalty," Stimson observed, our constitutional theories of individual liberty would die. Stimson went on the point out that the American lawyer must recognize that he is both a potential officer of his government and a "defender of its laws and Constitution." And most ominously: "I felt that if the time should ever come when this tradition had faded out and the members of the bar had become merely the servants of business, the future of our liberties would be gloomy indeed."[25]

In their wisdom and their broad understanding of both the law and human nature, the lawyer statesmen reflected the values of the large firms with which they were generally associated. Today, these firms (which typically pluck the elite from the top law schools) continue to exert a major influence on legal practice. It is here that so many of the changes in

22. Burke, "Tools of Man," 18.
23. Tocqueville, *Democracy in America*, 125.
24. Kronman, *Lost Lawyer*, 11–52.
25. Linowitz, *Betrayed Profession*, 1.

American society in recent decades are most apparent—and here, as we shall see, that the loss of meaning in the legal profession has been most keenly felt.

The wisdom and breadth of understanding that were essential to the lawyer statesmen of the postwar period was largely a function of education. This notion dated back to Jefferson, who asserted that "history, politics, ethics, physics, oratory, poetry, criticism, etc. [are] as necessary as law to form an accomplished lawyer."[26] Leaders of the bar in postwar America often made literary references in their briefs, and were not only trained by the Socratic method, but knew who Socrates was. (Even Jackson, who lacked both a BA and a JD, liked to reference the Bible and the poets in his briefs.) Knowledge like this was no mere window dressing. Humanities education framed the legal profession with a larger system of ideas and values that gave it enormous meaning. Law was then a calling, whose purpose was not only to help clients but to improve society. Lawyers were counselors and family friends—more like clergymen than like soldiers and generals, as one older lawyer has put it.[27]

A striking example of the emphasis placed upon humanities education in preparation for a legal career comes from a 1958 letter from Supreme Court Justice Felix Frankfurter. Frankfurter was responding to a twelve-year-old boy who had asked for advice on becoming a lawyer. The letter is notable not only for what it says about one notion of proper legal preparation, but for what it reveals about the values once enshrined in humanities education generally:

> My dear Paul:
> No one can be a truly competent lawyer unless he is a cultivated man. If I were you I would forget all about any technical preparation for the law. The best way to prepare for the law is to come to the study of the law as a well-read person. Thus alone can one acquire the capacity to use the English language on paper and in speech and with the habits of clear thinking which only a truly liberal education can give. No less important for a lawyer is the cultivation of the imaginative faculties by reading poetry, seeing great paintings, in the original or in easily available reproductions, and listening to great music. Stock your mind with the deposit of much good reading, and widen and deepen your feelings by experiencing vicariously as much as possible the

---

26. Linowitz, *Betrayed Profession*, 135.
27. Linowitz, *Betrayed Profession*, 12.

wonderful mysteries of the universe, and forget all about your future career.[28]

Today, an email to a prospective law student would probably recommend any curriculum that indicates academic rigor and contributes to higher LSAT scores. English courses would still be recognized as valuable for developing reading and writing skills but not for the psychological insights of a great novel or the deep meanings so often available in poetry. Business and economics courses would be regarded as more useful than the humanities regimen Frankfurter has in mind. So, too, would courses in chemistry and environmental science since they would give young students a leg up on legal positions in these industries. Of course, the Western Civilization background that gave the sort of broad insights Frankfurter so values disappeared long ago, giving way to popular courses on television, contemporary film, and other mostly forgettable diversions.

While law students have been entering upon their careers without the humanities background once deemed essential, law education has changed in ways detrimental to meaning. Anthony Kronman has noted how legal education in recent decades has been heavily impacted by the law and economics trend of the sixties and the critical legal studies movement of the seventies.[29] Each has roots in scientific realism, and each is antithetical to the claims of practical wisdom in scholarly work. At the same time, the larger meanings available from the practice of law have begun to lose their hold. Impelled by a fear of "elitism," law professors in the eighties began challenging the old moral principles that once gave the profession so much weight. Sol Linowitz has pointed to the writings of one scholar who argues that lawyers should embrace the notion that they are simply hired guns. And further: "Instead of seeking to justify their actions by reference to process values that allegedly produce truth and justice, lawyers must concede—indeed, affirm—that they actively promote the objectives of their clients and justify their own behavior in terms of the substantive justice of their clients' goals."[30] Indeed, it appears that law today has entered that perilous time of which Stimson once spoke.

The loss of higher values in law is perhaps most apparent in the fate of the idea of law as a "calling."[31] Kronman traces the roots of this notion

28. Linowitz, *Betrayed Profession*, 137–38.
29. Kronman, *Lost Lawyer*, 225–64.
30. Linowitz, *Betrayed Profession*, 10.
31. Kronman, *Lost Lawyer*, 368–75.

to seventeenth-century Protestant sects who believed in the inscrutability of God's will and the need for believers to "complete" God's creation through their labors. When such religious notions collapsed, believers turned to work that promised self-improvement and the betterment of society. Kronman argues that the notion of the "professions" took root here, and that the "lawyer statesman" ideal was one expression of a vision that found widespread expression before it began to collapse. Writing at the end of the twentieth century, Kronman sees this collapse across the broad spectrum of the professions, although, as we have seen, traces of the old notion can still be found here and there among the labors:

> The present crisis in the professional self-understanding of lawyers is merely one expression of a broader development in which all the great professions of the nineteenth century have lost their saving power. Today, in fact, the whole ethos of professionalism seems like a doomed attempt to sustain the idea of a calling within certain traditionally prestigious lines of work—an attempt that has clearly failed. . . . At the end of the twentieth century we have returned, then, to a democratic regime like that which existed in the seventh-century Puritan's imagination but with one important difference. For while the Puritan's vocational democracy rested on the equal capacity of every kind of work to bring salvation, ours is based upon the equal incapacity of all to offer any.[32]

In addition to the notion of law as a "calling," traditional legal practice took on meaning from the familial atmosphere that the best of the big firms once sought to cultivate. From the postwar years into the eighties, young associates were regarded here not merely as employees but as students whose education would be completed through the tutelage of older lawyers. Associates then worked closely with one partner, but became familiar with other partners and associates both through labor and by means of the popular social events. Firms then had frequent dinners or firm outings, and some had afternoon teas or cocktail hours designed especially for partner and associate interaction. One such firm was Arnold & Porter in Washington, which had an open bar in the library every day at six o'clock (Paul Porter called it "the children's hour") where older lawyers would drop by to discuss law and cases with the associates.[33]

Partners in the old firms also freely associated with each other at a time when lunch gatherings were common and closed doors rare. The

---

32. Kronman, *Lost Lawyer*, 372.
33. Linowitz, *Betrayed Profession*, 97.

combination of social interaction and legal discussion and debate was immensely meaningful, if not always financially profitable. As Sol Linowitz points out:

> Some of the happiest memories of law practice in the middle decades of the twentieth century are the recollections of impromptu conferences in a senior partner's office, talking over some odd problem the firm had just been handed, engaging in discussions that challenged one's intellect, knowledge and judgment. No client was billed for that time, or, as an ordinary matter, for the time the juniors took discussing the problems they couldn't handle.[34]

The notion that the older lawyers had accumulated wisdom along with legal expertise was reflected in compensation, which, with a few exceptions, was based upon seniority, with the salary of the highest paid partners being about three or four times that of the lowest (today, the range is forty-three to one in at least one large firm).[35] Before the new values took hold, the vast majority of partners came from the ranks of the associates and stayed with the firm for life, creating a strong familial atmosphere. The sense of family extended to clients, who took "retainers" on firms and developed life-long relationships not only with their lawyer, but with the larger firm, since new generations of clients were generally passed along to new generations of lawyers. Such bonds in no way compelled lawyers to adopt the clients' goals at the expense of their own standards. As the venerable Elihu Root reportedly advised one client, "The law lets you do it, but don't . . . It's a rotten thing to do."[36]

The most dramatic changes in legal practice followed from the economic boom of the eighties. In 1983, Americans spent $40 billion on legal services. By 1989, that number was $83 billion.[37] As lawyers began to compete for all that money, the old values began to decline. Now all the big firms began to hire marketing directors—a position that didn't exist in 1980. Firms also began to compete not only for clients but for client-rich partners ("rainmakers"), leading to a tripling in the number of headhunter firms in one five-year period in the eighties.[38] All this was accompanied by enormous growth in the big firms. In 1978 there were 15 firms in America

34. Linowitz, *Betrayed Profession*, 96–97.
35. Randazzo, "Flip Side," para. 19.
36. Linowitz, *Betrayed Profession*, 48.
37. Linowitz, *Betrayed Profession*, 101.
38. Kronman, *Lost Lawyer*, 280.

with 200 or more lawyers. By 1988, there were 115 firms of this size.[39] In 2018 there were 29 American firms with 1,000 or more attorneys.[40]

Lawyer dissatisfaction has accompanied such growth. An American Bar Association poll found that, between 1984 and 1990, the number of lawyers satisfied with their job dropped 20 percent, while only three in ten felt very satisfied with their work.[41] A study from 1992 showed that fully 72 percent of respondents enjoyed legal practice less than they had when they began.[42] Lawyer dissatisfaction remains a problem in the twenty-first century, where it now takes a major psychological toll. An American Bar Association study from a few years back chronicled the many personal issues of today's lawyers, including tendencies toward depression (28 percent), chronic stress (23 percent), anxiety (19 percent) and drinking problems (20 percent).[43]

Of all the factors working against the available meanings to be found in the legal profession, perhaps none is more important than the extraordinary increase in workload. Hourly billing was rare in law firms prior to the fifties. Today, it is every lawyer's bane. In the seventies, billable hour numbers at the big firms were about 1,500 per year. By the second decade of the twenty-first century, the number had jumped to between 2,000 to 2,200 hours. At some big firms, an ambitious young lawyer today may bill more than 2,500 hours to impress the partners. Given the amount of unbillable time in each work day, this amounts to 80 or more hours of work a week.[44] Hours like these not only preclude socializing within the firm; they leave little outside time for spouses and children, church choirs, book clubs, and so much else that enhances life and gives it meaning.

Given all these changes, it should not surprise us that few attorneys today would recommend the practice to others. Meanwhile, Americans appear to have lost the confidence in lawyers they once had. A 2018 Gallup poll rating twenty occupations on the basis of "honesty and ethical standards" put lawyers in fourteenth place, with 19 percent rating them "high" or "very high," and 28 percent "low" or "very low."[45] While this still places lawyers above car salesmen, telemarketers, and members of

---

39. Kronman, *Lost Lawyer*, 274.
40. Randazzo, "Flip Side," para. 12.
41. Stefanic and Delgado, *How Lawyers Lose*, 52–53.
42. Stefanic and Delgado, *How Lawyers Lose*, 53.
43. Cho, "Why Are Lawyers," para. 1.
44. Randazzo, "Flip Side," para. 37.
45. See chart in Brenan, "Nurses Again Outpace."

Congress (who perennially rate at the bottom), it signifies a major change from Tocqueville's era. More significantly, it appears to reflect a loss of meaning in recent decades that so many lawyers themselves have described.

Since the beginning of public schools, teachers in America have been confronted with a variety of issues in attempting to find meaning in their work. Foremost of these have been behavior problems and the difficulty in reaching students and awakening them to the joys and necessities of learning. As we shall see, these perennial difficulties have worsened considerably with the many social changes since the postwar years. But this is not all. In today's schools, teachers confront an array of social issues their forebearers could not have imagined. Today, it seems as if the public schools, on their own, are expected to resolve conflicts and disputes that the larger society has no idea how to address.

While the trope of the boy who dips the girls' pigtails in the inkwell is an old one, schools were once remarkably safe places for teachers and pupils. During the Depression, school violence was rare, with lying and truancy cited as the chief concerns by teachers. Obedient children were also characteristic of the World War II years, and good behavior persisted through the decade. When teachers in the forties were asked to list the primary behavioral problems encountered in the classroom they named issues such as too much noise, getting out of place in line, littering, and gum chewing.[46]

The relative placidity of the forties classroom appeared to be threatened in the mid-fifties by a perceived epidemic of juvenile delinquency.[47] During the decade, juvenile misbehavior was the subject of Senate hearings, American Bar Association investigations, and periodic warnings from FBI head J. Edgar Hoover. Violence in the public schools became a real concern with the film *The Blackboard Jungle* (1955), in which actor Glen Ford portrayed a first-year teacher struggling with violence in an inner city school.[48] However, while conditions seemed to be deteriorating in some large cities, reports from the hinterlands told a very different story.[49] A sociological study of the high schools of northern Illinois during the late fifties revealed that only about a quarter of students ever smoked

46. Crews and Counts, *Evolution of School Disturbance*, 69.
47. G. Gilbert, *Cycle of Outrage*.
48. Brooks, *Blackboard Jungle*.
49. Ravitch, *Left Back*, 367–71.

or drank and that sexual promiscuity was limited by the view—shared by some 90 percent of girls—that, in order to be popular, a girl must have a "good reputation." Here, as in most American communities, school officials and families shared the same values, discipline and morale were high, and rules about dress and behavior were, for the most part, implicit. If there were any complaints about the group that would become known as the "silent generation," it was that they tended toward conformity and were largely apolitical—a failing many today would regard with nostalgia.

Like so much else, the real change in American schools began in the late sixties. From that time through the end of the century, public schools often served as battlegrounds rife with weapons offenses, student assaults, rape, and attempted rape.[50] Student assaults on teachers provide a good barometer of the period. In 1964, a total of 253 assaults on teachers were reported in the American public schools. Between 1994 and 1998, teachers were the victims of 668,000 violent crimes at school—a more than 600-percent increase per year compared to the early sixties.

While assaults in the school was certainly one concern, lesser behavioral issues were just as likely to cause teachers to question their choice of profession. Gerald Grant has described how, during the seventies, moral order disappeared in many American classrooms, as "absenteeism rose, cheating was widespread, drug use became more common, fighting and backtalk increased."[51] In schools like these, teachers not only lost community support but were fearful of attack for either failing to achieve equal outcomes in the classroom or for attempting to exercise the authority necessary if equality was ever to be achieved. Many reacted by retreating into the classroom and closing their doors, while others responded by smoking pot with the kids. Looking back at the changes in the late eighties, Grant characterized the era this way: "The balance between getting and giving has grown more disproportionate in recent decades. Expectations, complaints, even lawsuits have multiplied, while rewards have diminished. Responsibilities have increased as authority has weakened."[52]

In the wake of increased security measures school violence began to decline in the early twenty-first century. However, as students returned to school following the recent COVID crisis, violence saw a upsurge, with firearms in the classroom too often leading to tragedy.[53] Meanwhile, the

50. Midlarsky and Klain, "History of Violence," 44–46.
51. G. Grant, "World We Created," 31.
52. G. Grant, "World We Created," 31.
53. Pierce, "As Students Return."

twenty-first century has been plagued by an epidemic of mass school shootings, which began in Littleton, Colorado, on April 20, 1999, and showed no signs of letting up twenty-three years later, when an eighteen-year-old gunman murdered nineteen students and two teachers in an elementary school in Uvalde, Texas. While a surfeit of firearms is certainly part of the problem, the root cause appears to lie in an anomie that most often afflicts young men lacking the social bonds and sense of purpose in life (including a hitch in the military) that were once common.

Teachers in the twenty-first century also have to deal with the dangers of cyber bullying, which has reached epidemic proportions in many of our schools. Meanwhile, the many hours spent online each day (estimates are as high as six to nine hours) have been cited as a major contributor to a dramatic rise in anxiety and depression, which afflicts young women especially.[54] Beyond all this are the many social issues that were virtually nonexistent a few generations ago. We get a glimpse of these from a diary entry that paints a rather disheartening picture of the beginning of a teachers work day in postmodern America:

> Back to school after two snow days—good to be back although I have a slight flu. Mary looking wan from weeks of strep and family turmoil. Ralph, with bad cough and sore throat and looking feverish, pulled me close to him and said they'd won the custody case I testified in last week. Althea, full of anxious chatter about their moving date in three weeks. Frannie and Carol both on medication which requires reminders to be taken periodically. Chris brings friend who speaks no English to visit for the day. Fei's mother weeps from homesickness for Taiwan. All this while taking attendance and collecting lunch money between 8:35 and 8:45.[55]

If postwar American schools were generally more placid places for teachers, it was also a time when they had a clearer sense of both the purposes of public education and its limitations. In the fifties, God and country occupied a central place in the classroom, where the work day typically began with a brief nondenominational prayer and the pledge of allegiance. Many schools of the era included religious instruction in the form of Bible stories which were intended to convey simple moral lessons. Character formation was then regarded as more important than academics, with the result that good manners, good behavior, and "citizenship" were a vital part of learning. These ideas were inculcated largely by the

54. Pipher and Gilliam, "Lonely Burden."
55. G. Grant, "World We Created," 1–2.

study of the heroes of American history. Garrison Keillor has fondly recalled that many old classrooms contained faded portraits of Washington and Lincoln, displayed like "an old married couple on the wall."[56]

In most communities, learning was facilitated by active (though seldom overactive) parents. Parental involvement was especially apparent in the popularity of the Parent Teachers Association, which fostered parent-teacher interaction through monthly meetings, fundraisers and other planned activities. In the postwar era, PTA membership flourished, the percentage of parents who were members doubling between 1945 and 1960.[57] The result was that, in 1960, the PTA was the largest secular organization in America, with about twelve million members. By 2016, and despite the extraordinary growth in the school age population, that number was down to about four million.[58] Today fewer than half of American public schools have a PTA chapter, and only about one quarter of parents even know that the organization exists. All this despite the fact that study after study has concluded that parental involvement is vital to academic success.

Learning in postwar America was also fostered by the prevalence of small neighborhood schools, whose numbers dwindled with the move toward school consolidation and the spread of busing. A Federal Highway Commission study a few years ago pointed out that, in 1969, 48 percent of public school students still walked to school. By 2009, the number was 13 percent.[59] And while time spent on buses may be relatively short for kids living in urban and suburban areas, children living in rural America have a very different story to tell. A 2014 Arkansas study found that the median daily commute by school bus in the state was over one and a half hours. Some students spent as much as five and a half hours a day going to and from school.[60] The toll of busing on students like these extends far beyond the loss of time for work and play. Children who must be at the bus stop before dawn suffer from serious sleep deprivation—a situation that has clearly been shown to correlate with lower academic performance.

Schools of the fifties recognized that schoolwork went better when the day was punctuated by breaks. In addition to lunch periods (which actually occurred at lunchtime), little children had naps and milk breaks.

56. Reese, *America's Public Schools*, 254.
57. Putnam, *Bowling Alone*, 56.
58. March, "Students, Parents Pay Price."
59. Ehrenhalt, "Is Education Reform Worth," para. 10.
60. Ehrenhalt, "Is Education Reform Worth," para. 2.

In the fifties, recess was standard, with one or even two play periods a day. Many schools today have curtailed recess or eliminated it altogether to make available more time for study—this despite warnings from pediatricians that "the importance of playful learning cannot be overemphasized."[61] Today's pediatricians are aware that, for little children especially, play is a vital opportunity to discover and learn with little or minimal teacher interference. This belies the current notion of "preschool readiness," which seeks intellectual development at an age and in a manner inconsistent with the way little children learn best. Once again, we are far from the postwar era, when children, at most, spent a year in the "little red schoolhouse."

In spite of the dominant progressive educational philosophy of the day, fifties schools typically stressed rote learning, in accordance with the experience of teachers who had generally learned that way. Still, there was time for music and art (especially in the early grades) and for the many school projects that allowed creative students to shine. Differences in learning ability were unabashedly acknowledged in the postwar era, and it was understood that, by middle school, some students would transition to vocational studies. The typical means of separating the college bound from the others was the standardized test. However, standardized tests were relatively rare and seldom elicited the sort of recriminations so typical today.

The late sixties saw a move toward high school graduation for all at the very time student behavior was going to the dogs. Schools responded to the turmoil by beating a hasty retreat from high academic standards.[62] Less demanding elective courses now replaced academic subjects as students flocked to the "general track" curriculum. Grade inflation and social promotion were rampant, and one study showed that students had only three hours a day of instruction time. Over the course of the seventies, the number of students who scored six hundred on the verbal SAT fell from 116,585 to 66,292. The percent of students who needed remedial math soared from 4 percent to 30 percent. But dramatic academic decline was only part of the problem, as Diane Ravitch has explained:

> Many common practices in the schools—grade inflation, social promotion, lowered standards—taught students not to value hard work, personal effort, diligence, and perseverance. Allowing students to turn their assignments in late or not at all taught them

61. Sahlberg and Doyle, "To Really Learn," para. 14.
62. Ravitch, *Left Back*, 402–15.

that personal responsibility was unimportant. The reduction in homework not only shortened the amount of time that students spent reading, writing, and practicing their schoolwork but reduced the level of self-discipline that was expected of them.[63]

Through it all, only self-esteem flourished.[64] In 1982, 50 percent of high school graduates entered college despite the fact that a paltry 9 percent had taken a college preparatory regimen of math, English, foreign language, science, and social studies. Colleges responded not only with lower entrance requirements but with remedial courses and grade inflation of their own. It wasn't enough. Between 1984 and 1987, nearly half of white students and two thirds of black students left college without obtaining a degree.

In contrast to the relative consensus of the postwar years, schools in recent decades have been roiled by never-ending debates concerning teacher tenure, self-esteem, common core, and school choice. Disagreements have also arisen regarding the best way to teach multiculturalism, math ("new" versus "old"), reading (phonics versus "whole language") and other subjects. Teacher dissatisfaction has also grown with the teacher-evaluation and performance-pay programs that began in the Obama years, and most recently has been heightened by the controversies surrounding gender identity and the teaching of critical race theory. This issue of what schools should teach threatens the future of public education going forward. An article in *U.S. News and World Report* from the spring of 2023 observed that, in the last two years, more states than ever were choosing to provide options to public education.[65]

Yet another issue that has generated intense debate is the notion that all children should achieve academic success. The ideal emerged in the early eighties before attaining legislative status in the No Child Left Behind (2002) and Every Student Succeeds Acts (2015). The two laws are alike in expecting the states to set challenging standards for all students in math, science, and reading and in using frequent testing to establish students' progress. Every Student Succeeds chiefly differs in giving greater flexibility to the states in matters like teaching and testing, and it focuses more on children with special needs. In fact, the act encourages states to

---

63. Ravitch, *Left Back*, 406.
64. Ravitch, *Left Back*, 402–10.
65. Durrani, "What School Choice Is," para. 3.

develop teaching methods geared to those with the greatest needs, while providing "personalized" instruction for all.

The belief that all children must flourish has placed enormous burdens on teachers and bred unrealistic expectations in parents. That the latter fail to grasp the limitations of their children is clear from a 2016 nationwide study of parents of children from kindergarten through eighth grade. According to the survey, 90 percent of parents thought their children were on track in reading and math. In fact, just over a third of the students had met the standards set forth in these areas by the National Assessment of Educational Progress.[66] The recent COVID outbreak has, of course dropped more students even further behind. This according to a report issued in the spring of 2023, which found math and reading scores for America's thirteen-year-olds to be at their lowest level in decades.[67]

The broader loss of meaning occasioned by the new ideas (for both teachers and students alike) has been notable. Despite the fact that both federal programs insist upon the vital importance of arts education, efforts to implement the new ideal has resulted in a decline in these inherently meaning-rich subjects. This according to a study cited in a 2021 press release by the American Academy of Arts & Sciences, which noted a dramatic loss in support for the arts in America's public schools.[68] Meanwhile, the study of American history, which had once united students of different backgrounds and given them a sense of pride in their country, is in serious decline. Only here a disregard for subjects that are not tested has gone hand in hand with critical perspectives on the nation and its history in generating truly disturbing outcomes. In a recent survey by the American Association of Alumni and Trustees more than half of respondents thought that the Civil War occurred *before* the American Revolution.[69] History becomes meaningful only when we grasp it as a story. Today, this story has been lost and the resulting vacuum filled by tribalists.

One final negative outcome of the embrace of the new educational standards is the loss of those higher values that were once at the very core of learning. We are very far indeed from the ideal of "excellence" that was so valued in the brief John Kennedy presidency. Former HEW head John Gardner—whose little book *Excellence* (1961) had caught the president's

66. Learning Heroes, "Perspectives," para. 5.
67. Carrillo, "US Reading and Math," paras. 1–2.
68. Franklin, "New Report."
69. Boot, "If Schools Stop Teaching," para. 3.

attention—revisited his theme some twenty years later in response to what he saw as a rising tide of mediocrity throughout the nation and in his beloved schools especially. "Have the American people lost their sense of purpose and the drive that would make it possible for them to achieve excellence?" Gardner wondered. And more forcefully: "Extreme equalitarianism, or, as I would prefer to say, *equalitarianism wrongly conceived*—which ignores differences in native ability and achievement and eliminates incentives to individual performance—has not served democracy well. Carried far enough, it means the end of that striving for excellence that has produced history's greatest achievements."[70]

The difficulty of reconciling today's notion of "equity" with an ideal of equality that makes room for excellence was on display across America beginning in the spring of 2021. At issue was the problem of racial disparities in standardized math scores, and the larger question as to whether or not some children were innately "gifted" in certain areas of study. Matters eventually came to a head in California, where the state's Instructional Quality Commission proposed to enlarge the state's math curriculum with alternatives to traditional math courses and to eliminate advanced math in the middle grades—thereby keeping all students on the same track through sophomore year.[71] Needless to say, many parents and educators took exception to the idea. For some, this was simply another instance of the "dumbing down" that has been destroying excellence across the whole spectrum of American culture (sports, of course, excepted) for decades.

It was not always this way. Once, a teacher who worked to educate all her charges might still have been expected to take special delight in the child of rare talents, realizing that nurturing such ability may be the most meaningful reward of the profession. These teachers—whether in the sciences, the humanities, or the arts—once had a place of importance in American education. One of them appears in the childhood classic *Rebecca of Sunnybrook Farm*, written more than a century ago by educator Kate Douglas Wiggin. In the book, a young English instructor, Emily Maxwell, writes a letter to her father lamenting having to cram knowledge into the heads of children without aptitude or interest, and of the abject sense of failure that comes of it. She continues, before turning to young Rebecca:

---

70. Gardner, *Excellence*, 30; emphasis original.
71. Fortin, "California Tries to Close."

... in English literature and composition one yearns for brains, for appreciation, for imagination. Month after month I toil on, opening oyster after oyster, but seldom finding a pearl. Fancy my joy this term when, without any violent effort at shell-splitting, I came upon a rare pearl.... Fancy the joy of finding a real mind; of dropping seed in a soil so warm, so fertile, that one knows there are sure to be foliage, blossoms, and fruit all in good time! ... The pearl writes quaint, countrified little verses—doggerel they are; but somehow or other she always contrives to put in one line, one thought, one image, that shows you she is, quite unconsciously to herself, in possession of the secret.[72]

---

72. Wiggin, *Rebecca of Sunnybrook Farm*, 143–44.

8

Death, War, and Politics

HUMAN HISTORY GIVES POWERFUL evidence that meaning is found not only in positive encounters. It is also found in events that prove emotionally difficult and debilitating, including suffering, war, and death. The power of culture to give meaning to all of life is nowhere more evident than in events like these.

The reality of death may well be the experience that casts the longest shadow over the whole notion of meaning in life. Yet the ability of death to serve as a source of meaning is everywhere evident in traditional art, literature and music. From ancient wartime epics, to the dramatic demise of Wagner's heroes, to the tragic endings that typify many a great novel or film, the end of life has been capable of taking on extraordinary meaning through the work of a great creative mind. By dealing with subjects like suffering and death, the arts are able to convey something of that enormity and mystery that are vital components of the most deeply meaningful experiences.

In fact, the only limitations upon the meaning to be derived from any event lies in our ability to interpret it within a larger framework that gives it true significance. Art does this by creating a larger universe of order and beauty that takes death unto itself. Religion gives meaning to death by placing it within a cosmic framework whereby each life has significance and each individual has a small part in the eternal.

This belies the criticism of religion that it is nothing more than a means of avoiding the reality of death. While it is true that religion typically attempts to resolve the dilemma of death by resorting to conceptions that lie outside the realm of rational proof, this particular criticism is more fairly directed at those technologies that extend life beyond its reasonable limits while depriving death of the significance it once possessed. The tendency of contemporary medicine is to obscure death behind a welter of technology in which the suffering individual is lost. In religion, by comparison, the dying individual is front and center for the simple reason that only by acknowledging death can religion lay claim to ultimate meaning.

The reality of death, and the value of rituals in preparing Americans for it, was evident in 1945, when most deaths still occurred in the home.[1] At the time, multiple generations often occupied the same household, or lived close enough that children could see elder family members on a regular basis. This, and the still relatively high rate of mortality from disease, meant that children were more aware of the aging process and the inevitability of death as a natural occurrence. Many were even instructed in the reality of death by the little bedtime prayer repeated by so many youngsters:

> Now I lay me down to sleep,
> I pray the Lord my soul to keep.
> If I should die before I wake,
> I pray the Lord my soul to take.

The prevalence of home deaths not only provided comfort for the dying individual; it kept technology at bay and allowed for the introduction of the clergy and those religious conceptions that brought meaning to the event. The administering of last rites by Catholic priests and the deathbed rituals valued by Jews were more readily available. We will return to these later.

The end of death as a family affair began with the removal of the elderly—first from the home and, eventually, from the community. The first was largely a consequence of postwar prosperity, the second, of the emergence of retirement communities that began to take hold in the early sixties. The latter not only removed older Americans from the immediate environment; it took many to far flung areas of the country where warmer climes not only took off the chill but promised to keep the reality of death at bay by providing an Indian summer of activities. Meanwhile, changes in public health and the vast growth of medical technology were extending life (or, depending upon one's point of view, drawing out death) in ways that assured that more and more of later life would be spent in the presence of health specialists. The result was that, by the eighties, only

---

1. Gawande, *Being Mortal*, 6.

17 percent of deaths occurred in the home.[2] And while the percentage of home deaths has increased significantly since then, a clear majority of deaths still occur in hospitals, hospice facilities, and nursing homes. This, despite the fact that most Americans would prefer a home death.[3]

Like so much else, death became an issue in the late sixties. Between 1968 and 1972, some 1,200 books on death and dying were published in America. This was equal the number that had been issued on the subject in the previous eighteen years. Kenneth Woodward, who cites these numbers, observes that the period seemed to mark a turning point in our understanding of this vital subject: "[It was] a moment in American history when death had ceased to be a metaphysical mystery or a summons from God, but rather a managerial problem for the medical and other technicians charged with supervising nature's planned obsolescence."[4]

Included in the literature on death was Dr. Kübler-Ross's now classic *On Death and Dying*, where the author put forth her five stages whereby the terminally ill attempt to deal with disease and the approach of death. Kübler-Ross's book was designed to give a sense of dignity and meaning to people who were often being pushed aside by the medical community as "hopeless cases." *The Tibetan Book of the Dead* was also reissued during the period, speaking to many in the counterculture who looked to Tibetan Buddhism and its notion of reincarnation as a source of meaning to fill the gap created by the decline of orthodox faith.

By 1976, another eight hundred books had been added to the list, including physician Raymond Moody's enormously popular *Life after Life* (1975). Moody's book is not an isolated phenomenon. Since it appeared there have been other compelling studies of near death experiences. But Moody's was the first, and his interviews with individuals who puzzled over these events, unaware that others had experienced them, makes his account especially compelling. For many, it gave (and continues to give) meaning to death by providing tangible confirmation of age-old principles of faith.

Life after Life presents a "model" based upon some 150 survivors' stories of events that transpired during brushes with death (e.g., potentially fatal accidents) or apparent clinical deaths (e.g., during hospital surgeries). Moody's model includes the following events: hearing unpleasant

---

2. Gawande, *Being Mortal*, 6.
3. S. Cross and Warraich, "Changes in the Place."
4. Woodward, *Getting Religion*, 300.

noises and having a sense of moving rapidly through a tunnel or other enclosure; "out-of-body" experiences, including patients witnessing efforts at their resuscitation; emotions of disorder and distress which soon give way to feelings of joy and love; a gradual awareness of other disembodied, spiritual beings, including deceased loved ones and an all-powerful "being of light," who leads the individual in a review of the events of their life; the awareness of a divide or barrier, beyond which lies a realm of joy and fulfillment to which the individual is unable to proceed.

Moody has been criticized for "cherry-picking" his data and for a general lack of methodological rigor. More importantly, critics (and Moody himself) have noted the vital point that these events took place in brains that were still very much alive. How we view Moody's book ultimately depends upon how we understand the slippery matter of consciousness—that is, whether we see it as merely an epiphenomenon of the brain, or whether we believe, as the religions do, that it opens out onto transcendent realms of being.

From the perspective of meaning, this scarcely matters. What counts is the extraordinary *meaning* that comes from experiences like these. Those who have them no longer fear death. They also have a heightened sense of the value of life that makes them more determined to love others and to seek knowledge. One survivor noted that, following the event, their sense of self made a radical shift from the body, which had been her primary concern, to the mind, which she now knew to be all-important. Another simply observed: "I try to do things that have more meaning, and that makes my mind and soul feel better."[5]

There is great deal of irony in the fact that Moody's book became possible by developments in medical technology that extended life for many who, just a few generations earlier, would have never recovered to recount their experiences. Yet this same medical technology now defines our worldview such that we find it difficult to ascribe any great value to near death experiences, attributing them to the effects of drugs or regarding them as purely psychological responses to trauma. A telling feature of Moody's stories is the disconnect they illuminate between a religious perspective capable of giving so much meaning to death and a purely physical world-view that keeps meaning out of the picture. This disconnect is apparent in the experience of patients who witnessed heroic efforts at resuscitation. As one describes the event:

5. Moody, *Life after Life*, 90.

Just then, I saw them roll this machine in there, and they put the shocks on my chest. When they did, I saw my whole body just jump right up off the bed, and I heard every bone in my body crack and pop. It was the most awful thing! As I saw them below beating on my chest and rubbing my arms and legs, I thought, "Why are they going to so much trouble? I'm just fine now."[6]

For the foreseeable future, the experience of death for most will remain what it has been in recent decades: that is, a point of interaction between body and machine rather than the soul and its Creator. Today, our unwavering faith in modern medicine too often leads to the intensive care unit, and to the diminishment and dehumanization of the dying individual in their last days. Nearly all of us are familiar with such experiences. Nearly all have witnessed a loved one in the last stages of life, when doctors inevitably become focused on the challenging medical issues at hand and lose sight of the suffering individual. Most have had the experience of attempting to comfort a loved one who is highly medicated and tethered to winking and blinking medical devices by a welter of cables and tubes. This is a person who is isolated like a goldfish in a goldfish bowl atop an ICU bed, their rest constantly interrupted by well-meaning nurses and technicians. All this and more as a television drones on idiotically overhead.

One clear indication of our obsession with health and the associated fear of death is our surfeit of drugs and diet supplements, and our obsession with routine testing of all sorts. Much of this is familiar to Americans of all ages through television commercials. In the postwar period, a general lack of concern with health issues was evident by the shortage of television commercials on health products generally, and by the absence of any reference to truly serious or embarrassing ailments. Today, toilet tissue ads encouraging us to "Enjoy the go!," and ads for colon cancer screening are accessible to all—and especially during the dinner hour. The 2021 baseball playoffs even saw erectile dysfunction commercials in which young men and women smiled coyly at the camera as they danced off to the bedroom—this, as scores of young boys and girls watched. We have come very far indeed from the cheerful songs of Speedy Alka-Seltzer.

In postmodern America, our inability to accept aging and acknowledge the inevitability of illness and death is in direct proportion to our inability to any longer envision the whole of life in some way that gives it meaning. Today, death is not an inevitable eventuality of the body but

---

6. Moody, *Life after Life*, 36.

evidence of failure. Someone dies because they failed to exercise, did the wrong exercises, or exercised too much—because they ate too much, too little, or the wrong foods. Death could be prevented, or at least indefinitely delayed, by more and better laws, by more and better medical care, and by constant vigilance. For many, death elicits incomprehension and anger. Hence the mission to "fight" disease, from aggressive funding campaigns to demanding fitness routines.

As a sign of both personal and social failure (not to mention evidence of a spiritual shortcoming of colossal proportions), death has no place in postmodern America.

The future holds out little hope that death will someday have the meaning it traditionally possessed within a religious worldview. We get a sense of this in Barbara Ehrenreich's book *Natural Causes*, where the author examines the large number of high tech leaders who regard death as the ultimate medical and technological challenge. These include inventor and author Ray Kurzweil, who seeks to reprogram his own biochemistry the same way he reprograms his computers. Kurzweil's regimen involves "about 250" nutritional supplements taken daily in hopes of helping him live to about 2040—by which time he believes he should be able to ward off illness by means of millions of disease-fighting nanobots injected into his body. Another internet giant plans to live ten thousand years, while a third seeks to "cure death." Then there is Larry Ellison, co-founder of Oracle. Ellison finds the acceptance of mortality "incomprehensible." Hence the hundreds of million dollars he has spent in anti-aging research.[7]

Many may wonder whether these notions of extending life to such extraordinary lengths are feasible. From the perspective of meaning—and especially in regard to what this tells us about our changing understanding of ourselves and our place in the universe—the more probing questions concern what sorts of people harbor such ideas and what a world dominated by them will look like a few generations hence.

While immortality may not be as near at hand as our current tech leaders hope, we have a good sense of where we are going and the people who will take us there from Yuval Harari's *Homo Deus: A Brief History of Tomorrow*. Harari reminds us that death is today a technical, not a metaphysical, problem. Like all technical problems, it has a solution. Harari happily accepts the necessity of remaking ourselves over time that immortality will likely bring. Lifelong allegiances to spouse, children,

---

7. Ehrenreich, *Natural Causes*, 79–80.

and community—which once proved so meaningful to so many—will undoubtedly be jettisoned. By then, the larger cultural allegiances will already be gone:

> Once people think (with or without good reason) that they have a serious chance of escaping death, the desire for life will refuse to go on pulling the rickety wagon of art, ideology and religion, and will sweep forward like an avalanche.[8]

Harari is undoubtedly right about this, as the cart is already breaking down. But he is wrong to think, as is evident here and elsewhere in his book, that meaning will not suffer. For death is among the great teachers—and one whose chief lesson, as we shall see, has to do with meaning in life.

That death could still prove meaningful in the postwar years is apparent not only from the prominent place of religion but from the enormous popularity of existentialism. Existentialism dates to the nineteenth-century Danish religious philosopher Søren Kierkegaard and gained modern currency with the publication of Martin Heidegger's *Being and Time*, in 1927. From there, the rise of existentialism coincided with the move toward war, and took on enormous urgency following the invasion of France.[9] It was during the war years, in Paris and Algiers, that existentialist luminary Albert Camus completed his "three absurds" (*The Stranger, Caligula, The Myth of Sisyphus*). It was also during wartime that, imprisoned in a POW camp, Jean Paul Sartre began a second, closer reading of *Being and Time* and was inspired to write *Being and Nothingness* (1943). Sartre was not only a philosopher but a playwright and political activist. It was he who did more than anyone else to popularize the movement in the decades after the war's end.

In the fifties, death had an especially important place in the American iterations of existentialism through psychologist Rollo May and theologian Paul Tillich. Following Heidegger, the Americans understood death in the context of the notion of *nonbeing*. By this term, they had in mind not merely the terminal event. Nonbeing referred to death as an ongoing reality—the ever-present shadow side of life itself. Our natural tendency is to flee from the reality of death, which is the source of enormous anxiety. To do so, however, is to flee from life. It is only by confronting our own mortality, the existentialists argued, that we are able to act in full accordance with

---

8. Harari, *Homo Deus*, 29.
9. Bakewell, *At the Existentialist Café*, 139–74.

the human condition, and to live in a manner that is truly free and authentic. In our terms, we may say that reflection is joined here with the deepest emotion, opening us to the fullness of life in a deeply meaningful way.

American Abstract Expressionist Willem de Kooning once recalled of the postwar years that existentialism was "in the air," and that artists "were in touch with the mood," without knowing too much about it.[10] However, not only artists were impacted. A lengthy *Life* magazine article from 1964, featuring Sartre, included a full page with pictures of a number of American authors (e.g., Bellow, Baldwin, Heller, Updike) who were said to have been influenced by existentialism in their works.[11] Of course, the ideas of the existentialists did not blossom in a cultural vacuum. Many of the themes resonated in the currents of Zen Buddhism and Jungian psychology that were also in vogue in the period. According to this line of reasoning one may say that the Abstract Expressionist's determination to "act" upon the blank canvas was a gesture of existential authenticity, his slashes and swirls manifestations of a Zen-like artistry, and the forms themselves revelations of the collective unconscious. It was such notions of something "larger" that enabled the arts to take on so much depth of meaning during the era.

Early in the rise of existentialism in America, in 1946, psychologist Viktor Frankl published *From Death Camp to Existentialism* (currently titled *Man's Search for Meaning*). Frankl's book has none of the deeper philosophical analysis of Heidegger's or Sartre's works. Rather, it an intensely personal inquiry into the meanings found in suffering and deprivation by a man who had experienced these first hand as a prisoner in the death camps.

Frankl was a rising young Viennese psychiatrist when, in 1942, he and his family were arrested by Austrian authorities. Frankl was separated from the others (most of whom, including his wife, soon died) and spent the remaining war years in Auschwitz and Dachau. While imprisoned, Frankl witnessed the ability of a few men to rise above the degradation all around them, and to find meaning in suffering and death. The camps had taken away everything except their freedom to respond to their suffering on their own terms. There were also moments of revelation. Frankl recalled an early morning march when his wife's face appeared to him as an image "more luminous than the sun that was beginning to rise."[12]

10. Sandler, *Triumph of American Painting*, 98.
11. Kappler, "Sartre and Existentialism."
12. Frankl, *Man's Search for Meaning*, 37.

Man's salvation, he thought to himself, is in and through love. Thoughts of his wife came again early one grey morning, when hope seemed to be embodied in the light of a distant farmhouse. Later that morning, as he labored at the icy ground, he felt his wife's presence more strongly than ever. At that very moment, a bird flew down, perched on a clod of soil, and steadily looked up at him.

Frankl came to the conclusion that the will to meaning was a fundamental and irreducible feature of human existence. And what is the meaning of life? Frankl makes it clear what, at least for the prisoners, the meaning of life was *not*:

> Long ago we had passed the stage of asking what was the meaning of life, a naïve query which understands life as the attainment of some aim through the active creation of something of value. For us, the meaning of life embraced the wider cycles of life and death, of suffering and of dying.[13]

Like the existentialists, Frankl held that meaning could be found only in embracing suffering and death as the "other" side of life. He refers to Rilke, and notes with approval Rilke's notion that we must "get through" our sufferings, much as we must get through our work. For Frankl, meaning is an ongoing *process* in which we continually assume responsibility for our actions, confronting the tasks and obstacles at hand with all the courage we can muster. Frankl firmly rejects the notion of some existentialists that life is an absurdity. While meaning is incomprehensible in rational terms, Frankl believed that there is compelling and irrefutable meaningfulness at the core of life—a meaning that is evident in love and labor, in the light of a distant window and the movements of a curious bird.[14] At heart, Frankl is a poet as much as a psychiatrist. Like most poets, he holds that life is rife with meaning. Like a good psychiatrist, he believes that it is our purpose and our deepest need to search for it, and to discover our connection to things beyond ourselves.

While the work of most of the existentialists have lost their hold upon American readers in recent years, Frankl's book continues to draw attention. A notable example of a popular work that gives an important place to it is Daniel Pink's best-seller *A Whole New Mind: Why Right-Brainers Will Rule the Future* (2005). I now want to briefly look at Pink's treatment

---

13. Frankl, *Man's Search for Meaning*, 78.
14. Frankl, *Man's Search for Meaning*, 37.

of Frankl for the evidence it gives of how the notion of meaning, especially in regards to death, has been greatly diminished in recent years.

In his book, Pink speaks of meaning as one of six "high concept and high touch" senses whose development he regards as vital to success and happiness in a dawning "Conceptual Age." It is important to note that meaning here is only one of the six. We should also observe that at least two other senses discussed by Pink—i.e., "story" and "symphony"—also have a place in our analysis, but *within* the context of meaning (this will become apparent shortly). These details should alert us to the vital point that meaning, as Pink sees it, has a much more modest scope and significance than we attribute to it.

We may also point out that Pink is careful to distinguish meaning from religion, apparently believing that, rather than enhancing meaning, religion profanes it. On the other hand, Pink believes that meaning and business are a marriage made in heaven. Pink cites studies that show that companies capable of aligning the spiritual values of employees with company goals outperformed others. Since meaning affects the bottom line, we will likely see more businesses trying to profit from it in this way. But this is not all. In the future we are likely to see a growth of the spiritual *as* business. Here, Pink cites the views of a savvy Forbes publisher who has foreseen the rise of products to satisfy the meaning-hungry masses:

> Meaning. Purpose. Deep life experience. Use whatever word or phrase you like, but know that consumer desire for these qualities is on the rise. Remember your Abraham Maslow and your Viktor Frankl. Bet your business on it.[15]

Words like these reflect the flavor of Pink's chapter on meaning, which is ultimately a mash up of the serious and the trivial that has all the hallmarks of the many fads whereby so many today profess to search for meaning but settle for reading the right books and donning the right exercise attire instead. It is precisely the technology and material wealth that Pink sees as ushering in a new age of meaning that militate against it, depriving us of the quiet, the time, and, above all, the depth of experience that meaning requires. It is this that makes Frankl's appearance in the book so incongruous. For while Frankl would undoubtedly have applauded Pink's apparent regard for meaning, he was acutely aware of how easily we may lose our humanity. Frankl's world was one of war and the death camps. His notion of meaning relies heavily upon terms like

15. Pink, *Whole New Mind*, 225.

"responsibility," "love," and "suffering"—words that today lack the resonance they had for earlier generations.

In the last analysis, Pink's book deserves to be placed alongside *All Things Shining* and the writings of the positive psychologists as compelling evidence of meaning loss. It comes as no surprise, then, that Pink ultimately turns to the gurus of happiness and to Martin Seligman's notion of meaning as an aspect of happiness in his book. Ultimately, Pink's understanding of meaning belongs to the sunny world of high tech, where the Dalai Lama is a "rock star" capable of stirring Hollywood stars like Richard Gere and Goldie Hawn to a show of reverence.[16] It is a world alien to those icy realms of the spirit where Frankl found revelation and monks still meditate upon suffering and death.

While Frankl was able to find meaning amid the horrors and ravages of war, others have found it in war itself. The virtues of combat have been acclaimed since at least the time of Homer, and continue to be a staple of popular literature and entertainment. The reason for this attraction is not difficult to discern. Drawing upon his many years in war zones—from insurgencies in El Salvador, to the horrors of Serbia—war correspondent Chris Hedges made the following observation:

> The enduring attraction of war is this: Even with its destruction and carnage it can give us what we long for in life. It can give us purpose, meaning, a reason for living. Only when we are in the midst of conflict does the shallowness and vapidness of much of our lives become apparent. Trivia dominates our conversations and increasingly our airwaves. And war is an enticing elixir. It gives us resolve, a cause. It allows us to be noble.[17]

Like the existentialists, Hedges recognizes the power of a life lived on the precipice of death to focus our lives and heighten our experience, thereby giving us the meaning we crave. But war does more than impact us as individuals. War provides a sense of shared experience and purpose which is so strong that, despite its dangers and deprivations, those who have suffered through it may long for it in peacetime.

In his book *Tribe: On Homecoming and Belonging*, Sebastian Junger focuses on the capacity of war to give meaning both by heightening the

---

16. Pink, *Whole New Mind*, 220.
17. Hedges, *War Is a Force*, 3.

significance of individual acts and fulfilling our need for powerful communal experience. Junger's account includes interviews and anecdotes from Bosnians who recall wartime experiences in the ethnic conflicts following the breakup of the former Yugoslavia. These include a taxi driver who had been in a special unit that made daring trips behind enemy lines during the war. "And now look at me," he says dismissively in reference to his current occupation.[18] Another interview was with a young woman who suffered deprivation and injury prior to finding safety by escaping to Italy. Despite the danger, she wanted desperately to return to her homeland. She missed being so close to other people, she explained, and being loved in the way that only a fearful and protecting community can love. People then were happier, she insisted, and they laughed more. "We didn't learn the lesson of the war," she continued," which is how important it is to share everything you have with human beings close to you."[19]

Evidence of the power of war to give meaning is not merely anecdotal. Since the time of the great sociologist Emile Durkheim it has been apparent that suicides and mental disorders decline during wartime, when life becomes precious and people band together for the common good. Durkheim's findings have been confirmed over and over again.[20] Despite predictions of mass hysteria and psychological breakdown, psychiatric hospitals in England during World War II actually saw admissions decline. Similar results were witnessed in Paris. During their civil wars, Spain, Algeria, Lebanon, and Northern Ireland saw a similar decline in the psychiatric wards. More recently, New York City saw violent crime, psychiatric disorders, and suicides all drop in the aftermath of the September 11 attacks.

What holds for the population generally in wartime is even truer for soldiers. Recent evidence indicates that incidences of post-traumatic stress disorder may have less to do with the trauma of battle than the loss of that sense of shared experience that comes with the return to civilian life. Junger argues that this need for common bonds is inbred in human nature, harking back to the time when we struggled for survival and worked and slept in proximity to one another:

> A modern soldier returning from combat—or a survivor of Sarajevo—goes from the kind of close-knit group that humans evolved for, back into a society where most people work outside

---

18. Junger, *Tribe*, 67.
19. Junger, *Tribe*, 70.
20. Junger, *Tribe*, 47–49.

the home, children are educated by strangers, families are isolated from wider communities, and personal gain almost completely eclipses collective good. Even if he or she is part of a family, that is not the same as belonging to a group that shares resources and experiences almost everything collectively. Whatever the technological advances of modern society—and they're nearly miraculous—the individualized lifestyles that those technologies spawn seem to be deeply brutalizing to the human spirit.[21]

It should not surprise us that, having been through war, even at a remove, Americans had something of this sense of community in the late forties and fifties, when neighbors not only knew neighbors but knew they could rely upon them. We may recall the neighborhood schools, local clubs, and neighborly socializing which were so prominent then—as well as the broader communal atmosphere (not only the coffee klatches and bridge clubs, but the sharing of resources) that was so evident in many of the new housing developments of the era.

Beyond all this, war gives meaning by immersing the individual in a broader ideology in which struggle and even death take on enormous significance. This is doubly true when ideology is backed by strong religious belief, as in the various Islamic militant groups who, despite their small numbers and modest firepower, have terrorized the West in recent decades. For many Westerners, the appeal of radical Islam—with its call to violent murder and death—seems impossible to fathom. But for young men and women isolated in the West, and too often lacking in any sense of purpose, the possibility of joining with others in an activity that promises to give ultimate value stands in sharp contrast to a culture that seems dead to all higher meanings.

And this leads to the issue of the potentially dangerous consequences of meaning. For the power of meaning to enrich life also makes it a force of unparalleled destruction when left unchecked by appeals to larger principles. Many would reasonably argue that this is what happened in America when the powerful political meanings prevalent in the postwar years (meanings we shall be examining shortly) led to disaster in Southeast Asia by blinding the nation to the evils of combat and the humanity of our enemy. In a sense, America has been politically divided ever since—so much so that, today, a basic love of country and culture are regarded as the opponent in what is nothing less than civil war. But there are still countries that value these things. Indeed, the tendency elsewhere in recent years has

21. Junger, *Tribe*, 93.

been to increasingly stress the value of country and culture as powerful sources of meaning. This has important implications for our larger political world. For while such efforts elsewhere will always lack power absent some genuine moral underpinning (something that democracy supplies) there is no denying the weakness of any nation that has lost the power of meaning because it no longer believes in itself.

While the relative strength of radical Islam contrasts notably to the ideological confusion and uncertainty of purpose that typifies the political landscape of contemporary America, it was not always so. The postwar years were a time of extraordinary political unity in the country, as biblical themes and American history each played a vital role in giving Americans a sense of common purpose. Even when divisions did appear, America's leaders were generally able to draw upon common values and a common language of symbols that brought the country together and gave enormous meaning to political life.

At the heart of these years was the presidency of Dwight David Eisenhower (1952–60). That Americans should overwhelmingly favor the great general to lead them during the perilous Cold War is not surprising. When asked about the prospects of war, one 1954 survey found that a majority of Americans agreed that a conflict with nuclear weapons was likely in the next five years.[22] What is surprising is that, from the first, Eisenhower sought to fortify the nation not chiefly through increased military might but by means of an alliance of politics and religion that goes by the name of American civil religion.

The term *civil religion* dates from the eighteenth-century French philosopher Jean-Jacques Rousseau, though the basic principles are apparent in the words of America's Founding Fathers. These men were not generally orthodox in their faith. However, they were schooled in the Bible and held to certain broad religious convictions rooted in biblical themes. These included belief in the following: the spiritual worth of the individual as created by God; the struggle for freedom and the Good in human history; God's essential role in bringing about justice in each individual life and in the affairs of human beings. American civil religion recognizes the presence of God in these and similar ways throughout America's history, and celebrates this in word, symbol and song.

---

22. Dallek, *Unfinished Life*, 183–84.

Many scholars have questioned the depth of Ike's religious beliefs, citing as evidence the president's famous line "Our form of government has no sense unless it is founded in a deeply-felt religious faith, and I don't care what it is."[23] The words are from a speech given just a month prior to the president's first inauguration. In the speech the future president said that the great struggle of the day was one of "spirit," and that a strong nation must first be strong in its "spiritual convictions." Ours is a religious civilization, argued Ike, because the Founding Fathers said it was a religious conception that they were seeking to translate into the political world. He added that it was this evocation of "the Creator" in the preamble to the Declaration of Independence that formed the foundation of America's religious heritage. All this is in accord with the tradition of American civil religion—as is the phrase "I don't care what it is," which made perfect sense given the bedrock biblical concepts that had formed the nation and continued to unite the faiths that dominated political debate in the era.

Nor is there any reason to doubt the sincerity of the president's own faith. Eisenhower was named after the evangelist Dwight Moody, and grew up in a fundamentalist family that sometimes changed religious denominations but remained unwavering in their commitment to the Bible, which was read daily. Although he was understandably "nonconformist" in denominational allegiance in his military years, aides of the general recounted that he was well versed in the Scriptures and quoted them frequently in making points at staff meetings. Speaking several years after the war, but prior to his nomination, Eisenhower noted how his religious faith had been so critical to him during the war years. "I am the most intensely religious man I know," he proclaimed. "Nobody goes through six years of war without faith."[24]

Ike not only spoke of the need for an alliance of faith and country; he acted upon his belief. At a meeting with his potential cabinet members, Eisenhower announced that they were all invited to join the family at a special religious service at National Presbyterian Church before his inauguration. That morning, the church was filled to overflowing, and other D.C. churches and synagogues (even one mosque) also celebrated the event. Prayer highlighted the inauguration, including a short private prayer that the president offered immediately upon taking the oath of office. In his address Eisenhower spoke of the need for Americans to renew their

---

23. Kruse, *One Nation under God*, 67.
24. Church, *American Creed*, 102.

faith. This faith was the creed of our fathers, who believed in "the deathless dignity of man, governed by eternal moral and natural laws."[25] Such words, again, fit in perfectly with the American civil religion tradition.

Soon after his inauguration, Eisenhower returned to National Presbyterian to be baptized—the first president to have the rite performed during his tenure in office. Four days later he was the guest of honor at the first national prayer breakfast. Ike is also remembered for beginning each cabinet meeting with a silent prayer. During his presidency, Congress added the phrases "under God" to the Pledge of Allegiance and "In God We Trust" to postage stamps—and, later, to paper money. Church and synagogue membership at the end of his presidency in 1960 stood at a remarkable 114.5 million—an increase of 50 million since 1940.[26]

In spreading the gospel of American civil religion, Ike was fortunate to have as an ally evangelist Billy Graham. Graham's religious revivals had varying degrees of success prior to the fall of 1949, when President Truman announced that the Soviets had successfully tested an atomic bomb. Speaking in Los Angeles the next Sunday, Graham made the event the headline for his sermon. Americans were now presented with the desperate choice of revival or divine judgment he proclaimed. This message, in conjunction with supporters like newspaper magnate William Randolph Hearst, forever changed Graham's career. The original stay in Los Angeles was extended from three weeks to eight, during which 350,000 people came to services.[27]

In 1952, Graham spent several days with Eisenhower on the campaign trail, advising him and suggesting passages from Scripture for Ike's use at his rallies. By 1954, the evangelist had led "crusades" in twenty-five major American cities; had a column, "My Answer," that appeared in seventy-three newspapers; and conducted a popular weekly radio program, *Hour of Decision*, that highlighted a biblical reading of current events. Graham was now a regular visitor in the White House. This practice would continue under succeeding presidents.

At the end of Eisenhower's second term, Americans turned to the good-looking war hero John F. Kennedy to carry on the crusade against the Communist menace. Like Ike, the young president was aware of the power of religion in public life. As Robert Bellah has observed, Kennedy's inaugural address was framed in the language of American civil

25. Kruse, *One Nation under God*, xii.
26. O'Neil, *American High*, 212.
27. Fitzgerald, *Evangelicals*, 174–75.

religion.[28] There is, for example, the following line, which occurs at the very beginning of the speech: "The same revolutionary beliefs for which our forebears fought are still at issue around the globe—the belief that the rights of man come not from the generosity of the state but from the hand of God."[29] The address concludes on the following note of inspiration: "Here on earth God's work must truly be our own."[30]

But while religion had a place in Kennedy's rhetoric, it was overshadowed by an array of myths and symbols designed to inspire Americans and give meaning to national life. One of these was the myth of the American frontier. The choice was timely, given that the American West was everywhere in popular culture during the period. In drawing upon it, Kennedy was making reference to a foremost symbol of American courage, strength and self-sacrifice.

The theme of a "New Frontier" was unveiled in Kennedy's speech accepting the party's nomination. Appearing in a packed Los Angeles Coliseum (with millions more watching on television) Kennedy reminded listeners of how American settlers had given up their comforts and joined together to expand the nation's horizons. The New Frontier demanded nothing less. Kennedy was not offering something to the American people but asking something of them. The New Frontier was not a set of promises but a set of challenges intended to appeal to their pride and capacity for self-sacrifice. The notion of challenging Americans would be reiterated in the famous last line of Kennedy's inaugural address, where the new president advised: "Ask not what your country can do for you—ask what you can do for your country."[31] This ideal took tangible form almost immediately after the inauguration with the creation of the Peace Corps, which offered young people a demanding yet peaceful means of serving both their country and the world.

Later that spring, Kennedy unveiled his plan to safely send and return a manned space craft to the moon. The project was not only a means of establishing American preeminence over the Soviet Union in the all-important race for space. Given that, in popular story and song, the moon signified the unattainable and had strong romantic connotations,

---

28. See Bellah, "Civil Religion in America."
29. See Bellah, "Civil Religion in America," 1.
30. Bellah, "Civil Religion in America," 1.
31. Kennedy, "Ask Not," para. 25.

the project was nothing less than a declaration of love for America by her president with the promise of fulfilling all her hopes and dreams.

In his ambitions to unify and inspire the country through story and symbol, Kennedy was aided by his lovely wife Jackie. Jackie Kennedy's contributions to the meanings of the Kennedy presidency went far beyond her efforts to add historical distinction to the interior of the White House. Many of the ceremonies now associated with the presidency (i.e., formal welcoming events on the South Lawn, fife and drum, people in colonial costume) were initiated by Jackie.[32] Mrs. Kennedy and the president also did much to promote the future development of American science and culture by staging elaborate dinner parties for leaders in these areas. One guest recalling the famous Nobel Prize dinner of 1962 spoke not only for the attendees, but for millions of Americans of the day. As Joseph Esposito recounts her words:

> "Because it was Camelot," she said, "we were all excited, impressed, moved by the promise of his presidency, which we thought was the peak of American accomplishment and hope." For her, and surely for many others at the dinner that night, the experience was etched in their minds. She recalls, "We all had a common cause which was America in those days." And for her, it was a dividing line: "We never again thought of our country the way we had that night."[33]

The myth of Camelot referenced here was the most memorable of Jackie's contributions to the Kennedy legacy, and it is all the more remarkable for having been forged in the immediate aftermath of the president's assassination. Like many an American boy, young Kennedy had been inspired by stories of the glorious courts of kings with fair maidens and dashing knights. Then, in 1960, the musical *Camelot* appeared on Broadway. The play recounts the story of King Arthur, Queen Guinevere, Lancelot, and the rest as depicted in T. H. White's popular novel, *The Once and Future King*. *Camelot* would spawn a national tour and a popular film. It also generated a best-selling album, which the president was said to listen to before retiring for the night.

At Jackie's initiative, Camelot as the symbol of the brief Kennedy presidency first took shape in a *Life* magazine article published on December 6, 1963. Although she discussed the idea with historian and political

---

32. Noonan, "Secrets of Great Spouse," para. 15.
33. Esposito, *Dinner in Camelot*, 174.

writer Theodore White, Jackie not only wrote and edited the piece, but resisted efforts by *Life*'s editors to tone down her references to Camelot. Larry Sabato puts it all in perspective:

> His widow had decreed that JFK had been King Arthur, his aides and cabinet the Round Table, and the time of John Kennedy would never be forgot. At that moment, after the strength she had shown and the sadness she had borne, Jackie Kennedy had more power to influence America than President Johnson, Congress and the Supreme Court put together. Her word was cultural law.[34]

The last figure of the era capable of portraying political events in a way that gave them extraordinary meaning was Martin Luther King Jr. King's rich background in theology and philosophy, combined with a thorough knowledge of Scripture, provided a strong intellectual foundation for his sermons, speeches, and writings. But King's ability to pack so much meaning into his words had a more vital source. Soon after becoming the preacher at Dexter Avenue Baptist Church in Montgomery, Alabama, King began to adopt the southern black church's technique of call-and-response dialogue between preacher and congregation. The method, which dates back to Africa, is effective in generating strong emotions in the speaker and his listeners. In a man of King's education and rhetorical talents, the result was a union of thought and feeling that proved extraordinarily meaningful—especially when joining timeless religious and political themes.

Soon after arriving in Montgomery, King became involved in a boycott of the city's buses in an effort to ensure fair treatment for African American passengers and employees. At the frequent community meetings to maintain support for the boycott, he laid out principles of nonviolent political action gleaned from his reading of Thoreau and Gandhi. The tone of the meetings was set with hymns, prayers, and Scripture readings. Then King addressed the crowd, calling upon them to meet brute force with the power of love. Here, as in all his speeches, poetry played a vital role in bringing King's words to life and instilling them with a unifying power. We must always be aware, he said, that we have "cosmic companionship" with a universe that "bends toward justice." Then, employing the biblical story that defined the movement, King proclaimed that the group was moving "from the black night of segregation to the daybreak of joy," and from "the midnight of Egyptian captivity to the glittering light

---

34. Sabato, *Kennedy Half Century*, 262.

of Canaan freedom."[35] One woman journalist of the time said that King's delivery was like "a narrative poem." A churchwoman observed: "When I hears Dr. King, I see angel's wings flying 'round his head."[36]

A highlight of King's crusade came in the summer of 1963 when some 250,000 mostly African Americans gathered at the Lincoln Memorial during the March on Washington. The event began with "The Star-Spangled Banner" and proceeded through an array of speakers and performers before King finally moved to the podium. King opened his speech by evoking the language and deeds of Lincoln. He then moved to his theme of the "check" African Americans now sought to cash in accordance with the promises of the Founding Fathers. At one point he proclaimed, "I still have a dream." From here on, and with the encouragement of those around him, King moved away from the scripted text, waxing poetic in his descriptions of the American landscape and his vision of a nation where little black and white children would one day join hands as brothers and sisters. There will be a day, he promised, "when all God's children will be able to sing with new meaning 'My country 'tis of thee, sweet land of liberty, of thee I sing. Land where my father's died, land of the pilgrims' pride, from every mountainside, let freedom ring.'"[37] King concluded by speaking of an America where all God's children of whatever race or religion would join in singing the words of the old Negro spiritual: "Free at last! Free at last! Thank God Almighty, we are free at last!"

As remarkable as King's words was the behavior of a crowd that was the largest ever to gather at the capital.[38] Four thousand soldiers and marines had been put on standby should violence erupt. They were never called. The District's fifty-nine hundred policeman had nothing to do but direct traffic.

By the summer of 1966 King's attention was shifting to the "Pharaohs" of Chicago, where injustices of poverty proved to be as oppressive (and, ultimately, more intractable) as the injustices of segregation. During the mid-sixties, massive riots roiled the ghettos of America's cities. This, along with the growing acceptance of violence among African American leaders, concerned King deeply.

The last issue was impressed upon him during "The James Meredith March against Fear" in June of 1966. On the March, King was accompanied

35. Oates, *Let the Trumpet Sound*, 77.
36. Oates, *Let the Trumpet Sound*, 80.
37. Church, *American Creed*, 114.
38. Manchester, *Glory and the Dream*, 982.

by the new national director of the Congress on Racial Equality, Floyd McKissick, and by Stokely Carmichael, the new chairman of the Student Nonviolent Coordinating Committee. Each man adhered to the new "Black Power" doctrine, which held that African Americans must forsake nonviolence. King disliked the term, which he felt conveyed an image of black superiority and separatism. Black Americans, he argued, must gain power as other minorities had, through group talent, creativity and determination. Regarding the use of violence: "Some people are telling us to be like our oppressor, who has a history of using Molotov cocktails, who has a history of dropping the atomic bomb, who has a history of lynching Negroes. Now people are telling me to stoop down to that level. I'm sick and tired of violence! I'm tired of the war in Vietnam! I'm not going to use violence, no matter who says so!"[39] As one journalist observed at the time, the Black Power slogan signaled that leaders like McKissick and Carmichael had given up appealing to the best in their supporters and were now appealing to the worst.[40]

In our first chapter we suggested that King's assassination on April 4, 1968, marked the beginning of a series of national upheavals that would soon include the assassination of Bobby Kennedy and eventually lead to the presidency of Richard Nixon and the official end of postwar America. This is but part of the story. In the coming months and years, violence would give way to the decline of the nation's highest ideals and degradation of many of its most cherished symbols. Indeed, from the perspective of the meanings to be found in political life, the years from the late sixties to 1980 are among the worst in the nation's history.

The tarnishing of Camelot and its nobility was one notable chapter in this story. In July 1969, John and Bobby Kennedy's younger brother, Teddy, was the driver in an automobile accident in which young Mary Jo Kopechne drowned on Chappaquiddick Island while Teddy swam away. The incident stood in sharp contrast to the wartime heroics of older brother John, who had famously towed a wounded crew member to safety, swimming with a life jacket strap between his teeth. Sandwiched between Bobby's murder and Teddy's disgrace was the announcement in October 1968 that Jackie Kennedy was to marry Greek shipping tycoon Aristotle Onassis. That the lovely young widow should remarry seemed

---

39. Oates, *Let the Trumpet Sound*, 401.
40. Oates, *Let the Trumpet Sound*, 405.

natural enough. But many assumed that, like actress Grace Kelly before her, Camelot's widow would find a new prince. Millions in the US and Europe were therefore shocked to learn that Onassis was a wealthy man who was divorced, much older, two inches shorter, and had none of the social conscience of his bride. A simple headline in a Stockholm newspaper said it all: "JACKIE, HOW COULD YOU?"[41]

Even the New Frontier was not spared. Although the Peace Corps maintained its vitality through the Johnson years, the Nixon presidency witnessed political infighting within the organization that sapped morale and diminished its effectiveness. Nor did things improve under Democrat Jimmy Carter. Now the problem was radical activist Sam Brown, who attempted to hijack the organization and take it in a political direction at odds with its original purpose of aiding foreign nations and establishing goodwill.[42]

The space program also failed to achieve anything like the popular successes of the sixties. When the Apollo program ended in 1972, human space exploration became limited to the low-earth orbit of the international space station. That same year, President Nixon announced that government support would now shift to the space shuttle program. By the early eighties the space shuttle was having significant success. Then, in January of 1986, the space shuttle *Challenger* burst into flames shortly after takeoff, killing schoolteacher Christa McAuliffe and six other crewmen. The tragedy set some space projects back a generation and caused others to be scuttled. For the millions of schoolchildren who tuned in—primarily to watch the teacher who was supposed to instruct them from space—the explosion had much the same emotional impact as the Kennedy assassination on an earlier generation of America's youth.

Politics in the seventies followed the rest of American culture, leaving the public dismayed as one tawdry act after another made its way upon the national stage. At the core was Watergate. The bare details of the scandal are well known. Police discovery of the June 1972 break-in at the Democratic National Committee Office in the Watergate Complex in Washington eventually led all the way to President Nixon, who was heavily involved in covering up the illegalities. By early 1974, the cover up was beginning to unravel. In July, the Supreme Court ordered the release of secret tapes recording conversations in the oval office. When the

---

41. Manchester, *Glory and the Dream*, 1140.
42. See T. Zane Reeves, *Politics of Peace Corps*.

president refused, the House voted to impeach him. On August 5, the tapes were released. Three days later, the president resigned.

What the bare facts fail to capture is the way the scandal inexorably seeped, drop by drop, as one unsavory detail after another emerged over the many months. A central actor in the story was the anonymous whistleblower known as "Deep Throat." The term was taken from the title of a recent porno film that had created quite a stir in New York City, where everyone from well-dressed middle-aged couples to celebrities and even diplomats from the UN joined in the fun. Along with the profanity-laced tirades of the president (which appeared on the tapes), the term added a tawdry note to the illegalities and contributed to a political atmosphere of disgust and depravity that would have been unimaginable ten years earlier.

Even Nixon's resignation was unable to put an end to the nation's trauma. Many were upset when successor Gerald Ford pardoned Nixon soon after taking the oath of office. Then there were the Watergate-spawned investigations into CIA activities. Along with unsavory details regarding assassination plots and spying on prominent Americans, these produced the first public revelations of Kennedy's lengthy affairs with Judith Campbell and Mary Pinchot Meyer. One political cartoonist of the times said it best. In early January of 1976, *The Birmingham News* featured a Charles Brooks drawing in which the label "John F. Kennedy's Secret Sex Life While President" appeared on a stuffed garbage can behind a phony castle marked "Camelot."[43]

The mood of the country during the period was captured by Billy Graham, who had been a close confidant of Nixon and was especially disturbed by the revelation of the president's fulsome profanity on the tapes. Although he would continue to visit with presidents, henceforth Graham paid less attention to politics and more to his role as a Christian leader in the world. From this point, his influence upon the American political scene diminished.

In 1977, Graham spoke with *Newsweek* writer Kenneth Woodward, who had met with him often over the years and was struck by the changes in the evangelist. Graham had just returned from Hungary, where he had completed his first preaching tour inside the Soviet bloc. "I no longer think we are a Christian nation," Graham confided. America was now a secular society, he said, where many Christians happened to live. Then the once avid anti-Communist made a startling observation about the changing character

---

43. Sabato, *Kennedy Half Century*, 318.

of American culture: "I wonder whether Christians don't have a harder time coping with the temptations of our society than the Christians in Hungary have in coping with the difficulties of living under a socialist system."[44]

Mere weeks before the decade's end, America suffered yet another blow to national pride when Iranian students seized control of the American Embassy in Tehran and took fifty Americans hostage. Their captivity lasted 444 days, ending on President Ronald Reagan's Inauguration Day. If America ever needed a cheerleader to breathe meaning into the political life of the country, it was now. In this, the new president succeeded remarkably well. From the first, Reagan had shown himself a master of the language of American civil religion. In his speech accepting his party's nomination, the candidate proclaimed the nation's greatness and declared that its best days lay ahead. Near the end, he departed from his text. Looking out at the crowd, Reagan averred that only "divine Providence" could have created the United States as an "island of freedom" in the world. He then silenced the throng with a call for silent prayer. The silence was finally broken with Reagan's simple declaration "God bless America."

In the following months, Reagan spoke of a "spiritual renewal" in America, and proclaimed that the motto "In God we trust" (which Ike had placed upon the currency) would not be removed—that, in fact, Americans needed the reminder more than ever. Though he seldom attended church, Reagan presided at the national prayer breakfasts, and he spoke at the National Religious Broadcasters conventions and the National Association of Evangelicals gatherings. At the 1982 prayer breakfast, the President made the point of emphasizing that God had been expelled from the classroom. That same year he pushed for a Constitutional amendment allowing voluntary prayer in the schools. Although the amendment ultimately failed, Reagan proclaimed the value of the Bible at the meeting of the National Religious Broadcasters held the next year. It was in the Bible, in the Sermon on the Mount, that Reagan found his symbol of America as "a shining city upon a hill." The image had first appeared in America in 1630, when John Winthrop used it in describing a colony that would be a model for the world.[45] Reagan employed it in much the same way—sometimes accompanied by Lincoln's characterization of America as "the last best hope of man on earth."[46]

---

44. Woodward, *Getting Religion*, 153.
45. Church, *American Creed*, 5–8.
46. E.g., Reagan, "Time for Choosing Speech," para. 48.

While Reagan's campaign and presidency were thus grounded in the themes of American civil religion, he also borrowed heavily from JFK. As Larry Sabato has pointed out, Reagan, more than any of Kennedy's successors, embodied "the Kennedy mystique."[47] Handsome, self-assured, with a ready wit, and an attractive wife in her designer outfits, Reagan often seemed to be an older version of JFK. In his first term, Reagan quoted Kennedy a remarkable 133 times—much more than he quoted any former president.[48]

One way where Reagan differed from Kennedy was his predilection for stories as a way of proclaiming his values and making sense of the world. Some have questioned the reliability of these tales, noting that they often came from old films. How much this matters may depend upon one's point of view. As we have noted, and will again, stories are an ideal way of giving meaning to utterance, and are therefore usually preferable to those political platitudes that are so common. Much depends, of course, upon whether one believes the story articulates some fundamental truth or is used as a way of avoiding it.

The link between Reagan and Kennedy also extended to matters of policy. Regarding defense, Reagan even mirrored Kennedy in word and action. Kennedy had famously visited Berlin at the height of the cold war, proclaiming, "Ich bin ein Berliner." Twenty-four years later, Reagan stood before the Berlin Wall and challenged Soviet Premier Mikhail Gorbachev to tear it down. Unlike Kennedy, who was opposed by the harsh and unrelenting Nikita Khrushchev, Reagan was fortunate in having the more pliable Gorbachev as his adversary. The President's massive military buildup, coupled with his dogged insistence upon the Strategic Defense Initiative, succeeded in eventually wearing down Soviet resistance. The Berlin Wall began to come down in 1990. Two years later, the Soviet Union was dissolved. It was a foreign policy victory worthy of JFK, and had it been initiated by a Kennedy, its author would have received more credit.

Reagan also followed Kennedy by pushing through tax cuts to spur economic growth. In defending his actions, he even went so far as to adopt Kennedy's phrase, "A rising tide lifts all boats." However, much had changed in America since Kennedy was president and Reagan first formulated his economic principles. In the late sixties, belief in the value of "the exceptional man" and the economic virtues of self-interest had paved the way

---

47. Sabato, *Kennedy Half Century*, 337.
48. Sabato, *Kennedy Half Century*, 348.

for the "greed is good" philosophy of the eighties, whose immediate effects we have witnessed in labor. Meanwhile, Reagan's tax cuts did wonders for wealthier Americans but nothing for the poor, leading millions to feel left out of the picture. As notable as the new wealth were the goods this wealth was used to obtain. It was during the eighties that the spiritual ambitions of the counterculture came undone, and personal identity became less a matter of what one was than what one owned. As Paul Roberts has said, self-discovery had become "an orgy of self-gratification."[49] Roberts notes how computers played a key role here both by enabling banks to make credit more readily available and by helping businesses supply a wider array of goods and services than ever before. By 1990, the average supermarket was able to make available ten times the number of different items ("stock-keeping units") as a supermarket in the fifties. But it wasn't simply sugar-free jams and low-salt peanuts that consumers wanted. In the eighties, the demand for designer jeans peaked, as consumers began to look to brand names without regard for quality or design. By the nineties, the SUV was becoming popular in America, its gas-guzzling engine and fearsome exterior reflecting ideals that stood in sharp contrast to the emblematic counterculture vehicle, the Volkswagen. Where consumption was concerned, the postmodern world was now firmly in place.

This is the dark side of the Reagan years, and a development that has had enormous consequences for meaning. And while Reagan obviously cannot assume all the blame for such a momentous shift—while he was, in Lou Cannon's words, "personally closer to Main Street than to Wall Street"[50]—no decade in recent history has had the negative economic impact upon the search for meaning in America.

At some point early in the twenty-first century, American civil religion died, as older Americans who embraced the idea passed from the scene and younger Americans (taught to see little of value in organized religion and even less in their nation's heritage) came of age. With its death seemed to go any possibility of joining the religious and political life of Americans in any deeply meaningful way for the foreseeable future, if ever again. Evidence of the chasm between young and old came from a survey on American civil religion conducted by Robert Wuthnow in 2003.[51] When researchers asked whether the country had been strong because of its faith in God, 69 percent

49. Roberts, *Impulse Society*, 64.
50. Cannon, *President Reagan*, 748.
51. Wuthnow, *After the Baby Boomers*, 274n14.

of Americans sixty-five and older strongly agreed—compared to only 39 percent of young adults (ages twenty to twenty-nine). Only 37 percent of the young strongly believed that their nation was founded upon Christian principles, compared to 71 percent of their elders. Most notable were the scores on what researchers called a Civil Religion Index, based upon these and two additional questions. Here, 70 percent of older Americans scored high compared to only 31 percent of young adults.[52]

In 2008, many Americans hoped that the old unifying themes might be resurrected in the candidacy of young Illinois Senator Barak Obama. The Senator had already demonstrated his grasp of American civil religion. In a stirring speech delivered at the 2004 Democratic Convention, Obama claimed a share of the tradition for Democrats, noting that "we worship an 'awesome God' in the blue states." He proceeded to stress the role of religious faith in uniting Americans ("We are one people, all of us pledging allegiance to the Stars and Stripes") while observing that not only the rights but the responsibilities of the American people derived from God. Finally, giving his own twist to the old theme, Obama proclaimed that God's great gift to America—indeed, the bedrock of the nation—was the audacity of hope.[53]

Obama returned to the theme during the Democratic primaries four years later. However, at that time, not only his association with the civil religion tradition, but his entire candidacy almost came undone when the fiery words of his minister, Jeremiah Wright (including the pulpit proclamation, "God damn America!"), came to light. Obama not only overcame the controversy, but emerged as a figure of racial reconciliation in a remarkable speech given in Philadelphia just days after the controversy broke. In the speech, entitled "A More Perfect Union," Obama explained how he understood not only the anger of African Americans but the fears and frustrations of white workers who had seen manufacturing jobs disappear while their children struggled without the benefits of affirmative action. Finally, and most emphatically, he returned to American civil religion: "I have asserted a firm conviction—a conviction rooted in my faith in God and my faith in the American people, that working together we can move beyond some of our old racial wounds, and that in fact we have no choice if we are to continue on the path of a more perfect union."[54]

---

52. Wuthnow, *After the Baby Boomers*, 164–65.
53. Kruse, *One Nation under God*, 290.
54. Kruse, *One Nation under God*, 291.

With the support of John Kennedy's brother Teddy and daughter Caroline Kennedy Schlossberg, Obama won a tight race with Hillary Clinton for the nomination. Some months later, he defeated Republican nominee John McCain by garnering 365 electoral votes. "He makes us believe in ourselves again," said Schlossberg, "that when we act as one nation we can overcome any challenge."[55] However, the new president was not JFK. Although very intelligent, and possessed of a ready wit, Obama was quieter and more laid back than his predecessor. Nor did Obama demonstrate that bold ambition that was once capable of uniting the country in common cause. In fact, astronauts Neil Armstrong, Gene Cernan, and Jim Lovell sharply criticized the young president for failing to adequately support the space program. But 2008 was not 1960. Perhaps all that could be expected of any president now was to maintain peace between warring parties. And here, Obama began his presidency as well as could be expected given the obvious drift of the Democratic Party.

Illegal immigration, gay marriage, transgender rights, payments for birth control, and the killings of Trayvon Martin and Michael Brown were among the hot-button issues where Democrats eventually pressed the issue during the Obama years. Opponents were not spared. Despite eventual jury findings that he killed Trayvon Martin in self-defense, George Zimmerman was subject to countless death threats and a $10,000 bounty for his capture by the New Black Panther Party. Nuns, bakers, florists, and photographers were sued when they failed to comply with laws regarding gay marriage or birth control that violated their religious principles. Soon, states, cities, and corporations were being blackballed, boycotted, or threatened with violence for a wrong word, deed, or image. More broadly, anyone who didn't fall into line with the new views was a racist, homophobe, xenophobe, and/or a nationalist—the last a term that once had mostly positive connotations but was now a badge of shame. Little wonder that, in a poll taken as he was leaving office, only 27 percent of Americans felt that the country was more united as a result of the Obama presidency.[56]

The final bill for all this came due in November of 2016, in the form of a shocking victory for Republican Donald J. Trump. Seldom, if ever, had America elected a man who seemed less qualified for the job. The opposition responded with an extraordinary effort to remove the president and

---

55. Sabato, *Kennedy Half Century*, 397.
56. Pew Research, "Poll Watch."

prevent him from ever again holding elective office that began even before he was inaugurated and continued long after he had left Washington.

America would have been better served had Trump's opponents attempted to understand the forces that had put him in the White House. Statistical evidence indicated that Trump's base tended to be people who desperately wanted meaning in their lives but didn't know where to find it and feared losing what little meaning they still had.[57] Trump voters were more likely than most Americans to be unemployed, less likely to marry, and more likely to divorce when they did. They were less engaged in civic affairs and less likely to attend church services regularly—even though they were more likely to say that religion was "very important" to them. Eight years earlier, Obama had spoken to these people. Now it was clear that they had been forgotten.

Counties that went for Trump in the general election were also more likely to be unsettled by "demographic change."[58] That is, they tended to be small, predominantly white communities that had seen a sudden influx of nonwhite immigrants. Here, the cultural fires still smoldered. Here, people felt that the things that still bound them to something larger and of more lasting value—their history, values, and culture—were being threatened at home. They were already gone elsewhere. As Amy Chua explains:

> Many whites feel an intense cultural anxiety. America's culture wars are nothing if not a fight for the right to define our national identity—and it's a bitter, race-inflected battle. After Beyoncé channeled Black Lives Matter at the 2016 Super Bowl, half the country deified her while the other half accused her of "cop killer entertainment." . . . White male heroes like John Wayne have given way to the clueless white male, who doesn't even realize how racist he is, and is regularly made into television sport (as on "Saturday Night Live"). For tens of millions of white Americans today, mainstream popular culture displays an un-Christian, minority-glorifying, LGBTQ America they can't and don't want to recognize as their country—an America that seems to exclude them, to treat them as the enemy.[59]

The statistics confirm all this. White working-class voters who supported Trump were three and one half times more likely than working-class

---

57. Carney, *Alienated America*, 203.
58. Chua, *Political Tribes*, 170.
59. Chua, *Political Tribes*, 173.

whites who didn't support the candidate to agree with the statement that they felt like strangers in their own country.[60]

To understand our contemporary political crisis, we must understand the loss of meaning that has infected politics like the rest of society since leaders like Kennedy and King graced the American political stage. When a new vision of society takes form within the broad parameters of religion, and evokes the best of America's character and history, it opens up world of meaning difficult to ignore. To embrace such a vision is, in effect, to participate in a broader, truer perspective of what America has been and may become. This is precisely what occurred when Kennedy spoke of the New Frontier and appealed to young Americans to "ask not what your country can do for you. Ask what you can do for your country." It occurred again when King evoked the poetry of "My Country 'Tis of Thee" and dreamed of a society where people "will not be judged by the color of their skin but by the content of their character." Such meaningful words—appealing to love of country and recognizing beliefs and values that supersede individual self-interest—are hopelessly out of date in the twenty-first century.

When calls for social change emerge outside religion and are accompanied by attacks on America's character and her past, the possibilities of meaning narrow. This occurred in the late sixties as the appeals of Kennedy and King gave way to the demands of the Students for a Democratic Society and the Black Panthers—groups who were proudly secular and for whom American history was merely a story of oppression. It is this point of view that dominates Progressive political discourse in the twenty-first century. Now the love of country and its history that inspired Kennedy is said to be hopelessly "nationalistic." Today King's appeal to strength of character has given way to a Black Lives Matter movement that stresses its secular foundations and proudly proclaims, "This Ain't Yo Mama's Civil Rights Movement."[61]

The new political atmosphere would be on prominent display in the aftermath of the killing of black American George Floyd by a Minneapolis police officer in late May of 2020. In the following days and weeks, Black Lives Matter supporters would behead, deface, remove, or force the removal of scores of monuments to American history across the country.[62]

60. Carney, *Alienated America*, 203.
61. Tesfamariam, "How Modern Civil Rights," para. 1.
62. Gottschalk, "List of 183 Monuments."

Not only were monuments to Confederate leaders and their supporters damaged, destroyed, or removed; statues honoring George Washington, Thomas Jefferson, Abraham Lincoln, Andrew Jackson, Ulysses S. Grant, the pioneer and pioneer mother, William Clark (of Lewis and Clark), John Marshall, Theodore Roosevelt, and Benjamin Franklin were among the victims of the group's anger. A statue of abolitionist Hans Christian Heg, who had been killed fighting for the Union in the Civil War, was inexplicably taken down and destroyed in Madison, Wisconsin. In Saratoga, New York, a 145-year-old statue honoring Union veterans was destroyed, while in Rochester, an image of legendary abolitionist Stephen Douglas was toppled and seriously damaged. Protesters in Philadelphia defaced a statue of abolitionist Matthias Baldwin with the words "colonizer," while the University of Pennsylvania removed a statue of evangelist George Whitefield for his sins. In Boston, both an Abigail Adams statue and a memorial to the all-black Fifty-Fourth Massachusetts Regiment were defaced for no apparent reason. In California, BLM protesters defaced the statue of poet and abolitionist John Greenleaf Whittier in his namesake city. To the north, in San Francisco's Golden State Park, protesters toppled a statue of Francis Scott Key, a slave owner who was better known as author of "The Star-Spangled Banner."

Many American cities sought to stay ahead of the iconoclasts by voluntarily removing the offending images. Most notable here was the effort of city leaders to rid themselves of the blight of Christopher Columbus. Among the cities who ordered memorials to the explorer removed were Sacramento, Buffalo, Detroit, Philadelphia, St. Louis, Providence, Austin, and San Antonio. The Connecticut cities of Bridgeport, New Haven, Norwalk, Hartford, and Middletown also wanted Columbus gone—as did the New Jersey cities of Trenton, Atlantic City, Newark, and West Orange. In Columbus, Ohio; Columbia, South Carolina; and New Haven and Waterbury, Connecticut, statues of Columbus were removed after suffering serious damage by protestors. In Boston, Baltimore, Camden, and Minneapolis, protesters were able to do the job of destruction by themselves.

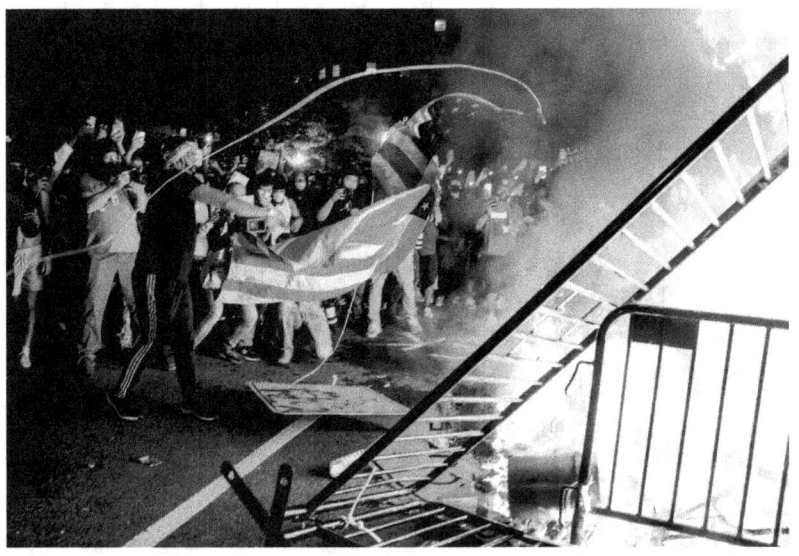

Violent protesters in Washington, D.C. in the summer of 2020
Photo by Samuel Corum/AFP via Getty Images.

Of course, the nation's capital was not spared.[63] In Washington, protesters set fire to ancient St. John's Church, which had been the "Church of the Presidents" since 1816. Fires were also started in the AFL-CIO union federation headquarters, while elsewhere in the city cars were burned, windows smashed, and looting took place. At one point, the White House was surrounded by smoke, and the president, his wife, and son were taken to the bunker for safety. Many undoubtedly wondered if Americans had ever forced a president to flee his living quarters for protection.

All this, and more, led many Americans to wonder if the assault was not simply aimed at the nation's transgressions but at American history generally. Of course, in the contemporary reading of the past, these two are essentially the same.

Our irreconcilable views on reckoning with the past and addressing social concerns going forward are at the heart of a political divide that today goes far beyond anything postwar Americans could have imagined. A poll from 2021 revealed that 43 percent of Americans believed our political system needed major changes, and nearly as many (42 percent) thought it should be completely overhauled.[64] Others think that nothing

63. Borger, "Fires Light Up Washington."
64. Galloway, *Adrift*, 158.

less than a political division of the country will do. This is suggested in a poll of voters in the 2020 election, which found that two in five Biden supporters believed that America should be separated along party lines, while more than half of Trump voters agreed.[65] Opinions like these inevitably affect the way we view those closest to us. A poll from 2018 showed that almost half of Democratic voters and a third of Republican voters were concerned that their children might marry someone of the opposition party. In 1960, only 4 percent of American parents had this worry.[66]

And this leads us to ponder what will become of all the powerful meanings enshrined in the words American schoolchildren once repeated each morning:

> I pledge allegiance to the flag of the United States of America, and to the republic for which it stands, one nation, under God, indivisible, with liberty and justice for all.

Can there be a "United States of America" when its flag and the author of its anthem are held in such disrepute by so many? And what about the "republic"? However, one understands the term, the fact that only 30 percent of millennials believe it "essential" to live in a democracy should give us pause.[67] As we have indicated, the phrase "one nation, under God" is incomprehensible to most younger Americans, and survey after survey indicates that the once "indivisible" nation is coming apart. The notion of "liberty" certainly seems hollow when so many are so willing to condemn others for expressing views with which they disagree. This leaves only "justice for all." For the young, at least, this notion appears to still have resonance. But justice, as defined by law, requires a verdict rendered by "our peers." The peers of the men and women whose monuments were defaced and removed in the summer of 2020 generally held them in high esteem. One wonders what *they* would think of *us*.

---

65. Galloway, *Adrift*, 139.
66. Galloway, *Adrift*, 148.
67. Howe, "Are Millennials Giving Up," para. 6.

# 9

Sports and Religion

IN ITS DIVISIVENESS, CONTEMPORARY politics is reminiscent of sports, whose rise to preeminence is one of the most remarkable developments in American culture since World War II. Our current preoccupation with athletics would indeed have seemed strange to the Founding Fathers. For while sports in America dates to the very beginning of the country, organized athletic contests, as we now known them, only begin around the middle of the nineteenth century. And even then things went slowly until technology lent a hand. The beginning of our obsession with sports dates to the invention of the radio, and gathered strength in the postwar period with the increasing popularity of television.

Still, for most of the twentieth century, professional sports continued to have a relatively modest place in society. In 1955, the Super Bowl didn't exist, the men's NCAA basketball tournament was not yet March Madness, and professional basketball still had franchises in cities like Fort Wayne and Syracuse. When the Philadelphia Athletics moved to Kansas City in 1954, it represented the furthermost Western baseball franchise. Th next year, fifteen million Americans paid to attend a major league baseball game. This compared to thirty-five million who paid to attend classical music concerts.[1] Even the World Series, which was the most popular competition in 1960, failed to have anything like the national presence it has today. In that year, it was a first-to-four-wins match between the champions of the National and American Leagues.

1. Woodward, *Getting Religion*, 38.

In 2022, it marked the culmination of a playoff system that included ten teams and took a month to complete.

In the fifties, organized sports for the young and fitness as an imperative for the middle classes were still on the distant horizon. At the time, boys and girls still played a variety of games together, including tag, dodge ball, kickball, red rover, cops and robbers, red light, kick the can, and hide-and-seek. Organized sports was for boys only and, prior to adolescence, consisted chiefly of Little League Baseball. This was scarcely a hardship. In small towns there was nearly always a vacant lot suited to football or baseball. In the cities, where open space was at a premium, the young adapted with games of their own invention like stickball and stoopball. All this was done without adult supervision or the critical eyes of parents. This is not surprising given that athletic scholarships (by today's standards) were rare and athletics was not usually a significant feature of the college résumé.

For their part, adults in the fifties seldom exercised, aside from the occasional game of golf or tennis, or the modest in-home exercise routines of many moms. Saunas and massages were more popular than swimming or squash. The exception to this was league bowling, which experienced a sharp rise in the fifties. Yet even bowling was less popular than bridge, which seemed better suited to the quiet socializing most preferred.

Scholars date the beginning of our current sports obsession to the mid-sixties. Around 1960, the ABC network, trailing CBS and NBC in revenue, made the decision to emphasize sports in programming. The very next year, Congress passed the Sports Broadcasting Act, which allowed sports franchises to negotiate with the networks as a body when selling broadcast rights for major sports events. While the financial future of sports was thus being guaranteed, technology was making sporting events more appealing to television viewers. Here, the change was initiated by ABC's Roone Arledge, who recognized that sporting events were not merely games but spectacles, in which the faces of coaches and fans, the gyrations of marching bands and cheerleaders, and all the rest were a vital part of the action.[2] Arledge's use of cameras and microphones not only brought viewers into the game; it encouraged fans to carry banners, don jerseys and costumes, and, in general, mug for the cameras. In the midst of all this, instant replay was being perfected. The results proved

---

2. Grundy and Rader, *American Sports*, 199.

popular not only for football fans but for baseball fans and other sports enthusiasts.

This increasing popularity inevitably bred increasing competition. In 1960, a new and financially strapped professional football league, the AFL, succeeded in securing a network contract with ABC. In 1966, the new league merged with the NFL, leading to the first Super Bowl (the name was given later) in 1967. In that same year, a new professional basketball league, the ABA, appeared, with a red, white, and blue basketball and the promise of a more wide-open, entertaining style of play. The ABA and NBA would merge in 1976. In order to avoid competition like this, Major League Baseball had already added two teams in 1961 and would add another four in 1969.

While college and professional sports were gaining popularity in the sixties, athletics had little significance for members of the counterculture. Youth of the day were generally skinny (by today's standards) with little musculature. "Jocks" were viewed by many young people with indifference or disdain. However, the young were happy to engage in a game of volleyball as long as all were welcome, there was plenty of laughter and no recriminations. Frisbees were also popular, appearing in the air above fields, beaches, or college campuses. Frisbee golf and football, which were just beginning, were generally not in keeping with counterculture values. The real emergence of today's competitive zeal came in the wake of the jogging craze and the implementation of Title IX during the seventies. However, neither seemed destined at first to give birth to the religion of sport we know today.

In the early seventies, many turned to jogging precisely because it required no real athletic skills, and because outcomes were measured by the improvement of mental or physical well-being rather than winning or losing. Some saw jogging as an environmental statement; others as a religious or metaphysical quest. This began to change when the term "jogging" gave way to the notion of "running."

This shift is apparent in the 1978 best-seller *Running & Being: The Total Experience*, by Dr. George Sheehan. Sheehan's book is rife with references to poets and philosophers, and seems to run counter to the growing impulse toward competitiveness by stressing the meanings to be found in the simple act of running. "For every runner who tours the world running marathons," says Sheehan, "there are thousands who run to hear leaves and listen to rain and look to the day when it all is suddenly as easy as a bird in flight."[3] At its best, running is for Sheehan a "peak experience," in which one has intimations of the Creator. At other times, his analysis seems not merely to begin with the body but to end there—the body and its drives not simply being the conduit of the spirit but its embodiment.

Running & Being also provides a fascinating insider's look at the changes taking place in jogging in the last half century or so. Sheehan observes how his first Boston Marathon, in the early sixties, basically involved a "club" of some 225 participants, all of whom were welcome.[4] Some runners were overweight. Many wore sneakers. One runner who led Sheehan all the way to Framingham had donned a derby. Sheehan notes how, by the late seventies, the field had swelled to over two thousand and was limited to those who had recorded acceptable times the previous year. By now, running clothes and running periodicals were big businesses, and races like the Boston Marathon were becoming cultural phenomena. This tendency has persisted into the twenty-first century. The 2023 Boston Marathon was "limited" to thirty thousand runners. Today, success is paramount, whether this is measured by one's place in the vast parade of runners or by the achievement of a "personal best" over the distance.

The seventies saw a parallel move toward competitiveness in women's sports as educators attempted to understand how best to apply the dictates of Title IX.[5] In 1972, women's collegiate sports came under the control of the Association for Intercollegiate Athletics for Women (AIAW). At the time, the powerful NCAA had no interest in women athletes. This was fine with the AIAW, who felt the NCAA was too driven by profit and failed to recognize that athletics was only one reason students attended school rather than the *raison d'être*. The AIAW hoped to avoid the hypercompetitiveness that typified men's athletics and the scandals that followed in its wake. Toward this end, the organization originally forbade athletic scholarships.

However, under pressure from the courts, institutions began offering athletic scholarships to women in 1973. By the late seventies, the number and monetary value of athletic scholarships had become the principle test for compliance with Title IX. By now, the most popular women's sports were also demonstrating that they could be profitable—which naturally drew the attention of the NCAA. In 1982, schools were

---

3. Sheehan, *Running & Being*, 75.
4. Sheehan, *Running & Being*, 201.
5. Grundy and Rader, *American Sports*, 249–52.

given the option of competing in Division I women's championships in the AIAW or the wealthier NCAA. The choice was clear, and the AIAW and its ideals were out of business.

As women's sports have proliferated, young women have been encouraged to put on their game face and abandon the impulse to cooperate (an impulse that is essential to the cohesion of human communities). In the twenty-first century, being a fierce competitor in play and at work is considered desirable in young women—at least as long as it does not carry over in to all phases of life. However, this is a difficult balancing act for anyone, and for young women especially. Researchers in a study published in the *Journal of Adolescent Research* have noted that competition is a more complex issue for girls than boys "because their relationships are more essential to their well-being."[6] Many young women struggle to develop that fiercely competitive attitude that now seems to be so desirable in all phases of our lives, and from cradle to grave. The result for young women is a sense of failure that may be manifest in anxiety, stress, and low self-esteem.

At the other extreme are those women who find success today not only in basketball and tennis but in boxing and mixed martial arts. This is a telling development regarding the premium put on cutthroat competition, the lure of spectacle, and the limitations of equality as a vehicle of meaning for young women. Many believed that men's boxing would be banned in America following the death of fighter Bennie Paret in 1962. But violence in sports was the wave of the future. Today, both women and men may achieve fame and fortune in mixed martial arts, a sport whose unrestrained violence led to its being banned until the beginning of the twenty-first century. Some see in such developments another indication of women's continuing gains in equality. Others may wonder if any of these women, having attained equal footing with men, aren't beginning to realize that the ground is low indeed.

Even as women's sports in the eighties were becoming more like men's, women began appearing alongside the opposite sex at the many fitness centers popping up across America. Although anticipated by an earlier generation of Jack LeLaine's and Debbie Drake's, the new fitness gurus—with their admonitions to "pump iron" and "feel the burn"—encouraged an intensity and competitiveness hitherto unseen. The new gurus included body builder Arnold Schwarzenegger and

---

6. Wallace, "Teaching Girls," para. 4.

actress-turned-aerobics instructor Jane Fonda. Schwarzenegger's over-the-top physique was unlike the old movie heroes of the past. Fonda's physical attributes typified a new generation of women who had enhanced the effects of exercise with plastic surgery.

Shelley McKenzie attributes the fitness revolution to the militarism and aggressive economics of the Reagan years.[7] However, it is worth noting that most of the values that spawned the movement were already in place prior to 1980. Competitiveness and a tendency toward self-absorption had always been dangers of the counterculture, as evident in its confrontational political stance and its goal of self-actualization. All that was necessary was a shift in focus from the political to the economic, from mind to body. Having reached something of a dead end in politics, and lacking both the opportunities and the commitment needed for real spiritual growth, young people by the late seventies were ready for a change. We can see the move in counterculture stars like Jerry Rubin, the Yuppie leader who turned to EST, meditation, and yoga before transforming himself into a physical fitness entrepreneur. A similar shift was apparent in Fonda, who had famously visited Hanoi to protest the war in Vietnam prior to her daily treks to the gym.

The results of the athletic revolutions of the seventies and eighties are now evident in America, where the goal of a well-toned body is a cult, and success in sports the American ideal. Now physical activity is the proving ground for competence generally and the clearest proof of self-worth. In America, a Phi Beta Kappa student is more likely to be proud of completing a marathon than of her academic success. Today, citizens suffering an impairment are expected to prove themselves by means of physical achievements like a cross country hike or staggering through a long distance race. Ours is indeed a very different world from the one in which a blind and deaf Helen Keller could inspire as a writer, speaker, and social activist. Today, it is the body that is the locus of meaning, and the individual in pursuit of fitness or athletic prowess the embodiment of the search for purpose.

The limitations in meaning to be derived from our obsession with physical activity are obvious. While the team player may find a significant source of meaning in the camaraderie of teammates, the serious athlete, like the fitness enthusiast, finds in the long hours of training meanings of a more modest sort. Here, meaning comes from the creation of a new

---

7. McKenzie, *Getting Physical*.

"self," as defined by a slimmer waist, firmer thighs, and large, well-toned muscles. Such an individual does not look upward or outward for meaning but to his own form in the mirror. Hence the narcissism that is so evident in the fitness craze and on the sports field—and the limitations of meanings that depend upon the transient joys and beauty of the human form.

Beyond all this is an abusive atmosphere in sports—from bullying (and much worse) teammates to taunting (and worse yet) coaches. People like these may leave deep and abiding emotional scars. An elite gymnast, who was one of many victims of sex abuse by trainer Larry Nassar, has been equally direct in her accusations of famed coach John Geddert. Among Geddert's endearing traits was his proclivity for allowing the girls to fall when he was supposed to be spotting them, tossing clipboards at them, and blaming the girls for their injuries. This gymnast's current physical condition and her account of her experiences should serve as reminders to all who worship at the shrine of competitive athletics:

> Today she wears a metal knee brace from old gymnastics injuries. Physical pain is a part of her everyday life. Then there are the psychological scars. 'People don't realize how many broken girls it takes to produce an elite athlete,' she says, delivering the haunting words with the perfect posture of a gymnast. 'A coach can easily go through 300 girls, or more.'[8]

While participatory sports are important, it is the spectator sports that are the primary source of meaning for most Americans. The reasons for this have already been noted in an earlier chapter. When we watch a game we are not only emotionally but cognitively engaged, analyzing physical actions, considering strategies, and calculating scores and odds. When this occurs in company with a larger "tribe" of supporters who share our interests and concerns, our emotional highs and lows, the result may be a sense of meaning that is both powerful and far-reaching. There is much evidence for this.[9] Studies indicate that fans of local teams are especially likely to benefit from their teams' success, which gives them a sense of belonging. Such success can even ward off depression, while creating a lasting sense of self-worth among those who most closely identify with the team.

---

8. Pesta, "Survivor," 48.
9. Healy, "Be a Fan."

This and other similarities have led some scholars to argue that sports is like a religion, and that games are a form of religious practice. Obviously, the question turns upon what we mean by religion. For most traditional peoples, religion is nothing less than an all-encompassing belief system regarding the origins and purposes of life. Anyone claiming to find this in sports (and some seem to) must have a narrow worldview indeed.

However, scholars looking at religion from a phenomenological perspective—that is, by examining not what people believe but what they *do* in religious practice—will note a number of very real similarities. They will observe that both religion and sports occur in a special area that has been carefully arranged for the activity and set apart from the world of everyday affairs. They will point out that each has a prescribed order of events, with uniforms, symbols, rules of behavior, and the like. They may even argue that sports is like religion in expressing and reinforcing basic social values, that sports emerged to real prominence precisely when religion began to decline, and that sports satisfies the same basic emotional needs as religion but does it better.

The last is the view of character Annie Savoy, in the popular sports film, *Bull Durham*. As Annie put the matter: "I've tried 'em all, I really have. And the only church that truly feeds the soul day in and day out is the Church of Baseball."[10] Anyone familiar with the film will recall that Annie was a knowledgeable participant in the Church of Baseball, and one whose yearly rituals included a hook up with a new ballplayer. Annie believed that, much like Dante's Beatrice, she could lead her latest in a string of lovers to the heavenly realm of the big leagues.

Comments like Savoy's ultimately have more to tell us about ourselves than about religion and sports. The raucous behavior at a good game differs fundamentally from the reverential attitude at a traditional church service. In the latter, the focus is twofold: upward, toward the transcendent, and inward, toward the deeper regions of our own experience. The vital place of transcendence is evident in traditional churches, with their tall windows and high ceilings—an effect dramatized in the Middle Ages, when religious faith was at its apogee. By comparison, all attention in the ballpark is downward, to the field, where players perform as we cheer them on. It is this dimension of transcendence,

---

10. Shelton, *Bull Durham*, 3:23.

and the lasting meanings that may follow from it, that is missing—not only in sports, but in our lives generally.

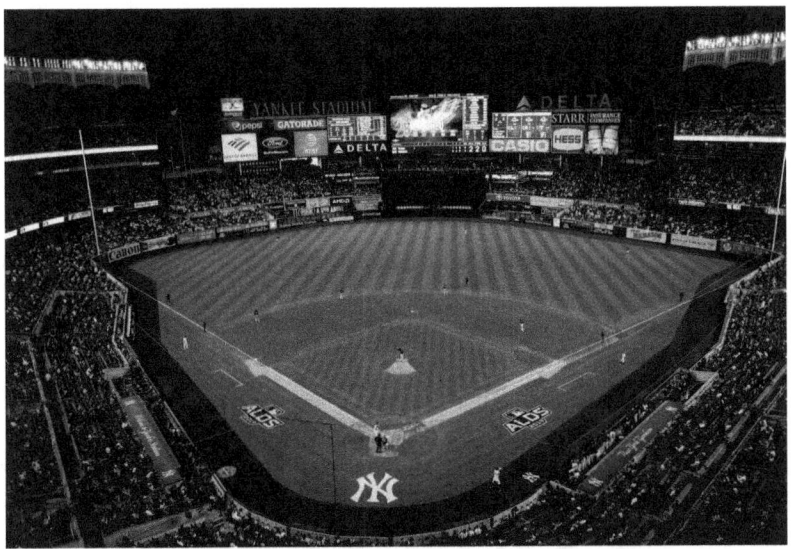

A Major League Baseball Stadium at Night
Photo by Mary DeCicco/MLB Photos via Getty Images.

Sports and religion also differ in having diametrically opposed social goals. As famed anthropologist Claude Lévi-Strauss put it, a game begins with the equality of the two teams and works to achieve inequality. A religious ritual begins from the many inequalities among individuals and seeks to join them into a meaningful unity.[11] Lévi-Strauss emphasizes this distinction by citing the example of the Gahuku-Gama of New Guinea, who, having been taught the game of football, will play several days running in an effort to achieve the same score. As the anthropologist points out, this is treating sports as a religious ritual.

And this leads us to one final difference between religion and sports, which is the hyper-competitive atmosphere of the latter. Like politics, sports serve to join us to some people, only to strongly separate us from others. In many cases, this "us" versus "them" mentality produces disturbing outcomes. We have already noted statistics indicating the psychological virtues of athletic competition for spectators. Now we want to

---

11. Lévi-Strauss, *Savage Mind*, 30–31.

look at the downside, which follows from setting one group of supporters against another and, too often, fans against themselves.[12]

Studies have indicated that fans enjoy watching rivals fail almost as much as they enjoy winning and take satisfaction in heckling opponents. Fans respond positively to reports of an opponent's injury and feel let down when the opponent experiences a speedy recovery. Sometimes fans assault and occasionally murder opposition fans. Following a loss, they tend to be unproductive at work and (at least after the Super Bowl) have a greater risk of dying from a heart attack. A few even commit suicide. And all this is despite the fact that the rewards of spectator sports are so short lived. Indeed, there are now so many sports, so many teams, and such long seasons that winning fans have little opportunity to bask in the reflected glory of their heroes. For there is always one more game, one more season, and one more sport ahead.

In this sense, sports is like a drug "fix," whose highs lead only to the pursuit of another high rather than to something of more lasting value. Little wonder that groups like the Gahuka-Gama, for whom the group stability and cohesion fostered by religion is essential to a meaningful life, have little use for athletic competition as we know it.

Hence the crux of the matter regarding the emergence of sports as a chief source of meaning today, which is this: as activities that are uniting yet divisive, spectacular yet shallow, demanding of time while fleeting in their consequences, sports are the perfect vehicle for the modest meanings now available in America.

The primary difference between sports and religion is apparent in the word "religion," which comes from the Latin *religio*, meaning to bind together. This sense of radically joining the individual to others, to the larger world and its Creator, and to infinite realms of being has made religion the greatest source of meaning in human history. The capacity of religion to give meaning is most obvious in traditional societies. However, it was also apparent, to a remarkable extent, in postwar America.

We have observed the popularity of churches and synagogues in the postwar period. We have also noted the alliance of religion and politics, and have seen how this alliance proved enormously effective in uniting the country and giving enormous meaning to national life. We have even

12. Healy, "Be a Fan."

touched upon the vital role of the language of religion and spirituality in the larger culture, where it proved invaluable to the arts. All this is but a part of the story. The postwar era was a time when the Bible generally, and Christianity in particular, was everywhere in America. It is vital that we understand this if we are to grasp the enormity of meaning loss that has followed from the nationwide decline of religion and accompanying efforts to remove it to the periphery of society.

For TV viewers in the fifties, the day began and ended with brief "sermonettes," which were usually delivered by local clergymen, although in a few urban areas a rabbi would sometimes be chosen to give the homily. At night, these were followed by the national anthem—thereby cementing in the mind of night owls the integral relation of God and country. The workweek then had a religious structure with its conclusion on the "day of rest," Sunday, when many families did indeed avoid not only labor, but virtually all commerce (especially where it was restricted by blue laws). Then, as now, religion shaped the school year, and few hesitated to refer to "Christmas" or "Easter" holidays. Many public schools had some form of daily prayer in the fifties, while most churches and synagogues prominently displayed American flags in their sanctuaries. In some schools, children learned Bible stories, touched on religious themes in school plays, and sang religious songs in assembly. Evidence of the last comes from *The Golden Book of Favorite Songs*, a songbook for school children of the era that includes, along with old standards and patriotic pieces, works like "O God, beneath Thy Guiding Hand," "Now Thank We All our God," and "Jesus Loves Me"—as well as a number of Christmas carols.[13]

As we will observe later on, biblical epics were everywhere in film from the late forties into the early sixties. Religious songs also had a modest place among the popular recordings then, with Frankie Laine's "I Believe" (1953) and Laurie London's "He's Got the Whole World in His Hands" (1958) becoming big hits in the US and the UK. Other religious songs that proved popular during the era were Al Hibblers's "He" (1955), The Browns' "Little Jimmy Brown" (1959) and "Crying in the Chapel"— the last of which appeared in a number of versions in 1953, and was later a big Presley hit. TV in the fifties also seemed relatively unafraid to touch upon religious stories and symbols. There is, among many examples, a notable episode from the crime drama *Dragnet* (1953), which concerns

13. Beattie et al., *Golden Book*.

the apparent theft of the figure of the Christ child from the local parish church's nativity. As it turns out, a little boy had borrowed the statue to give Baby Jesus a ride in his new wagon.

For the majority of Americans, this union of religion and culture was remarkably meaningful. Of course, nonbelievers and members of minority faiths felt left out. Worse yet, their children were sometimes expected to take part in the religious activities in school. These presented special difficulties for Jews, who had the additional burden of the real economic hardship imposed by blue laws.

By 1950, there were a number of organizations eager to reduce the overwhelming presence of religion in American society. Their legal effort would focus upon the First Amendment's Establishment Clause, which prohibits the federal government from establishing an official religion or restricting religious freedom. To better understand the founders' intent on the issue, special attention was given to Thomas Jefferson's 1802 letter in support of Connecticut Baptists seeking relief from their state's established Congregational faith. It was here that Jefferson's famous reference to "a wall of separation between Church & State" had appeared.[14] Historically, the idea of separation had most often been evoked by natavists concerned with the rising tide of Catholicism. Now it would be used as a weapon against all Christians to reduce the impact of the faith upon American culture.

The first real threat to the alliance of religion and culture had come in 1940, when the Supreme Court decreed that the First Amendment's prohibition against established religion applied to the states as well as the federal government. Then, in 1947, the court for the first time made Jefferson's notion of separation the primary factor in rendering a decision. The case of *Everson v. Board of Education of the Township of Ewing* (1947) concerned a New Jersey law that subsidized school busing in private institutions, including many Catholic schools. Counsel for the plaintiff argued the case on the grounds of separation. The defense responded by acknowledging the importance of the principle but asserted that church and state are nevertheless not "irretrievably committed to perpetual hostility."[15] In an amicus brief, two Catholic organizations made the point in another way. Jefferson's wall of separation, they argued, should not be an "'iron curtain' separating areas between which there should be free

---

14. Jefferson, "Jefferson's Letter," para. 2.
15. Hamburger, *Separation of Church*, 459.

passage."[16] A majority of the justices agreed with this line of reasoning, and the state was permitted to continue funding transportation to religious schools.[17]

In 1962 and again in 1963, the court revisited the matter of church and state in public education. Only now, at issue was the thorny question of religious *practice*. *Engel v. Vitale* (1962) concerned a school prayer written by the New York state regents and prescribed for all public school children. Speaking for the majority, Justice Black noted that the practice violated the prohibition on established religion. The court reaffirmed its position the next year by ruling against ritual Bible reading and recitation of the Lord's Prayer in the public schools of Abingdon, Pennsylvania. Only now the court went further. The First Amendment's purpose was not only to prohibit the establishment of religion, it ruled; it was to "uproot all such relationships," including voluntary ones.

Public outcry at the rulings prompted a wave of Congressional amendments in the coming years designed to permit school prayer while accommodating the court's viewpoint. This legislative effort culminated in 1984, in an amendment proposed by President Ronald Reagan. Reagan's proposal said, in effect, that prayer in any public place should neither be compelled nor prohibited. But by now public opinion had shifted too far for even this modest proposal. After weeks of debate, the Senate finally voted for the Reagan amendment. However, supporters lacked the necessary two-thirds majority in both houses required for the amendment to move on to possible ratification by the states.

Today, any notion of providing a meaningful moral or religious basis for public education has been rendered impossible by the increasing unpopularity of organized religion, growing religious diversity in America and a broader inability to reach consensus on any issue of substance. Now any public display of religious belief is likely to inspire lawsuits. In recent years, this attack upon religion in the public sphere has often focused upon public displays of religious themes, including Christmas decorations that include nativity scenes. However, in the broader attack on anything that sniffs of religion—including Santa Claus, Christmas trees, wreaths, treetop stars, Christmas music, and public caroling (what other kind is there?)—critics have felt compelled to engage in legal fisticuffs.[18]

16. Hamburger, *Separation of Church*, 460.
17. Hamburger, *Separation of Church*, 454–63.
18. Gibson, *War on Christmas*.

Most recently, the issue of religion in the public sphere has involved cases calling for the removal of the many monuments to the Ten Commandments that have sprung up over the years in the public schools, parks, and courthouses of America, reminding citizens of the religious foundations of our legal system and joining the two in a way many find meaningful. In nearly all these cases—Tennessee (2003), Alabama, (2003), Kentucky (1980, 2004), Oklahoma (2009, 2015), and New Mexico (2014)—the monuments have been found to violate the Establishment Clause.[19]

It is worth pondering how the current hullabaloo over public displays of Moses's tablets might have appeared to Benjamin Franklin and Thomas Jefferson—hardly the most religiously orthodox of the nation's founders. Immediately following the signing of the Declaration of Independence, on July 4, 1776, these men, along with John Adams, were assigned the task of designing the great seal of the new nation. Both Jefferson and Franklin looked to the Bible for inspiration. Jefferson, author of the famous "wall of separation" metaphor, proposed an image with the children of Israel in the wilderness. Franklin's plan had Moses parting the Red Sea, with rays extending to the prophet from a pillar of fire to demonstrate that he "acts by Command of the Deity."[20] For these men, a defining moment of Judaism and an image of God guiding the chief prophet of that faith were fitting public symbols for the birth of the nation.

From the perspective of meaning, the journey of religion in the public sphere has witnessed the extraordinary triumph of religion in postwar America to a recent effort to remove all public evidence of faith that goes far beyond anything the founders intended. As the author of *Separation of Church and State*, Philip Hamburger, has summarized our current understanding of separation:

> On the basis of this principle, many Americans question the right of others to bring their distinct religious views to bear on politics, and some courts limit the rights of religious organizations to receive government benefits distributed on entirely secular grounds. Put more generally, separation has barred otherwise constitutional connections between church and state ... the First Amendment, which was written to limit government, has been interpreted directly to constrain religion.[21]

---

19. Getto and Harjai, "8 Times."
20. Church, *American Creed*, xvi.
21. Hamburger, *Separation of Church*, 484.

In 1960, religious affiliation among some 179 million Americans was as follows: 63 million Protestants, 42 million Roman Catholics, 5.3 million Jews, 2.7 million Eastern Orthodox Christians, and 589,000 more Christians not included in these categories.[22] The numbers of other faiths (e.g., Muslims, Buddhists, etc.) were negligible. About half of Protestants belonged to the mainline denominations—that is, Episcopalians, Presbyterians, Methodists, Congregationalists, American Baptists, Lutherans, and Disciples of Christ. The majority of the remaining were religious conservatives, led by Evangelicals like the Southern Baptists. The heyday of the Evangelicals would come soon enough. In 1960, mainline Protestantism exerted the major influence upon American culture. However, with the recent election of America's first Catholic president, it was Catholicism that first drew national attention as the decade began.

That the sixties held enormous promise for American Catholics seemed certain not only from the election of John Kennedy, but from the opening of the Vatican Council by Pope John XXIII in October 1962. The pope possessed a warm and compelling personality, as well as a progressive vision of the Church that seemed to be in tune with the times. He had been inspired by the Holy Spirit, he said, to summon the bishops and other delegates to Rome for the purpose of renewing the Church's Christian tradition. When he died the following June, his successor, Pope Paul VI, shepherded in a number of important changes in accordance with the views of his predecessor.

A decree announcing sweeping changes in the Mass was issued in December 1963. The new Mass was to be spoken in the vernacular, and the liturgies simplified, with laypeople sometimes participating in the ceremony. Scripture was read facing the congregation, and an offertory procession brought the bread and wine from the back of the sanctuary to the altar. To further the communal atmosphere, churches added a passing of the peace and congregational singing. The last sometimes consisted of folk music with upbeat lyrics, sung to the accompaniment of guitars.

Kenneth Woodward, a Catholic who was for many years religion editor at *Newsweek*, has described these and other changes and has noted their impact upon younger generations of the faithful.[23] Regarding the new Mass, he says it was "about as moving as a freight train." Of the hymns, Woodward observes that they were "relentlessly upbeat," with

---

22. Ellwood, *Sixties Spiritual Awakening*, 36.
23. Woodward, *Getting Religion*, 83–84.

the message of a thoroughly pleasant deity who was all love and nothing more. There was "no awe, no hint of the Biblical fear of the Lord," Woodward laments. The children loved it all since they were being fed the same insipid diet in Sunday School—a development that led Woodward and his wife to chose to home educate them on the fundamentals of the faith. Concludes Woodward: "The church's failure to pass on the faith, through the liturgy or the classroom, would eventually snip two generations of young Catholics from their own religious roots."[24]

In fact, what Rudolf Otto had called the "numinous"—that sense of God as both a fearful and ultimately unknowable reality—was disappearing everywhere in Catholicism. By the eighties, the old Mass for the Dead (which rendered God's terrible judgment in black vestments, somber prayers and the terrible *Dies Irae*) had given way to a new Mass that stressed the loving nature of God. Gone, too, was the strong sense of sin, that had taken on visible reality in the dark confessional boxes that once did such a brisk business on Saturdays. Confessional boxes were also notably absent in the many suburban churches now being built—as were the old kneelers.

In many Catholic churches there now appeared a style of design that had lost sight of the old symbols when it didn't distort them. Anthony Esolen has described his experience of the new or redecorated churches in this way:

> I have seen, in Catholic churches, minimalist Stations of the Cross that can hardly be recognized as depictions of the Passion. I have seen crosses that look as if a modernist Jesus were flying with wings outspread, like a theological pterodactyl. I have seen the Eucharist relegated to what looks like a broom closet. I have seen a baptismal font that bubbles. I have seen beautifully tiled floors, with intricate cruciform patterns, covered over with plush red carpet.[25]

This inability to appreciate not only the beauty but the power of the old symbols—to, as it were, sweep them under the carpet—especially galls Esolen, who echoes Woodward when he speaks not only of seeing plywood on the walls, but of "hearing plywood from the pulpit, and singing plywood instead of hymns."[26]

---

24. Woodward, *Getting Religion*, 84.
25. Esolen, "Free Our Churches," para. 1.
26. Esolen, "Free Our Churches," para. 4.

During the sixties, those little rituals that had separated Catholics from others were also on the way out. These included the rosary and meatless Fridays—the former of which made prayer, the latter, prohibition, a vital part of the believers' ordinary routine. The Index of Forbidden Books disappeared then, as did the old prohibition against Catholics attending Protestant worship services. By such means the flock was being pushed more and more into the larger, secular world.

The result was a loss of certainty and a remarkable confusion of purpose that was perhaps most apparent among nuns. Nuns were the most visible face of the church from their prominence in hospitals, orphanages and, especially, parochial schools. Upon entering the convent nuns took the name of one of the saints. This, along with their conservative attire, gave them their identity as virgins consecrated to Christ. The "new nun" of the mid-sixties reclaimed her family name and was encouraged not only to don new clothes but to forsake the cloister and seek work and accommodation closer to the flock. Deprived of these little rituals of meaning thousands of nuns defected during the decade and the number of new novices dropped.

In the midst of all this change, in 1968, Pope Paul VI seemed to do an about face when he issued *Humanae Vitae*, affirming the Church's traditional opposition to contraception. Expressions of anger and dismay were immediate. In fact, the decision is widely cited as having engendered a crisis within the Church, leading to an even more dramatic decline in contributions and regular attendance at Mass. For us, this issue deserves attention. For what it indicates is the Church's determination to reaffirm a distinction between body and spirit that may be antithetical to our postmodern point of view but basic not only to Christianity but to the traditional religious viewpoint generally.

Dismay over *Humanae Vitae* was not only evident among the larger body of Catholics; it was also apparent among many members of the pope's Commission for the Study of Population, Family and Births, which spent three years in the mid-sixties studying the issue.[27] Having begun as a small, all-male group, the commission was eventually expanded to fifty-eight members, thirty-four of whom were laypersons, including three married couples. Among the latter were Americans Pat and Patty Crowley, who headed the Christian Family Movement. Another American was John C. Ford, SJ, a moral theologian who had been teaching at

27. McClory, *Turning Point*.

The Catholic University of America when summoned to Rome. At the conclusion of their work, the Crowleys were among the vast majority who voted in favor of lifting all bans on contraception. Ford was among a handful whose opinion in favor of maintaining the Church's prohibition eventually carried the day.

Many argue that the pope's position was merely a reassertion of papal authority and was rooted in an unwillingness to acknowledge that the Church had been in error on the issue in the past. But the pope and his supporters seem to have been acting to reaffirm the vital place of the spirit in a world that was rapidly losing sight of its role in human life.

By the spirit, I have in mind that part of reality that is regarded as being not only above and beyond the physical world, but anterior to it as the vital force from which all things come into being. The biblical creation story acknowledges this by placing the Spirit of God at the beginning, prior to the emergence of the physical world, which is born not through heroic feats or machinations, but by the creative power of the Word (another attribute of the Spirit). Christian cosmology sees human existence as a battleground between spirit and body, good and evil. Christian belief places the spiritual life alongside love of others as the other pole of religion. As this is rendered in Jas 1:27–28 RSV:

> Religion that is pure religion and undefiled before God and the Father is this; to visit orphans and widows in their affliction, and to keep oneself unstained from the world.

The ultimate goal of Christianity (as of most other religions) is to bring as much of the physical world as possible within the realm of the spirit, thereby giving it enormous value and meaning. It is precisely this ambition that seems to have guided the pope's view on contraception in *Humanae Vitae*.

In the encyclical, the pope stressed that the issue of contraception must be understood in light of recent efforts to place all of human nature within the purview of the physical and social sciences. In distinction to these, Christianity asserts that, in addition to their physical and temporal qualities, human beings are creatures of spirit—that is, that they possess "supernatural, eternal aspects." Marriage, which establishes the union of the couple with a loving God, is one expression of this union. In conjugal relations, husband and wife provide the matter for the transmission of life. God provides the spirit.

In the commission's discussions, Ford pointed this out by reference to the Sistine Chapel's great ceiling fresco, *The Creation of Man*, where Michelangelo has shown the outstretched hand of God giving life to the supine figure of Adam through the Spirit's spark. This is the moment we are talking about," Ford explained. And further: "Your conception is your very origin, your link to the community of living persons before you, the first of all gifts received from your parents, your first relationship with God as he stretched out his finger to touch you . . ."[28] It follows that, to engage in sexual relations without the possibility of engendering new life is to eliminate God from the act and to deprive it of any higher meaning.

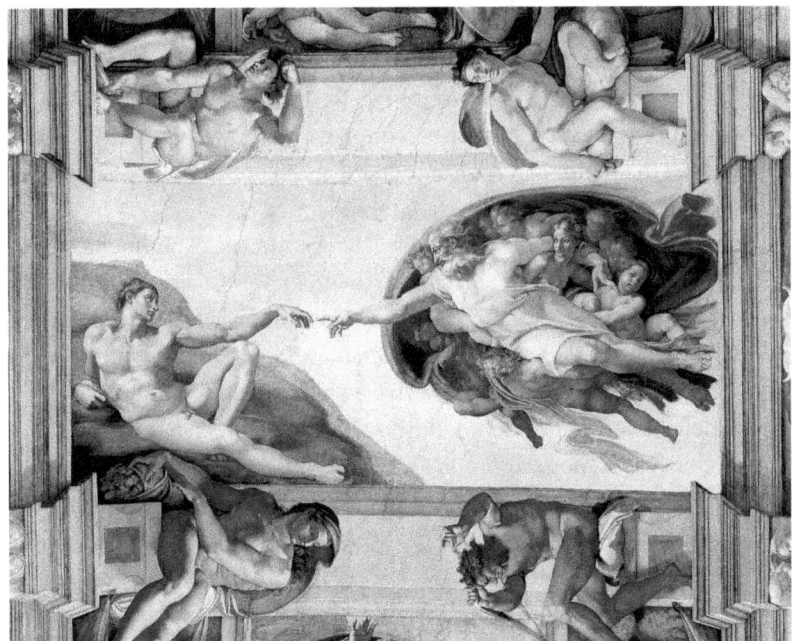

Sistine Chapel: *The Creation of Adam* by Michelangelo. Photo copyright ©Governorate of the Vatican City State—Directorate of the Vatican Museums.

The Crowleys were stunned by the pope's encyclical and later placed the decision on a par with the loss of Martin Luther King Jr. and John Kennedy as among the great tragedies of the sixties. Ford also fared poorly. Upon assuming a teaching position at Weston College, in Massachusetts, he was greeted with such cool disdain by faculty and students that he soon resigned.

28. McClory, *Turning Point*, 124.

More than fifty years after *Humanae Vitae*, Catholics remain divided over the issue of artificial contraception. In 2018, nearly five hundred British priests signed a statement supporting the pope's decision, noting that social changes over the decades regarding the issues of sex and the family had developed "to the detriment of human life and love."[29] Still, most priests have hesitated to take a firm stand on the issue, and a Pew poll from 2016 found that, of US Catholics who regularly attend Mass, only 13 percent think that artificial birth control is wrong.[30] None of this is surprising. In seeking to reaffirm the vital place of the spirit in all of life, *Humanae Vitae* sets an extraordinarily high bar. Where meaning is concerned, the Church might have been better served retaining more of the spiritual in the various little rituals of the faith and leaving sex to its many and varied postmodern expressions.

Growing modernization and a search for increasing relevance were also apparent in the mainline Protestant churches beginning in the sixties, although, at least in regard to the traditional service, the changes came slower and were far less radical. Of course, some churches experimented with guitars and dancing. For the most part, however, things didn't go so fast or so far. Greater informality simply became apparent with gradual additions like the passing of the peace and the brief interlude when the children came to the front of the sanctuary to receive a simple homily (an event which, to the delight of many, often had humorous consequences). Applauding in church became more common and a growing emphasis on social issues was apparent in the pulpit and the hymnal. While the new hymns may or may not have been as bad as the ones Woodward describes, they usually lacked the heartfelt poetry of the old pieces. Too often, hymn writers settled for a mix of liberal theology and political phrases, with poetry confined to simple end rhymes. Many churchgoers regretted the loss of works which, like old familiar faces, were gradually disappearing from the pews.

Poetry was also disappearing from the pulpit. This occurred with the gradual replacement of the Authorized Version of the King James Bible (which had been standard for some 250 years) with the new Revised Standard Version, which appeared in 1953. Advocates stressing the greater clarity of the new text seemed unconcerned that this change

---

29. Caldwell, "Nearly 500 British Priests," para. 9.
30. O'Loughlin, "Poll," para. 6.

came at a cost. For what the King James Bible lacked in clarity it had more than made up for in poetry.

Two short translations from the Christmas story demonstrate the difference. As Luke's account appears in chapter 2 of the RSV:

> And in that region there were shepherds out in the field, keeping watch over their flocks by night. And an angel of the Lord appeared to them, and the glory of the Lord shown around them, and they were filled with fear (Luke 2:8–9 RSV).

And in the old King James Bible:

> And there were in the same country shepherds abiding in the field, keeping watch over their flock by night. And, lo, the angel of the Lord came upon them, and the glory of the Lord shown round about them: and they were sore afraid (Luke 2:8–9 KJV).

Although there appears to be no real difference in the content of the two translations, there are telling differences in the language. We will note that the first verse in the King James version possesses subtle alliterations ("there" and "were," "same" and "shepherds") that link the words and take us more quickly into the scene. The word "abiding" has a gentle, peaceful quality lacking in the prosaic "out in the field," and better sets the stage for the drama that follows. The sudden impact of the angel's appearance ("And lo, the angel of the Lord came upon them . . . and they were sore afraid") is more apparent in the language of the King James translation—as is the wonderful sense of an encircling power conveyed by the alliterative *os* in "shown round about."

At least the modern translators had the good judgment to leave the many "ands" in the text to drive the narrative. This device is everywhere in the Hebrew and King James Bibles but generally absent in the RSV (cf. the story of Rebekah at the well in Gen 24:15–16). The result of this and so many omissions is, as I see it, a loss of the poetry that adheres to the King James text. Scholar Eric Ormsby puts it this way: "For all its flaws, the King James truly reflects the beauty of the original Hebrew. That beauty is not one of mere embellishment. It is intrinsic to the way in which the Hebrew writers sought to drive home the truth of their words; indeed, it is inseparable from that truth."[31] To sacrifice this for the modest gain in accuracy of the RSV is to give up much of the meaning that, as in the Latin Mass, adheres to words that speak not merely to the mind but to the spirit.

---

31. Ormsby, "Hebrew Bible," para. 17.

The spirit was, in fact, something mainline Protestants, like many Catholics, increasingly had little use for. Liberal Protestant leadership in the sixties embraced the secular *as* sacred, according to the notion that if God was to be found anywhere, it was in the secular world, not the church. In the early sixties many liberal northern churches became heavily involved in the civil rights movement in the South. Soon, political activism spread, with many ministers taking the unprecedented step of endorsing liberal candidates. And when civil rights started to fade from the front pages, the escalating war in Vietnam engaged many mainline churches and their leaders. Much of this was clearly commendable. Liberal Protestants rendered a great service to the drive for civil rights by working and suffering with African Americans. However, as the decade wore on, both the civil rights and anti-war movements took on a militancy that the churches were slow to recognize for what it was. Having lost touch with the religious foundations that had legitimized their acts and imbued them with meaning, the churches were now venturing into ethically grey area.

Popular liberal Christian literature of the sixties demonstrated just how far this line of thought could go. Most notable here was Harvey Cox's *The Secular City* (1965), which appeared to popular acclaim as America's metropolises were beginning their annual summer ritual of rioting and burning. In the book, Cox defined secularization as the "liberation of man from religious and metaphysical tutelage, the turning of his attention away from other worlds and toward this one."[32] For Cox, the city, with its anonymity, its impersonality and, above all, its dynamism, was the site of the coming Kingdom of God. The role of the church was to be God's "avant-garde," looking for signs of the approach of God's kingdom and working towards its realization.

Liberal theologians like Cox typically embraced the new morality and the situation ethics that was thought to sustain it. In an article appearing in *Playboy* magazine in 1968, Cox went so far as to compare hippie "love-ins" to the old Methodist camp meetings.[33] As farfetched as this notion was, it exemplified the fuzzy thinking of the period (much of which found a home in *Playboy*). It was a time when many in the church, and in society, found in the Beatles' popular refrain "All You Need Is Love" profound theology.[34] Few seemed to notice that the agape so prized by situation ethics quickly dissipated amid the heat of Eros.

32. Ellwood, *Sixties Spiritual Awakening*, 132.
33. Ellwood, *Sixties Spiritual Awakening*, 199.
34. See "All You Need."

Such tendencies to lose sight of Christian fundamentals had always been a danger of the this-worldly concerns of the social gospel. Writing of, and for, an earlier generation, theologian H. Richard Niebuhr had characterized this sort of religion in this way: "A God without wrath brought men without sin into a kingdom without judgment through the ministrations of a Christ without a cross."[35] For meaning, the problem was the narrowing of the soul and its universe. Like today's positive psychology, the new liberal theology had no room for the angels and demons so essential to traditional Christian theology. Many longed for the old Christianity and disparaged Christianity lite. These included George Weigel, who put it like this:

> The only Christianity worth considering... is the kind of Christianity that, in Henrik Ibsen's phrase, is far more deep-down-diving and mud-upbringing. A Christianity that takes itself seriously as the bearer of great truths about the human person, human community, and human destiny is a Christianity to contend with. A Christianity indistinguishable from the editorial page of the *New York Times* is hardly worth anyone's bother.[36]

In fact, mainline church pews were probably as likely to be populated by readers of the editorial page of the *Wall Street Journal* as the *New York Times*. This disconnect undoubtedly contributed to declining numbers of churchgoers. Between 1965 and 1990, the mainline denominations lost between 20 and 30 percent of their members.[37] This decline, as a proportion of the population, has persisted. In 1993, the once-powerful mainline churches accounted for only about 20 percent of America's Christians. By 2018, that number was down to about 11 percent.[38] Although there are a number of reasons for this decline, many scholars point to the willing involvement in "the secular and the faddish" as the leading cause. As a Methodist theologian put is some years back: "God is killing mainline Protestantism in America, and we goddam well deserve it."[39]

In his book, *Why Conservative Churches Are Growing* (1972), Dean Kelley added his voice to those who felt that a loss of traditional ideas and practices was chiefly to blame for the decline of mainline Protestantism. Liberal churches, Kelley argued, had lost the "traits of strictness" that were

35. Weigel, "Christian Citizen," 176.
36. Weigel, "Christian Citizen," 176.
37. Thomas Reeves, "Collapse of Mainline Churches," 207.
38. Burge, "Mainline Protestants," para. 6.
39. Thomas Reeves, "Collapse of Mainline Churches," 208.

essential to a religion of real substance. "Strong" churches, on the other hand, "provide firm beliefs about the meaning of life," teach clear moral principles, and expect firm commitments from their congregations in return.[40] Kelley was referring to a range of conservative religious bodies, including Mormons, Orthodox Jews, and those evangelical churches that began to flourish as mainline Protestants began their decline. During the eighties, evangelical membership passed the mainline Protestants for the first time since the numbers were counted. By 2018, they were 22 percent of Americans—or twice the mainline Protestant numbers.[41]

The largest evangelical group is the Southern Baptists, like Thomas Road Baptist in Lynchburg, Virginia. Thomas Road Baptist was founded by Jerry Falwell in 1956 at an old factory building in a rundown section of town. By 1980, it had sixty pastors and weekly attendance of about eight thousand at its three Sunday services and Wednesday night prayer meetings. Frances Fitzgerald has provided a valuable account of Thomas Road at that time that heavily informs the following discussion.[42] As she makes clear, the mission of Thomas Grove, like many evangelical churches of the era, was to proclaim both a meaningful Christian message to those who had lost their way and provide sanctuary from the "secularists and liberals" who now seemed intent on eradicating all the old values.

In 1980, services at Thomas Grove Baptist looked much as they might in any conservative Protestant church of the era. Churchgoers were clean cut and appropriately dressed, the men in double-knit suits, the women in modest print dresses. Worship began with a robed choir singing traditional Baptist hymns. This was followed by solos of inspirational music and, on occasion, a performance by the student choir from nearby Liberty University. Falwell's sermons were then delivered. Sometimes Falwell spoke as a sage counselor might, clarifying religious and moral issues. At other times, he was more impassioned, calling the congregation to combat the secular humanists of the day. Fitzgerald points out that, in the summer of 1980, Falwell delivered a series of sermons warning that the tribulations of the last days, as described in the Bible, may well be close at hand.[43] Where meaning is concerned, the potential of such prophecies and exhortations is enormous.

Falwell's message should be understood within the context of the need for meaning of so many in his congregation, and of Falwell's own

---

40. Woodward, *Getting Religion*, 126.
41. Burge, "Mainline Protestants," para. 12.
42. See Fitzgerald, *Evangelicals*, 265–90.
43. Fitzgerald, *Evangelicals*, 309–10.

experience as a wayward youth whose father was a sometimes violent alcoholic. There were prohibitions against alcohol, dancing, pornography, and drugs, and churchgoers were warned against Hollywood films and many TV shows (including *Charlie's Angels*). While many Americans would undoubtedly chafe under such strictures, the effort here was to preserve the home from the many temptations posing a threat to family stability and to preserve the spiritual life from the debasement that had become so prevalent in society. As Fitzgerald points out, even the church's dictate that wives submit to their husbands should be understood within the context of the lives of so many in the congregation:

> As for the Thomas Road women, they might have invented the church, so heavily did the prohibitions fall on traditional male vices like drinking, running around and paying no heed to the children. To tell 'Dad' that he made all the decisions might be a small price to pay to get the father of your children to become a respectable middle-class citizen.[44]

Thomas Road Baptist was much more than Sundays and Wednesday evenings. The church was a hub of activity throughout the week, with special programs for children, young people, adults, the elderly, and the deaf. There were Bible study groups, lectures, special trips and outings, picnics, and programs for unmarried adults and the divorced. Voluntarism was also a vital part of the church's ministry. Groups of volunteers regularly visited hospitals, nursing homes, and prisons, providing aid while carrying the church's message. The program was so comprehensive that members could (and some did) devote all their free time to the church and its many ministries.

In addition to giving meaning to daily activity, the church provided an overarching theology that framed the believer's worldview in a powerful way. While churchgoers were typically friendly, engaging people, they viewed themselves as somewhat apart from the surrounding world. They had a sense of the guiding power of the spirit that took form in the belief that God had a plan for their lives and had led them to Lynchburg and to Thomas Road. In this they were like many fundamentalists, who found in their faith a clear path forward in a world of increasing chaos. There was no need to look beyond the church and the Bible for answers, including answers to the thorny political issues of the day. For folks like these, their own point of view was not preeminent in all things—including,

---

44. Fitzgerald, *Evangelicals*, 281.

most especially, matters of faith. Needless to say, theirs was a vision with enormous capacity for meaning—as well as disappointment in a world that seemed more and more to reject the will of God.

In the twenty-first century, mainline Protestantism has found new ways to make its brand of Christianity almost indistinguishable from the editorial pages of the *New York Times*. Evidence for this comes from an edition of *Presbyterians Today* that appeared in the late summer of 2022.[45] One article in the magazine suggests that those churches that employ marketing techniques to highlight their liberal credentials are better than less savvy congregations that rely upon old fashioned methods to aid the needy. Another praises radical changes in traditional church architecture to make sanctuaries more relevant. These include one historic structure (said to have seated Abraham and Mary Todd Lincoln) that was being reconfigured into a design intended for the 6 percent of Americans who will struggle with PTSD at some point in their lives. Some black Presbyterian churches have even recently gotten their white counterparts to reach into healthy endowments to provide reparations for the black community. The assumption in all this seems to be that the eternal realities of the faith lack power unless reclothed in contemporary economic philosophy or the political cause *du jour*.

Meanwhile, Evangelical Christianity has now sought to bridge the gap between sacred and secular through the emergence of "megachurches" (that is, churches having two thousand or more weekly attendees). Today, megachurches are the public face of Christianity in America. A number of these churches, like Thomas Road Baptist (which moved into a reconfigured electronics plant when Jerry Falwell died) still maintain their links to the Southern Baptist Convention. Others, including Joel Osteen's enormous Lakewood Church in Houston, long ago severed their Southern Baptist ties. In fact, megachurches are a diverse phenomenon, and not easily reduced to simple characterization or formula. Although generally conservative on social issues, they typically avoid the adversarial stance on popular culture that was such a prominent feature of Falwell's ministry. On the contrary, megachurches employ the styles and methods of the contemporary world in the service of salvation.

---

45. *Presbyterians Today* 112 (Sept./Oct. 2022).

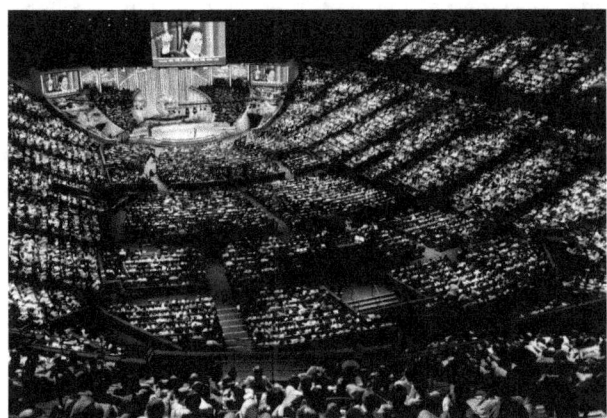

Lakewood Church in Houston. Photo by Timothy Fadek/Corbis via Getty Images.

Like Thomas Road Baptist, the typical megachurch today occupies a renovated warehouse, which has been remodeled into a movie theater with a stage, sophisticated lighting, and a huge HD screen. Every effort is made to welcome visitors and make them feel at home. Here, the hard pews of traditional churches have given way to cushioned seats, and well-dressed churchgoers have often been replaced by "come-as-you-are" congregants—some of whom are attired in jeans and flip-flops and have a cup of coffee in hand. All this appears to be vital to the warm, communal feeling that is essential if the service is to have the desired effect. Attendees come for a powerful emotional experience that they themselves liken to the atmosphere of a football game or a rock concert. Everything in the service is done to achieve this effect. And when it is absent—and vacant seats become apparent on Sundays—the megachurch is on its last legs.

In their book *High on God: How Megachurches Won the Heart of America*, authors James Wellman, Katie Corcoran, and Kate Stockly stress that megachurches aim not to enlighten, but to create a "powerful, effective experience of the divine."[46] Their surveys of attendees bear this out. When asked on a scale of one to five to rate their reasons for remaining in their church, about 80 percent gave the worship style either a four or five. Of the words used to describe their worship experience, "feeling" was by far the most common.[47] Indeed, from the warm greeting through the mood of growing expectation to the powerful altar call,

---

46. Wellman et al., *High on God*, 71.
47. Wellman et al., *High on God*, 104.

everything is designed to heighten the emotional atmosphere. In their book, the authors cite one lighting director who described his efforts to make sure attendees felt, in turn, welcomed, engaged and fulfilled.[48] The huge screen is vital here, unifying participants through the words of the hymns, highlighting the face of the senior pastor or lead singer, and scanning the throng for emotionally involved members.

The pastor is the central player, and many a megachurch folds when an otherwise able leader is called upon to replace his charismatic predecessor. Music is also vital, and, while it varies from church to church, it is generally loud and emotion laden, in sharp contrast to the slower, more contemplative hymns of old. The singing, too, is more dynamic, as members of the congregation raise their hands, close their eyes, and rock back and forth.

While all this is clearly meaningful, it is the nature of the meanings that are at issue. And here, results are unclear. In their book, the authors of *High on God* praise megachurches for delivering an uplifting and enriching experience, and they note that participation carries over into weekly activities that are not only emotionally but cognitively engaging and of enormous value to surrounding communities. Still, it is emotion that is the real star here—so much so that megachurch members often experience emotional withdrawal after Sunday services and note their need to be "filled up" again soon afterward.[49] It's hard to ignore this or the many ways contemporary culture has been used to orchestrate emotion and harness it to a one-dimensional vision of the Christian faith. Ultimately, our view of megachurches will likely turn upon whether we believe they are bringing the secular more and more into the service of the spirit, or further forsaking that sense of "otherness" that is the spirits true realm.

The new service style may be necessary to hold generations who expect to be entertained. However, it seems unlikely that even this will for long stem the tide. In 1999, membership in religious organizations in America (church, synagogue, or mosque) was at 70 percent. In 2020, the percent dropped below 50 percent for the first time since these statistics have been recorded. Among millennials, the number was only 36 percent.[50] Nor do the youngest generation of Americans hold out much

---

48. Wellman et al., *High on God*, 282–83.
49. Wellman et al., *High on God*, 173–74.
50. S. Bailey, "Church Membership in U.S.," paras. 1, 9.

hope for the future. As Jean Twenge points out, our iGeners are on track to be the least religious group in recorded history.[51]

If the emergence of the megachurch represents one major trend in the accommodation of religion and secular society, today's pursuit of an amorphous "spirituality" signifies another. As we noted earlier, the notion of the "spirit" in religion has historically taken meaning from opposition to the material and bodily. This was clearly the case among the Christians of early America, as Leigh Schmidt points out:

> Puritans and evangelicals emphasized practices of piety; they pursued devout, holy, or godly lives; like the Apostle Paul, they juxtaposed the spiritual with the carnal, but rarely did they label their regimen of sanctification "spirituality." Far from being a keyword in the early Protestant vernacular of personal devotionalism, *spirituality* was usually employed as a theological term in opposition to *materiality*. It pointed, in other words, to the fundamental contrast between the physical and metaphysical worlds, matter and spirit.[52]

Schmidt notes how this began to change around the middle of the nineteenth century, when the notion of an inward and much broader "religion of the spirit" began to appear in men like Emerson and Whitman. From there the notion of spirituality continued to take form from a variety of philosophers, spiritualists, Theosophists, and liberal and ecumenical spokesmen of the many faiths who found support in America. The result today is a tendency to dissociate "spirituality" from religion and to accept accommodations between spirit and the material or bodily that are antithetical to the traditional religious point of view. And in matters of the spirit, as in so much else, the real transition dates to the late sixties and seventies.

While spirituality of the sixties and seventies usually involved nothing more than the purchase of incense, a few books and records, and the adoption of a number of popular phrases, many young people of the era searched for a deeper, truly transformative experience. The vast majority would be disappointed. Sometimes the sages who came to America lost their way amid the temptations of the West. Other times, they taught a watered-down spiritual practice that had modest health benefits but

---

51. Twenge, *iGen*, 119–42.
52. Schmidt, *Restless Souls*, 4; emphasis original.

nothing more. In either case, a culture that was geared to the body rather than the spirit and valued the quick sale rather than the slow journey to salvation was largely to blame.

Typical of those who lost their way was Guru Maharaj Ji, who promulgated meditation as a means of discovering the God within. Maharaj Ji brought his father's Divine Light Mission to America in 1971 at the tender age of fourteen. As DLM membership grew and ashrams began to spring up across America, the young man heralded as the Avatar of the Age began to acquire a lavish lifestyle. Things started to go downhill in November of 1973, when a big festival at the Houston Astrodome failed to draw anything like the expected attendance, leaving the organization seriously in debt. Then, in 1974, the guru forsook his vow of celibacy for marriage, causing his mother and brother to return to India. By the early eighties he had abandoned the religious features of the movement, renounced his claim to semi-divine status, and closed the American ashrams. Today, the man known as Prem Ramat proclaims a simple message of peace and brotherhood.

Things went even worse for other expatriates, including many of the Buddhist teachers who came to America. Notable here was Chögyam Trungpa, a master of mindfulness meditation who followed the Dalai Lama into exile and later founded the famous Naropa Institute in Boulder, Colorado. Soon after settling in Scotland, in 1967, Trungpa gave up his monastic vows and adopted a lifestyle that included smoking and drinking. Kenneth Woodward recalls watching Trungpa swill sake as he discoursed on dharma and recalls that the sage "died bloated and disoriented from alcoholism at the age of forty-seven" in 1987.[53] Trungpa's predilection for sleeping with students (which dates to the Scotland years) was another failing, and one he shared with many other gurus. As Woodward recalls: "In the mid-Eighties, scores of Buddhist teachers, foreign-born lamas, Zen-masters, as well as Americans who had acquired those titles, were discovered to have seduced their students, male as well as female."[54] Needless to say, all this is completely at odds with the Buddhist notion that meditation is a way of disciplining the self and eliminating desire.

When the gurus were not discrediting themselves by their behavior, they were watering down their message so that its underlying soteriological purpose was lost. While both Maharaj Ji and Trungpa have been accused

---

53. Woodward, *Getting Religion*, 274.
54. Woodward, *Getting Religion*, 274.

of this, perhaps the most notable example is the Maharishi Mahesh Yogi, who was widely known for his early association with the Beatles. For a while, this quintet seemed to promise a spiritual reawakening of historic proportions. However, when the yogi's relation with the band cooled, he looked to various means of popularizing his method of "Transcendental Meditation" to schools, businesses, and individuals for its health benefits. By the seventies, hundreds of TM centers manned by thousands of trained instructors were appearing across America. Meanwhile, the scientific study of meditation, which the yogi had encouraged and facilitated, demonstrated that the technique's value for the body had nothing to do with its religious components. Whether one evoked the sacred syllable *om* or the name of the family cat in religious practice, the results were the same.

Among the Maharishi's most famous pupils is Dr. Deepak Chopra, a star of New Age spirituality who is known for applying the insights of TM in his medical practice. In 2010, Chopra engaged in a debate with physician Aseem Shukla, who headed the American "Take Back Yoga" campaign.[55] Shukla has pointed out that the secularization of yoga, as practiced in TM and elsewhere, is a betrayal of the tradition. American yoga is really nothing more than a stripped-down version of hatha yoga, which has to do with posture and breathing. The real yogi knows that this is but part of the practice. The spiritual core of yoga lies in raja yoga, which concerns the eightfold path to salvation.[56] This involves, in addition to bodily control, strenuous moral and mental exercises designed to reveal the God within. To imply that one is much the same as the other, points out Shukla, is little more than heresy.

Shukla has not been alone in attacking this trend toward secularization. In 2014, India's prime minister, Narendra Modi, began a campaign to return yoga to its spiritual roots. This was at the middle of a yoga boom in America. Between 2012 and 2016, the number of Americans engaged in yoga almost doubled to close to thirty-seven million, making yoga a $17 billion industry.[57] In order to attract enthusiasts, American yoga centers began to adopt a variety of gimmicks. One California yoga instructor added marijuana to the votive candles and sitar music. There was also "bold and naked yoga," tantrum yoga, karaoke yoga, hip-hop yoga, and yoga with a trampoline. Those who have come to yoga chiefly to lose

55. Shukla, "Yoga."
56. H. Smith, *Religions of Man*, 32–36, 51–61.
57. K. Heller, "Are Gimmicks a Buzzkill," para. 24.

weight have been drawn to hot yoga and power yoga. Some prefer yoga with animals. Baby goats are especially popular.

Rivaling yoga in popularity is mindfulness meditation, which began in America in the fifties and gained a real foothold the next decade with the large influx of Asian expatriates. Mindfulness is an ancient Buddhist yoga technique involving dispassionately observing our thoughts, feelings, and sensations as a means of quieting the many distractions in life (the "monkey mind") and recognizing the illusory character of the self. The goal here is the attainment of Nirvana, in which the desiring (hence, continuously suffering) self is extinguished like a burning candle. However, mindfulness was forever changed in 1979, when a New York scientist, Jon Kabat-Zinn, pioneered a mindfulness course to treat patients with chronic pain and cancer. Kabat-Zinn made every effort to eliminate all the religious and metaphysical trappings of the practice. It worked. Today, mindfulness is touted simply as a way to "health and happiness."

A recent magazine on mindfulness meditation (with a lovely young woman on the cover) advises the reader that the practice can alleviate the stresses of work and parenting in as little as five minutes a day. There is also an article on a mindfulness diet (touted as a way to lose weight) and another on how to mindfully eat your mindfulness food. One piece tells us how to turn our iPhones into miniature mindfulness coaches, and another features popular TV shows and movies that may help us "find our center."[58] Among the most promising articles is one that describes the early morning routines of high achievers like Michelle Obama and Mark Zuckerberg. The tagline here reads: "Many billionaires say the first thing they do each day is meditate and seek answers to the big questions in life."[59] The assumptions seem to be that meditation is the key to fame and fortune and that anyone able to achieve these should be well on the way to discovering the answer to life's meaning.

If we wish to discover a truly meaningful form of Buddhist thought and practice amid today's wealth of superficial, materialist trappings, we should look to the aging Dalai Lama. Tibetans regard His Holiness as nothing less than a living Buddha, possessed of the wisdom capable of putting an end to the suffering that comes with each turn of the "wheel of life" (*Bhavachakra*). However, as Ken Woodward points out, the Dalai Lama's American followers are largely "Designer Buddhists," who have a

---

58. See "Mindfulness: The New Science of Health and Happiness," special issue, *TIME* (Sept. 2016).

59. Bova, "Power A.M. Routines," 68.

strong streak of individualism and a goal of enhancing their this-worldly existence rather than transcending it.[60] People like these are unlikely to care for the Dalai Lama's daily routine, which begins at four a.m. with a five-hour meditation and includes exercises in which he envisions his own death. Nor are they fully on board with His Holiness's social and political views. As Woodward explains:

> They pay him heed when he talks about the environment and promotes religious tolerance. But, he noticed, this was not the case when he declared that abortion and euthanasia are violations of the Buddhist principle of "nonviolence toward all sentient beings," or when, in San Francisco (of all places), he declared that one could not be a Buddhist and have sex with others of the same gender. Despite his popularity, he said, he sometimes thinks his influence is no deeper than a "screensaver on computer."[61]

The Dalai Lama's way of life and his views on the issues remind us once more about the traditional religious understanding of the relation of spirit to matter. As we have pointed out, religion privileges spirit as the much greater of the two, while our chief concern is with the physical. Indeed, ours is a world where the spirit is, at best, an ever-diminishing reality. It is this difference that puts us at odds with the Pope, the Dalai Lama, and Christian fundamentalists on issues like contraception, abortion and gay marriage. While their view may be out of step with the times, it reflects a distinction that is vital to religion. And the same vital distinction is apparent in the various traditional forms of meditation, which seek to rein in the body so that the spirit may shine forth. Americans fail to recognize the value of all such efforts because, for most of us, the body is all there is.

So ingrained has our notion of the primacy of the physical become that it has everywhere displaced the old language of the spirit. We have already observed this in popular film and song, and will deal with it again when we look in more detail at romance. For the moment we simply want to note how this loss is evident in everyday speech. This is vital because, as we have said, language is both a reflection of how we view the world and the lens through which the young will come to know it.

Andrew Klavan has noted how today's language reflects our changing view of human nature. Klavan observes that we now like to say that we experienced an "adrenaline rush" rather than we were aroused, or

---

60. Woodward, *Getting Religion*, 272–74.
61. Woodward, *Getting Religion*, 274.

speak of a "dopamine high" in characterizing feelings of invigoration.[62] Words like these reflect a view of the self as nothing more than a series of chemical reactions. Meanwhile, computers have become the primary model for understanding the human brain.[63] This is not only apparent in the language of psychiatry and neuroscience; it is evident in daily discourse—as when, for example, we say we are "hardwired" for this behavior or "programmed" for that. "A human being is a cross between a chemistry set and a computer," notes Klavan, "his actions governed solely by a series of discharges and sparks." It follows that there is no higher moral authority in our lives, nor any deeper experiences like love and faith. As Klavan puts it: "Emotional states are not to be examined for truth content, merely adjusted to taste with various medications."[64]

All this reinforces what we have said regarding the changing climate in religion and spirituality while pointing the way toward what is to come. And it makes a mockery of those who anticipate a "spiritual awakening in America"—an event that could never be more than a twitch of the eye.[65] Contemporary spiritual practice here is nothing more than another abject lesson in how far true spirituality has retreated from our world—and with it, the likelihood of finding any deep and abiding meaning in religion or in life.

62. Klavan, "Faith That Upholds," para. 1.
63. T. Burns, *Our Necessary Shadow*, 278–79.
64. Klavan, "Faith that Upholds," para. 2.
65. Dias, "8 Questions."

PART FOUR

Stories of Meaning

10

Music, the Novel, Drama, and Dance

WHILE MEANING SOMETIMES APPEARS suddenly, it may also evolve slowly over minutes, days, months, or even years. In these cases, meaning usually becomes apparent when we are able to discern a pattern amid the welter of words, images, sounds or gestures. Quiet, patience, and a willingness to engage in the various rituals and languages of meaning are sometimes necessary if we are to find value in experiences like these.

In addition to the cognitive component, meaning requires that such experiences have a significant emotional element. Any public speaker should be aware of this. This is why he or she so often inserts a joke or story into the discourse. Such insertions are not simply efforts to "lighten" the mood but "enliven it"—by which I mean to instill it with meaning by giving it something of the emotion of lived experience.

The great religious and ethical teachers have always known that truths couched in the language of daily life have a special power. We see this in the parables of Jesus, which engage emotionally and cognitively, confronting us at the deeper levels of life. The fables of Aesop work in much the same way, as do the Sufi stories, Jewish folktales, the Jataka tales, and the stories of Chuang Tzu. All these recognize that there is an enormous difference between being "told" a truth and "feeling it in our bones"—that is, at those levels of inwardness where meaning occurs.

The story is the prototypical form for meanings that develop over time. Some stories are meaning writ large. These tales have the capacity not only to suggest an image of life but to render it in its vastness and depth. Such stories are commonly found in the great myths of the religions, where, as enacted in ritual, they become tangible realities. The novel and drama have their roots in works like these. Elements of the story can also be found in music and dance, each of which also dates back to myth and religion. Even poetry and painting look back to the story. Poetry has roots in the ancient epics, and continued to flourish in lengthy religious expositions like Dante's *Commedia* and Milton's *Paradise Lost*. Early art also aspired to the story. This is evident, for example, in the imagery of prehistoric caves, the paintings of Native Americans, and the Bayeux Tapestry.

This triad of the story, the arts, and myth underlies much of our discussion in the next few chapters. We will begin by looking at music, drama, the novel, and dance. In our discussion of each of these, there has obviously been no effort to trace all the developments over the decades. That would be a book in itself. The concern is to emphasize a common shift in which the capacity of each art to evoke in their public something of "greater and more lasting value" was largely lost, and what has become known as a "postmodern" art was born. It is this shift, rather than the era more broadly, that is our concern. In our next section we will look at American film, which was once the most popular source of stories for Americans and continues to have broad appeal today. We then conclude by looking at romance. As we shall see, stories of romance dominated popular culture in the postwar years—in film, music, and that remarkable American invention, the Broadway musical. It is in romance, perhaps more than anywhere else, that ordinary Americans once looked for stories of meaning. And it is here, as perhaps nowhere else, that the end of meaning in recent decades is most apparent.

A classical music concert is one activity where meaning develops over time. To the lover of the more popular musical genres, the apparent passivity of the symphony goer may seem to be indicative of a lack of engagement. But what appears to be a lack of emotion is really emotion in contact with thought and imagination, resulting in a powerful process of discovery and integration. In all this, "serious" music differs from today's more popular musical forms, which stress a rhythmic impulse that plays directly upon the senses and does little to encourage any deeper emotional or intellectual engagement.

Beginning in the eighteenth century, the forms of serious Western music (symphony, concerto, sonata) assumed a three-part organization referred to as the "sonata form." The sonata form was a constructive framework within which simple musical motifs could be developed.

A popular example of such development occurs in Beethoven's Fifth Symphony, where the powerful opening notes, da-da-da-*dum*, persist in various guises to the very end of the work. The sonata form gave a good deal of freedom to the composer. However, it structured thematic development in such a way that the work assumed something of a literary character. As one author describes the form:

> The basic concept was to present the idea or ideas to be elaborated in a first section, which our theorists call "exposition," develop this material in the middle or "development" section, then prepare and execute a "recapitulation" or "reprise" in such a manner as to reconcile the warring, antithetical tonalities by restoring the unequivocal supremacy of the main key.[1]

The literary nature of the sonata form became even clearer with the symphonies of the Romantic composers, who strengthened the linear dynamic by better integrating the movements. The Romantics also shifted emphasis from the first allegro (which had been primary in the eighteenth century) to the finale, giving the work a strong conclusion. The literary potential of music was further enhanced by development of the popular "programmatic" effects. In this technique, visual imagery is conveyed solely through sound. The twitter of birds, clamor of a summer storm, or whir of a spinning wheel are just a few popular examples. The tone poem and the Lied—both of which became popular during the Romantic period—also indicate the strengthening of the bond between music and literature. With the emergence of opera—and, especially, the musical dramas of Wagner—this union reached its highest level of development.

The literary character of classical music was apparent to most Americans from film, where composers used orchestral compositions to enhance the effect of the stories. Cartoons also introduced the public to classical masterworks. The most notable example of this was Walt Disney's critically acclaimed film *Fantasia* (1940). Here, a variety of famous classical compositions (including richly programmatic pieces like *Night on Bald Mountain* and *The Sorcerer's Apprentice*) were illustrated by the Disney studios to music performed by the Philadelphia Orchestra under the direction of Leopold Stokowski. All this helps to account for the enormous popularity of classical music in America in the thirties, forties, and fifties.

However, film was only part of the story. In the twenties, a series of technological breakthroughs had made it possible for ordinary Americans

---

1. Lang, *Symphony*, xi.

to hear classical music in quality recordings and radio programs. Radio executives quickly became aware of the potential of the technology to bring the meanings of this music into the homes of ordinary citizens. At its height, during the thirties and forties, both the NBC and CBS radio networks scheduled at least twenty different radio shows of classical music a season.[2] Nor was musical education ignored. For some four decades, radio (and later, television) offered a variety of programs aimed to educate its listeners (and viewers). The most notable example of this, on radio, was NBC's *Music Appreciation Hour*, hosted by Walter Damrosch, which ran a remarkable fourteen years (1928–42).

Opera also entered the mainstream during the period. This began in 1931, when the financially strapped Metropolitan Opera Company began live radio broadcasts from New York. Although works were presented piecemeal at first, by the 1933–34 season complete performances were being broadcast on Saturday afternoons. The popularity of this music was still apparent in 1955, when 15 million (out of a population of 165 million Americans) could be heard listening (and sometimes singing) to live opera performances on a typical Saturday afternoon.[3]

During the Depression years, the growing regard for classical music was also spurred by the Federal Music Project, which dramatically expanded the number of America's orchestras while bringing the works of American composers to receptive listeners. Recalling the period, composer Aaron Copland noted that composers now felt needed as never before, and wrote in a manner designed to "satisfy both our collaborators and ourselves."[4] In their compositions, American composers often made reference to jazz, spirituals, American hymns, and folk tunes. The public responded accordingly. As Tawa observes: "Listening to music, they said, carried them swiftly to a different world and deepened their lives. They were able to join others in the audience in common appreciation of art at the finest expressive level. In a world as drab and incoherent as theirs had become, this sort of experience was prized."[5]

Copland was the foremost composer of the period, and a man whose music captured something of the "mythology of the frontier and the Wild West."[6] Copland's ballet *Billy the Kid* envisions the outlaw as both a latter-

2. Brian Rose, *Television and Performing Arts*, 92.
3. Woodward, *Getting Religion*, 38.
4. Tawa, *Great American Symphony*, 13.
5. Tawa, *Great American Symphony*, 4.
6. Ross, *Rest Is Noise*, 290.

day Robin Hood and as a symbol of a frontier wilderness which, in the music, still maintains its mystique. The opening and closing processional of the piece, "The Open Prairie," evokes not only a vast landscape, but the slow progression of settlers who will tame the wilderness and shrink the expanse. A number of reshaped cowboy tunes—e.g., "Great Granddad," "Whoopee Ti Yi Yo (Git Along Little Dogies)," "The Old Chisholm Trail"—add an additional Western flavor.

Copland also produced notable film scores for John Steinbeck's *Of Mice and Men* and *The Red Pony*, as well as two commissioned pieces with a strong American flavor: *Lincoln Portrait* (whose reciters have included luminaries like Eleanor Roosevelt, Carl Sandburg, and Coretta Scott King) and the enormously popular *Fanfare for the Common Man*. Copland's "open prairie" style also pervades *Oklahoma!*, while the spirited dances of Rodgers and Hammerstein's enormously influential musical look back to the composer's cowboy ballet *Rodeo*.[7]

Classical music remained popular into the early television years thanks in large measure to Arturo Toscanini, the great maestro of the NBC Symphony Orchestra. Toscanini's ten TV concerts between 1948 and 1952 remain among the most powerful musical performances ever recorded. In 1954, when he retired, television was fortunate in finding another star in Leonard Bernstein. Bernstein was conductor of the New York Philharmonic Orchestra and a composer whose musicals (including *West Side Story*) captured New York's vibrancy, exaltation, and despair. Although Bernstein also produced a number of outstanding instrumental works, his greatest contribution to classical music may have come in his role as teacher. In November 1954, Bernstein appeared on the famous *Omnibus* series to discuss Beethoven's Fifth Symphony. Shortly after his final *Omnibus* show, in 1957, Bernstein became a TV regular with the New York Philharmonic *Young People's Concerts*, which ran to 1972.

Bernstein was a natural on TV and a man whose instructional programs might well have had a major impact upon generations of the young. Unfortunately, his youngest audience members had grown up on rock and roll. Despite Bernstein's best efforts, the young people's telecasts could never maintain a youthful audience. This was evident from a 1964 survey that revealed that 83 percent of Bernstein's viewers were adults, and a mere 5 percent teenagers.[8]

---

7. Ross, *Rest Is Noise*, 313.
8. Brian Rose, *Television and Performing Arts*, 102.

During the sixties, the marriage of classical music and network TV began to unravel. By the eighties, classical music on commercial television had become a curiosity. Since then, full-length programs devoted to serious music have been the province of PBS. This is telling, since, at its best, PBS has never been able to draw the percentage of Americans who tuned in to classical music on radio and early television.

Even as classical music began to lose favor with the American public, the old forms gave way to styles of composition that could have little meaning for the vast majority of listeners. The new "serious" music of the fifties and sixties came in three varieties, i.e., random, computer, or electronic. Random music is widely associated with American composer John Cage, who created one piece whose every performance was determined by tosses of the *I Ching* and another that calls for the "performers" to simultaneously "play" twelve radios, each tuned to a different station. In electronic music, sound fragments are recorded on tape, then rerecorded at varying tempi, pitches, or volumes, "backwards and forwards, upside down, and so forth," in order to achieve a finished work.[9] Computer music relies upon a set of instructions that are fed into a computer that proceeds to "compose" by choosing notes from a random series. As the name implies, chance is a vital component of random music, although it is widely employed in electronic and computer music as well.

The result of these methods are works that lack that sense of literary development we associate with classical composition. As Leonard Meyer points out, music like this has no apparent purpose or goal. Meyer proceeds to observe the implications of the new forms for meaning: "Since no event or action refers to or leads us to expect any other event or action, the sequence of events is, in any ordinary sense of the term, meaningless."[10]

In an effort to establish a meaningful foundation for the new musical forms, reference has often been made to Chinese metaphysics, Zen Buddhism and the like. Unfortunately, neither the ideas nor their relevance to the work is readily apparent to the listening public, to scholars, or to critics (not to mention composers, who seem to have only the vaguest notion of the real significance of such ideas). The same problem is evident in the efforts of the minimalists, whose works took hold in the late sixties and remain popular today. As Martha Bayles explains:

---

9. Meyer, *Music, Arts, and Ideas*, 70.
10. Meyer, *Music, Arts, and Ideas*, 78.

Like the blank canvases of radical nonobjective painters, the monotonous compositions of minimalist composers are routinely praised for inducing the aesthetic equivalent of religious trance. But . . . to what purpose? The unavoidable fact is that, without a meaningful connection with the symbols and disciplines of a shared religious tradition, such as Hindus possess when they listen to ragas, most of us (including most music lovers) find it hard to stick with trancelike music for its own sake. We may become mesmerized for a while, but when nothing much happens, we become unmesmerized.[11]

Brian Eno has characterized the shift from classical composition to minimalism as "a drift away from narrative and towards landscape."[12] This is one reason why minimalist composer Philip Glass's score for the film *Koyaanisqatsi*, with its images of cities, deserts, and countrysides, proves so effective. Unfortunately, the music is a one-note samba that more often fails to satisfy. Glass's musical accompaniment to Jean Cocteau's magical fairy tale *La belle et la bête*, for example, has all the meaning of the pairing of a swan and a vacuum cleaner.

Of course, minimalism is not the only form of composition available today. Serious music in the twenty-first century is known for its variety of styles and its borrowing from a wide array of musical modes. But the shift beginning in mid-century is notable for what has been lost in the way of meaning. Copland and his contemporaries drew upon traditional melodies in imaginative compositions with clear and discernible movements and an unambiguous beginning, middle and end. This music spoke to Americans of all walks of life—not only to those living in the major cities but to those in the towns and open spaces. Such music was determined to inspire and unite. As one author explains it:

> [the music] embraced an entire society, not just the artist, and embodied both the creative individual's and the society's profoundest expressions. Music thus understood included the modes for dealing with and explaining reality, the special mindset for interpreting the circumstances of human existence, and the artistic institutions that made available this interpretation to the community. In this way individuals could direct their thinking to matters beyond and above themselves.[13]

---

11. Bayles, *Hole in Our Soul*, 226.
12. Ross, *Rest Is Noise*, 517.
13. Tawa, *Great American Symphony*, x.

Many composers of the late fifties and sixties derided all this and wrote works that were often designed to confuse the listening public. This hastened a decline that the appearance of rock and roll aided and abetted.

Today, American symphony and chamber orchestras face significant economic challenges. Nor has the decline of humanities education helped. At today's colleges one often finds relatively few young people among the listeners at serious music concerts. This would have been unthinkable in 1960, when surveys showed that classical recordings were the most popular among college students.[14] During that period, one could expect young people to look forward to a concert, to dress appropriately, and to prepare for the performance by reading the program notes. Today, the few students who can be seen straggling into performances typically appear underdressed and unprepared.

However, unprepared concert goers may be the least of the problems for music that appears headed for extinction. The year 2002 saw a significant decline in classical music programming on National Public Radio, which heretofore had been its foremost supporter. The apparent reason for this is that market concerns are increasingly driving public radio (a body whose charter ironically proclaims its desire to "serve groups whose voices go unheard").[15] In 2002, only 11.6 percent of Americans had heard a live classical music performance in the last year. By 2012, the percentage had dropped more than a quarter, to 8.8.[16] Little wonder that recent years have seen a rise in bankruptcies among orchestras and chamber ensembles—or that books heralding the end of classical music appear every few years like clockwork.

Classical music was by no means the only meaningful music available to Americans in the postwar years. Later on we will look at the romantic singers who largely defined the era. These included not only the great crooners, but major country performers and most of the stars of rock and roll. Romance also had an important place in the flourishing of folk music, which elsewhere added a much needed poetry to issues of social justice. In the following, we limit ourselves to jazz. Like the other popular music forms, jazz found great popularity in an era that seemed to look for meaning everywhere.

14. Hobsbawm, *Jazz Scene*, 208.
15. Bowman, "Day the Music Died."
16. Joelle Lee, "Is Classical Music Dying," para. 2.

At its best, jazz is a truly meaningful art form, the emotional force and creative dexterity of the performer both touching and stimulating the listener. This is why the serious jazz aficionado often seems to be engaged with the music much like the knowing symphony goer, responding not merely to its rhythms but its creative forms. Like classical music, jazz needs time to develop its themes, which is why a jazz rendering of a popular melody may take several minutes to unfold. We may say that the jazz musicians, like an orchestra, are taking listeners on a journey—the difference being that the orchestra follows a well-known path, while the journey in jazz is largely one of exploration and discovery.

What we have said of jazz is especially evident in the style of jazz known as bebop or simply bop. Bop emerged in the postwar years, replacing the popular big bands with a small cadre of musicians who took swing music's association with high culture and learning to a new level. Bebop musicians were said to converse freely on topics like philosophy, modern art, and psychoanalysis, and their music naturally attracted a different sort of listener than swing. As one scholar explains: "The music was often too fast, and too difficult, to dance to, but that was rather as it should be, as bop artists promoted an environment in which patrons sat and attended quietly instead of talking, drinking, and most especially dancing during performances."[17] The birth of bebop meant the flowering of an array of jazz greats, including Miles Davis, Charles Mingus, Dizzy Gillespie, Charlie Parker, John Coltrane, Dexter Gordon, and Thelonious Monk. Speaking of the period, Gillespie later recalled: "We had some fundamental background training in European harmony and music theory superimposed on our own knowledge from Afro-American musical traditions." Gillespie added that the jazz musicians had their own way "of getting from one place to the next."[18] Indeed they did. While jazz performers of the day saw themselves as serious musicians, the music always maintained its original creative energy.

Postwar jazz found its first adherents among hipsters and intellectuals. However, the music reached a larger audience following the appearance of Art Kane's famous photo of jazz greats, *Harlem 1958*, in *Esquire* magazine in January of 1959.[19] *Esquire* was popular among college aged men, who now began appearing with their dates at jazz concerts and festivals. A survey of music preferences of college students in 1960 showed that

17. Foertsch, *American Culture in 1940s*, 91.
18. Ross, *Rest Is Noise*, 519.
19. See Myers, "Great Day in Harlem."

a healthy 22 percent favored jazz.[20] Preferred listening at the time were the top-selling albums of jazz greats Miles Davis (*Kind of Blue*), Art Blakey (*Moanin'*), and Dave Brubeck (*Time Out*). By 1962, college students were being drawn to jazz by the bossa nova craze, which featured tenor sax great Stan Getz's classics "Desafinado" and "The Girl from Ipanema."

The problem for jazz began with a new generation of baby boomers who had known only rock and roll and who were interested only in what they already knew. The decline of jazz is told in the experiences of performers like tenor saxophonist Ben Webster. Webster had enjoyed success during the fifties and early sixties, playing concerts, recording for major record companies, and even appearing on television. All this changed following the British Invasion. As Dominic Green points out:

> After Beatlemania, though, important jazz labels like Verve and Fantasy concentrated on white folk and rock acts. Verve signed Frank Zappa. Fantasy, once San Francisco's in-house jazz label, had hits with Credence Clearwater Revival. Webster eked out his last years without a steady record label, playing clubs and festivals in Europe.[21]

Although jazz is today a shadow of its former self, the music has rebounded somewhat from its low point in the late sixties and early seventies. Today, jazz boasts several stars, foremost of whom is Wynton Marsalis, whose style fits generally within the bebop tradition. Like some other outstanding jazz musicians of the past, Marsalis also has a classical background. Over the years, he has promoted both musical forms through tours, records, and visits to public schools. During that time he has amassed numerous Grammy's and one Pulitzer Prize—the last for his *Blood on the Fields* (1994), the first jazz composition ever to be so honored.

Marsalis's early recordings, *Marsalis Standard Time, Vol. I* (1987) and *Live at Blues Alley* (1987) had put him at the forefront of the jazz avant-garde. But the musician was unhappy with the style of playing ("all those really complex rhythms, playing fast, wild"), which seemed to be an abandonment of the traditional African American roots of jazz—and especially the music of his native New Orleans.[22] He was now determined, he explained, "to put together an approach through which I can create a

---

20. Hobsbawm, *Jazz Scene*, 208.
21. D. Green, "When Rock Killed Jazz," para. 20.
22. T. Gioia, *History of Jazz*, 351.

more accurate picture of the world I came out of, of the things in my life that have the deepest meanings to me."²³

Marsalis's embrace of the blues and his preference for a more controlled style of playing have been widely criticized by many jazz critics and performers. So, too, have his criticisms of those who would sacrifice tradition to make common cause with more popular styles. These have included jazz great Miles Davis, who spent the seventies trying to bridge the gap between jazz and rock before turning to hip hop in his last years. With reference to Davis, Marsalis once observed that he had little patience with jazz musicians who try "to act like rock stars." Davis responded by refusing to let him sit in with his group when Marsalis once attempted to do so at a jazz festival.²⁴

While the "jazz wars" have waned, Marsalis has proven controversial for his criticism of the sorry state of popular black music—a decline he dates to its incorporation of the music of the black church. When once asked if he had any use for rap, Marsalis explained: "I look at it in relation to all of the American music that's available to me, and in terms of the level of musicianship and improvisation . . . and I don't have that much respect for it. And I feel that from a musical standpoint, it would be very difficult for me to be proven incorrect about that."²⁵ Rap, we may say, is rejected for the inability of the music to engage the mind in any significant way. In this it is the opposite of postmodern jazz, which has lost the emotional power from which the music originated. Marsalis seems to be insisting on music that has both strong cognitive and emotional capacities—even as it maintains strong ties to its roots. Which is to say that Marsalis prefers music rich in meaning.

In literature, the continued success of the novel appears to give evidence of the capacity of the verbal arts to unfold meaning in ways readers still find rewarding. A good novel enables the reader to experience life lived in all its depth and complexity, providing, through the very tangible world of its characters, insights into the deepest realities of the human experience. A great novel may do more, chronicling what writer Saul Bellow

---

23. T. Gioia, *History of Jazz*, 351.
24. T. Gioia, *History of Jazz*, 352.
25. DeLuca, "Marsalis Straight," para. 17.

has called "true impressions."[26] The term, which appears in the author's Nobel Prize lecture, refers to intimations of a spiritual reality that was once accepted by novelists (as it was by artists and poets) but has been lost in a society that now regards such things as taboo. We have noted how these moments are not only vital to traditional poetry, but occupy an important place in the novels of writers like Faulkner, Joyce, and Woolf. Bellow observes their presence in the fiction of Proust and Tolstoy. As an example of what Bellow has in mind, we may cite such an experience as described in Tolstoy's *Anna Karenina*. It is a moment, Tolstoy tells us, when a trio of things reveal themselves to Konstantin Levin as being "not earthly creatures":

> It all happened at the same time: a boy ran toward a dove and glanced smiling at Levin; the dove, with a whir of her wings, darted away, flashing in the sun amid grains of snow that quivered in the air, while from a little window there came a smell of fresh-baked bread, and the loaves were put out. All of this together was so extraordinarily nice that Levin laughed and cried with delight.[27]

In his lecture, Bellow observes that a novel moves between the world of objects and experiences and the spiritual reality from which such "true impressions" originate, leading us to conclude that our belief in an inherent truth and goodness at the core of life is no illusion. Bellow notes a turning from this notion in French literature of the sixties, and he cites writer Robbe-Grillet as one who laid the spiritual universe low by reducing all of reality to the realm of "things."[28] Something of the same thing was becoming apparent at about the same time in American literature, although our clearest counterpart was pop art, where the radiance of Chardin's kitchen utensils or the evocative power of Cornell's clay pipes and shells gave way to Warhol's lifeless soup cans. The sixties, of course, was only the beginning. As we shall see, the death of serious novels has to do not only with the loss of the spiritual, but with the ongoing politicization of life and with technologies that so privilege speed over substance that we no longer have time to consider a Cornell box or ponder Levin's moment of revelation.

Our current state of decline contrasts notably to the situation a few generations ago. Postwar America witnessed the late productivity of some

---

26. Bellow, *Simply Too Much*, 300.
27. Tolstoy, *Anna Karenina*, 424.
28. Bellow, *Simply Too Much*, 292–93.

of her greatest novelists, and the beginning careers of a number of young authors of enormous promise. Foremost among the mature writers was William Faulkner. In accepting the Nobel Prize for Literature in 1949, Faulkner had urged younger writers to make room for "the old verities and truths of the heart, the old universal truths lacking which any story is ephemeral and doomed—love and honor and pity and pride and compassion and sacrifice."[29] Faulkner had found such truths in Bible stories and Greek mythology. In his novels he reconfigured them in his own mythic south—even as George Steinbeck revisited them in California, in books whose very titles (e.g., *East of Eden, Of Mice and Men, The Grapes of Wrath*) evoked the old stories, poems, and songs. Steinbeck would win the Nobel Prize for Literature in 1962.

The winner of the prize in 1954 was Ernest Hemingway, whose world in the last years was chiefly Cuba, the Florida Keys, and the surrounding waters of the Caribbean. Hemingway's Nobel Prize came in recognition of the last novel published in his lifetime, *The Old Man and the Sea*. Some took exception to the book, including Norman Mailer, who called it "a bad piece of work."[30] Faulkner knew better. Faulkner regarded *The Old Man and the Sea* as the best of Hemingway's books, and possibly the best work of his generation.[31] Here, said Faulkner, Hemingway had expanded his fictional world from men and women who made themselves and their fortunes to the realm of a God who made not only them, but the entire Creation. In its scope, Hemingway's book is indeed comparable, in a small way, to Melville's great masterpiece, *Moby Dick*. Only now the great fish signifies not some malevolent power that destroys a man but a majestic force that ennobles him.

Of the new writers, Faulkner most admired J. D. Salinger, in whose first novel, *The Catcher in the Rye*, he discerned the author's ambition "to save mankind from being desouled."[32] Another fan of Salinger's was Bellow, who won his Nobel Prize in 1976. Writing a decade after Faulkner, and with an eye toward Salinger's later work, Bellow praised the writer for clinging "to his fragile idealism." "There is a nobility of feeling in his stories that is, unfortunately, rare in contemporary literature," said Bellow.[33] Along with Salinger and Bellow, other prominent young novelists

29. Faulkner, *Essays, Speeches*, 120.
30. Mailer, *Advertisements for Myself*, 12.
31. Faulkner, *Essays, Speeches*, 193.
32. Faulkner, *Essays, Speeches*, 165.
33. Bellow, *Simply Too Much*, 186.

of the fifties were Mailer, John Updike and Ralph Ellison. To these would be added, in the sixties, Phillip Roth, Walker Percy and Joseph Heller.

The postwar years were generally good ones for serious American novelists. During the period, interviews with writers were often featured in popular periodicals, serious fiction frequently appeared on the best seller list, and the works of many gifted writers (e.g., Faulkner, Steinbeck, Hemingway, Mailer, Salinger) were made into motion pictures. And while a growing dissatisfaction with American society was apparent among writers as the decade wore on, many looked to a rebirth of American culture with the Kennedy presidency. Writers James Baldwin, Katherine Anne Porter, William Styron, Robert Frost, Pearl Buck, and John Dos Passos were among the guests at the famous 1962 "Dinner in Camelot" in which the president and Mrs. Kennedy honored the nation's Nobel Prize winners. Authors John Hersey, Robert Penn Warren, Archibald MacLeish, Thornton Wilder, Tennessee Williams, and Bellow attended an elegant White House dinner hosted soon afterward to honor André Malraux. Many of the writers at these dinners felt that, spurred on by the new administration, America was on the verge of an extraordinary cultural awakening. In his *Dinner at Camelot*, Joseph Esposito has said of the time that "the value that we place on the contributions of artists, writers, scientists, and thinkers was at its apogee."[34]

As the sixties wore on, writers began to question their belief that writing was essentially a sacred calling—a search for what Alvin Kernan, echoing Bellow, has called "a mystically true meaning" that is be found at the core of the best literary works.[35] In fact, few of the young writers who came of age in the postwar period escaped the decade unscathed. During the sixties Salinger ceased to publish, while Heller published little of note following the appearance of *Catch 22*. In 1964, at age thirty-nine, Flannery O'Connor died, following a twelve-year struggle with lupus. Ralph Ellison, whose *Invisible Man* had won the National Book Award in 1953, lived another forty years, but never published another work of fiction. Mailer turned from fiction to journalism at this time, while Updike and Roth, though continuing to write fiction, had by the late sixties entered postmodern hells from which, in the minds of many of the public, they would never escape—Updike's, a suburban world of marital infidelity; Roth's, an inner realm of masturbation and psychoanalysis. Both were

---

34. Esposito, *Dinner in Camelot*, xiii.
35. Kernan, *Death of Literature*, 203.

emblematic of a new type of writer who, as Faulkner had warned, writes "not of the heart, but of the glands."[36]

Of the young writers who showed such promise in the postwar years, Bellow and Walker Percy were the ones who best seemed to understand the significance of the change in America. In novels like *The Last Gentleman* (1966), *Love in the Ruins* (1971), and *The Thanatos Syndrome* (1987), Percy examined the old moral and religious questions in a world of ethical and spiritual collapse—a world of promiscuity, consumerism, and boredom, where sex, science, and materialism had conspired to diminish the soul. Bellow's novels *Mr. Sammler's Planet* (1970) and *Humboldt's Gift* (1975) are similarly accounts of cultural collapse. The first is the story of a Holocaust survivor subjected to the decay of New York City; the second the tale of a poet whose ideals are badly out of step with the times.

Bellow's first great popular success, *Herzog* (1964), had appeared just as America was beginning its decline. The title character is something of an older Holden Caulfield who fires off unmailed letters not only to family and friends, but to politicians, scientists, rude salesmen, and even world-renowned philosophers (i.e., "Dear Doktor Heidegger, I should like to know what you mean by the expression 'the fall into the quotidian'"[37]), all while attempting to maintain a life of higher ideas and ideals as the men and women around him try to bring him down (ex-wife Madeline and her lover, Gersbach) or, at least, down to earth (current lover Ramona). In *Herzog*, Bellow provided many insights into the temper of the times, including the following little snapshot:

> This generation thinks—and this is its thought of Thoughts—that nothing faithful, vulnerable, fragile can be durable or have any true power. Death waits for these things as a cement floor waits for a dropping light bulb.[38]

The decline of the novel became apparent on college campuses in the seventies, where "texts" were decoded so as to destroy notions of authorial intent. Alvin Kerman points out how, after the Marxists and the deconstructionists have had at it, "the literary text has no meaning, or, what comes to the same thing, it has as many and whatever meanings

---

36. Faulkner, *Essays, Speeches*, 120.
37. Bellow, *Herzog*, 55.
38. Bellow, *Herzog*, 315.

anyone wants to find in it."[39] Elsewhere universities have reaffirmed their political slant by transforming freshman literature courses into parallel education tracks where required readings are geared to race, gender, or sexual preference. No universal meanings here either—nor, presumably, in a society where such groups are still expected to find common ground. By the nineties, required literature courses had been eliminated in many schools in favor of courses in composition. This trend has continued into the twenty-first century. As of 2015, only 37.5 percent of American universities required any literature courses of their students.[40]

Today, the sad fate of serious literature is everywhere to be seen in America. Like poetry, prose now suffers from its incestuous relation with the American universities, whose more than eight hundred creative writing programs turn out not only our poets but our novelists. Now fiction that might have appeared in more than a dozen national periodicals (e.g., *The Atlantic, Esquire*) not so long ago is largely confined to university literary magazines. This unhealthy relationship is also evident in the content of contemporary fiction. Like today's poets, today's masters of prose seem unable to develop a distinctive style, or to engage in the larger realm of ideas that gave so much heft to the fiction of the forties and fifties. As Ted Genoways has said of (and to) the new generation: "Writers need to venture out from under the protective wing of academia, to put themselves and their work on the line. . . . Treat writing like your lifeblood instead of your livelihood. And for Christ's sake, write something we might want to read."[41]

As serious literature has declined, the romance and mystery genres have emerged to prominence. Writer Gore Vidal put it this was in 1993: "The serious novel is going. Novels by lawyers and thrillers by Stephen King should not have driven out serious books, but they have."[42] The trend observed by Vidal has continued into the twenty-first century. In 2018–19, mysteries were the most popular genre of fiction in America, and romance novels the most profitable—their $1.44 billion in profits far outdistancing mysteries ($728.2 million).[43] Not that such works lack meaning. The triumph of love and justice are evidence of an order in the world that many find compelling. The problem is that contemporary

39. Kernan, *Death of Literature*, 212.
40. Linz, "Guest Blog."
41. Genoways, "Death of Fiction," para. 11.
42. Washburn and Thornton, *Dumbing Down*, 41.
43. Herold, "Book Publishing Market," paras. 11–14.

"page-turners" satisfy our need for speed at the cost of a deeper (and lengthier) probing into ourselves and our world. In effect, we no longer have the time for those insights into the greater and more lasting realities that give great literature so much significance.

However, the issue today may not be so much the quality of our fiction, but whether or not any writing of substance has a future.[44] In the late seventies, most teens still read a book or magazine every day. By 2015, only 16 percent did. By then, one out of three high school seniors acknowledged that they had not read any books for pleasure at all in the last year. This was three times the number of nonreaders in 1976. Today, not only are college students reading less than ever before, but newspaper and magazine readership among the young is virtually extinct. IGeners are simply not into reading, and lower SAT scores in writing and critical reading in recent years reflect this. As one young person explained to the *Chronicle of Higher Education* a few years ago, the internet has replaced "the whole book thing."[45]

By the eighties, the sense that the writer no longer had anything meaningful to say was also apparent to playwrights like Arthur Miller, who observed that postmodern drama too often settled for entertainment rather than confronting the deeper issues of life. Such plays, said Miller, seem "to have no reason for existing at all," but "to be an effusion of some kind, under the license of I don't know what—free association or something."[46] Miller believed that plays like these lacked those deeper insights into human nature that the old stories provided:

> What we take away from the Bible may seem like characters— Abraham and Isaac, Bathsheba and David—but really, they're psychic situations. That kind of storytelling was always fantastic to me. And it's the same thing with the Greeks. Look at Oedipus—we don't know much about him, apart from his situation, but his story bears in itself the deepest paradoxes in the most adept shorthand.[47]

---

44. Twenge, *iGen*, 59–65.
45. Twenge, *iGen*, 63.
46. Roudané, *Conversations with Arthur Miller*, 381.
47. May, *Cry for Myth*, 43.

Miller often spoke of his love for the Bible and for Greek and Elizabethan drama, the last two of which drew upon a storehouse of myth. He believed that good drama required "symphonic organization"—that is, a clear sense of development that was now mostly missing in plays. Miller had found this structure in Greek drama, and he proclaimed its discovery the greatest in his professional life.[48] The newest playwrights had lost their roots in the old tales, he felt, and had lost any sense of the development of the story. "We don't have any past anymore," Miller pointed out in one interview. "And we've got little plays as a result. They're little in the sense that they're about one small aspect of an event."[49]

For Miller and his fellow dramatists of the forties and fifties, there had been no shortage of stories. The Greek drama had been a source of inspiration in modern American theatre since Eugene O'Neil's *Mourning Becomes Electra* (1931), which resets Aeschylus's great trilogy in the Civil War era. The old stories were reborn in Miller's tragic masterpiece *The Death of a Salesman*, and again in Tennessee Williams's *A Streetcar Named Desire*, which redefines the theme of the "damsel in distress" in terms of the southern ideal of refinement and gentility and the onslaught of a new brutalizing spirit in America. The old themes of love and loneliness, as experienced in small-town America, drive the plays of William Inge, like *Picnic* and *Bus Stop*, each of which proved popular not only on stage but in film during the fifties.

Like serious music, serious drama had an important place on network TV in the postwar years, chiefly through the popularity of the anthology series. Conceived by the New York theater community (and enacted by a huge number of noted performers of stage and screen), the anthologies gave significant freedom to playwrights and producers, requiring only that the dramas fit the appointed time length and studio capabilities. In 1953, the series included *Philco Television Playhouse, Goodyear Television Playhouse, Kraft Television Theater, Studio One, Robert Montgomery Presents, U.S. Steel Hour, Revlon Theater,* and *Medallion Theater*. The most notable of these was *Kraft Television Theater*, which, by the end of 1953, had already produced 169 Broadway plays, 23 adaptations from the London stage, and 22 classics.[50]

Restaging the classics held particular appeal for TV, which saw four adaptations of *Macbeth* alone between 1949 and 1951. Classic drama

---

48. Roudané, *Conversations with Arthur Miller*, 386.
49. Roudané, *Conversations with Arthur Miller*, 384–85.
50. Brian Rose, *Television and Performing Arts*, 198.

had also been a vital part of the extraordinary *Omnibus* series that ran for ninety minutes on Sunday evenings between 1952 and 1959. In 1953 *Omnibus* put on a ninety-minute uninterrupted version of *King Lear*, with Orson Welles in the title role and a score composed and conducted by Virgil Thompson. In fact, *Omnibus* ranged widely over the arts, producing original theater works by William Saroyan and James Agee, interviews with prominent Americans like architect Frank Lloyd Wright, classical plays and condensed operas, lectures by Leonard Bernstein and Agnes DeMille, and introductions to (among others) "Indian music and dance, Japanese Noh theater, and Yugoslavian ballet."[51] And this while attracting millions of American viewers on any given Sunday night.

During the fifties and early sixties, drama was also readily available in popular films, which treated not only musicals, comedies, and romantic tales, but dark stories (e.g., *Long Day's Journey into Night*, *Suddenly Last Summer*, *A Streetcar Named Desire*). In highlighting such films, Terry Teachhout sheds enormous light on the significant place of culture in postwar America:

> Why were such movies made? Because the plays on which they were based had high name recognition, not just in New York but across America. You didn't have to be a bred-in-the-bone Manhattanite to know who Lillian Hellman, William Inge and Tennessee Williams were: You could read about them in *Time*, *Life* and *Newsweek*, which routinely covered Broadway openings, just as stage actors and playwrights appeared no less routinely on popular TV shows like "Tonight" and "What's My Line." Because of this coverage, theater was part of the national cultural conversation.[52]

Like serious music, serious drama began to disappear from network TV during the sixties. The link to film remained stronger, although this, too, began to weaken as the decade wore on. Teachout refers to the film *A Man for All Seasons*, from 1966, which is notable in this regard. Appearing just as new Hollywood was being born, *A Man for All Seasons* was traditional Hollywood history fare, produced with a heavy British accent. As Teachout makes the point:

> *A Man for All Seasons* grossed $28,350,000 in the U.S. at a time when it cost about a dollar to go to the movies. That's a lot of

---

51. McCarthy, *Citizen Machine*, 124.
52. Teachout, "Films for all Seasons," para. 3.

tickets—especially for the film version of a play that ran for just 637 performances in a Broadway theater that seated 1,228 people. Run the numbers and I suspect you'll come away feeling, as I do, that we are diminished as a culture because we no longer share the mass experience of coming together to see such eloquent tales told on the big screen.⁵³

While American playwrights told their stories in words, Martha Graham told hers chiefly through the movements and gestures of the human body. Graham's notion that her work originated from "the drama of an idea" is reminiscent of Arthur Miller, with whom she found inspiration in Greek tragedy and Bible stories.⁵⁴ Graham was also a strong advocate of Wagner's notion of the *Gesamtkunstwerk* (total work of art) and, like Wagner, recognized the supreme value of myth in rendering the unchanging verities of human experience. "[Myths] were read to me when I was a child," she once observed. "They contain truths, the constancy of return to the essentials of life."⁵⁵ Graham's philosophy of dance followed from her rejection of ballet as an artificial, European art form, and her determination to craft a distinctively American art. As she once put the matter: "To be great art must become indigenous, it must belong to the country in which it flourishes, not be a pale copy of some art form perfected by another culture and another people."⁵⁶ Like many novelists, dramatists, composers, and painters of the forties and fifties, Graham grounded her work in the American experience in such a way that it had enormous meaning for viewers.

Graham first wed dance and native mythology in *Primitive Mysteries* (1931), which was inspired by the rituals of the Southwest American cultures. This was followed by *American Provincials* (1934) and *Frontier* (1935)—the first, an attack on American puritanism, the second, an exploration of boundaries, both personal and geographical. In *American Documents* (1938), Graham's style came to maturity. *American Documents* sees American history as an antagonism between puritanism and sensuality, the opposition dramatized by a speaker who reads alternately from the Song of Songs and the hellfire sermons of Jonathan Edwards.

---

53. Teachout, "Films for all Seasons," para. 6.
54. Mazo, *Prime Movers*, 195.
55. Mazo, *Prime Movers*, 198.
56. Mazo, *Prime Movers*, 162.

Graham's dispute with puritanism reappears in the conflict between love and duty in *Letter to the World* (1940)—a work loosely based upon the poetry of Emily Dickinson.

Graham generally designed her own costumes, which served as visual complements to the dance, adding a symbolism of form and color and occasionally engaging directly with the body of the dancer in meaningful ways. Many of the dances draw force from Isamu Noguchi's sparse, evocative sets. Like Graham's dances, these are modernism at its best—rooted in reality, they eschew the material, engaging the mind and leading it to something truer and more poetic. A strong sense of the modern is also evident in the various musical works commissioned for the performances. Although these naturally varied, Graham's preferences were those in the mold of her guide and early music director Louis Horst, who thought strings too reminiscent of ballet and that horns gave brilliance and reeds lent a needed sense of the primitive to the dance performances.

Above all, of course, Graham's work is a language of the body. As Joseph H. Mazo puts it, Graham always concentrated on movement "as a vehicle for meaning rather than on movement as an end in itself."[57] Mazo has provided a wonderful summary of the many and various meanings conveyed by the characteristic movements of the torso and legs in Graham's dances. But not only these have meaning. Mazo points out how, as Graham's work developed, the gestures of the dancers' hands also took on a meaningful role. As he describes the significance of some of these:

> The little clappings, a cross between prayer and applause, that are the theme gesture of the four young followers of *The Revivalist* are a major example. A peculiar fluttering of hands recurs in several dances—the Abbess uses it, as does Clytemnestra—and this gesture has the connotation of trying to sweep the past from the eyes and, at the same time, of attempting to bat away the mists that cloud vision.[58]

Anyone who has seen Graham or her company perform can attest to how effective such movements are in giving meaning to the dance.

Graham's exploration of American myth culminated in 1944 in *Appalachian Spring*, a work often regarded as her masterpiece. Here the music was provided by Copland, whose score was chiefly inspired by the old Shaker melody "Simple Gifts." *Appalachian Spring* deals broadly with

57. Mazo, *Prime Movers*, 190.
58. Mazo, *Prime Movers*, 190.

the myth of frontier life, including its hardships and promises. The story is set in a Pennsylvania farmhouse, and, like most myths, is populated by a range of archetypal characters: the husbandman and his spunky young bride; the pioneer woman, who signifies the American dream; and the revivalist, who shows up at the home with his followers. The work concludes with the union of the husbandman and the bride. This dance unfolds in music evocative of a slow Sunday afternoon, conveying both a mood of reverence and a sense of renewal promised in the days ahead.

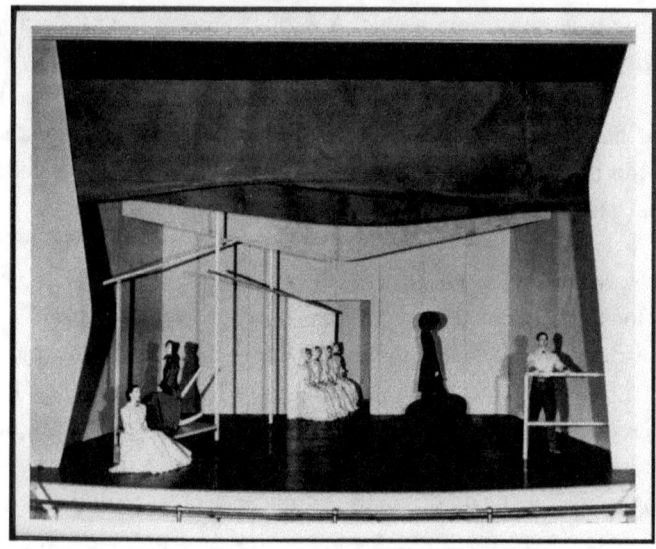

Appalachian Spring, 1944. Martha Graham, choreographer; Isamu Noguchi, set design.

While *Appalachian Spring* marked the culmination of Graham's exploration of American myth, it by no means signaled the end of myth in her work generally. Following her consultation with a Jungian analyst in 1945, Graham turned alternately to the Greeks, the Bible, and Christian history for inspiration. The masterpiece of this period is the lengthy *Clytemnestra* (1958), based upon the Greek tragedy of the queen who betrays her husband, Agamemnon, and is eventually murdered by her son, Orestes. A notable feature of the dance is Graham's use of Agamemnon's robe, which demonstrates her enormous capacity to meaningfully draw together costume, gesture and dance:

> [Graham] uses a red-purple drapery, first as a regal cloak for Clytemnestra, then as the carpet Agamemnon follows to his

death, and finally as the curtain which opens to reveal the stabbing of the king and of his mistress, Cassandra. Graham knew that the walk on a carpet of purple, the royal color, told the Greeks that Agamemnon was guilty of *hubris* . . . for which sin he died. She also knew that in the Greek theater acts of violence were not acted out. . . . In her dance, the audience does witness the stabbings, but the use of the curtain reminds spectators of the classical practice.[59]

Graham was not only a great dancer and choreographer; she was also a great mentor, whose pupils have been among America's greatest dancers and choreographers. Chief among these was Merce Cunningham, who is commonly acknowledged as the father of postmodern dance. What Graham joined together, Cunningham tore asunder. The result is not only the end of narrative, but the loss of all those other connections— e.g., between gesture and theme, dance and the other arts—whereby Graham's work proved so meaningful.

From the first, Cunningham forsook narrative and drama and rejected the notion that dance has any significance other than itself. As one authority on postmodern dance has put it, "meanings are precisely the sort of things that Cunningham's work is designed to deter and deflect."[60] In a Cunningham performance, all the parts exist independently of one another. Cunningham did not collaborate with designers. He simply told them how long the dance would be and requested that the props not unnecessarily interfere with the dancers movements. When things do come together, it seems to be purely by chance. As often as not, they work in opposition to one another. The dancers in *Rainforest* (1968) must contend with Andy Warhol's huge, helium-filled silver Mylar pillows. The tension in *How to Pass, Kick, Fall and Run* (1965) comes from the juxtaposition of the dancers alongside readers who sit to the side of the stage narrating one-minute long stories. Here, the opposition between dancers and story—which detract from one another—could be taken as a metaphor for Cunningham's work generally, where narrative and dance never meaningfully occupy the same stage.

The same disintegration of parts is evidence in the dances themselves. Cunningham often created new works by splicing together phrases and dances from other works. Hence the notion of an underlying narrative was rejected from the outset. The same lack of integration is

59. Mazo, *Prime Movers*, 179.
60. Banes, *Writing Dancing*, 113.

apparent in the dancers, who, even when they come together, seem to do so by accident rather than intention. As Sally Banes describes the effect:

> Since Cunningham's dances are not dramatic, his dancers do not appear impelled by motivations. But, if they are not personal agents, neither are they social agents. They often seem unaware of each other as they dance different phrases juxtaposed at opposite ends of the stage. Undoubtedly, a large measure of this effect derives from their performance masks, which are generally free from every emotion save concentration.[61]

Cunningham was an exceptional dancer, and his works, as expressions of the imaginative possibilities of the human form, have a capacity to engage as most other postmodern art does not. However, his dances not only disavow the potential for meaning that is inherent in narrative; they are visual testaments to the view that life is random and momentary—that it has no "greater or more lasting value." Cunningham is thus another of the many postmodern practitioners of "Rorschach" art—here so called because, as in the famous ink blot test, the viewer (or reader or listener) is invited to find whatever meaning he or she may. Like the ink blot, the work itself is meaningless.

---

61. Banes, *Writing Dancing*, 111–12.

11

Film

WHILE THE STORY ONCE had a home in the novel and drama, music and dance, today it is chiefly to be found in the multiplex, where it appears wrapped in surround sound with color and, perhaps, 3D. This is an important distinction. For as surely as suggestion and ambiguity stimulate the search for meaning, realism quells it by providing little room for imagination or inquiry. By realism I am clearly not referring to the subject matter of recent movies but to a major shift in cinematic style—i.e., to that *explicitness* that is now so evident in writing, cinematography, and sound. In today's entertainment, every assault upon the screen (and there are many) is accompanied by a second assault upon the senses of the viewer, with meaning the victim.

The traditional American movie house was usually a dramatic theater with curtains, stadium seating, and a balcony. Films were often referred to as "dramas"—a quaint notion but one that was often reinforced by movie sets, which lent an intimate mood to the story. The early movie screen was large, and the theater held a large audience. In this way it served as a gathering place for a community whose members came regularly to see shows they would often discuss with their neighbors. During the Depression years, movies were one of the few affordable family entertainments. Movies were still enormously popular in the mid-forties, when some 80–100 million (out of a population of only 140 million) saw films weekly in the 18,719 movie theaters (and 300 drive-ins) of America.[1]

---

1. Ellis, *History of Film*, 272.

The central place of the movie house in the community was evident by its location. From the twenties well into the sixties, movie houses tended to be located at the center of towns near churches, stores, and municipal buildings. While Saturday mornings were often reserved for children's shows, films were generally family fare. There was no need for a ratings system like the one that today serves to segregate audiences by age. Moviegoers could generally depend upon the discretion of filmmakers and would, in any case, learn of questionable content from their friends and neighbors.

Movies served not merely as centers of entertainment but as places of modest instruction where traditional values were upheld. The movie was accompanied by a cartoon that lightened the mood of even the darkest film noir, and by newsreels, travelogues, and other short subjects that provided information that spoke to all Americans and appealed to common interests. Although filmmakers often played fast and loose with history, both movie shorts and features provided meaningful accounts of inventors, political figures, folk heroes, and the like. And while directors drew upon the best popular fiction of the day (including stories from the many periodicals then available), they also looked for inspiration to the classics, including in their films works by Shakespeare, Melville, Kipling, Stevenson, Austen, the Brontës, Dickens, Verne, Crane, Dumas, Cooper, and Twain, among others.

Although the arts were a secondary concern for filmmakers, they were by no means ignored. As Alex Ross has pointed out, classical music was especially popular in film:

> Say this for the movie people: they were certainly mad for music ... there were biopics of Schubert (*Melody Master*), Chopin (*A Song to Remember*), Robert and Clara Schumann (*Song of Love*), even Rimsky-Korsakov (*Song of Scheherazade*). John Garfield played a violinist in *Humoresque*; Bette Davis played a pianist entangled with a cellist and a composer in *Deception*; Leopold Stokowski played Leopold Stokowski in the Deanne Durbin comedy *One Hundred Men and a Girl*. Each major studio assembled a symphony orchestra to record its scores, providing employment to the throngs of Jewish musical émigrés who had been driven out of the great ensembles of Central Europe.[2]

Most of the above films date from the mid-forties. In the fifties, classical music was evident in film chiefly in the form of the great tenor Mario Lanza, whose nine popular films (and three-million-selling records) attested to the continued popularity of the music for Americans.

---

2. Ross, *Rest Is Noise*, 316.

By the fifties, filmmakers were also beginning to take advantage of color to make powerful films on artists like Toulouse Lautrec (*Moulin Rouge*), Van Gogh (*Lust for Life*), and Michelangelo (*The Agony and the Ecstasy*). Such films typically portrayed their subject in a sympathetic or inspirational light, thereby highlighting the meaning of their work and its value to viewers. Filmmakers were also capable of drawing upon great art in framing their scenes. A notable example of this is the musical *An American in Paris*, where Gene Kelley dances in colorful sets adapted from the works of the French Postimpressionists Utrillo, Toulouse-Lautrec, Rousseau, and Dufy.

As we may imagine, the forties saw a wave of heroic films designed to instill patriotism in Americans. While war films had become more nuanced by the fifties, the notion of the inherent goodness of the American serviceman and the righteousness of his cause persisted into the sixties. The years following the war also marked the triumph of the American hero in the Western, which flourished in films like *My Darling Clementine*, *Red River*, *She Wore a Yellow Ribbon*, *Shane*, *The Searchers*, and *High Noon*. Western heroes embodied the same values as the American soldier. Successful actors of the day (e.g., Kirk Douglas, John Wayne, Gregory Peck, Henry Fonda) merely had to switch from military attire to spurs and Stetsons to effectively play their roles.

The Cold War also spurred an interest in the heroes of American history. The most famous examples of this were the TV shows and movies of Davy Crockett, which inspired a craze among the very young for coonskin caps. However, Crockett was only one of numerous heroes capable of instilling a love of America and its history in the young. Michael Medved gives a vivid account of his experience in growing up among the many Hollywood heroes of American history:

> At age seven I went three times to see *The Great Locomotive Chase* (1956), starring Fess Parker as a fearless Union officer who leads a daring raid behind enemy lines to steal a key Confederate train. The next year I thrilled to *Johnny Tremain*, which took me to colonial Boston along with a poor but courageous boy who joins the Sons of Liberty and takes part in the early stages of the struggle for Independence. I also loved *The Buccaneer* (1958), with Andrew Jackson and pirate Jean Lafitte winning the battle of New Orleans; *The Horse Soldiers* (1959) starring John Wayne and William Holden as Union cavalry officers in the Civil War; *John Paul Jones* (1959) with Robert Stack as the great naval hero of the American Revolution; and, of course, John Wayne's

two-hour-and-forty-minute epic, *The Alamo*, with Davy Crockett, Jim Bowie, and Colonel Travis sacrificing their lives with incomparable gallantry for the cause of Texas independence.³

Movies of the postwar years also provided powerful religious meanings through their treatment of basic Judeo-Christian themes. Religion had, of course, had a significant presence in earlier film, usually in the form of the kindly priest, who assumed center stage in the films of Pat O'Brien (*Angels with Dirty Faces, The Fighting 69th*), Bing Crosby (*Going My Way, Bells of St. Mary's*), and Spencer Tracy (*Boy's Town, Men of Boy's Town*). Beyond this, the pious nun or priest was a standard figure in many films, helping the down-and-out, comforting the sick or injured, and teaching the orphan or runaway the value of honesty and good sportsmanship. Now, in the postwar years, Hollywood turned to biblical epics in films like *Samson and Delilah, David and Bathsheba, The Robe, Quo Vadis, The Ten Commandments, Solomon and Sheba, Ben Hur, Barabbas,* and *King of Kings*.

Notable here is the generally high quality of the films. *The Ten Commandments* (1956), for example, was a marvel of film production, and a story whose general faithfulness to the biblical account led many religious leaders to commend it to young viewers. *Ben Hur* (1959), although a fictionalized story, was exceptional filmmaking, garnering a record eleven Academy Awards, including Best Picture, Best Director, and Best Actor both in lead and supporting roles. *Ben Hur* proved to be the second-largest grossing film in Hollywood history (after *Gone with the Wind*). This, along with the success of other biblical epics, was scarcely surprising in an era when so many citizens could be expected to attend church on Sundays. Thus movies had an extraordinary unifying role in America—one that combined elements of synagogue and church, patriotic civic institutions and schools all rolled into one.

Film critics and historians often speak of Hollywood's Golden Age in reference to films dating from the mid-thirties into the early sixties. The period nicely coincides with the implementation of the Production Code among the major studios. The code was basically a series of documents that eventually led, in 1934, to the practice of issuing seals to films that met basic moral standards. Directors, producers, and writers often chafed under such strictures. However, as a reflection of basic American values, the code did much to establish film as the central form of American entertainment. Nor is it easy to reconcile the limitations imposed by

3. Medved, *Hollywood vs. America*, 231–32.

such standards with the extraordinary films of the era. One could even argue that, far from being a hindrance, the code had a major role in the flourishing of Hollywood cinema.

One way the code did this was by encouraging and even mandating that directors forego graphic sex and violence and appeal to the viewer's imagination. Not surprisingly, the greatest kissing scenes in Hollywood history date from the code era. One such scene occurs in *Casablanca* (1942) as Rick (Humphrey Bogart) and Ilsa (Ingrid Bergman) await the German troops' advance toward Paris. The scene actually includes three kisses, which grow more intense as the German guns grow louder in the distance. In the last kiss, Ilsa pleads with Rick to kiss her "as if it were for the last time." Rick rises up, gathering himself for a kiss that will conclude with Ilsa's outstretched hand toppling over a wine glass.[4] The gesture conveys both the passion and reckless abandon of the lovers while foreshadowing the loss and despair that follow in the story.

Hollywood directors of the Golden Age commonly employ props like the overturned glass to convey violence or passion or to serve as clues to coming events—clues to be deciphered by the viewer. But directors also had other means of conveying intense romantic feelings. The kissing scene in *Casablanca*, for example, employs the popular three-point lighting scheme to lighten Ilsa's face and create a "halo effect" around it. The result, in a light-skinned woman like Ilsa, is to make the woman appear to "glow with a light that works to purify the darker lusts their kisses may evoke."[5] It is precisely this sense of something "higher" and "purer"—conveyed to a wartime audience for whom such notions had real and immediate significance—that is at the heart of *Casablanca*, giving the romantic tale so much force and meaning. And, as we shall see, it is chiefly the lack of belief in anything "higher" or "purer" that has doomed romantic love in postmodern film.

Even the more graphic displays of sexual attraction gained force through suggestion in film. A perfect example of this occurs in *From Here to Eternity* (1953), in a kissing scene involving Sergeant Milton Warden (Burt Lancaster) and his superior officer's wife, Karen Holmes (Deborah Kerr).[6] The kiss occurs following a brief nighttime dip in the ocean as the couple fall at the water's edge. The scene is richly poetic, the surging waves and foam that engulf them serving to join the lovers' passions to

4. Curtiz, *Casablanca*, 46:27.
5. Williams, *Screening Sex*, 37.
6. Zimmerman, *From Here to Eternity*, 35:40.

nature's own, giving the act a remarkable intensity. The waves also evoke that sense of wild disregard for convention displayed by the lovers—even as the surrounding foam becomes a symbol for intercourse that, given the drama of the setting, it seems superfluous to otherwise indicate.

What is perhaps most remarkable is the ability of classic cinema not only to convey passion without sex, but to employ this limitation in creating some of the greatest films ever made. I am referring here to the screwball comedy. The screwball comedy revolves around the differences between the sexes while referencing basic social and economic divisions of the thirties, forties, and fifties. In the screwball comedy, conflicts are heightened and compressed, with the result that the relationship between the couple develops over a brief period of time. Here, differences are resolved not through reasoned thought or discussion, but by means of madcap activity fueled by sublimated sexual energy.

Many screwball comedies acknowledge that such energy underlies the action. Near the end of *Bringing Up Baby* (1938), Susan (Katherine Hepburn) confesses to David (Cary Grant) that the wild escapades of the previous day (chiefly involving the search for a dinosaur bone and the rounding up of a stray leopard) resulted from her desire to keep him near her.[7] In a similar vein, *My Man Godfrey* (1936) contains one memorable scene that immediately follows Godfrey's (William Powell) immersion of a fully clothed Cordelia (Carole Lombard) in the shower. In the scene, a drenched Cordelia is seen running around the house, gleefully crying, "Godfrey loves me! Godfrey loves me!"[8]

The heyday of the screwball comedy was from the early thirties through the World War II years. However, the genre continued into the early sixties before beginning to fade from the scene with the popular Doris Day romps. The reason for this decline is clear enough. In a society where anything goes—a society where divorce, infidelity, and illicit sex were on the rise—the screwball comedy had run out of the steam supplied by social constraints and sexual sublimation.

During the Golden Age, violent scenes also relied heavily upon suggestion in ways that heightened their impact upon the viewer. A notable example of this occurs in Alfred Hitchcock's classic *Psycho* (1960). Hitchcock was a master of suspense who generally shunned unnecessary displays of violence. The plot for *Psycho*, however, revolved around a shower

---

7. Hawks, *Bringing Up Baby*.
8. La Cava, *My Man Godfrey*.

stabbing that required not only nudity but graphic violence, raising concerns of censorship among the director and his crew. Hitchcock's solution managed to satisfy not only the censors but his own artistic values. It also resulted in what is arguably the most terrifying scene in film history.

The setting of the scene is the isolated Bates Motel, where Marion (Janet Leigh) has stopped for the night. Marion had stolen money from her Phoenix employer and, escaping in a driving rain, has wandered far from the main road. The mood is one of foreboding, the rain, isolation, and loneliness made palpable through black-and-white photography and Bernard Herrmann's powerful score. As in many of the later Hitchcock films, the composer employed long stretches of music without harmonic resolution in *Psycho*, thus conveying a mood of expectancy in the viewer. Only Herrmann went further here, adopting a strings-only score that complemented the black-and-white photography, effectively cutting off the viewer (much as Marion is cut off) from the world of everyday experience.[9]

Marion's sense of isolation is lessened somewhat by a light supper with proprietor Norman Bates (Anthony Perkins) in the motel office. The subsequent scene in her motel room (where she is watched by Bates through a peephole) is accompanied by slow, suspenseful music. Marion is now resigned to the fact that she must return to Phoenix the following day and return the money. To further set the stage, Hitchcock directed Leigh to wash thoroughly in the shower, as if attempting to remove the stain of her crime. This sense of relief and hope of new beginnings makes the shadowy entrance of the murderer behind the shower curtain more surprising. His rapid knife thrusts, accompanied by the piercing cries of the strings, caused many viewers of the day to turn away in terror.[10]

Hitchcock later claimed that the murder scene required some seventy camera setups and seven days of shooting—all for just forty-five seconds of film. As he explained the process:

> *Psycho* is probably one of the most cinematic pictures I've ever made. Because there you had montage in the bathtub killing where the whole thing is purely an illusion. No knife ever touched any woman's body in that scene. Ever. But the rapidity of the shots. . . . The little pieces of film were probably not more than four or five inches long. They were on the screen for a fraction of a second.[11]

9. R. Brown, "Herrmann, Hitchcock."
10. Hitchcock, *Psycho*, 47:37.
11. Hitchcock, *Hitchcock on Hitchcock*, 288.

"Illusion" it may have been, but the graphic nature of the murder—its pure visceral power—was unusual for Hitchcock and indicative of a new direction in Hollywood that would fully take hold before the decade's end.

Changing, too, was the vital role of music, that had been so central in heightening the meanings of classical film. Speaking of his long and fruitful collaboration with Hitchcock, Herrmann once claimed that Hitchcock did only 60 percent of the film—he did the rest.[12] This was no mere boast. Herrmann was among the last of a number of great composers (e.g., Max Steiner, Alfred Newman, Erich Wolfgang Korngold) who played a vital role in classic Hollywood films through musical scores that fully complemented the characters and their activity, cuing in the moviegoer and heightening the film's cognitive and emotional power. These men were classically trained musicians, and the studios provided them with a symphony orchestra to bring their works to life. By 1960 the studio orchestras were gone. Now composers were being encouraged to adopt pop and jazz in their compositions—a development that led Herrmann to break with Hitchcock when the director insisted on a more contemporary score for his film *Torn Curtain* (1966).

While the classical scoring technique did not completely disappear in the sixties, new Hollywood was inclined to adopt soundtracks attuned to the times but not the story—music which, hopefully, would prove financially profitable on its own. On some occasions (e.g., Simon and Garfunkel's music for *The Graduate*) the music managed to complement the overall mood, thereby heightening the meaning of the film. Too often music and story went their separate ways, with a consequent loss of meaning. Sometimes the music even created a sharp disconnect with the action. A notable example occurs in the getaway scene in *Bonnie and Clyde*, where the tense, sinister music we would once have expected in the circumstances gives way to the playful banjo music of Flatt and Scruggs's "Foggy Mountain Breakdown." As we shall see, in this mood of irony and loss of meaning, *Bonnie and Clyde* set the standard for what was to come.

Movie viewership declined in the prosperous postwar years, when rising incomes permitted other amusements and the increasing popularity of television kept more and more potential moviegoers in their homes. Still, the first half of the sixties witnessed the production of a remarkable number of outstanding films. These included: *The Apartment, Psycho,*

---

12. R. Brown, "Herrmann, Hitchcock," 102.

Judgment at Nuremberg, West Side Story, Spartacus, To Kill a Mockingbird, The Miracle Worker, Long Day's Journey into Night, Lawrence of Arabia, Elmer Gantry, Ship of Fools, My Fair Lady, The Longest Day, The Train, The Night of the Iguana, and *Dr. Strangelove.* Then, almost overnight, the Hollywood well of creativity began to run dry.

The best films of 1966—Robert Bolt's *A Man for All Seasons* and Edward Albee's *Who's Afraid of Virginia Woolf*—were taken from the theater. These films show a Hollywood divided: Bolt's tale looked back to the great films of the Golden Age and to traditional notions of heroism; Albee's story pointed to a new type of film attacking traditional values and laced with profanity and sexual content. This division was even more apparent in the films of 1967, which saw the simultaneous release of traditional Hollywood fare (e.g., *The Jungle Book, Fitzwilly, Camelot, Doctor Doolittle, Hotel*) alongside films that seemed designed to shock traditional viewers (*In Cold Blood, Bonnie and Clyde, The Graduate, The Dirty Dozen, Point Blank*).

Of these films, *Bonnie and Clyde* has come to be regarded as most emblematic of the new Hollywood values.[13] The story is Arthur Penn's freewheeling rendition of the life and death of Depression-era bank robbers Bonnie Parker and Clyde Barrow. In the film, Bonnie (Faye Dunaway) is portrayed as a lovely, self-absorbed young women who is bored with life and looks to Clyde (Warren Beatty) for romance and good times. Her needs will not be altogether satisfied. From the start, Clyde proves to be mostly inept both in bed and in the bank-robbing business. Still, things eventually pick up for the couple. As the movie unfolds, the Barrow gang grows—along with a palpable sense of doom following the horrific murder of a bank clerk in one botched robbery. The film ends with the gang's betrayal and subsequent ambush by authorities led by Texas Ranger Frank Hamer (Denver Pyle).

13. Penn, *Bonnie and Clyde.*

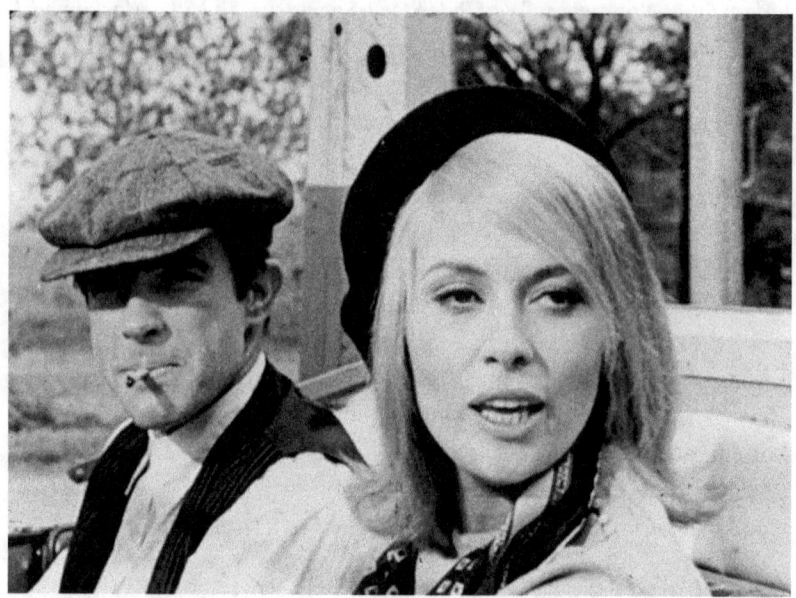

American actors Warren Beatty and Faye Dunaway sit in a car in a still from the film *Bonnie and Clyde*, directed by Arthur Penn, 1967.
Photo by Fotos International/Courtesy Getty Images.

Bonnie and Clyde is today widely recognized as a film whose break with the moral strictures of the times set the stage for a revolution in Hollywood filmmaking. Judged by Golden Age standards, the film did have much that was new. *Bonnie and Clyde* was ahead of its time in the frank treatment of sexuality, although the sexual content is tame by today's standards. It is the movie's blend of humor and violence and its gratuitous display of the latter that truly distinguished it from old Hollywood. In the earlier crime stories, criminals are typically hard-nosed villains whose hubris and ruthless disregard for decency make them fodder for audiences who willingly accepted their demise. Penn made Bonnie and Clyde not only attractive, but likeable, delineating them as "jes folks" who were always willing to lend a hand—people who had troubles just like everyone else, although not everyone else was wanted for murder. Among Penn's liberties with history was his depiction of Hamer as an inept, scheming official. His ambush of the duo unfolds as a grisly danse macabre that concludes the film, leaving many in the audience to depart in stunned silence.

When *Bonnie and Clyde* opened the Montreal Film festival in August of 1967, the dean of American reviewers, Bosley Crowther, savaged it in the *New York Times*, expressing dismay that "so callous and callow a film should represent [the] country in these times."[14] Crowther was disturbed by the way the film's violence had been treated with humor, and troubled that moviegoers responded with laughter and applause. Others agreed. Jimmy Breslin seemed to capture the essence of the film for many when he characterized it as a story of "pretty people who kill, and the killing they do is pretty too." Breslin recounted how Bobby Kennedy refused to watch the film, having heard that it was "the most immoral movie ever made."[15]

As it turned out, *Bonnie and Clyde* was a test on where viewers stood in the great divide now taking place in America. While most older Americans shared Crowther's and Kennedy's points of view, a new generation seemed genuinely moved by what they saw on the screen. When *TIME* panned the film, one young woman responded by arguing that *Bonnie and Clyde* was "not a film for adults," and that young people *liked* the protagonists and wanted to be like them. Young black viewers were especially receptive. Penn described the response of a black audience at a private screening in this way: "'Five Negroes present . . . completely identified with Bonnie and Clyde. They were delighted. They said, "This is the way; that's the way to go baby. Those cats were all right."'[16] In Penn's view, Bonnie and Clyde had emerged as "heroic" figures in the film.

Within months of his critical review, Crowther and his old-fashioned views were out at the *New York Times*. His place as the dean of critics would be taken by Pauline Kael, who had given *Bonnie and Clyde* a rave review, repeating the old bromide that any work of art that elicits such strong reactions among so many *must* be good. Kael would find fame championing the new cinema and trashing the old Hollywood values. Like many at the time, she seemed unconcerned about the resulting debris. Commenting on her career, at her death, film director Paul Schrader tellingly observed: "It was fun watching the applecart being upset, but now where do we go for apples?"[17]

14. Hoberman, "*Bonnie and Clyde*," 318.
15. Hoberman, "*Bonnie and Clyde*," 320.
16. Hoberman, "*Bonnie and Clyde*," 321.
17. Monteith, *American Culture in 1960s*, 78.

American film was the most visible manifestation of what Andrew Delbanco has termed a "culture of irony," which had taken hold broadly by the late sixties.[18] Irony is not unknown in traditional societies. In fact, it has an important place there as a means of temporarily relieving the heavy hand of tradition (even while putting it in sharp relief) in ceremonies in which bedrock principles are upended, so that the high is made low, order becomes disorder and the sacred is profaned. Among a Pueblo tribe, the Hopi, this occurs in rituals where the spirit beings, the kachinas, assume the form of clowns. Clown kachinas are everything ordinary kachinas are not. As David Maybury-Lewis describes their ceremonial antics:

> [They] swarm into the plaza from the rooftops, climbing down the ladders head-first, falling, stumbling, rushing out to grasp the sacred paraphernalia for themselves.... They act out life as it should *not* be—they are irreverent, ignorant, they squabble with their wives, they seek fame, they hoard food.[19]

While a taste of irony is beneficial to society, the irony that took hold in sixties America was more in the way of a sustained attack upon values that succeeded in eventually wearing them down. We have noted signs of a change in music, drama, and dance—as well as in pop art, where the Abstract Expressionist brushstroke simply became another "technique" of picture making and archetypal forms that had carried so much meaning gave way to comic strip characters and soup cans. Film was simply a logical extension of Warhol's nihilism. *Ramparts* writer Peter Collier pointed this out early on, when he characterized *Bonnie and Clyde* as "Andy Warhol's serial put-ons packaged in a dramatic context with all of Hollywood's savvy behind it."[20]

Even some who valued the new style eventually became aware that something vital was being lost. These included writer and intellectual Susan Sontag, who had championed early sixties irony as a counterpart to "serious" culture but had begun to question it by 1974.[21] Looking back from the late eighties, Sontag spoke of a "cultural nihilism" that had taken hold in America. And further: "The cultural situation has changed even more radically for the worse than I would have predicted 25 years ago. And so I find myself moved to support things which I did not think

---

18. Delbanco, *Death of Satan*, 185–217.
19. Maybury-Lewis, *Millennium*, 212.
20. Haberski, *Freedom to Offend*, 193.
21. Haberski, *Freedom to Offend*, 228.

would be necessary to support at all in the past. Like seriousness, for instance. I really did not think one would have to defend seriousness, and I do now."[22]

On a larger stage, the emergence of irony in the sixties was apparent in films (e.g., *Dr. Strangelove, Catch 22, M*A*S*H**) that attacked war by parodying mindless authority and patriotism. This was irony as a spur to thought and as a relief valve for the mindless absurdity of war. But there was another, more disturbing undercurrent of irony that took form in works like Truman Capote's account of a real-life horror story, *In Cold Blood* (1965), where the author can scarcely conceal his preference for the two killers rather than for the wholesome Midwestern family who are their victims.[23] *In Cold Blood*, like *Bonnie and Clyde*, was indicative of what Nietzsche had called a "transformation of values," where villains emerge as heroes and law-abiding citizens and their protectors become the enemy. This shift would emerge as a prominent feature of film from the late sixties on.

Bonnie and Clyde also initiated a glorification of violence that has had far-reaching impact. As one writer has observed:

> One can see the influence of *Bonnie and Clyde's* aestheticism of violence in the slasher/horror films of the 70s and 80s in which the narrative acts as a mere pretext for moments of gory spectacle. We can trace a clear line of development from *Bonnie and Clyde, The Wild Bunch* (1969), *Billy Jack* (1971), *Straw Dogs* (1971), *Dirty Harry* (1972), and *The Exorcist* (1973) to *The Texas Chainsaw Massacre* (1974), *Halloween* (1978), *Friday, the 13th* (1980), and their sequels, in which violence is at the center of each highly staged sequence and exists solely for its own sake; shocking, yes, but also predictable and campy, detaching an audience aware of its stock conventions.[24]

"Campy" indeed, although perhaps not so very "detaching." In fact, *Bonnie and Clyde* resonated with a generation who were inclined to play with the old values like rich children with expensive toys, breaking them beyond repair in the process. Hence the influence of the film upon a new political activism that became more destructive as the era wore on.

That new Hollywood did not sit well with the old Hollywood crowd was evident from declining movie attendance. Despite the advent of TV,

22. Poague, *Conversations with Susan Sontag*, 240.
23. Delbanco, *Death of Satan*, 205.
24. Man, *Radical Visions*, 10.

the number of Americans who went to movies weekly had remained relatively stable between 1953 and 1965, at some 40 to 49 million. Between 1965 and 1969, however, weekly movie attendance plummeted to a mere 17.5 million viewers, wiping out an extraordinary 60 percent of what had for years been a stable viewership.[25] That the change in Hollywood fare was chiefly responsible was evident to theater owners, who blamed much of the decline on "a commensurate drop in the morality quotient of films."[26] The change was also evident in Hollywood's notion of its best productions. In 1965, the Academy Award for Best Motion Picture went to *The Sound of Music*—a tale whose blend of natural beauty, music, romance, love of family, love of God, and devotion to country made it one of the most meaningful films ever made. But meaning was out, as was apparent in critics like Kael, who mocked the film, calling it 'The Sound of Money'. The shift from meaning was even clearer by 1969. In that year, the award for Best Picture was given to *Midnight Cowboy*, a powerful but ultimately despairing tale of poverty, prostitution, and death.

Midnight Cowboy could be regarded as a metaphor for the sad state of the cowboy generally in postmodern cinema. Long gone were the fifties, when the Western was a bigger draw than all other genres *combined*. Writing in the early nineties, the authors of *Hollywood's America* noted that, since the early seventies, the only Westerns to break into the yearly top-ten box office draws (*Blazing Saddles* and *The Electric Horseman*) were hardly traditional fare. Even Clint Eastwood's more conventional Western, *Unforgiven* (1992), showed its postmodern lineage in the form of "a racist and sadistic" sheriff (Gene Hackman) and a protagonist who appears as an "uncontrollably violent, albeit reluctant, hired killer."[27] In fact, from Arthur Penn's *Little Big Man* (1970) through *Dances With Wolves* (1990) and *Brokeback Mountain* (2005), the postmodern Western is more often a vehicle for social commentary than a means of reinforcing common values.

While the classic Western hero today appears to be riding off into the sunset, he is not alone. Beside him, like Tonto to his Lone Ranger, is the war hero. In their survey of selected films from 1946 to 1990, the authors of *Hollywood's America* noted in military films a dramatic rise in individual acts of violence and a dramatic erosion of faith in the military generally, and in its authority structure especially. Once again, the change

---

25. Medved, *Hollywood vs. America*, 277.
26. Medved, *Hollywood vs. America*, 284.
27. S. Powers et al., *Hollywood's America*, 27.

dates to late sixties, although it was in the eighties that the trend really came into its own:

> The changes are particularly clear in Vietnam films like *Platoon* (1986) and *Good Morning Vietnam* (1987), not to mention the *Rambo* films. In these films and others like them, authority figures are often portrayed as incompetent, if not vile. The sense of community or fraternity, once a prominent feature of the military movie, barely survives, or if it does, becomes a source of sadism and evil. No better example can be found in our sample of the complete breakdown in loyalty and trust among soldiers than Barnes' (Tom Berenger) murder of Elias (Willem Dafoe) in *Platoon*.[28]

The point here has little to do with the quality of these films. From the perspective of meaning, the issue concerns the picture they paint of a world that lacks order and a sense of common values and purposes that are essential to meaning in life. One may reasonably argue that postmodern Hollywood has provided a corrective to old Hollywood's dream world where belief in authority (if not all authority figures), the rule of law, and the eventual triumph of good over evil held sway. But evidence is clear that films of recent decades have gone much further than Americans generally in rejecting the old values. In effect, the new Hollywood films replaced one vision with another, the dream world of the past giving way to a nightmare where not only has the applecart been overturned but the apples intentionally scattered.

With the heroes of the past either disappearing or looking more and more like the villains, where did viewers in postmodern America look for apples? Certainly not to religion. Although religion and the supernatural were still popular in the seventies, eighties and nineties, the helpful priest had long ago gone the way of the stolid cop on his beat. In *Hollywood vs. America*, Michael Medved makes the point in this way: "Whenever someone turns up in a film with the title 'Reverend,' 'Father,' or 'Rabbi' in front of their name you can count on the fact that he will turn out to be corrupt or crazy—or probably both."[29] Medved cites some two dozen films from the eighties and nineties that either "jab" Jews, "bash" born-again Christians, or "kick" Catholics. He also notes the double standard whereby filmmakers hesitate to insult any social group *except* the religious—faith having become the one agreed upon subject of attack.

28. S. Powers et al., *Hollywood's America*, 95–96.
29. Medved, *Hollywood vs. America*, 52.

By the eighties, the simple Bible tale had long disappeared. In its place was a new type of film more in accord with the new values. In earlier movies with a strong Christian flavor (e.g., *The Robe, Ben-Hur, Barabbas*), the Savior appears as a shadowy, spiritual presence, the focus rightly being upon those who come under his influence. Postmodern cinema brought Christ down to earth by asserting his sexuality (e.g., *The Da Vinci Code, The Last Temptation of Christ*) or by graphic displays of violence. The latter was most apparent in Mel Gibson's heartfelt *The Passion of the Christ* (2004), where it becomes, for many, a hindrance in what is otherwise a powerfully meaningful tale.

Even as Hollywood began to bring the supernatural down to earth, it sought to relocate the earthy in the heavens. This is evident in the extraordinary popularity of the fantasy genre, which gained a foothold in the seventies with the first Star Wars films, saw a big upsurge with the Harry Potter and Lord of the Rings movies, and has come to dominate in the twenty-first century with the Marvel and DC comics films. By 2018, 80 percent of the top-grossing American films were of the fantasy genre. This represents a complete reversal from 1968, when only 20 percent of films were fantasies.[30] This is an extraordinary change, and one that is telling both in regard to our inability to conceive of meaning in everyday experience and our unwillingness to engage with cinematic tales in the depth necessary for meaning to unfold.

The leader of the fantasy genre are the Marvel movies, which today have passed both the DC comics and the Star Wars stories in popularity. Some may see in these movies the rebirth of the hero. But the Marvel universe is not old Hollywood, where characters faced real-life challenges without resort to pyrotechnics. There is a shallowness and superficiality here that evinces that same willingness to play with the old values that marked the dawn of new Hollywood more than a half century ago. Professor Richard Goldstein, who teaches film (and enjoys the Marvel movies), acknowledges this in speaking of the mash-up of myth in the popular and critically acclaimed *Thor: Ragnarok*:

> Why was the Hulk rampaging through the distant planet Sakaar? (Isn't that like pouring Velveeta on Swedish meatballs?) And what's with Thor's self-actualization pitch to Loki, his adopted brother: "You'll always be the god of mischief, but you could be more." I complained to my students that Loki is supposed to be a trickster, not a candidate for cognitive behavior therapy, but

---

30. Cort, "Our Love Affair," 54.

they replied that knowing the source of a superhero myth can ruin it.... Every legend is up for grabs in the Marvel blender. Set the dial on hyper-explosive, add colors that make Day-Glo look dull, and you've got a style.[31]

This merging of mythologies dates back to Marvel's originator Stan Lee, who realized that connecting the different characters in the Marvel Comics universe was a way of boosting sales.[32] Lee recognized that baby boomers were hesitant to move on to adulthood, and, in the sixties, he began marketing to young men, creating lifelong fans and quickly passing the tamer DC comics in popularity. By the seventies, Marvel fans were being fed a more adult diet in films that violated the standards of the industries' censorship board (the CCA). Today, the Marvel world is an even darker and more troubled one, and its moral message blurred when not altogether lost. Fantasy scholar Jess Nevins, who grew up during the years of transition in fantasy films, has had this to say regarding the changing nature of the hero in these stories: "The deliberately maintained innocence of the superheroes of my youth is long gone and has been replaced by what is too often a ghastly combination of post-9/11 ruthlessness and postmodern, even nihilistic, cynicism."[33]

Today's fantasy world has other difficulties endemic to the genre. By totally removing these stories from the everyday world and relying so much upon special effects for impact, the new films encourage that pure escapism that now largely defines film in America. This accords with the artificial world of a younger generation of viewers. As Goldstein observes: "They expect entertainment to immerse them in alternative realities. They don't bring literary standards to these films, and neither should you. Abandon PBS, ye who enter here! Accept the invitation to regress, sink into a daydreaming delight, and you'll find the pleasure in these films."[34] Regress indeed. At least the Rowling and Tolkien series (although better in print) keep one foot in reality while demonstrating that real heroism can be found among the smallest and gentlest of creatures. In fact, the journey from Sergeant York and Davy Crockett through droids, muggles, and hobbits to the latest Marvel heroes is

31. Goldstein, "My Students Love Marvel," para. 6.
32. Daurer and Fingeroth, "Superhero of the Comics."
33. Dirda, "From Beowulf to Batman," para. 10.
34. Goldstein, "My Students Love Marvel," para. 10.

another chapter in the story of the loss of meaning in American culture, and the emergence of mere spectacle in its stead.

Of course, not all Americans are enthralled by the new cinema. And this narrowing of the cinematic world to a small segment of the population is another telling feature of film today. Classic Hollywood cinema drew viewers from all ages and walks of life, reconfiguring age old stories and instilling common values, awakening patriotic feelings and proudly proclaiming the history of America. This all changed when cynicism and irony began to dominate the cinematic world in the late sixties. But the loss of the old ideals and stories is but part of the story. Along with the loss of common values there has been a loss of the larger meanings of the film experience, which dates to the advent of streaming in 2010. Today, even as the old movie houses are being shuttered, the multiplexes that followed are becoming passé. For the youngest Americans (many of whom grew up alone before a TV screen), neither the raucous response to a Popeye cartoon nor the cool communal spirit of the little black boxes in the mall will do. For today's youth, movies are all about *me*. As one iGener recently explained:

> With today's technology, you can stream the movie online, wear your most bum-like outfit . . . and eat snacks straight from your fridge and pantry. You can also pause, rewind and fast-forward the movie as you please, something that does not happen in a movie theatre. Ever.[35]

---

35. Twenge, *iGen*, 67–68.

12

Romantic Love

IT IS DIFFICULT TO know where romance should be placed in our study of meaning. In the middle of the twentieth century, romantic love was at the very heart of popular culture. For this reason, it could reasonably be placed in our "meaning writ large" section. But romance (at least as traditionally understood) is also a story. In fact, the word "romance" originated in the Middle Ages in reference to a fantastic tale that was often told in verse. This is an important point. For the progression of romantic love has all the elements of narrative, including the slow unfolding of its theme, the various complications that ensue, and a resolution in which the various strands finally come together—or not. Indeed, the most remarkable feature of the romantic tale may be the fact that, even when its ending is a sad one, we may still find it extraordinarily meaningful. This is because, to be caught up in a romance (even a tragic one) is to be temporarily elevated beyond the realm of ordinary experience into a world of greater and more lasting value.

The source of such power is largely spiritual. Since the Middle Ages, it is the "otherworldly" language of religion that has shaped romance and given it its extraordinary meaning. This was the case at least until the late sixties, when the spiritual began to fade and romance to lose its luster.

While romantic love had been around for generations, it truly emerged in the postwar years, when the courtship behavior of young Americans underwent a profound change. During the thirties and early forties, dating practice had placed a premium upon popularity and "playing the field," while discouraging serious romance until young people were of a suitable age. Now, in the aftermath of war, the popularity system was replaced by the practice of "going steady."[1] Of course, having a steady beau as a prelude to marriage was nothing new. However, by the fifties, it was becoming the norm not only for college-age women and men but for their younger brothers and sisters.

In response to what many regarded as a serious moral crisis, American families turned to a welter of magazines and books designed to provide guidance in the thorny issue of premarital relations. In the years immediately after the war, teen magazines proliferated, while the most popular magazine for parents, *Parents Magazine*, saw its circulation double.[2] These periodicals were unanimous in urging restraint among the young. And while many older teens solved the dilemma by early marriage, the value of delay still held sway—at least in theory. As late as 1966, a Roper poll indicated that over half of Americans believed that both the bride and groom should be virgins on marrying. This was the same number as in 1937.[3]

All this seems hopelessly naive in an age in which promiscuity is regarded as nothing more than good clean fun. But we should note that restraint is not only vital to ethical development but essential in giving meaning to the romantic atmosphere that characterizes the early stages of courtship. The medievals who invented romantic love were well aware of this. The early troubadour Marcabru said it best when he professed that his lady did right in making him wait for what she had promised him. As he explained: "He who is disposed to love with sensual love goes to war with himself, for a fool after he has emptied his purse cuts a poor figure!"[4]

Like the medievals, dating couples in the postwar years followed a series of little rituals designed to slow down the process of courtship, build trust, and test the mettle of young gentlemen as romance grew and blossomed. Generally speaking, dating etiquette required that the young man assume the initiative and provide for the needs of his date. This was in accordance with the courtly tradition by which knights held their lady in esteem, and were expected to come to the assistance of all women. A contemporary author may reasonably see in these roles a pattern of male "dominance" and feminine "submission."[5] However, a popular guidebook

1. B. Bailey, *From Front Porch*, 25–26.
2. Altschuler, *All Shook Up*, 69.
3. Skolnick, *Embattled Paradise*, 77.
4. Rougemont, *Love in Western World*, 118.
5. B. Bailey, *From Front Porch*, 110.

for young men from the era advises "always treat your date like a queen."[6] Nor did young women object. During the period they consistently rated "a knowledge of proper etiquette" highly as a valued quality in young men.[7]

Dating etiquette continued on the dance floor, where a young man was expected not only to request dances of his date but to occasionally seek out unoccupied girls for dances to make sure that they were not left out. Of course, the old system of the "once-rounder," whereby a girl was expected to never dance with a young man more than once, came to ruin amid the practice of going steady. At dances, couples often paired off, in violation of the social principles that had once held sway. Now some of the old dance steps also began to lose favor. While elements of the jitterbug persisted for a while in fast dancing, the sixties would see the growing popularity of dances that didn't allow for hand holding. The impact upon romance was enormous, as young men and women "watusied" and "mash-potatoed" at a distance, each to the beat of their own drummer. Fortunately, slow dancing remained a bit longer, although the fox trot, which had been popular in the swing era, generally gave way to young people simply swaying rhythmically to the music.

"Slow dancing" was invariably performed to one of the many romantic ballads that became a staple of popular American music in the postwar period. Romantic ballads had, of course, occupied an important place in the repertoire of the big bands. However, listeners now preferred the "schmaltz" turned out by crooners and violins to the "jump" tunes that were so popular a few years earlier. When Frank Sinatra left the Tommy Dorsey Orchestra for Columbia Records in 1943, it marked the beginning of an era of independent singers who would fill the popular music industry with romantic ballads well into the sixties.

We get a good sense of popular music at the midpoint of the postwar era by looking at Donald Horton's landmark 1957 essay, "The Dialogue of Courtship in Popular Songs." Horton studied the lyrics of 225 popular songs from June of 1955. The preoccupation with romance was evident from the fact that, if religious songs are excluded (yes, religious songs) some 90 percent of the songs were romantic. In fact, 83.4 percent of the songs deal with the issue of "dating and courtship," as this theme is expressed in what Horton characterizes as an intimate musical conversation between lover and beloved.[8] The value of these songs, from Horton's

6. H. B. Powers and Putnam, *Manners Make Men*.
7. B. Bailey, *From Front Porch*, 9.
8. Horton, "Dialogue of Courtship."

point of view, is that they provide a model by which young people were expected to learn the language of courtship and romance.

In the music, courtship is a "drama" that unfolds in various scenes and acts. It begins with a prologue whose theme is youthful anticipations of love. Examples of this can be found in songs where the young woman seeks a man who will truly care for her ("Someone to Watch over Me") or the young man waits with open arms for a partner ("A Girl to Love"). The courtship continues with heartfelt promises ("For Your Love I'd Do Most Anything") or pleas for assurance ("Honestly"). Fulfillment or despair follow. Lost love may begin with subtle changes in the romance ("Kisses Don't Lie"). This may lead the lover, in despair, to ponder whether a broken heart will ever live again—or find a heaven when it dies ("Where Does a Broken Heart Go?").

Two essential points emerge from the survey. One is the intensity of love as expressed in an array of poetic imagery revolving around heaven and earth, eternity and death, heady transport and endless tears. The other is the lack of overt sexuality. In the fifties, a reassuring phrase or a lover's touch are popular motifs, as lovers demonstrate their sensitivity to a word or a kiss. Songs like these speak of a time when love progressed slowly, moving from one state of anticipation to another. This was an era when romance played heavily upon the imagination of lovers, raising feelings to a fever pitch and lifting the entire event to levels of meaning difficult to imagine in a youth culture impatient for fulfillment and saturated with sex.

A very real threat to romantic song seemed to come with the appearance of Elvis Presley on *Ed Sullivan* on September 9, 1956. Elvis was, indeed, a phenomenon. But Elvis was also an expert balladeer, and rock and roll, in some sense, merely the return of those "jump tunes" that had lost much of their value after the war. It is important to note, too, that ballad singers like Perry Como, Nat King Cole, Frankie Laine, Dinah Shore, Andy Williams, Frank Sinatra, and Dean Martin had popular TV shows during the postwar years. With only three major networks (and one TV in the house), the impact on young people of these singers and the romantic ballads that were their staple was enormous.

As the big bands began to fade from the scene, a few band leaders found success by emphasizing strings to create a lush, romantic effect in comparison to the brass instruments featured previously. Among these was Percy Faith, who had the Billboard number-one song of the year in 1954 with his wistful "The Song of Moulin Rouge." Such romantic "mood" music was enormously popular into the early sixties, when "Wonderland by Night" (Bert Kaempfert), "Stranger on the Shore" (Acker Bilk), and "Moon River" (Henry Mancini) became enormous hits. By the sixties, strings had also become popular in teen music through the hits of Johnny Mathis, Little Anthony and the Imperials, the Shirelles, and country stars like Skeeter Davis and Brenda Lee, among many others. The combination of lush instrumentation and soulful singing was also key to Ray Charles's enormously popular album *Modern Sounds of Country and Western*, which includes plaintive romantic tunes like "You Don't Know Me" and "I Can't Stop Loving You," each of which became a number-one hit.

It is important to recognize these developments because accounts of popular music of the era have repeatedly demonstrated a bias against the soft, romantic sounds young people craved. Histories of the formative years of rock and roll give enormous weight to rockabilly stars Jerry Lee Lewis and Buddy Holly, and to rhythm and blues singers Little Richard and Chuck Berry, regarding them as figures who, with Elvis, essentially defined an age. What such writers appear to have forgotten is that the current reputation of these four performers far outstrips their popularity during the heyday of rock and roll. During the period, these four had a *combined* total of five songs in the Billboard yearly top-thirty singles. This is the same number as the Platters, who were notable for smooth, romantic ballads like "My Prayer" and "Twilight Time."

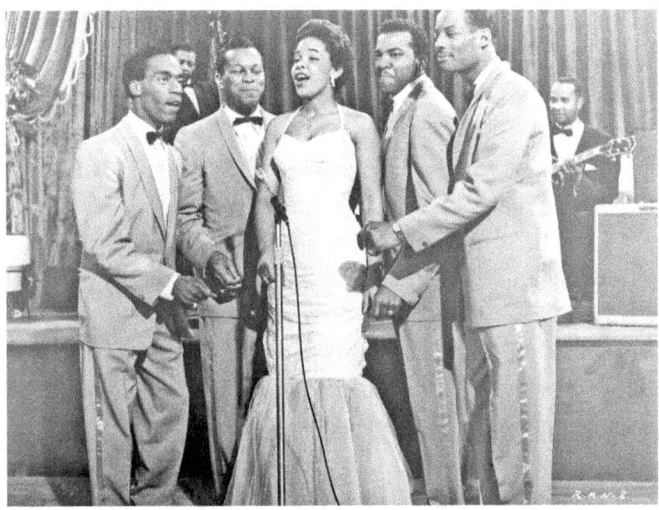

Circa 1955: (L-R) Herb Reed, Tony Williams Zola Taylor, Paul Robi, and Dave Lynch of the early rock and roll group "The Platters" perform onstage in circa 1955. Photo by Michael Ochs Archives/Getty Images.

From the early fifties until the British Invasion, doo-wop performers like the Platters sang many of the greatest love songs ever recorded. Doo-wop may be ignored by rock historians, who prefer the "sweaty sex" of R&B to the "hearts and kisses" of the doo-wop sound. But romantic love realizes that it is the "preliminaries" that speak to the imagination, providing meanings that last. This was apparent to one sixty-two-year-old fan of doo-wop, who put the matter this way in 1998: "There's no sex in it, there's no 'goin to bed,' none of that. You have to imagine, and I think there's something in the mystique of imagination."[9]

A young Shelley Winters once observed that she had detected "an almost animal scent" in only two men she had ever known. One was Elvis; Marlon Brando was the other.[10] Brando came first. Presley was reported to have worn his sideburns long in imitation of the rebellious biker Johnny, played by Brando in the film *The Wild One* (1954). Elvis's performance in his film *Jailhouse Rock* (1957) was also based upon Johnny. With his mumbled phrases and monosyllabic words, Presley even sounded like Brando.

In *The Wild One*, Brando's character is the black leather jacket–clad leader of a motorcycle gang who terrorizes a small Western town.[11] Johnny's love interest is Kathie (Mary Murphy), a pretty waitress whose father runs the local café. The disconnect between the pair is apparent from the first. When Johnny proclaims that sometimes "Ya gotta wail!" Kathie sympathizes by recalling being disappointed by a cancelled fishing trip with her father. The only real language the gang comprehends is the raucous jazz of the jukebox—music that is again heard in the film's scenes of violence. That such violence often extends to young women is apparent in Johnny's rough treatment of Kathie in what at first appears to be a prelude to a rape. Kathie's ultimate rejection of Johnny signifies the victory of love and romance over the allure of pure sexuality.

Johnny's character reappears in the form of the gang leader Buzz (Corey Allen) in *Rebel without a Cause* (1955).[12] However, the central figure in *Rebel* is Jim Stark (James Dean). Through Stark, Dean expresses the feelings of so many fifties teens who might have rebelled against their parents, but still held fast to most of the old values, including the essentials of romantic love. While prone to violent outbursts, Jim also

9. Runowicz, *Forever Doo-Wop*, 98.
10. Downing, *Marlon Brando*, 22.
11. Benedek, *Wild One*.
12. Ray, *Rebel without a Cause*.

possesses a soft, caring nature that is evident early on in his friendship with Plato (Sal Mineo), a smaller, insecure teen who idolizes him. When Buzz is accidentally killed, his girlfriend Judy (Natalie Wood) turns to Jim, recognizing in him not only strength but a tenderness she desperately needs. Unlike Buzz, Jim is a romantic partner she can trust—one she could marry. A highlight of the film is a scene where Jim, Judy, and Plato playfully recreate their own "family" in an abandoned mansion where they are hiding from Buzz's friends.

That tenderness and caring win out over sex is apparent throughout Hollywood films of the fifties and early sixties. In many of these, the man proves his worth by willingly sacrificing for the woman (e.g., *Roman Holiday, The Apartment, Gigi, Brigadoon, An Affair to Remember*). In at least one instance, the sacrifice helps to save the young woman from a seducer (i.e., *The Apartment*). Other times it comes at the expense of the man's previous life as a playboy (i.e., *Gigi, An Affair to Remember*).

An Affair to Remember (1957) has remained popular largely through its role as backdrop in Nora Ephron's film, *Sleepless in Seattle* (1993).[13] The film is no simple love story. It is the tale of a man's reformation in accordance with popular notions of romance. Only through true love is Nickie Ferrante (Cary Grant) transformed from an internationally renowned playboy to a man who actually woos proposed partner Terry McKay (Deborah Kerr); from an idler to a man who will work to be "worthy" of his wife; and from a selfish Don Juan to someone who remains true to his beloved despite what appears to be her crippling injury. Such behavior is unthinkable in one of Ephron's men, of whom a few hugs and a little commiseration are the most that can be expected. *Sleepless in Seattle*'s Annie Reed (Meg Ryan) must look to the other side of the country and to a widower (Tom Hanks) with a young son to find a suitable mate.[14]

In 1959 Hollywood responded to the romantic ideals of the young with the popular summertime teen romance *A Summer Place*, which included Percy Faith's enormously popular rendition of "Theme from *A Summer Place*." The same year, *A Summer Place*'s young lead, Sandra Dee, appeared in *Gidget*, the first of a series of teen romances focused around surfing. By the early sixties, such beach movies were proving enormously popular. The first (and best known) of the genre was *Beach Party* (1963), starring ex-Mouseketeer Annette Funicello and teen idol Frankie Avalon.

13. McCarey, *Affair to Remember*.
14. Ephron, *Sleepless in Seattle*.

Avalon and Funicello would be paired in a number of the films, which featured girls in bikinis and young people making out, but (despite Avalon's best efforts) retained a virginal quality.

An interesting feature in the beach movies is the evocation of *The Wild One* by the appearance of a group of bikers in black leather jackets. Although the group frequently stirs up trouble, their leader, Eric von Zipper (Harvey Lembeck), is a bumbler who serves as a parody of Brando's character. By the early sixties, the bad boys of the fifties were little more than a running joke. Then, almost overnight, all this seemed to change.

The main outlines of the sexual revolution are well-known. They include: the growing popularity of the pill as the preferred method of birth control not only for married women but, increasingly, young unmarried women; a general relaxation of moral standards among the middle classes, which was visible in trends like open marriage; an increasing leniency in the courts, evident in everything from contraception to abortion, literary censorship to divorce; new standards in television, music, the stage, and cinema—in the last of which, hard-core sex films became popular; and a general preoccupation with sex as a matter of public interest as indicated in the rise of the scientific study of sex, an increasing emphasis on sex education in the schools, and the popularity of self-help books dealing with sexual matters.

The implications of these developments for the meanings of romantic love were enormous, although the precise way the new ideas would play out was at first unclear. What was clear is that these changes encouraged sexual relations outside romance, heightening the disconnect between sex and commitment and depriving the activity of much of the larger meanings it had traditionally possessed. It thus fueled that culture of pure enjoyment that signified both an assault upon the old morality and the end of romantic love.

While it is impossible to pinpoint the beginnings of the sexual revolution, a reasonable starting date may be the year 1962. For our purposes, the year is important because of two events. The first is the publication of Helen Gurley Brown's immensely popular *Sex and the Single Girl*. The second is the release of the first of an enormously influential series of spy movies based upon Ian Fleming's popular fictional character, James Bond. Of course, the book and the movie are only part of the story. Each found echoes in larger cultural developments that would eventually separate sex from any essential relationship to romantic love.

Sex and the Single Girl is revolutionary in its rejection of romance and its embrace of sex as a pleasurable commodity. Brown applauds the Don Juans of the world for helping young women get over the romantic ideal ("white knight, white charger") and argues that a life of sexual escapades is preferable to waiting for "Mr. Right." In Brown's view, the young woman who maintains her virginity is invariably unhappy and, perhaps, unhealthy. For Brown, sex is a basic bodily function that suffers under societal constraints:

> Well, the truth is everybody starts out sexy . . . or with terrific potential. A sixteen-month-old baby girl is the prototype of sexiness. Watch her play peekaboo, wiggle her lovely fanny, or turn to give you a last melting look before wriggling off to bed. . . . She will be sexy all her life if nobody interferes. Unfortunately, in our society somebody nearly always interferes![15]

The era's widespread praise of the "naturalness" of sex was an effort to abandon the role of culture in turning the act into something "higher" and more meaningful through romance. However, by elevating the natural to supremacy, advocates of the new sexual freedom were also abandoning the one sure defense against the depersonalization of sex. This is apparent in Brown's views of men as "usable" commodities that women acquire through various forms of "man bait" (unless they come "gift wrapped" from a female friend). Even married men are useful as "pets" to add spice to a girl's life, although Brown cautions that "one married man is dangerous. A potpourri can be fun."[16] For their part, women are encouraged to market themselves as suitable sex partners. In addition to diet, flattering attire, and exercise, Brown argues for plenty of makeup. She also sings the praises of cosmetic surgery, citing both her own experiences and those of friends who have "bought" new faces and breasts and been delighted with the results.

The second important event from 1962 was the release of the James Bond spy thriller, *Dr. No*.[17] Compared to Brown's book, the impact of the movie—which was number nine on the American box office list for the year—may seem modest. However, in 1963, two more Bond films were released, each placing among the top-five grossing movies of the year: *Goldfinger* and *From Russia with Love*. Thus began a string of Bond movies that persists today, helping to shape the vision of romance among

---

15. H. Brown, *Sex and Single Girl*, 66–67.
16. H. Brown, *Sex and Single Girl*, 24.
17. Young, *Dr. No*.

generations of young people and making the series the most popular in cinematic history.

The basic formula for the Bond series was a mixture of violence, cruelty, and sex. The formula was not new, having been a Hollywood staple since James Cagney smashed a grapefruit in Mae Clark's face in *Public Enemy* (1931). What was unprecedented was the dramatization of the hero's numerous sexual encounters and his attitude toward the women he seduced, which ranged from cruelty to cool indifference to a temporary regard for them merely as mates. Bond was not a brawling gangster like Cagney. He was a man of shallow sophistication with a knowledge of cars, fine wines, and proper attire. Bond was also something of a hero since he managed to save the damsel in distress (not to mention the world) before seducing her.

Like the Ian Fleming novels upon which the movies were based, the Bond series tended to take a voyeuristic approach to the female.[18] We see this in Bond's encounters with his *Dr. No* heroine, Honey Ryder (Ursula Andress). In the movie, Honey first appears emerging from the ocean, two huge conch shells held provocatively at chest level in her outstretched arms. When she asks Bond (Sean Connery) if he is looking for shells, he coyly responds: "No, just looking." This treatment of women as mere sex objects continues in subsequent movies, where it extends to include a range of other sexually-laden names that typify the series, viz. Pussy Galore (*Goldfinger*), Kissy Suzuki (*You Only Live Twice*), Plenty O'Toole (*Diamonds Are Forever*), Holly Goodhead (*Moonraker*), and Octopussy (*Octopussy*).

Although *Dr. No*'s depiction of violence, cruelty, and sex drew the condemnation of the Vatican, the movie received generally favorable reviews from critics who regarded it as little more than an enjoyable diversion. In fact, the climate had changed significantly in the years since Brando's film, *The Wild One*, had been widely condemned. While there were many reasons for the changing climate toward sex, one major cause was the slow ascent to respectability of the men's magazine, *Playboy*.

Scholars have observed the many parallels between *Playboy* and the Bond movies.[19] In fact, the magazine's features corresponded closely to Bond's interests. They included: sections on lifestyle (including the three A's, viz. alcohol, automobiles, and attire); fiction; racy gag cartoons and cartoon features; a humor page and, of course, a photo layout of the "Playmate of the Month." For us (as for "readers"), the last was especially

---

18. Lindner, *James Bond Phenomenon*, 68–73.
19. Lindner, *James Bond Phenomenon*, 89–105.

important. Here was the visual counterpart to that dehumanization of women—and corresponding trivialization of sexuality—that typified both the Bond movies and the magazine.

In its success as the periodical epicenter of the sexual revolution, *Playboy* did not remain alone for long. In 1965, *Playboy's* hegemony in the market of soft pornography for men was challenged by the appearance of *Penthouse* magazine. In that same year, Helen Gurley Brown parlayed the success of *Sex and the Single Girl* into the editorship of *Cosmopolitan*, which soon became the center of the sexual revolution for women. There were many parallels between *Playboy* and *Cosmopolitan*. Each featured celebrities while providing readers with tips on grooming, fashion, and other contemporary trends. And most importantly:

> Both were out to create a new kind of person defined not by class or connections but by consumption. Both put bosomy women on their covers, the difference being that in *Playboy* sex was the prize and in *Cosmopolitan* sex was how you got the prize. In both, sex was a commodity.[20]

If we really want to understand the cultural shifts in romance that began in the mid-sixties, we need look no further than soul music. As a popular vehicle for romantic love, soul first emerged in the soft sounds of Sam Cook's "Send Me," which replaced Presley's "Jailhouse Rock" as the number-one song in America in 1957. While Cook and Ray Charles largely defined the music early on, by the mid-sixties, soul was associated with a variety of performers, including balladeers like Solomon Burke, Percy Sledge, Ben E. King, and Otis Redding; the "blue-eyed" soul of the Righteous Brothers; and the Motown groups (e.g., the Miracles, the Supremes, the Four Tops, the Temptations) whose repertoire of smooth romantic songs sparked accusations of "schmaltz" but delighted teens.

Signs of a change came with the emergence of soul stars Aretha Franklin and James Brown. Franklin's youthful struggles and rich gospel heritage fueled a remarkable vocal talent. Upon coming to New York in 1960, at the age of eighteen, Franklin embraced a variety of styles of singing before finding herself and emerging to national prominence in 1967, when her version of Otis Redding's song, "Respect," made its way to the top of the charts. Redding's rendition possessed a plaintive, beseeching quality that typified so many soul ballads of the era. Not so Franklin's version, which was highlighted by shouts of anger and pride that spoke directly to a new

20. Allen, "Woman Who Made."

generation of African Americans—and, more broadly, to young Americans who were growing impatient with war in South Asia and the slow pace of social change at home.

Brown had been an R&B favorite since the mid-fifties before enjoying broader success in 1965 when "Papa's Got a Brand New Bag" and "I Got You (I Feel Good)" both became big pop hits. Brown's new songs possessed a raw, sexual power that had nothing to do with the words (which were few and mostly inconsequential) but emerged from a frenetic performance style that featured screams and energetic dance moves. "I Got You (I Feel Good)" starts with an unalloyed shriek. This is followed by the din of instrumental riffs, drums that sound like machine guns, rapid running guitar patterns and a voice filled with energy and passion. As musicologist Robert Palmer has described the new music: "The rhythmic elements *became* the song. There were few chord changes, or none at all, but there were plenty of trick rhythmic interludes and suspensions. . . . Brown and his musicians began to treat every instrument and voice in the group as if it were a drum."[21]

Brown's new sound signaled the beginning of funk music, while his influence persisted into the seventies in disco, whose pulsating, rhythmic beat, solo dance movements, and inane lyrics epitomized the narcissistic, pleasure-seeking atmosphere of the times. Disco's big hits included Donna Summer's "Love to Love You Baby" (1975), which has more than two dozen repetitions of the title phrase, rendered as moans of pleasure. Brown's primal power also influenced rap, which, in the twenty-first century, is not only the most popular music genre in America, but the world. It is the ultimate realization of Brown's desire that every voice and instrument should be a drum.

Many young people of the sixties responded to the loss of the old values and a growing disconnect between themselves and their elders by attempting to give new meanings to sexuality. If sex was no longer merely an expression of love between committed couples, neither was it simply a pleasurable commodity. Sex, they believed, could now have much broader significance.

At its best, the counterculture understood sex as a vital part of a broader embrace of life that encompassed mind, body, and spirit, and included all of nature. In this new view, far from losing meaning, sex appeared to

---

21. Guralnick, *Sweet Soul Music*, 240.

gain meaning by being part of a larger worldview. The naked young people frolicking in the water in the documentary *Woodstock* (1970) is one well-known expression of what was essentially an Edenic vision. A similar scene in the counterculture classic *Easy Rider* (1969) linked this vision to the communal movement, where nature was encountered on a daily basis.

Yet however much one sought to get "back to the garden" (as Joni Mitchell's popular song advised[22]) human beings remained hopelessly divided between body and spirit. Achieving the union of sex and the spiritual was like attempting to educate a small child on the beauties of art by a trip to the museum. Although the parent may stress the harmony and proportions of the human form, the child seems to notice only the private parts.

The coarsening of romance was the result not only of the immaturity of youth; it was constantly being fueled by evidence of social injustice at home and military dangers abroad. According to the logic of the day, the obscenities of war and racial injustice were ample justification for obscenities of language and sexual behavior. This view was especially popular among the young men of the radical Left, who regarded the spiritual notions held in certain quarters of the counterculture as nothing more than false consciousness. These young men saw marriage as a form of private property, but did not hesitate to assert proprietary rights of their own. As one author summarizes their view: "In the radical organizations of the New Left, women found that they were often taken for granted: they were expected to answer phones, cook meals, do laundry, and provide sexual companionship—in other words, to be secretaries, housekeepers and concubines.... A Students for a Democratic Society brochure stated: 'The system is like a woman; you've got to fuck it to make it change.'"[23]

Things were no better at the epicenter of the counterculture, Haight-Asbury. One hippie noted that rape was "as common as bullshit on Haight street." Others described the scene in this way: "Guys were running around [the Haight] saying 'I'm you and you are me and everything is beautiful so get down and suck my dick.'" Artist and activist Shulamith Firestone wrote that a woman who refused to have sex with a man was called a "ballbreaker," or a "cockteaser," a "real drag" and a "bad trip." Some hippie men were not ashamed to pressure a woman to have sex as much as conventional society pressured her *not* to.[24]

22. Mitchell, "Woodstock."
23. Allyn, *Make Love, Not War*, 102.
24. Allyn, *Make Love, Not War*, 103-4.

The last cinematic gasp of youthful romance came in Mike Nichols's enormously popular film *The Graduate* (1967). *The Graduate* tells the tale of recent college graduate Benjamin Braddock (Dustin Hoffman), whose summer given over to pondering his future is punctuated by an affair with the family friend, Mrs. Robinson (Anne Bancroft). Benjamin views the relationship as nothing more than "just shaking hands" and soon falls madly in love with daughter Elaine (Katherine Ross). From this point he moves heaven and earth to get Elaine back from her parents, who are now determined to marry her off to a handsome medical student. Benjamin ultimately succeeds in rescuing Elaine at the altar, the couple escaping pursuers to catch a bus in the nick of time.

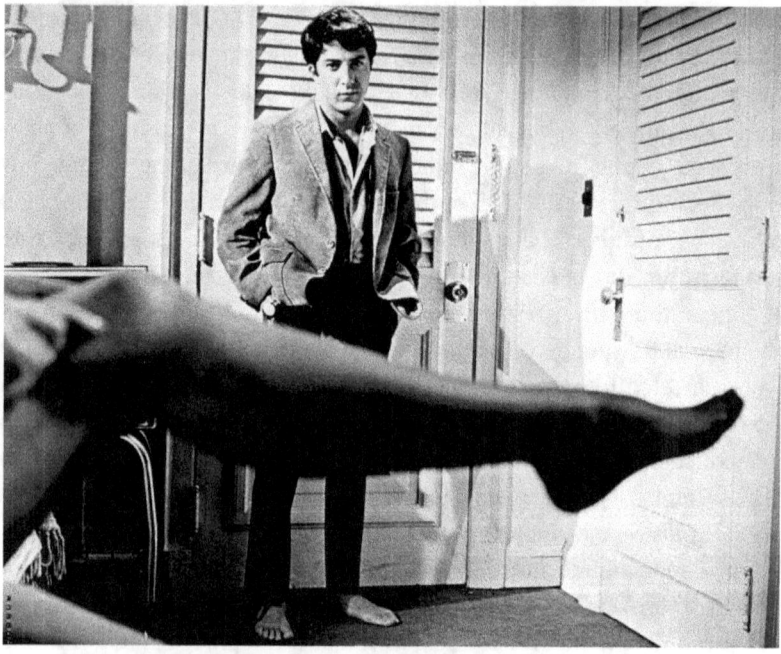

American actor Dustin Hoffman as Benjamin Braddock, watching his older lover Mrs. Robinson get dressed in a promotional still from the film *The Graduate*, 1967. Photo by Silver Screen Collection/Getty Images.

Critics generally see the film as a broadside on middle-class mores generally. But it is loveless sex that is the real temptation here, and Nichols has highlighted the issue by making Benjamin a more innocent character than he appears in Charles Webb's novel. The film celebrates the triumph of young love—over not only the soulless sexuality of Mrs.

Robinson, but the loveless sex of the frat boys and the raw sexual power of the strip joint. In the last, the attack upon innocence is dramatized by the humiliation of Elaine, dressed all in white, as the tassels of a stripper lash her hair to the accompaniment of a James Brownian drum solo. At this sight, Benjamin awakens as from a bad dream, removes his sunglasses, and again becomes the earnest young man he really is.

From this point, the defense of young love is the object of Benjamin's tireless quest to win Elaine. Now the little red sports car with which he pursues her is his charger, the gold cross he wields at the church, both his sword and shield. All this (plus the haunting beauty of lost love in Simon and Garfunkel's "Scarborough Fair/Canticle" and "April Come She Will") spoke to young people brought up on romance but about to enter the wide world of sexuality. Surveys from the period showed that, while young people were laxer than their parents regarding sexual behavior, an overwhelming majority were opposed to promiscuity. Most agreed with the situation ethicists of the day, who put the matter like this: "This is the difference between lust and love: lust treats a sexual partner as an object, love as a subject. Charity is more important than chastity, but there is no such thing as 'free love.' There must be some care and commitment in premarital sex acts or they are immoral."[25]

In 1966, Massachusetts's highest court decided that it could not be sure that William Burroughs's novel *Naked Lunch* was devoid of literary significance. The decision initiated an era of literary freedom that was mostly apparent in works designed for titillation and profit. Soon the venerable romance genre was taking love into the bedroom, as witnessed by the publication of *The Flame and the Flower* (1972). Now *Playboy* found itself competing with magazines like *Hustler* that not only made no claim to literary merit but often made the *Playboy* brand of erotica seem tame. By 1969, the courts had reached the conclusion that, if they didn't recognize obscenity when they read it, they probably didn't know it when they saw it either. Thus, during the seventies, nudity and sexual acts became commonplace in movies. The critical and financial ($25 million) success of *Deep Throat* (1972) signaled the widespread public acceptance of pornography. *Deep Throat* had little redeeming social value. However, Bernardo Bertolucci's X-rated *Last Tango in Paris* came with a stinger.

Last Tango (1972) tells the tale of Paul (Marlon Brando), who, while still in emotional turmoil over his wife's suicide, begins an affair with

---

25. Fletcher, *Moral Responsibility*, 138.

pretty young Jeanne (Maria Schneider). In a rented apartment over a period of weeks, the two engage in profanity-written, increasingly aggressive sex. No names or personal information are exchanged, in accordance with Paul's proclamation that he was better off with grunts and groans than with a name. Indeed, bestiality is a running theme in the affair, and it eventually leads to two controversial scenes of anal penetration—one by Paul, and the other (at his insistence) by Jeanne. The second, following Jeanne's professed need for Paul, serves as a proof of their love. During the scene, Paul makes angry, demeaning demands of Jeanne, to all of which (and more) she promises, "Yes!" Eventually, the relationship reverses course, with Paul pursuing Jeanne, revealing his hopes and dreams to her and proposing marriage. Jeanne will have nothing of it. When he insists on following her back to her apartment, she shoots him.

Many have criticized the ending, claiming that Jeanne's rejection of Paul is inconsistent with her previous behavior and that Paul's murder is simply a device to bring the drama to a close.[26] I disagree. While the murder may be a convenient way for Bertolucci to get rid of his protagonist, it is a perfectly logical way of killing off his idea. The problem with the erotic, as depicted in the film, is that it represents a way down-and-out of society that is ultimately untenable. Jeanne knows Paul (and wants him) only within their little world of lust, bestiality, and sadism—all of which serve as a needed counterpart to the insipid "pop" love of her boyfriend. In this sense, Paul's murder is a natural, if not inevitable, outcome of the affair.

Although *Last Tango* is a forceful film, it is not a truly "liberating" film, as critic Pauline Kael suggested it might prove to be.[27] Nor has it led to a wealth of filmmaking dedicated to exploring the untold wealth of sexuality. *Last Tango* is a dead end whose great virtue lies in powerfully demonstrating the limits of the erotic as a vehicle of meaning.

In the early years of rock and roll, the potential degradation of romance in popular song had been minimized by the general familiarity of youth culture to the larger society. But by the seventies, teenagers had TVs, radios, and stereos of their own. The coming decades saw the emergence of new technologies that would make entertainment even more private. This began with the Sony Walkman (1979) and led, through the development of computers, to the emergence of individual entertainment worlds where

---

26. Lev, *American Films of 70s*, 87.
27. Lev, *American Films of the 70s*, 80.

the impact of sound and image was more powerful than ever. And more pervasive. Research showed that, by 1980, teenagers between the seventh and twelfth grades had spent almost as many hours listening to music as they spent in the classroom between kindergarten and high school graduation.[28] As youth culture gained freedom from familial eyes, pop lyrics began to lose all constraints. Accompanying this change was the development of music television, which was commonly associated with the birth of MTV (1981). The MTV format was perfectly suited both to the anger and superficiality of the times, capturing these sentiments in images that largely bypassed the mind and spoke directly to the senses.

The changing nature of music in the eighties was heralded by Olivia Newton-John's big hit, "Physical," in which a young woman expresses her impatience with conversation and her eagerness to pursue relations at lower regions of the anatomy—and from a horizontal position.[29] Performed in a video amid scores of exercising young men, "Physical" could be said to capture the era's growing preoccupation with the body generally, and with sex especially. Yet "Physical" has a playful, tongue-in-cheek quality that looks back to the seventies and to the singer's performance in the musical *Grease*. If we wish to really understand where the eighties was headed we need to look at Emily Edwards's essay, "Does Love Really Stink? The 'Mean World' of Love and Sex in Popular Music of the 1980s." Edwards's observations are particularly useful when her findings are compared to the dialogue of courtship that we earlier observed in fifties song.

We may begin by noting that eighties popular music was not entirely without the exalted notions of love that dominated in the past. Any decade with recordings like Belinda Carlisle's "Heaven Is a Place on Earth" or the many love songs of Lionel Ritchie had not entirely lost touch with romance. But while heady transport could still find a small place in popular music it was now being slowly pushed aside. We get a clear sense of this by looking at the various roles of men and women in the songs studied in Edwards's survey.

Where young men might once have asked a young woman for a dance or a date, Edwards observed that, in the eighties, the role of seducer was the most popular, followed closely by that of victim. Women fared a bit better, though the roles of seducer and victim were popular here as well. In fact, seduction was not only the most popular game in eighties

---

28. Edwards, "Does Love Really Stink," 229.
29. Newton-John, "Olivia Newton-John-Physical."

song, but one in which either sex was becoming adapt. By now, the preliminaries of romance—i.e., the anticipatory dreams, the first meeting, the slow unfolding of love—were losing significance for young people who wanted to cut to the chase. This is clearly evident in music dealing with what Edwards tactfully refers to as "the first stage of a relationship":

> In picturing the first stage of a relationship, lyrics will often depict the couple's meeting and initial attraction to each other. Examples of this stage are reflected in songs like Joan Jett's (1982) "I Love Rock and Roll," in which the artist describes noticing a seventeen-year-old dancing by the record machine and asking the dancer for his name and a dance. Shortly afterward, she describes taking the young man home. The implications of the song are wholly sexual. There are no hints of a long-lasting relationship in the offing.... Similarly, Madonna's (1985) "Crazy for You" also emphasizes the sexual attraction of the first (and—in the case of a one-night affair—perhaps only) stage of a relationship. Madonna doesn't bother to ask for the name of her prospective lover, "I walk over to where you are . . . eye to eye, we need no words at all."[30]

By the eighties, the fifties mood, in which wayward kisses were often the theme, seemed a relic of Victorian times. Edwards observed that, in marked contrast to popular songs of an earlier era, the new songs rarely expressed any hesitancy about initiating sexual activity. In addition to casual sex, popular songs now touched upon hard-core subjects like fellatio and incest. A disturbing amount of music associated sex and violence. This trend, which had begun with heavy metal, found additional support with the rise of rap, which had evolved (if this is the right word) into "gangsta rap" by the decade's end. Now romantic relationships were not only unlikely to be viewed as ideal or even wholesome, but were sometimes equated with "mental illness, addiction, black magic."[31] Women often fared poorly. In fact, going back to the seventies, women were often viewed as "dependent and emotional or dangerous and seductive."[32] Now they were sometimes treated like commodities, or said to marry for money.

If wordless sex was increasingly the outcome of the end of romance among the youngest, soulless verbiage was the form it took among their elders. During the eighties, the language of the social scientist became

30. Edwards, "Does Love Really Stink," 237–38.
31. Edwards, "Does Love Really Stink," 242–43.
32. Edwards, "Does Love Really Stink," 232.

popular as young adults sought to navigate a sexual landscape where romance had lost its hold and analysis was the order of the day. By now, the notion of the "relationship" between men and women had become an important topic in a variety of publications aimed at couples in any stage of their affair. Books with titles like *Intimate Partners* and *Soul Mates* were not concerned with romance, but with how to build, repair, and sustain close friendships between men and women. As one young author said of her peers: "We do not fall in love, we build relationships."[33]

David Shumway has discussed the relationship ideal and noted how it differed from the old romantic notions in important ways. Where romance promised "enduring passion and spiritual transcendence," the relationship held out the possibility of lasting love based upon a deep, ever-evolving friendship. Shumway notes how the "relationship" story, as it took shape the movies of Woody Allen, Norah Ephron, and others, differed from the older "discourse of romance":

> If the premise of the discourse of romance is that love is natural and historically unchanging, then romantic stories need not, and perhaps could not, spend their time analyzing or commenting on love. Love used to be something that happened to the characters, its power lying precisely in its not being entirely comprehended by the rational mind. In relationship stories, on the contrary, the characters are almost continually in the process of struggling to comprehend their own feelings and actions, and those of their partners, and the patterns of relationships in general.[34]

The new ideal had little to say of passion, and tended to regard romance and "true love" with suspicion. However, it had much to say about sex. In the relationship ideal, greater communication and intimacy between partners was said to lead to the holy grail of great sex.

The problem of reconciling sex and the relationship ideal is the theme of Norah Ephron's enormously popular film *When Harry Met Sally* (1989).[35] The film tells the story of Harry Burns (Billy Crystal) and Sally Albright (Meg Ryan), who first meet as University of Chicago students to share driving duties on a trip to New York. Early in the trip, Harry makes casual reference to what will be the theme of the story by observing that men and women could never be friends because sex gets in the way. The

---

33. Hymowitz, "'L' Word," 27.
34. Shumway, *Modern Love*, 163.
35. Reiner, *When Harry Met Sally*.

film examines this notion while chronicling a twelve-year on-again-off-again friendship between the pair, who, in the interim, are involved in other failed relationships (i.e., Harry's marriage, Sally's long-standing affair with Joe). *When Harry Met Sally* ends with a blossoming love between the two and a New Year's Eve kiss to the strains of "Old Lang Syne."

Many regard the last as a powerful conclusion to a romantic tale. But Ephron's film lacks the spark nourished in an era when romance reigned supreme, and physical and emotional intimacy grew hand in hand through the rituals of courtship. As in her other films, Ephron has made her point here by placing her story against the backdrop of a classic Hollywood romance. In this case, the film is *Casablanca*, which becomes the basis of a heated debate on the trip to New York and makes a cameo later in the film.

Casablanca is the classic film chronicling the relationship between Rick Blaine (Humphrey Bogart) and Ilsa Lund (Ingrid Bergman), who meet and fall madly in love in Paris at the brink of World War II and rediscover each other many months later when Ilsa and her husband—famed Nazi antagonist Victor Laszlo (Paul Henreid)—stumble into Rick's café in Casablanca.[36] In their debate, Sally argues that Ilsa didn't really want to return to Rick, and that, being practical (like all women), she would prefer her chances with her husband. Harry refutes Sally by arguing that Ilsa would not willingly give up the "great sex" she has experienced with Rick in Paris. Both views signify a remarkable blindness to romance. The real question here is whether Harry and Sally will really be transformed by true love or (like so many of their generation) finally fall into one another's arms from sheer exhaustion.

Casablanca has to do with the power of love (not sex) as a driving force—not merely in the characters, but in ultimately knitting together what Rick refers to as a "mixed up" world. Love in *Casablanca* takes many forms. It is love of country that sparks a stirring display of French patriotism in Rick's café. It is a deep love for her husband and future children that impels a young refugee to assent to an affair with Inspector Renault (an affair that Rick will act to prevent). Above all, it is a love of humanity that forces Rick and Ilsa to forsake each other so that Ilsa's husband may carry on his campaign against the Nazis. The place of romance against this broader vision of life is wonderfully captured in the famous theme song, "As Time Goes By," which is the favorite of Rick and Ilsa.

---

36. Curtiz, *Casablanca*.

By comparison, the mood throughout *When Harry Met Sally* is one of a malaise that typifies postmodern relationships. We sense this mood in Sally's cool practicality and Harry's droll sense of humor, as well as in the ex-spouses and ex-lovers who move in and out of their lives like shadows, leaving little more than a little anger or a few tears in their wake. In a world that still firmly believed in romance, it is inconceivable that so many intimate partners should leave so little to remember them by. In the past, a Rick Blaine would react to lost love by burying himself in a little gin joint in North Africa. Such things do not happen in the postmodern romance. Harry's wife's declaration to him that she's not sure if she ever loved him seems to characterize the romantic feelings of all the young people in the film.

The last years of the twentieth century featured films in which popular British actor Hugh Grant seemed intent on separating sex either from marriage (*Four Wedding and a Funeral*) or romance (*Bridget Jones's Diary*). In this climate, those who still longed for the old values ran to Jane Austen for help. The result was the appearance of a host of works in print or on film that were either authored or inspired by the Regency period author. Among these, two treatments of Austen's masterpiece *Pride and Prejudice* stand out for what they tell us about the changing views on romantic love.

The first Austen adaptation was a BBC production starring Jennifer Ehle and Colin Firth that appeared on PBS on Sunday evenings in six fifty-minute segments beginning in January of 1996.[37] This spacing of the story was enormously useful as a stimulus to the viewer's imagination. By spreading the romantic tale of Elizabeth Bennet and Mr. Darcy over a number of weeks, the series was able to convey both the slow unfolding of courtship and the many uncertainties and upheavals that befall the romance of young couples. In the production, Darcy's smoldering passions are chiefly conveyed by his tortured expressions and by frequent difficulties conversing with Elizabeth. The tension and conflict between the two are rendered by the technique of framing their meetings so as to keep them apart, focusing our attention upon one then another so that we note every word and subtle change of expression. This is in accordance with Austen's realization that romance blooms from a close reading of word and gesture. The closest the film comes to sex occurs as the couple turn to one another after their wedding. Their kiss, having no place in Austen's text, occurs discreetly in the last frames of the film.

37. Langton, *Pride and Prejudice.*

It would be interesting to know the median age of the viewers of the BBC production. In any case, a few years later, moviemakers decided that it was time for a new film version designed to appeal to a new generation of viewers. This "postmodern" *Pride and Prejudice* (2005) lacks either the emotional or intellectual depth of the 1995 BBC adaptation.[38] It is film as spectacle, delivered at such speed and in such beautiful packaging that, presumably, no one will notice its many defects—chief of which is the absence of the deeper meanings of romantic love. With its rapid-fire dialogue and slapdash plot, the new *Pride and Prejudice* is designed for a youthful audience impatient for action and unwilling to imaginatively invest in what would otherwise be a slow unfolding of romance. Now the silliness of the two youngest Bennet sisters seems to have afflicted the entire household and to have spread to the frolicking partygoers among whom Bingley and Darcy make their first appearance. The filmmakers do retain much of Austen's dialogue. However, it is delivered at such speed, and interspersed with such lifeless prose, that the effect, rather than heightening the psychology of romance, detracts from it.

This postmodern version finally finds its voice in late scenes where Austen has effectively been jettisoned and Darcy (Matthew Macfadyen) and Elizabeth's (Keira Knightley) newfound love is rendered through stunning visual effects and beautiful music rather than subtle language and gesture. The concluding scene finds the pair in romantic conversation on the steps of Pemberley, their relaxed bearing and disheveled bed clothes indicating that this is a postcoital exchange. The scene is wildly inconsistent with Austen, for whom the culmination of the story is the couple's realization that they truly love one another, and that, the many obstacle's dividing them having finally been removed, a joyful wedding is at hand. Postmodern love sees things differently. Postmodern love sees love's culmination in a night of what Harry Burns would call "great sex."

The "relationship ideal" was only one way the icy hand of the social scientist was beginning to cool the heat of romance in the eighties. In response to the rise of AIDS in America, a group of researchers at the University of Chicago determined, in 1987, to make an extensive survey of sexual behavior that would replace the badly outdated Kinsey studies. The results, which were published in 1994, were enormously valuable not only as an image of America's sexual behavior in the period. From the vantage point

---

38. Wright, *Pride and Prejudice*.

of the present, *Sex in America: A Definitive Survey* is helpful in discerning new views on sex that would continue to grow in the twenty-first century.

In their introduction the authors point out that there is nothing magical nor especially complex about sex. Sex is merely "an animal instinct" and, as such, can be analyzed just like any other basic impulse. The authors even quote with apparent approval the views of television comedienne Roseanne Arnold, whose words managed to capture both the pronounced narcissism and diminished romanticism of the day: "The way I think about it is that anybody can have sex with anything. You're the one that's sexual. The person you're having it with doesn't do anything to make you one way or the other."[39]

In place of the old romantic ideas, *Sex in America* spoke of the "sexual marketplace." The notion goes back at least as far as Helen Gurley Brown. However, Brown's breezy style of writing conveyed a warmer, girl-to-girl tone than that of the researchers. Here, the term has callous connotations that the authors acknowledged may prove offensive to some. Undoubtedly it did. However, we will find that, by the twenty-first century, the notion of finding the best "deal" in the marketplace of relationships has essentially replaced the old values of romance.

The intent of the authors is apparent in the early chapter "Finding a Partner," which gave the lie to the old notion that we may fall in love with anyone in any place.[40] The authors argue that, contrary to such myths, the data shows that the vast majority of American men and women marry someone very similar to themselves in age, race, and education. This should not really come as a surprise. It is likely that the man or woman of our dreams will be someone of similar age, race, and social class. In fact, romance once occurred daily among couples who had the capacity to find "magic" where the social scientist sees only one more in a series of dreary tales of middle-class men and women meeting and marrying. This "magic" was nourished by culture in story and song. And if the social scientist wishes to dispel such myths, we may reasonably ask what meaning he or she proposes to put in their place. *Sex in America* tells us that our choice of a partner is likely to be a "strategic move" that benefits our "social network."[41]

Beyond this, *Sex in America* confirmed what most already knew—that younger Americans were having more sex with more partners than

39. Michael et al., *Sex in America*, 13.
40. Michael et al., *Sex in America*, "Finding a Partner," 67–87.
41. Michael et al., *Sex in America*, 53.

had their parents or grandparents. The old equation of "love and marriage" was badly out of date. While researchers found that 93 percent of older women (born between 1933 and 1942) married without having first lived with their partner, only 36 percent of younger women (born between 1963 and 1974) had not cohabitated first.[42] Sex with multiple partners also appeared to be on the rise. This was indicated by the fact that 90 percent of women in the older group were virgins upon being married or had had premarital sex only with their prospective spouse. By 1992, a third of young men and women (eighteen to twenty-four years old) had had two or more sex partners in the last twelve months alone.[43]

In fact, attitudes toward sex had changed more broadly, as evident from what researchers regarded as three distinctive groups in regard to views on premarital sex: traditionals, relationals, and recreationals.[44] Most of the first, which numbered about 30 percent of the population, believed that premarital sex, extramarital sex, and sex without affection are wrong. The second group, the relationals, were much more accepting of premarital sex but strongly agreed that sex without love is wrong. This was the largest group, at 44 percent. The recreationals, who numbered 26 percent, were more accepting of premarital sex than the other groups and much more favorable toward sex without affection.

Of particular interest for us is the breakdown of the numbers according to age and gender. For example, the percentage of men in the recreational group had remained fairly steady over the generations at about one third. However, young women (eighteen to twenty-four) were almost three times as likely to be recreationalists as their elders (25.3 and 9.6 percent).[45] In effect, sex purely for fun was growing significantly among young women. Still, the relational view of sex was clearly most popular among the young, with 47 percent of young men and 52 percent of young women falling into this category.

The other important feature of the survey concerned changes in the specific nature of sexual activity and the likely reasons for the change. One issue involved the factors that led to the beginning of sex. For older women, it was clearly affection, which was cited by 54 percent. Only 13 percent cited peer pressure. However, while 35 percent of young women cited affection, more (37 percent) gave peer pressure as the reason for

42. Michael et al., *Sex in America*, 97.
43. Michael et al., *Sex in America*, 102.
44. Michael et al., *Sex in America*, 236–46.
45. Michael et al., *Sex in America*, 236, table 19.

beginning sexual activity.[46] The survey further showed that young women were more likely to engage in oral and anal sex than their elders, despite the fact that most young women said they dislike the latter practice. And while only 5 percent of older women found the idea of sex with a stranger appealing, a healthy 10 percent of younger women did.[47] Numbers like these made the scenario of *Last Tango in Paris* seem more likely than would have seemed possible a generation earlier.

In fact, the researchers found that young women were now moving to the sort of sex men prefer, and they pondered the degree to which cultural change was responsible:

> The public world of sex, as portrayed in books and movies, increasingly is emphasizing the sort of sex that, our survey says, appeals to men. Censorship is weakening and anti-romantic scenes of raw, explicit sex, without the haze of romance, are starting to proliferate. Since these movies are made with an eye to huge box office receipts, the question arises: Are women really quite so repelled by this sort of sex as they have said they are?[48]

As to the last question, the data was suggestive. As we noted above, the young, moviegoing generation (eighteen to twenty-four) of women were much more likely to be recreationalists than older women. When we add this to evidence of increasing peer pressure on women to begin sex and to engage in sexual activities they don't like, the impact of external forces becomes clear. The researchers noted that nearly all women had fantasies that are "soft, hazy, romantic, that veer far from explicit sex."[49] It was men whose fantasies tended to pornography. Clearly, women were neglecting their own ideals to conform to the sexual fantasies of men. The only real question was the extent to which the view of young men was being shaped by changes in popular culture.

While the social scientists of *Sex in America* were providing a statistical survey of America's sexual behavior, another group was relating sex to love in a collection of studies entitled *Romantic Love and Sexual Behavior: Perspectives from the Social Sciences* (1998). Even here, where romance was the theme, a number of authors were applying "cost-benefit" and "investment" models in analyzing their subject. Others seemed to acknowledge

46. Michael et al., *Sex in America*, 94.
47. Michael et al., *Sex in America*, 146, table 12.
48. Michael et al., *Sex in America*, 150–51.
49. Michael et al., *Sex in America*, 150.

the end of romantic love in the not-so-distant future. In his essay "The Future of Love," Charles Lindholm explored the views of famed sociologist Anthony Giddens, who anticipated the eventual birth of "a new, pragmatic, non-transcendental form of relationship" without the "entangling ideals, commitments, or moral obligations" that have hampered enjoyment in the past.[50] In another essay, John Alan Lee looked to the day that love will be a commodity like computers and mutual funds—only more profitable. The bulk of his article was devoted to developing a typology of the various "lovestyles" and "sexstyles" that will facilitate this development.[51]

A different perspective, and one more consistent with past views, seemed to be indicated in Pamela Regan's paper "Romantic Love and Sexual Desire." Regan's essay was based upon a survey of college students designed to determine which of a total of 119 features of relationships was most closely associated with romance. Of these, sexual desire had the second-highest frequency rating at 65.8 percent. Only trust (80 percent) was rated higher. Compared to desire and trust, sexual activity rated low among Regan's students at only 25 percent.[52] These findings seem to be consistent with much that we have already observed. As we noted earlier, the creators of the old screwball comedies knew that it is unrequited desire that provided the energy for their romantic tales. Moreover, trust and desire are twins in the old rituals of romance, which recognize that these must develop hand in hand if romantic feelings are to blossom.

What would have startled many older readers is the extraordinarily low correlation among the students between romance and touching or hugging (17.5 percent) and kissing (10 percent). As we have seen, it is precisely such simple gestures, and *not* deeper sexual involvement, that defined romance in music and film for earlier generations. The kiss, especially, epitomized romance, in accordance with the old notion that the mouth is the conduit of the spirit and the eyes windows into the soul. This is why the great romantic films (e.g., *Casablanca*, *A Place in the Sun*) highlight the kiss, and focus so intently upon the facial expressions of lovers. It is here that both the poetry of romance and its spiritual ambitions come into focus, and it was by looking here that romantic story and song once made their claim to meaning. Apparently, all this has changed. For the kiss to be valued so lowly is a disturbing indication

---

50. Lindholm, "Future of Love," 19.
51. John Lee, "Ideologies of Lovestyle."
52. Regan, "Romantic Love and Sexual Desire," 104.

of how romance has lost its hold as interest has moved to lower regions of the anatomy. Young people today seem unable either to expect or to tolerate that slow unfolding of love that makes romance such a meaningful experience—one whose imprint remains strong in later years.

In its own way, this is as disturbing an indication of where romance was heading at the end of the twentieth century as any we have seen. And it supports the views of those social scientists who even then were looking to the end of romantic love—an end which, as we shall see, already seems to have come for most young Americans.

That the disconnect between sex, marriage, and romance continued to grow a generation or so after *Sex in America*, was evident from a 2011 study of sexual behavior among eighteen- to twenty-three-year-olds with the title *Premarital Sex in America: How Young Americans Meet, Mate, and Think About Marrying*. The title is suggestive. By now it was evident to any social scientist that mating came before most young people even "thought" about marrying. The authors even admitted that the term "premarital sex" may be outdated, since most relationships among the young no longer resulted in wedlock. As they discovered, almost 90 percent of unmarried young men and women who were currently in any sort of relationship were already having sex.[53]

Indeed, much had changed since the Chicago study. Sex now started earlier, anal sex was more common than ever, and oral sex, once considered an alternative to vaginal intercourse, was now just foreplay. In short, when it came to fooling around, the kids were not fooling around. Sixty-six percent of eighteen-year-olds had had vaginal sex. By the time they were twenty-three, two thirds had had two or more partners, and a quarter had had between five and ten.[54] There were limits, of course. Most young women thought that having ten or more sex partners was too many. Of course, they would never say so. Sex among the young was now nearly free of any moral connotations. In fact, almost nine out of ten young women agreed with the statement "I should not judge anyone's sexual conduct except my own."[55]

The new study showed that sexual economics had not only taken firm hold among the young, but had become more complex in the twenty-first century. However, one thing was clear. As to the question of how high the price of sex now was, the answer was "not very high

53. Regnerus and Uecker, *Premarital Sex*, 16.
54. Regnerus and Uecker, *Premarital Sex*, 25.
55. Regnerus and Uecker, *Premarital Sex*, 112.

at all." This was especially evident in colleges, where the numbers were decidedly against young women. In 1947 there were 245 men on college campuses for every 100 women. By 2010, the number of men per 100 women had shrunk to just 74.[56] Now, 20 percent of young men had engaged in sex on a first date, though only 14 percent of such relationships lasted as long as a year.[57] Hooking up, which was just beginning when the earlier study appeared, was now the name of the game on almost all college campuses—its chief virtue being, aside from convenience, that it allowed for no deeper feelings or commitment. There was also what the researchers called "friends with benefits." This involved frequent sex with a friend, or what the young called a "fuck buddy." Such relationships were almost always short lived and exhibited little in the way of passion, being more of a latter-day Benjamin Braddock and Mrs. Robinson affair.

Of course, some young people still engaged in sex within a romantic relationship. But the researchers discovered that these relationships tended to be less serious and of shorter duration than ever before. Less than one quarter lasted more than a year.[58] The primary reason for this failure, researchers believed, is that sex occurs so early, sucking all the mystery and romance out of the relationship. As feminist writer Naomi Wolf observed in recalling an interview with one young man:

> "I prefer to have sex right away just to get it over with. You know it's going to happen anyway, and it gets rid of the tension." "Isn't the tension kind of fun?" I asked. "Doesn't that also get rid of the mystery?" "Mystery?" He looked at me blankly. And then, without hesitating, he replied: "I don't know what you're talking about. Sex has no mystery."[59]

As the study indicated, today's acceptance of easy sex disrupts that coordination of emotional and physical intimacy that is vital to romance. As a result, romance is virtually dead. The basic message in relationships today is that sex and love are essentially unrelated. Thus young people move from one loveless encounter to another through the college years, into their later twenties, and beyond. When marriage finally occurs it usually has a "Harry and Sally" quality. I mean by this that it seems to be the consequence of exhaustion rather than the result of the spark of romance.

---

56. Regnerus and Uecker, *Premarital Sex*, 120.
57. Regnerus and Uecker, *Premarital Sex*, 60.
58. Regnerus and Uecker, *Premarital Sex*, 73.
59. Regnerus and Uecker, *Premarital Sex*, 75.

Premarital Sex also helps us understand how the current situation continues to be shaped by culture, which stresses the sort of sex men prefer while teaching young women that "freedom and equality" demands that they go along. In the early nineties, young people chiefly had films, books, and periodicals for reference. Now they have personal computers and the internet. In 2010, 86 percent of young men watched internet porn at least once a month.[60] Many of these men are addicted to it. And there are other difficulties. Porn websites depict sex as mechanical rather than affectionate, stress unnatural positions rather than the intimacy of face-to-face sex (the "missionary position"), and lead young men to believe that exclusive sexual relationships are atypical. Thus they further devalue sex in what is already a buyers' market.

The problem has become truly significant for iGeners, many of whom had sex introduced via computer at an age once unimaginable. In fact, many young boys begin watching internet porn when they learn how to disable the age filter on the family computer. In a few years, these children will begin encountering sexy selfies of young women of their age on computer screens. Little wonder that, as with the young man described above, all the "mystery" of sex will have disappeared for them well before college. Small wonder, too, that the number of young people who believe that sex among teens sixteen and younger is "not wrong at all," increased fivefold between 1986 and 2016.[61] It may well be that we are not so far from Helen Gurley Brown's notion of sexual activity among young children as we may imagine.

The good news today is that young people want to practice safe sex. The bad news is that this does not simply mean disease and pregnancy free intercourse. Today, "safe sex" means sex without any of the emotional contacts that may interfere with a successful career or limit the freedom that young people now associate with life in their twenties and beyond. One of the clearest indications of the death of romance is the inability of so many of the young today to contemplate "falling in love," with all the uncertainty and sacrifice it entails. Where their grandparents used to speak of the thrill of "falling," today's young speak of the dangers of "catching feelings" for one's sexual partner. Jean Twenge points out that the implication of the phrase is of a disease one would rather not have. As one iGen college student summarizes the idea: "The

---

60. Regnerus and Uecker, *Premarital Sex*, 95.
61. Twenge, *iGen*, 205.

worst thing you can get called on a college campus these days isn't what it used to be, 'slut,' and it isn't even the more hook-up-culture-consistent 'prude.' It's 'desperate.' Being clingy—acting as if you need someone—is considered pathetic."[62]

Little wonder that romance in film is now either dead or dying. Since its heyday in the nineties, romantic comedies have seen a decline at the box office as cinema undergoes a shift in style to "raunch-coms" like *Knocked-Up*, *Bridesmaids*, and *Trainwreck*. This, according to at least one writer, is in reaction to the "unprogressive cultural expectations regarding gender roles" and "idealized vision of love" evident in filmmakers like Nora Ephron.[63] That films like *When Harry Met Sally*, *Sleepless in Seattle*, and *You've Got Mail* should today be regarded as *too romantic* is extraordinary given that, as we have seen, they represent a dramatic decline in romance compared to their classic Hollywood prototypes. If Ephron's films should be relegated to "sci-fi" (as one young viewer has suggested) then classic romantic movies must belong to the "horror" genre.

When they finally do think about finding a partner, today's youth are determined to "shop around" for the best deal. This may be the most common economic metaphor in today's relationships, and it is worth noting that famed sex therapist, Dr. Ruth Westheimer, has noticed the practice among the young. When asked in a 2019 interview if her answers to any sexual issues had changed over the years, she replied that she didn't think so. She then added: "I'll tell you what has changed. I get more questions about people who, in a relationship, may be always looking [to see] is there something better."[64]

By 2020, the notion of the dating "market" was becoming more popular than ever as the young who were finally ready for a relationship began to employ not only the language of economics but the methods in looking for a companion. This is according to an article appearing in the *Atlantic* just before the COVID-19 pandemic struck America.[65] The authors argue that the economic model has become so ensconced in young people's thinking that it leads to a warped perspective on matters of "love." Specifically, shopping online now influences the way they "shop" for partners on dating apps that allow for filtering. Young people today think they know what they want in a companion, and that they

62. Twenge, *iGen*, 217.
63. Yahr, "Rom-Com Is Dead," para. 9.
64. Rothman, "9 Questions."
65. Fetters and Tiffany, "Dating Market."

should be able to order it up the way they would a new sofa or a Crock-Pot. They have forgotten (if they ever knew) that love is not a measurable quantity.

It appears that shopping for a mate today is really much like shopping for a car. As with a car, you want to make sure beforehand that all the boxes are checked. As with a car, you shouldn't expect to get more than about sixty thousand miles before trading it in. However, buying a car is not exactly like beginning a serious relationship. With a car, it's still easy to fall in love.

PART FIVE

Life's Journey of Meaning

THE NINETEENTH-CENTURY ENGLISH WRITER Samuel Butler once observed that life was like giving a violin concert while learning to play the instrument.[1] Most of us have a pretty good idea of what Butler was talking about. We all go through life learning as we go, inevitably making mistakes in the process. From this perspective, living seems to be little more than the struggle to obtain a skill that never really comes—or comes too late. The result is too often a sense of regret, failure, and the absence of any deep and abiding sense of meaning in life.

This state of affairs may seem to be characteristic of human beings generally. It is not. While all people make mistakes and suffer the pangs of regret, many take it for granted that life is still orderly and purposeful.

One popular expression of the idea that life has a purpose is the notion that events are guided by a higher power that values our needs while working for the greater good. We have observed this notion in the idea of work as a calling, in the belief that God guides us to a certain town or church, or in the belief in "the one" love that has such a prominent place in the lore of romance. I will attempt here neither to confirm nor dispute this idea. Each life is so complex, and touches so many others across the miles and the years, that it would be impossible to determine (much less evaluate) all the possible outcomes of a single event. I would simply note how extraordinarily rich in meaning life may be when viewed this way—and how much more likely we are to find (even in failures and tragedies) joy and a sustaining courage.

More commonly, the journey of life takes meaning according to the notion that individual existence follows an archetypal path that marks the major transitions (birth, puberty, marriage, and death) while extending

---

1. Bellow, *Simply Too Much*, 341.

far beyond earthly existence. Stories and myths illuminate this journey. So too, on occasion, do visual symbols.

Illustrations by Oswald White Bear Fredericks, copyright ©1963 by Frank Waters; from *The Book of the Hopi* by Frank Waters. Used by permission of Viking Books, an imprint of Penguin Publishing Group, a division of Penguin Random House LLC. All rights reserved.

One such image is the Mother Earth symbol of the Hopi. Frank Waters has described its significance in this way:

> The center line at the entrance is directly connected with the maze, and the center of the cross it forms symbolizes the Sun Father, the giver of life. Within the maze, lines end at four points. All the lines and passages within the maze form the universal plan of the Creator which man must follow on his Road of Life; and the four points represent the cardinal or directional points embraced within this universal plan of life. "Double security" or rebirth to one who follows the plan is guaranteed.[2]

By the last, Waters is referring to the Hopi belief that human life continues through a series of rebirths that proceed through the seven worlds and seven universes of the cosmos. The Hopi believe that, at death, the soul (or "breath body") is met by the god Tokonaka, who determines whether the deceased shall pass on to the next world or be consigned to

2. Waters, *Book of the Hopi*, 30.

the fire pits for purification. If allowed to pass, the soul is reborn into an underworld that is a mirror of the world he left behind. Life and death follow this pattern until all the levels of existence have been traversed.

The view that death is not an end point, but one more stage in a larger journey, is typical of traditional cultures. Such ideas are seldom subject to speculation. Says Waters: "The idea of personal reincarnation is no more explicitly expressed by the average Hopi than the idea of personal religiousness, honor and gain."[3] Elsie Clews Parsons observes the same attitude among a neighboring Pueblo tribe, the Zuni, where, in the words of one Catholic priest, it takes form as "a sense of assurance about life after death much greater than that afforded by the Church."[4] The important point here is the extraordinary sense of *meaning* that comes from the belief that life has an order and purpose that joins birth to death, past to future, time to eternity, this world to the beyond. It is in this notion of the journey of life that the answer to the question "What is the meaning of life?" is to be found. And the answer is all the more compelling for the reason that traditional peoples seldom think to ask the question.

Today belief in life's journey has eroded to such a degree that we may well ponder whether the notion still has any significance for the young. R. R. Reno recalls a discussion with a young friend that illuminates the views of so many today:

> A younger friend, agonizing over the choices he faced in life, asked for advice. I told him I couldn't help very much. For me, life has been like a train ride. The engine of strong cultural norms pulled me through life's stages: college, job, marriage, children. In its time, the train will take me to retirement and, of course, death. He replied, "No, no—life's not like that anymore. Now it's a sailboat that you pilot first this way and then that in order to make your way to the destination of your own choosing." It struck me as an exhausting way to live.[5]

Absent such knowledge of the stages of life, the decisions so many now struggle to make are not only exhausting, but time consuming. In 2000, researchers found that completing all the major transitions of life as these were understood at the time (i.e., leaving home, finishing school, becoming financially independent, getting married, and having a child)

---

3. Waters, *Book of the Hopi*, 235.
4. Parsons, *Pueblo Indian Religion*, 1:68.
5. Reno, *Return of Strong Gods*, 104.

was achieved by only 46 percent of women and 31 percent of men by age thirty. In 1960, the numbers were 77 percent of women and 65 percent of men—or almost twice as high.[6]

In most cultures, the journey of life is punctuated by rituals marking the stages of birth, puberty (or initiation), marriage, and death. In the following pages, we want to look at these stages in postwar America with frequent reference to traditional societies. Their example is useful because in this one instance the weakening of age-old practices was already well on its way in America prior to the middle of the twentieth century. Still, we will observe here, as elsewhere, a significant decline in meaning since the postwar years.

Some traditional cultures have rituals predating birth. This accords with the belief that the journey of life is a circle, that moves from death to rebirth and back again in endless cycles. As anthropologist Colin Turnbull points out, traditional peoples do not begin their life story with "When I was born," but with "When I was conceived." Life itself is thought to date back generations—even eons. The tribal philosopher, adds Turnbull, thinks "in terms of spiritual descent from the first ancestors, the continuity of one single life force."[7] Turnbull observes that the Mbuti of the Ituri Forest, in Africa, hold that conception begins the moment a child is wanted. Like many tribal peoples, the Mbuti also believe that the child-to-be is capable of hearing and learning. Expectant Mbuti women go on forests retreats, bedecking themselves with leaves and flowers and singing and conversing with the child. The purpose of these conversations is to inform the child of the world she will inhabit, and instill in her reverence for "mother forest, father forest."[8]

While rituals like these may precede birth, the act of giving birth is rarely subject to rituals. In much of the world, birth is one of the most private acts, and generally occurs alone, or the company of a midwife or female companions. In this regard, the American experience, where some 98 percent of women give birth attended by a team of medical professionals, is noteworthy for what it reveals about the available meanings of childbirth in our culture.

Robbie Davis-Floyd has pointed out how hospital births now are really rituals whose primary purpose is to stamp the imprimatur of

---

6. Wuthnow, *After the Baby Boomers*, 11.
7. Turnbull, *Human Cycle*, 26.
8. Turnbull, *Human Cycle*, 33–34.

technology on the defenseless body of the mother.[9] Davis-Floyd characterizes the postmodern American birth as an assembly line where the body is a machine and the doctors and their associates technicians. All this is one of a series of "separations" that have today destroyed the old ties of meaning. As another author has powerfully put the matter:

> The history of Western obstetrics is the history of technologies of separation. We've separated milk from breasts, mothers from babies, fetuses from pregnancies, sexuality from procreation, pregnancy from motherhood. And finally we're left with the image of the fetus as a free-floating being alone, analogous to man in space, with the umbilical cord tethering the placental ship, and the mother reduced to the empty space that surrounds it.[10]

The story of Davis-Floyd and her associates is another cautionary tale of the dangers to meaning posed by a culture where human beings today are often nothing more than machines, consumers, or statistics. Here, such "connections" as are now established are of little value for meaning—unless we believe that machines have the same value as people.

If the act of childbirth is rarely acknowledged ritually, the appearance of a child is universally celebrated with a variety of ritual acts. We now want to look briefly at such rituals as they occur among the Hopi and in traditional Jewish and Muslim communities.[11] This will provide a basis for comparison with common practice in contemporary America. It is a comparison we will pursue consistently in the following pages.

When a Hopi child is born, an ear of perfectly formed corn, signifying the Corn Mother, is placed beside it. In the culminating birth ritual, twenty days later, the Corn Mother is passed over the child as her mother lifts her to the rising sun, proclaiming: "Father Sun, this is your child." According to Muslim practice, the *shahādah* ("There is no God but God, and Muhammad is his messenger") is recited in each ear of the child as soon as possible after birth. This phrase captures the essence of the Muslim faith, and is, ideally, the last phrase the child will hear before dying. In Jewish tradition, the child's religious training begins in the womb, where an angel teaches it the whole of the Torah. Just before birth, the angel

---

9. Grimes, *Deeply into the Bone*, 22–23.
10. Davis-Floyd and Sergeant, *Childbirth and Authoritative Knowledge*, 315.
11. On Hopi practice, see Parsons, *Pueblo Indian Religion*, and Waters, *Book of the Hopi*. For Christian, Jewish and Muslim rites, see Holm and Bowker, *Rites of Passage*.

touches the child's lips, causing him to forget. Thus begins the lifelong study of the law that is such an essential part of Jewish tradition.

In contemporary America, the most popular baby ritual is the baby shower, which may occur before or after birth. At its best, today's baby shower is a valuable ritual in which friends and relatives gather to acknowledge the joy of the parents-to-be and to offer modest support in the form of useful gifts. Still, the popularity of the baby shower, with its party-like atmosphere, is a fairly recent phenomenon, and one that has much to tell us about the changing nature of meaning in America.

At least as late as 1937, the baby shower was clearly secondary to the ritual of christening. Evidence for this comes from the 1937 edition of Emily Post's authoritative book *Etiquette*. Post scarcely mentions the "stork shower" but devotes a whole chapter to christenings.[12] In the chapter the author provides details involving appropriate baby's clothes (white only) and food ("christening" cake and punch). Special attention is given to the role of the godmother, whose job is to remove the baby's cap and coat and clearly repeat its name to the clergyman for the christening. Such care befits the religious significance of the event. For it is only by immersion in water that the child becomes a member of the Christian community.

Given the importance of christening (or baptism, as it is often called) the decline of the practice and the emergence of the baby shower as an alternative for many couples is enormously significant. Among Protestants, this decline has followed the diminishment in church membership generally that began in the sixties. Despite an influx of Catholic immigrants, christenings among Catholics in America also appear to have significantly declined. In the Archdiocese of Philadelphia, for example, infant baptisms fell from about thirty-eight thousand in 1960 to only about eight thousand in 2023.[13] Meanwhile, there is a growing outcry against the practice generally from those who argue that it forces a child's obedience to precepts it cannot possibly understand. Once again, the individuality of the child is paramount—even when the child is totally dependent upon the parents not only for its values but its very survival.

Naming the child is another important birth ritual, and one that often occurs in the context of other early celebrations. In Hopi practice, the child is given a different clan name by each of its aunts on the morning it is presented to Father Sun. These names are maintained for years until one

---

12. Post, *Etiquette*, 277–83.
13. Gambino, "Decline in Baptisms, Marriages," para. 4.

is agreed upon—at which point the aunt who gave the name becomes the godmother. Muslims name newborn children at a ceremony known as the *Aqíqah*, which occurs seven days after birth. Here, the name is expected to be both beautiful and meaningful, with names of the prophets or compounds that include one of Allah's names preferred. In Jewish practice, a baby girl's naming ritual occurs on the first Sabbath after birth, a boy's on the eighth day, in the rite of circumcision. Custom has it that the newborn should be named for a close relative. Hence the prominence of the same first names in many Jewish families. Jews also hold that the name is chosen by God himself, and that it reflects the character of the bearer.

Naming also once had broader significance in America along the lines seen in traditional societies. In the thirties, forties, and fifties, family names were standard in America, with names of Biblical origins (e.g., Mary, James, John) among the most popular. This began to change in the sixties. Part of this had to do with a turning from tradition generally among young Americans. Therapists of the period also advised against giving children family names, arguing that names should designate the individuality of each child. The result has been a remarkable social change. In the fifties, one in three boys and one in four girls was given a "top ten" name. Now that number is less than 1 percent for both genders.[14]

The result is that, today, many Americans consider the bestowing of family names unacceptable. Now names are generally chosen according to trends that seem to place a premium on celebrity or uniqueness—until, of course, the celebrity or uniqueness wear off.

The current viewpoint was on display in 2017 in the public outcry following the rumor that celebrities Beyoncé and Jay-Z were considering giving variations of their own names to newborn twins.[15] The rumor turned out to be false, and the children were given names (Rumi and Sir) befitting the parents' notion of their own celebrity. Here, the entertainers were following the example of many American parents, who now regard naming as an act of self-expression and a means of giving the child a certain social cachet. Now there are even consultants who, for a fee, will troll the wide world of names to help parents win the baby-naming game. Hence the act of naming children is one more small chapter in the long-running story of American individualism triumphant—with meaning

---

14. Shea, "When Did Naming," para. 8.
15. Shea, "When Did Naming," paras. 2–4.

(understood again as a sense of *connection* to something of greater or more lasting value) the victim.

Some years ago the *Encyclopedia of World Problems and Human Potential* proclaimed the absence of rites of passage to be a global problem.[16] By rites of passage, the authors specifically had in mind initiation rituals whereby young men and women traditionally mark the transition to adulthood, receiving and sometimes professing sacred knowledge and assuming the responsibilities of adults in their society. At the end of the twentieth century, about half the world's societies had initiations for one or both sexes. Most of these were small-scale cultures.[17] In fact, Muslims have no initiation rituals. The Jewish *bar mitzvah* and *bat mitzvah* and Christian confirmation are sometimes regarded as initiation rites. However, these lack the emotional and physical intensity typical of initiation rituals in many parts of the world.

Today, the *bar mitzvah* (male) and *bat mitzvah* (female) generally follow the same pattern, the primary exception being among Orthodox and a few Reform Jews, who place limitations on the performance of the *bat mitzvah*. On a Sabbath following their birthday, Jewish boys of thirteen and girls of twelve (age thirteen for Reform Jews) are expected to take part in the weekly religious service as a way of demonstrating their readiness to assume the responsibilities of the faith and enter into public worship. In many congregations, this day follows a long period of study and attendance at prayer services. Thus prepared, the initiate appears before the congregation and reads from the weekly portion of the Torah. Further readings, prayers, and even brief orations by the initiate sometimes ensue. The *bar mitzvah* and *bat mitzvah* are followed by a party, where the young are showered with gifts such as jewelry, religious books, gift certificates, and money. In recent years, these parties have become so elaborate that efforts have been made to reassert a firm religious intent.

The Christian counterpart to the *bar mitzvah* and *bat mitzvah* is confirmation. In the early church, confirmation was a part of the ritual of baptism, and, as such, was a "coming of age" ritual. Today, it may take place among children as young as seven or eight. Confirmation is a means of confirming children in their religious faith in accordance with commitments made on the child's behalf at the christening. In some churches, the ritual is necessary for the attainment of full membership in

---

16. Grimes, *Deeply into the Bone*, 91.
17. Grimes, *Deeply into the Bone*, 108.

the congregation, and classes in religious instruction may be required. In the service, candidates may be asked to make a declaration of faith or answer a few simple questions regarding their beliefs. In the Catholic Church, the confirmand is anointed with consecrated oil by the bishop, who makes the sign of the cross on his forehead. As with the *bar mitzvah* and *bat mitzvah*, a party may follow the ceremony, though these are generally modest affairs as befits the young age of many initiates.

The Hopi rite of initiation differs from the Jewish and Christian rituals in a way more typical of small scale cultures. Here, the lessons learned are less intellectual and formulaic, and more dramatic and tactile. This does not mean that the Hopi shun religious instruction. Religious learning here is also a vital process, and one that occurs both in the family and in the many ceremonies that take place throughout the year. The difference is that Hopi initiation is intended to make a strong emotional imprint—an imprint that requires the infliction of pain.

Between the ages of six and eight, Hopi children are initiated into either of two societies: the Powamu Society or the Kachina Society. The initiations take place together in the yearly Powamu ceremony, in the kiva, which is an underground chamber with a ladder where Hopi rituals often occur. The ritual begins around midnight with the children and their godparents in attendance. During the ritual, the children are told stories of the sinful world they are leaving behind and undergo rites intended to impress upon them the role of Mother Earth (signified by the Corn Mother) and Father Sun as their true parents. Finally, a group of spirit beings, the kachinas, abruptly descend into the kiva, armed with yucca whips. All the children are terrified. Those who are being initiated into the Kachina Society are whipped amid general screaming and yelling. The initiation ends with the kachina chief's declaration: "I am the Father of all of you, yet as a father I have failed to protect you as my children, and it makes me sad to see this happen to you."[18]

Although the lashing marks the dramatic climax of the initiation, the ritual does not end here. The next evening the initiates are taken to a different kiva, where a beautiful sand painting of the whipper kachinas has been constructed. There, around midnight, a figure known as the Chowilawu kachina will appear, singing and jumping up and down on the painting to destroy it. When he leaves, the Powamu kachinas perform

---

18. Waters, *Book of the Hopi*, 219.

the bean dance, which is part of the Powamu ceremonies in which the bean plants are blessed and presents are given to the children. The dance will continue until dawn. During it, the Powamu kachinas unmask, revealing to the children that they are not really spirits at all.

The physical and emotional turmoil of the Hopi initiation ritual will be disturbing to most. But it is important to recognize what the ritual hopes to accomplish. By means of it, the Hopi mean to transform children into adults, with something of the wisdom and sense of responsibility needed to perform their roles in society.[19] "Tribal initiations involve pain and stress for a time," observes anthropologist David Maybury-Lewis, "but they enable the individual to move with a fair degree of certainty through clearly demarcated stages of life." Maybury-Lewis adds that such clarity and certainty contrast notably to our postmodern situation, "where families dither over their maturing and often resentful young, suggesting that they may be old enough but not yet mature enough, mature enough but not yet secure enough, and so on through an obstacle course that keeps being prolonged."[20]

And what constitutes adulthood? The rituals suggest that part of this is the ability to endure the physical pain signified by the yucca whips. There is also a lesson in the inevitable injustices of life, which is clear from the fact that some children are whipped and others spared, and some children are whipped harder than others. The godparents in attendance constantly point this out. Some may even ask to take one or two lashes for the child. However, neither they nor the kachina chief nor the Chowilawu kachina who destroys the image of the whipping figures can prevent the child from experiencing the pain and injustice of life.

Most important of all is the lesson that the gods who populate the yearly rituals are not really gods but men. The revelation of the kachinas may seem to have all the abruptness and cruelty of a Christmas Eve unmasking of Santa. But its significance is much deeper. What the children learn is that the gods are not tangible like men, nor readily subject to understanding or responsive to persuasion. This does not mean that they don't exist. In fact, nothing in the ceremony is likely to destroy the child's faith in his community or its gods. What is destroyed is the illusion that suffering is avoidable, and that the world exists to fulfill all our needs. In this fashion the initiation opens the child to a deeper realm of

---

19. Waters, *Book of the Hopi*, 215–24.
20. Maybury-Lewis, *Millennium*, 137.

experience whereby he recognizes his dependence on those around him and on those truly transcendent beings upon which all of life depends. Such depth and the radical sense of connection that follows from it are vital to any abiding sense of meaning in life.

An implicit recognition of the need for pain and emotional hardship explains why, in the absence of real rituals of initiation, many in our society have sought to create demanding rituals of their own. The results are invariably disappointing. Fraternity rituals or the rituals required for gang membership in many urban areas are notable examples. Both may add an element of physical trial and even danger to the initiation that most in our society will find unacceptable. Initiations by the young and for the young are almost always a bad idea. But without adults willing and able to instill knowledge in young people—adults who are respected members of society and who have the force of a compelling belief system to back them—the young are forced to make their way in life following the example of their peers or looking to popular culture for answers. Little wonder that adolescence now lasts through youth into middle age and even beyond.

Initiations supported by youth organizations, like the Boy Scouts, are much more worthwhile. Still, they inevitably lack the element of real hardship religious rituals may provide. Perhaps better in this regard are the various outdoor excursion groups like Outward Bound, who promise an experience that strengthens individual resolve and demands group bonding. However, here there is the absence of a larger, overriding belief system to add real depth to the experience. In any case, organizations like these provide opportunities that will, at best, become available to only a small number of potential young citizens.

The only place where initiation rituals of any real scope and substance occur today is in the military. Certainly the primary elements of initiation are here, including separation from larger society, the impartation of knowledge, physical trials, and the sense of being joined to something of greater and more lasting value. Military service was expected of all physically fit young men in America from World War II until the establishment of the All-Volunteer Force in 1973. It would be hard to calculate its loss upon the maturation of generations of young Americans.

That military service can be a powerful source of meaning for American youth should not be doubted. We get a strong sense of this from Neil Simon's semi-autobiographical *Biloxi Blues* (1984), a Pulitzer

Prize-winning drama that was made into a movie in 1986. Simon's story recounts the experiences of Eugene Morris Jerome, a young Jewish draftee from Brooklyn who has been sent to a military base in the deep South near the end of World War II. The movie vividly chronicles the many tribulations of basic training, including the physical trials, the thoroughly offensive behavior of a number of recruits, and the bizarre antics of an unbalanced drill sergeant. All of this occurs against the backdrop of the men's preparation for what they believe will be a dangerous assault upon the enemy in the Pacific.

Looking back, Simon's character recalls that the young men somehow found much to enjoy during their military days. Not that they liked the military—and certainly not because they liked the possibility of war. They didn't even like each other, though Jerome is surprised to realize, many years later, that he loves "every damn one of them." "I realize my time in the army," he concludes, "was the happiest time of my life."[21] He might also have said it was a time rich in meaning.

In most traditional societies, marriage has a very different meaning than it has in contemporary America. Although few cultures completely discount attraction between young men and women, marriages in the traditional world are typically arranged by parents, who seek out a good partner for their child. Here, too, the marriage ceremony is secondary to rituals leading up to it, which are concerned with achieving and cementing a favorable social and economic alliance. This goal is commonly realized by the exchange of gifts between the families. Gift giving often begins early in the courtship and sometimes carries over to the marriage festivities. In some cultures, the exchange of gifts continues until the new couple is firmly established in the community.

Like most traditional peoples, the Hopi place much less emphasis on the marriage ceremony than on the many religious ceremonies that mark the yearly ritual cycle. Waters gives no mention of it in his study of Hopi religion. In her study, Parsons briefly mentions it, reserving her attention for the rituals leading up to the event.

In traditional Hopi practice, girls often play the major role in the courtship process.[22] According to custom, a Hopi girl first makes known her interest in a young man by small gifts of food. Baking him a sweet

---

21. Nichols, *Biloxi Blues*, 1:43.
22. Parsons, *Pueblo Indian Religion*, 1:41–45.

corn loaf or carrying a basket of meal to his mother amounts to a proposal. The period leading up to the wedding is marked by frequent visits between the families, exchanges of food, and feasts. Parsons mentions a ceremonial hair washing of the couple just prior to the ceremony. She notes that weddings of a number of Pueblo peoples occur in a European setting but provides no further details. In fact, Western influences upon weddings can be found in many areas of the world where traditional cultures have come into close contact with Western practices.

Both Muslims and Jews have historically relied upon arranged marriages, in part because each has traditionally placed severe limitations upon interaction between young men and women. Each emphasizes the contractual nature of the union. In Judaism, this takes visible form in the *ketubah*, a document that lays out the financial obligations to the bride should her husband divorce or predecease her. In Islam, the contract appears in the form of the *mahr*, or marriage gift—a financial arrangement that is sometimes spelled out along with other pre-nuptial agreements prior to the marriage. Both Jews and Muslims give significant attention to the religious dimensions of the union. Biblical phrases and references occur throughout the Jewish wedding, which includes an address to the couple by the rabbi, who exhorts them to adhere to the traditions of the faith. In Islam, the service begins with a brief sermon setting forth the responsibilities and duties of marriage. The service itself is liberally sprinkled with prayers and recitations from the Koran.

In both Judaism and Islam, the "giving" of the bride and the joining of the couple by the officiant follows a pattern widely observed in other religious weddings. What distinguishes the two traditions from most is the enormous religious and psychological weight given to the union itself—an emphasis that looks back to the Genesis account of God's creation of Adam and Eve. Islam notes the importance of marriage by saying that Adam and Eve were created from a single soul. Jewish tradition says that Adam was an hermaphrodite who was separated by God to create man and woman. In either case, marriage is a restoration of that "one flesh" that characterized the original human condition. One cannot imagine a more meaningful way of expressing the unifying power of love between a man and woman.

In recent decades, marriage in America has seen an extraordinary decline in religious significance. This decline, which goes back as far as the baby boomers, has picked up steam in recent years. Religious congregations hosted 41 percent of weddings in 2009. By 2017, that number was down to 22 percent.[23] Favored settings today are country clubs, hotels, beaches, vineyards, rooftops, etc.—almost anywhere that is devoid of traditional religious significance. Disappearing, too, are the clergy, as civil magistrates or credentialed family members assume leadership in what was once a solemn religious rite. In fact, marriages generally are in decline. At the end of World War II, the marriage rate in America was sixteen per thousand adults. In 2019, the number was down to six per thousand—the lowest since numbers first began to be recorded in 1867.[24] This is yet another indication of how the old notion of life's stages has gotten lost in what is now an extended adolescence.

Where bride and groom were once key players in a sacred drama, today they are the stars in a performance whose secular atmosphere extends into the wedding venue, where noisy throngs and obtrusive photographers add to the spectacle-like environment. The brightest star in the wedding firmament is the bride. Today, the wedding is thought to be the highlight of a woman's life and the culmination of a childhood dream. The current view is reflected in a major growth in wedding expenditures since the postwar years. In 1950, wedding costs amounted to 9 percent of the average family's yearly income.[25] By 2022, that number was more than 40 percent—or some $30,000.[26] In order to understand where all this money goes, and to grasp the significance of the wedding in contemporary America, one only has to look at the many "bride" magazines currently available.

The overriding message to today's bride is to "be yourself" and make sure the wedding "tells *your* story." This begins with a careful selection of guests, each of whom is chosen on the basis of how well they will serve the couple's needs ("How can we be sure that we're only inviting guests who are truly there to support us in our own personal definition of marriage," one concerned couple writes a wedding advice columnist).[27] The focal point of planning is the wedding theme. This is an idea designed to capture the uniqueness of the couple, and it is supposed to be reflected in everything from the guest book and color palette to the wedding party ensemble. Personalized wedding vows, favored now by about half of married couples, and the perfect wedding poem further assure that

---

23. Lupfer, "Fewer Couples Are Marrying," para. 5.
24. Lupfer, "Fewer Couples Are Marrying," para. 3.
25. Grimes, *Deeply into the Bone*, 153.
26. Forrest, "Average Wedding Cost," para. 2.
27. Moorhead, "Brides Are Too Afraid," para. 8.

the occasion is unique. Today, even the right choice of last names may demand attention. How do the couple find a name that represents their union while preserving their individuality? The bride's magazine comes to the rescue with columns like "What's in a Name? YOU DECIDE" (deceptively located in a section of the periodical labeled "Traditions").[28] Here we learn of the creative couple who decided to merge their last names to form a new name. Another bride adopted the groom's name, but found consolation by changing her middle name to one she liked better.

Of chief concern, of course, is the wedding dress. Today's wedding dresses are usually white (as if this symbolism still mattered in a society where 84 percent of couples live together before marriage) but are otherwise very different from dresses of the past. Wedding dresses of the fifties were invariably long, had modest necklines, and came with cover-up accessories like a bridal veil and (often) full-length gloves. American brides of 2019 often dressed as if preparing for a swim—or something else. Brides' dresses in that year included sheer, low-cut, strapless affairs, or possessed open sides, bare backs or bare midriffs. Feathered minidresses were a popular style. Others included a lace jump suit and a very low-cut, mid-length gown with 3D embellishments. The newest wedding footwear for 2019 had four-inch heels, metallic shimmer, crystals, and feathers.

The notion that it's "all about you" continues to the lavish wedding reception, which will consume the lion's share of expenditures. Older Americans may remember when wedding receptions were modest affairs held in church basements with homemade dishes and amateurish decor. Those days are long gone. Today's reception begins with the introduction of the wedding party in a manner consistent with the naming of Academy Award winners or the starting lineups at a major sports competition. Some brides and grooms even opt for fireworks. Many couples today insist on their favorite dishes for the catered dinner while others will have a signature cocktail. Old traditions like the tossing of the garter or bouquet are now giving way to rituals that highlight the wedding party while rewarding onlookers with deafening music and an abundance of alcohol.

Expenditures increase at the "destination" wedding or should the bride otherwise choose to make extravagant financial demands on her guests. However, to do so runs the risk of being labeled a "Bridezilla." This term, which dates to the nineties, is widely applied now to any bride who loses her perspective amid all the festivities. Real-life "Bridezillas" include

28. Baragona, "What's in a Name."

one young woman who demanded that guests pay a $1,500 entrance fee—and then cancelled not only the wedding but the marriage when they refused.[29] At least she saved herself the cost of the honeymoon. Couples now have no intention of spending a few days at Niagara Falls or the beach. Preferred honeymoon venues in 2019 included a tent in the jungles of Kenya (complete with "claw footed tub and fully stocked minibar"[30]) or a tree house in India, which came with Bengal tigers and the modern amenities.[31] Once again, we are far from the family-oriented rituals of the past. At one time, honeymoons in America were primarily seen as an opportunity for the new bride and groom to visit far-flung family members.[32]

Today some couples choose to express their uniqueness in more creative ways. Where the traditional wedding was a purely religious affair, many today find inspiration in sci-fi or the macabre. This is apparent from a *Washington Post* series, "On Love," which highlights such festivities. One of these couples chose to get married in the Pharmacy Museum in New Orleans, where the bride, sporting emerald-green hair, laughed as the groom gave a speech with lines from *The Nightmare Before Christmas*. The wedding night ended with a visit to a "vampire-inspired" speakeasy. The party continued days later, when the couple held a get together for friends at a large D.C.-area cemetery. There the bride wore a white wig, a wine-red dress (with accompanying body suit), and zombie-inspired makeup. Guests to this affair appeared in costume. Many of them sported skull makeup.[33]

That weddings like these can be meaningful should not be doubted. Like major sports events, a big wedding is now one of the few real avenues of meaning still available to Americans. As in sports, it is the nature of these meanings and what they tell us about our culture that are the real issue. In the past, weddings were chiefly family and religious affairs, designed to link participants to kin, community and the sacred. Here, attention moved in two directions simultaneously—inward, toward the couple, and back out again to those larger social values represented by family, church, and community. Expectations followed the same pattern: much was given the couple, but much also expected from them in terms of their relationships to each other, to kith and kin, and to God.

29. Moorhead, "Brides Are Too Afraid," para. 4.
30. Bouselli, "Your Safari Adventure," 129.
31. Bouselli, "Your Safari Adventure," 130.
32. Grimes, *Deeply into the Bone*, 158.
33. McDonough, "Till Death," paras. 19–22.

In a typical wedding today, all attention is on the pair and "their story." Now a wedding's lasting value comes in the form of memories available from a copious record of events. But is this a reasonable exchange—mementoes of a glorious moment for an ongoing, larger world? It is hard to escape the notion that all our effort and expense is really an attempt to give weddings the larger meanings they now lack. Today's weddings may, indeed, be as unique as the individuals whose union they celebrate. But the postmodern tale they tell of the lure of spectacle, and of people with few large and lasting bonds of meaning is commonplace.

In a popular PBS series some years ago, anthropologist David Maybury-Lewis made the point that the value placed upon the elderly and the meanings given death are the most notable features distinguishing traditional cultures from our own.[34] In the traditional world, wisdom is thought to come with age, and is valued more highly than that wealth of trivia that for us usually passes for knowledge. In small-scale societies, the elderly are regarded as founts of information regarding tribal lore and etiquette, kin and community—not to mention the natural world upon which survival depends. In these societies the elderly are peacemakers and are prized for their judgment and interpersonal skills. Much of this knowledge is passed on to children, whom the elderly routinely care for, freeing their parents for necessary physical labor.

Above all, the aged are regarded as sources of sacred knowledge and power. This derives from the fact that, being closer to death, they are closer to the realm of the spirit. Turnbull observes this among the Mbuti, where the aged are expected to go on long sojourns in the forest to commune with "mother forest, father forest," much as they did as children. Turnbull sees a parallel between Mbuti practice and Hinduism, as laid out in the ancient *Dharma* texts.[35] Each tradition regards adulthood "as little more than a profane interlude" between a youth devoted to the acquisition of sacred knowledge and old age, when this knowledge takes hold in increased time spent in solitude and meditation (a stage Hinduism refers to as that of the *vanaprastha* or "forest dweller.") "In both these societies," says Turnbull, "old age is not seen as an end to life, but as a source of continuity, linking the future with the past, death to life."[36] Such notions contrast notably with the views held in contemporary America,

34. Maybury-Lewis, *Millennium*, 142.
35. Turnbull, *Human Cycle*, 228.
36. Turnbull, *Human Cycle*, 228.

where aging is a great evil, and the elderly are often pushed aside as reminders of a death that continues to lose the meanings it once had.

In the early twentieth century, aging Americans typically lived in the family home, surrounded by children and grandchildren. Even in the postwar years, multiple generations (not to mention uncles, aunts, and cousins) often lived in the same communities—or at least close enough that children and parents could visit elderly and ailing relatives on a regular basis. Here, they would hear the old stories and songs, learn about their kin, and receive any wisdom their elders had to offer. Here, too, they would come face-to-face with aging and the approach of death, since many deaths still occurred in the home.

Increasing mobility put an end to this arrangement, while a growing embrace of youth culture led to the removal of the old from a prominent place in society. Like so much else, this change dates to the early sixties, when the first retirement communities began to spring up across America. Since then, we have seen a continuing marginalization of the elderly, resulting in the severance of those ties between generations that are vital to meaning. When the elderly are present today, their primary role is to observe youthful athletic performances rather than to teach. This is an extraordinary change, and one that highlights both the enormous weight we now give to youth and physical activity, and the enormous lack of regard we have for age and the knowledge and wisdom that may come with it.

This tendency to ignore aging and deprive it of its significance carries over to contemporary rituals of death—as we will see from a comparison of traditional death rites and the postmodern celebrations that have begun to take their place. In the latter, too, the elderly seem to have no place. Today's popular death events are designed not only with no regard for the sacred but with a party-like atmosphere more appropriate to the young.

For traditional Jews and Muslims, death marks a transition from this world to the next and is regarded as a time for reaffirming the principles of the faith. At the approach of death, Jews should, ideally, confess their sins and end life by uttering the *shema*, which affirms the sovereignty and oneness of God. Muslims believe that the *shahādah* should be the last words on a dying mans lips. Both traditions reject embalming and the associated ritual of visitation. In both, the body is washed by relatives or designated community members, with burial to follow soon afterward. Muslims have specific rituals for cleansing and preparing the body, which will be wrapped in a simple white shroud. Jews place the body in a plain wooden coffin. Services for both typically include prayers and Scripture readings, as well as a few rituals distinctive of each faith.

After services in the mosque or synagogue, mourners proceed to the graveside, where more prayer and Scripture readings follow. It is here that the Jewish prayer the *kaddish* is recited for the first time. In both traditions, family members throw a handful of soil into the grave. Muslim mourners often repeat the *Fātihah* upon leaving the grave, and may repeat it forty paces further on. Tradition has it that, at this point, the angels Munkir and Nakir will appear to inform the deceased of their fate in the afterlife.

An important feature of death among both Jews and Muslims is the prescribed rituals of mourning. For Muslims, the first three days, during which family members are visited and comforted, are critical. Forty days after the burial, relatives and friends will gather again to remember the deceased and to offer prayers and readings from the Qur'ān. The Jewish mourning period is longer and more complex. Jews typically mark the first seven days of mourning with a variety of prohibitions and rituals. A lesser manner of mourning extends another thirty days. In Judaism, sons are expected to say the *kaddish* for eleven months, to help the soul rise to heaven. Here, the death anniversary is typically marked by rituals such as a memorial graveside service.

In postmodern America, medical technology, in close alliance with the funeral industry, has largely removed the dead from family and obscured the significance of death as a religious ritual. Not that this is all to the bad. Death is nearly always sudden and uncertain, and few would want to forgo the opportunity for medical intervention to help the ailing and ease their pain. Nor do many begrudge the role of professionals in preparing the body—a task that once fell to family and kin. The problem has to do with our inability to achieve a meaningful relation to death by acknowledging its reality while affirming the possibility of something greater that gives death meaning.

For traditional Catholics, death is the beginning of a journey that hopefully culminates in the soul's acceptance among the communion of saints in the presence of God. The journey starts with the ritual of the last rites that is comprised of the confession of sin, absolution, the anointing with oil, and last communion. These are all preparation for the journey—a notion that is apparent from the Latin term for last communion, the *viaticum*, which refers to provisions for a journey.[37] The physical journey traditionally involves a transition from home to church to cemetery. At the heart of this is the Mass for the dead, whose musical setting is referred to as the requiem Mass.

Today's requiem Mass typically takes either of two forms: the ordinary (new) rite or the extraordinary (old) rite. The difference dates to Vatican II and signifies a shift in viewpoint that is clear in the services themselves. The old rite is more severe and solemn. Emphasis here is upon the fearful and awe-inspiring nature of death—a mood that is apparent, for example, in the Collect, where participants pray not to be "delivered into the hands of the enemy" and to escape "the pains of hell."[38] At the center of the service is the *Dies Irae*, a beautiful but fearful segment that keeps attention focused on the power of God, the certainty of judgment and the terrible punishments that may follow. In the ordinary or new rite, emphasis has shifted to the love of God and the joys of the world to come. While the old ceremony puts the fear of God into believers, the new is intended to comfort through the message that God's mercy triumphs over all. This change accords with a broader tendency in organized religion to move from a fearful God to a God who is all love and forgiveness. Although the result is a loss in that powerful sense of the "otherness" of God, the Mass for the dead remains a vital service. By means of it, the reality of death becomes apparent while the event becomes meaningful as part of a larger, cosmic process that unfolds under the watchful eyes of the Creator.

In the mainline Protestant denominations, a religious atmosphere is created in the funeral service through the combination of prayer, Scripture reading, a brief homily, and the singing of beloved sacred music. This serves to remind the faithful of the centrality of the faith in death as in life and confirms the promise of everlasting life that is at the core of the Christian message. However, in comparison to Catholics, mainline Protestants have a tepid embrace of the afterlife that seriously limits the meanings found in death. We may say that most Protestants choose to keep one foot in the postmodern world, while holding out hope in something more. A traditional Catholic's allegiance is stronger and clearer. As one author explains:

---

37. Holm and Bowker, *Rites of Passage*, 54.
38. Phillips, "Old Rite Requiem," para. 5.

In the Catholic tradition the liturgy for the dead refers to the journey the soul undertakes as it moves to God and is welcomed by the saints. . . . The Protestant tradition has been far less ready to talk about and assume any knowledge of what awaits any particular individual; for this reason the prayers for the dead which are central to the Catholic tradition are largely missing among Protestants.[39]

Of course, any sort of religious setting is likely to prove more meaningful than the life celebrations that today seem to be elbowing the traditional church funeral aside. This should come as no surprise. Many baby boomers long ago forsook any notion of a "higher" reality for their own reflection in a mirror. Celebrations like these may be much like today's nonreligious weddings: plenty of laughter and gaiety, lots to eat and drink, lavish attention on the honored and, ideally, a theme or motif to hold it all together. Here, too, the message is individualistic and secular rather than communal and sacred. Little wonder that, in a 2023 website noting the best funeral songs for an older generation of Americans, Frank Sinatra's big hit "My Way" leads the list.[40]

Some celebrations may even go to macabre lengths. Evidence for this comes from the cable TV show *Best Funerals Ever*, which began airing in 2013. In one of these funerals, the body of the deceased was put on display atop a motorcycle. In another, she appeared at her party posed upright in a pink boa with a glass of champagne. Sometimes, the casket has the leading role in these affairs. In the celebration for a deceased bowler, the casket was sent careening down the alley for a strike. The death of one Olympic athlete saw the casket "sprinting" down the track to receive a gold medal. In the funeral of one chocolate lover, all were invited to take part as the casket was dipped in chocolate so that everyone could have a taste.[41]

Today, even cremations can acquire such personal touches. Now a family member may turn to a tattoo artist who will mix the ashes with ink to create a custom-made tattoo. One Alabama company will even put the ashes in ammunition so you can "blast them to the afterlife in a one-gun salute."[42]

At least the former appears to have some lasting value.

39. Holm and Bowker, *Rites of Passage*, 56.
40. Richard Martin, "21 Best Funeral Songs," para. 3.
41. See, e.g., https://www.amazon.com/Best-Funeral-Ever-Season-1/dp/B00H2E5T1W.
42. Pott, "6 Funeral Trends," para. 7.

Conclusion: American Dystopia and the Hero of Meaning

IN CHRONICLING A RAPIDLY approaching society without meaning I may be said to be painting a dystopian picture. I am not—at least as the notion of dystopia is generally understood today. In contemporary America, the term designates a genre of literature and film that usually views future social dysfunction through a political lens. Notable examples of this are Margaret Atwood's *The Handmaid's Tale* and Suzanne Collins's *The Hunger Games*. Atwood's book envisions a dystopian America that results from a takeover by religious fundamentalists. Collins's book sees it arising from a division between "haves" and "have nots." Each book rated in the top forty in a survey to determine the most popular one hundred novels that was taken in conjunction with PBS's 2018 television series *The Great American Read*.[43] Each has spawned popular films, with Atwood's story being expanded to a lengthy TV series.

This political focus also helps explain the continuing popularity of George Orwell's classic, *1984*, which was the highest-rated dystopian novel in the PBS survey at number eighteen. Books like these appeal because they assure us that things will never deteriorate as long as people like us—the "good" people—remain vigilant. Here, the enemy is "out there" rather than in ourselves. I believe that a truly dystopian novel would see things differently. Such a novel would foresee a future where there is no salvation because people have fundamentally changed. This society may be orderly and pleasant enough and its inhabitants content. However, it would be a society virtually without meaning.

The best work of this sort, in my view, is Aldous Huxley's *Brave New World*. This dystopian classic was nowhere to be found in the one

---

43. Great American Read, "Read the 100 List."

hundred books on PBS's list. However, it occupied a prominent place in the Modern Library's 1998 survey of the best twentieth-century novels.[44] The Modern Library list was determined by a panel of literary luminaries and intellectuals, including William Styron, A. S. Byatt, Vartan Gregorian, and Daniel Bornstein. Here, *Brave New World* placed number five—amid the works of writers like James Joyce and William Faulkner.

Huxley's book was likely omitted from the more recent survey because the dystopia it characterizes was already taking shape in America by the end of the twentieth century. Readers who took part in the PBS survey likely turned from the novel the way they may turn from an unflattering photo of themselves. We don't intend to do this. We intend to look at *Brave New World* in order to better understand the new type of human being assuming form in the twilight of American culture. This human being is not a victim of political tyranny. With few exceptions, he or she has readily embraced the beliefs and values of a culture where meaning is clearly in retreat.

The extraordinary relevance of Huxley's book may not be apparent from the first pages. Here, the action takes place in the Central London Hatchery and Conditioning Center, where a tour for new students is being led by the Director of Hatcheries and Conditioning (the D.H.C.). In the center, human embryos are genetically engineered, "decanted," and conditioned according to a caste system that extends from a small number of Alpha Plus elites all the way to Epsilons, who are bred in large, identical masses and conditioned to perform the most basic, mundane tasks. The result is a complete elimination of the notion of the family that may seem improbable to many readers today.

It is worth recalling, however, the steps we have taken in this direction in the decades since *Brave New World* appeared in 1932. These include a sexual revolution that has markedly destabilized the family, brought birth control to unmarried young women (as in *Brave New World*), and made abortion available to many (much as in *Brave New World*). We have also witnessed the increasing role of technology in pregnancy and childbirth. The result of these developments is a series of "separations" (e.g., "milk from breasts, mothers from babies, fetuses from pregnancies, sexuality from procreation, pregnancy from motherhood" in the words of

---

44. Paul Lewis, "*Ulysses* at Top."

CONCLUSION: AMERICAN DYSTOPIA AND THE HERO OF MEANING

writers quoted earlier[45]) that typify our tendency to sever all the old ties of meaning. We have also observed a growing disregard for family generally among younger Americans, as evidenced by drops in marriage rates and "replacement" fertility rates that are at record lows. More recently, government and public health officials have even taken to abandoning the term "mother" (in favor of "birthing people") in a way that seems to be at home in Huxley's society, where the word is an obscenity.

Huxley's vision of a conditioning system in which subliminal messages are nightly inscribed in the brains of sleeping infants is another idea that may seem farfetched. But to think so may blind us to the fact that our society has found other ways of achieving a world very much like Huxley's. This change began in the sixties, when shifts in law, politics, education, and the popular media joined to engender a society that favored the individual over those connections (to family, community, country, culture, and religious faith) that had once proven so meaningful. By the end of the eighties, additional changes in technology, the mass media, economics, and the social and physical sciences had determined that this new individual was a creature of base and bodily needs, and that the primary purpose of culture was to gratify these. By now, conditioning was virtually 'round the clock rather than (as in Huxley's world) a mere thief in the night.

I may add that *Brave New World* is situated sometime in the twenty-sixth century. This is long after a terrible Nine Years' War and an accompanying great Economic Collapse that began around the middle of the twenty-first century. Given our society's rapid move toward future catastrophe—whether from environmental degradation, social and political unrest, nuclear war, economic distress, or disease—it seems likely that we will experience some similar upheaval necessitating an even stronger move toward science and technology to insure social order. All that seems missing from Huxley's world, really, is computers and all that has come with them. As our futurists point out, this will almost certainly lead to an eventual merger of human and machine—an eventuality not even Huxley could have foreseen.[46]

The elimination of the family and the heavy reliance upon conditioning are two of the most significant ways *Brave New World* paints an image of a world that may, or may not, be on our horizon. We now want

---

45. Davis-Floyd and Sergeant, *Childbirth and Authoritative Knowledge*, 315.
46. Harari, *Homo Deus*, 43-49.

to focus on how the novel paints a picture of meaning loss that is already with us.

In the course of their tour, the students are joined by the exalted Resident Controller for Western Europe, Mustapha Mond. If the role of the D.H.C. is to familiarize students with the basic purpose of education (which here, as in contemporary America, is based upon the notion that "not philosophers, but fretsawyers and stamp collectors compose the backbone of society"[47]), Mond's job is to fill in a few little-known details from history. His first words to the students is Henry Ford's famous dictum: "History is bunk." To reinforce the message, Mond waves his hand as if brushing off a bit of dust with a feather whisk. Huxley's point here could serve as an account of the fate of the Western civ ideal on university campuses following the revolutions of the late sixties:

> Whisk—and those specks of dirt called Athens and Rome, Jerusalem and the Middle Kingdom—all were gone. Whisk—the place where Italy had been was empty. Whisk, the cathedrals; whisk, whisk, King Lear and the Thoughts of Pascal. Whisk, Passion; whisk, Requiem; whisk, Symphony; whisk . . .[48]

The Director proceeds to recite some facts from the Nine Years' War. One detail was a "campaign against the past," which, in an echo of our recent upheavals, involved blowing up historical monuments. To give muscle to the new, anti-history policy, all books published before the war have been banned as being not only irrelevant but "pornographic"—a fact that may remind us of our own efforts to deconstruct the classics or remove some of them from library shelves. There is also a brief reference to the murder of eight hundred "simple lifers" at Golders Green. The fate of the communal movements of the sixties and seventies and the ongoing elimination of the family farm are contemporary counterparts—although, thus far, we are managing to destroy rural life without resort to such acts of violence.

Where traditional cultures focus on meaning, Huxley's society, like ours, is concerned with happiness through the elimination of disturbing or unpleasant encounters and the fulfillment of all desires. Mond reminds the students of this and points out that their ancestors were so stupid as to want to hold on to their "horrible emotions." Much like our current positive psychologists, authorities in Huxley's world recognize a shallow psychological universe. "Everybody's happy now" is the popular refrain.

---

47. Huxley, *Brave New World*, 4.
48. Huxley, *Brave New World*, 35.

CONCLUSION: AMERICAN DYSTOPIA AND THE HERO OF MEANING

The Director is one of the very few who has any inkling of a higher reality, and it is his duty to censor any publication that threatens the happiness ideal. When one such paper makes its way to his desk, Mond rejects it for publication and directs that tabs be kept on its author. He then ponders the work's implications:

> It was the sort of idea that might easily decondition the more unsettled minds among the higher castes—make them lose their faith in happiness as the Sovereign Good and take to believing, instead, that the goal was somewhere beyond, somewhere outside the present human sphere; that the purpose of life was not the maintenance of well-being, but some intensification and refining of consciousness.[49]

It is precisely such "intensification and refining of consciousness" for which we now have neither the time nor the inclination.

As we may imagine, drugs have a prominent place in Huxley's world—or, rather, one drug. Each citizen is given a daily ration of the drug *soma*. In small doses, *soma* induces calm and a sense of well being. In larger amounts it creates blissful visions, which inhabitants refer to as a *soma* "holiday." We may recall the dramatic increase in the use of pharmaceuticals in America since the sixties, including anti-anxiety and anti-depression drugs for adults, and Ritalin to subdue the very young. As for hallucinogens, Americans today can look forward to the nationwide legalization of marijuana in the not-so-distant future. Of course, we may yet achieve the effects and convenience of *soma*, whose invention Huxley places at the end of the twenty-first century.

It is worth pausing here to note the reasoning behind the recent move to legalize marijuana, despite the fact that the drug may prove addictive and may be harmful to mind and body. According to a point of view that now dominates in such matters, pot should be legalized because people really want it, and it is easier to give in to desire than prohibit it. It is this attitude that shapes our moral universe, much as it does the culture of Brave New Worlders, which seeks to fulfill every whim and satisfy every itch. Mond points the latter out to the students, only one of whom acknowledges ever having to wait any significant period between the awareness of a desire and its fulfillment. We are moving rapidly along the same track. One sure sign of this is that actions or tendencies that not so long ago were regarded as evidence of character deficiency or even

---

49. Huxley, *Brave New World*, 177.

"sin"—e.g., sloth, avarice, irresponsibility, promiscuity, profanity, sacrilege, gluttony, gambling—now pass without censure.

Like today's Americans, Huxley's inhabitants regard age as the great enemy. They have even succeeded in holding back the aging process so that only at sixty does the body begin its rapid (mostly unwitnessed) descent toward death. With no natural parents, no marriage, a lifelong adolescence, and the prospect of a quick death, there are no stages in life's journey. It follows that there is no honoring of the aged nor any recognition of the wisdom and sense of sacred power that was once thought to come with the approach of death. As Mond puts the contrasting views to the students: "Work, play—at sixty our powers and tastes are what they were at seventeen. Old men in the bad old days used to renounce, retire, take to religion, spend their time reading, thinking—*thinking*!"[50] Huxley's world looks forward to an America where the elderly now train for marathons and cheer on youthful athletes rather than ponder life's meaning. We are very far indeed from a postwar world where grandparents imparted knowledge and wisdom to the young—and further yet from the elderly "forest dwellers" we observed in some traditional societies.

While Brave New Worlders remain active into old age much as we do, their sports are a little different. In Huxley's society, sports have taken form largely as variations on their prototypes (e.g., tennis, golf), the modifications having been added to increase sales of sporting equipment. Here, upper-class citizens often wear sporty attire, with women donning shorts and other close-fitting garments. As with young American women today, this is a visible expression of the importance of athletics and the preeminence of the body. Elites in Huxley's world also wear gray—a fact that would make them feel right at home in our world of visual and ethical "grayness." As in America, spectator sports are popular, and, along with "feelies" (motion pictures that can be "felt" through knobs on the arm rests), are basic dating activities. Like our society, Huxley's is inconducive to any but the most shallow and superficial entertainments. Bereft of humanities education and lacking any large and compelling vision of human nature, Huxley's society has no creators of serious art, literature, music, and dance—creators who are rapidly disappearing from our own society as well.

Like gifted young Americans today, talented Brave New Worlders gravitate toward jobs in teaching or work in the popular entertainments. One of these individuals is Helmholtz Watson, a handsome, athletic man

---

50. Huxley, *Brave New* World, 55.

CONCLUSION: AMERICAN DYSTOPIA AND THE HERO OF MEANING   325

who is a lecturer in the Writing Department of the College of Emotional Engineering. Watson is, in effect, a poet in a world without poetry. Thus while his remarkable facility for "slogans and hypnopaedic rhymes" has led to his commercial success in the "feelies," he has a sense that there must be a better way to use his gifts—another way of writing and one that deals with subjects of real significance. Watson tries to formulate his thoughts and feelings in private conversation with his friend Bernard Marx, who has strange ways of his own. How does one write "piercingly" about subjects like a Community Sing or the newest technical achievements in the scent organ, Hemholtz ponders. "Can you say something about nothing?" he wonders.[51]

One vital subject lost to the potential poet in Huxley's world is romantic love. The Director points this out to the students, noting that people in the bad old days had a thing called "romance." Like our own society, Huxley's is preoccupied instead with sex. In America today, sexual activity begins earlier than ever thanks to internet porn and the nude photos of young women posted on the internet. Sex education also seems poised to develop in ways unimaginable to earlier generations as many now push for sex and gender identity instruction for little preschoolers. Thus far, we have avoided the supervised erotic play that is a basic part of early childhood education in Huxley's society. However, we share the belief that sex is simply sex and that young men and women should enjoy ever-changing partners. A Brave New Worlder characterizes this view of a relationship in words that could be those of many an iGener: "Don't imagine . . . that I'd had any indecorous relation with the girl. Nothing emotional, nothing longdrawn. It was all perfectly healthy and normal."[52]

One young woman who seems to have the old romantic notions is lovely Lenina Crowne, who emerges as a central character in the story. Lenina's proclivity is apparent early on in her relationship with Henry Foster, whom she has been "having" exclusively for four months. This has drawn the notice of her friend, Fanny, who reminds Lenina that, for appearances' sake, she ought to be a bit more promiscuous. However, even Fanny is surprised when Lenina decides to go out with Bernard Marx.

Bernard's odd behavior is apparent early in the date with Lenina when the couple are returning by private helicopter from the Semi-Demi-Finals of the Women's Heavyweight Wrestling championship in

51. Huxley, *Brave New World*, 70.
52. Huxley, *Brave New World*, 97.

Denmark. Flying low over the North Sea, Bernard insists upon quietly hovering over the dark, windswept ocean. This sends Lenina frantically to the radio, where the refrain "skies are blue inside of you" can be heard. In a locker room scene some days earlier, Bernard became upset when he overheard two men talking about "having Lenina." He cannot help thinking that they regard her (and she regards herself) as nothing more than "mutton"—a term which, depending upon one's point of view, may or may not be as disparaging as our notion of the "fuck buddy."

Perhaps it is not so surprising that, the day after their date, Bernard tells Lenina that he regrets their not having delayed the obligatory sex. In explaining himself, he points out that his fellow citizens are adults in their working hours, but infants "where feeling and desire are concerned." One cannot imagine a more concise description of adulthood in contemporary America. This preoccupation with childish wants and preferences is perhaps the most visible change since the postwar years, and we have seen how it begins with toys that encourage escapism, continues in the absence of powerful rites of adulthood, assumes its most characteristic expression in sex without commitment, and persists in the youthful clothes, music, films, and furniture we prefer even in old age. And yet, young Americans today have greater "maturity fears" and anxiety about "adulting" than any previous generation. We may well wonder what "adulthood" will look like in another generation or two.

The turning point in the story occurs when Lenina and Bernard make an excursion to the rarely visited New Mexican Reservation, where a group of Pueblo tribes abide. These inhabitants—with their misshapen faces and figures, their smells, and their terrible religious ceremonies—are too much for Lenina, who desperately wishes she had her *soma* with her. Suddenly, the couple spot a handsome, light-haired youth who speaks flawless English. This is John, the son of a London couple who came to the reservation many years ago, only to be separated, and the woman presumed dead. Somehow, and despite all her precautions, the woman, Linda, found herself pregnant and gave birth to the boy. John leads Lenina and Bernard to his grossly overweight and prematurely aging mother, who lives in squalor at the outskirts of the village. Linda is overjoyed to see them, and plans are made for Linda and John's journey to London. This is made possible by Mond, who finds John ripe for scientific study.

Before they leave for London, Bernard asks John for details about his life in the rocky mesas of New Mexico. John recounts a childhood

CONCLUSION: AMERICAN DYSTOPIA AND THE HERO OF MEANING 327

lived between two cultures, and the meanings that have come both from living with the Pueblo and being an outsider.

There were happy times for John, as when Linda spoke glowingly of her world, and the old wise man, Mitsima, taught him to work the clay to fashion a pot. There was also the day he discovered the works of Shakespeare from an old and well-worn volume left in the house by Linda's lover, Popé. Huxley describes the effect in terms that capture great poetry's capacity for meaning:

> The strange words rolled through his mind; rumbled, like the drums at the summer dances, if the drums could have spoken; like the men singing the Corn Song, beautiful, beautiful, so that you cried; like old Mitsima saying magic over his feathers and his carved sticks and his bits of bone and stone . . . but better than Mitsima's magic, because it meant more, because it talked to *him*; talked wonderfully and only half-understandably, a terrible, beautiful magic.[53]

The words even made his hatred for Popé more real—made Popé himself more real. The result was John's attempted murder of Popé, resulting in two wounds to the man's shoulder and John's tears, which sent him fleeing from the dwelling as Popé laughed.

There was also one real crisis. This came when, because of his light skin, John was denied the opportunity of undergoing the initiation ceremony whereby the young boys became men. When he tried to enter the ceremonial kiva anyway, John was sent running out into the hills in the moonlight, bleeding from cuts received from stones the others threw at him. We earlier observed how such ceremonies were vital for young Pueblo men and women. To be prohibited from taking part, as John was, is to be effectively shut out of the adult world. But John now experiences his own rite of passage. Running into the desert, he eventually comes to a precipice where he sits, looking down into the dark below. Poised above the "black shadow of death," John holds out his hand so that drops of blood slowly fall. It is a confrontation with death that has all the character of an existential crisis and a religious awakening. As Huxley puts it: "He had discovered Time and Death and God."[54]

When the group returns to London, John becomes a celebrity, while Linda enters upon an extended *soma* holiday that will eventuate

---

53. Huxley, *Brave New World*, 131–32.
54. Huxley, *Brave New World*, 136.

in her death. As John's closest friend and confidant, Bernard also becomes popular, much to his great delight but eventual detriment, when this newfound acceptance goes to his head. John and Watson hit it off due to their common regard for poetry—a fact that stirs Bernard's jealousy. However, while Watson is delighted to discover Shakespeare, even he cannot abide listening to John read from *Romeo and Juliet*, with its family quarrels and endless squabbles over love and sex. When Watson begins to laugh uncontrollably, John closes the book and angrily puts it away. Watson professes that he now realizes that great poetry comes from pain and absurdity. Nevertheless, in explaining his reaction, he makes this point: "You can't expect me to keep a straight face about fathers and mothers. And who's going to get excited about a boy having a girl or not having her?"[55]

In the days after the return Lenina has come to realize that she is so taken with John that, despite continuing to have scores of men, she wants only him. John has adored Lenina from the first. He constantly associates Shakespeare's romantic phrases with her, and his thoughts and actions upon finding her asleep in her hotel room in New Mexico have all the elevated character of traditional romance:

> Very slowly, with the hesitating gesture of one who reaches forward to stroke a shy and possibly rather dangerous bird, he put out his hand. It hung there trembling, within an inch of those limp fingers, on the verge of contact. Did he dare? Dare to profane with his unworthiest hand that . . . No, he didn't. The bird was too dangerous. His hand dropped back. How beautiful she was! How beautiful![56]

The complexities of the situation become apparent in London, where John speaks to a confused Lenina about marriage. In accordance with his understanding of the rituals of romance, he professes the need to perform some heroic deed worthy of her (reminding us of Nickie Ferrante's desire to prove himself worthy of Terry in *An Affair to Remember*). Matters come to a head when Lenina attempts to seduce John. When she disrobes before him and quotes poetry of her own ("Hug me till you drug me honey") he becomes outraged and violently pushes her away. His subsequent cries of "damned whore" and "impudent strumpet" send Lenina fleeing to the bathroom.

55. Huxley, *Brave New World*, 185.
56. Huxley, *Brave New World*, 144.

At this point John receives a call that his mother is dying. He runs to the hospital and finds Linda much as we might see her today, heavily drugged, with a TV nearby, so that the inanities of a sports announcer interpose upon the deathbed scene. John's loud sobs create something of a scandal within the ward. In anger at his mother's ignoble, *soma*-induced death, John proceeds to an area in the hospital where a large group of Delta workers are receiving their daily *soma* ration. When he begins throwing away the *soma* boxes (all the while screaming of "freedom" and "manhood"), a riot breaks out. Having learned of the disturbance, Helmholtz and Bernard arrive. Soon, Helmholtz joins John, while Bernard looks on in fear and indecision. When the police arrive, the trio is arrested.

The next day, the three appear before the Director. Mond begins by addressing himself to John, who is surprised to learn that the Director has an extensive knowledge of Shakespeare. Mond explains that Shakespeare's works are not forbidden chiefly because they are old. They are forbidden because the world depicted there—a world of illness and death, passion and old age, wives, children, and all the rest—may be essential to art, but is incomprehensible to Brave New Worlders (much as it apparently seems strange to so many of us today). When John responds by noting that entertainments like the "feelies" and the "scent organ" have "no meaning," Mond cleverly counters by employing a different usage of the word—by using meaning, as it were, with a small *m*. "They mean themselves; they mean a lot of agreeable sensations to the audience," he proclaims.[57]

The precise wording of the phrase is telling. In the first part, Mond has indicated meanings that point only to "themselves," rather than evoking something of "greater and more lasting value." In the second, he uses the word in reference to the senses rather than referring to experiences that are both "cognitively and emotionally" engaging. This is understanding the word in a way that deprives it of any greater significance.

The discussion among the four ends with the controller telling Bernard and Watson that they will be exiled to a community of misfits on an island of their choosing. At this point, a visibly shaken Bernard leaves for a dose of *soma*. When Watson goes to comfort his friend, the conversation between the two remaining men moves on to the question of religion.

Religion and God are forbidden to Huxley's inhabitants, and the Christian crosses that were once so prominent have had their tops shorn to form a *t*—this to commemorate the famous automobile model of magnate

---

57. Huxley, *Brave New World*, 221.

Henry Ford, who has become a cult figure in Christ's absence. Early in the book, we witness Bernard's reluctant participation in a Fordian service, which has many features of a Christian communion. There are twelve participants (six men and six women), and they are seated around a table where *soma* tablets and *soma* ice cream are ritually consumed. Although the scene is an obvious parody of religion, the ritual is suggestive regarding the trend of religious services in many of our own churches. Rhythmic music is essential here, with drumbeats that grow louder and faster as the group becomes more animated. Lighting, too, is carefully orchestrated, rising and then falling to a rich red glow at the end. In the midst of all this a charismatic voice is heard. As Huxley describes the impact:

> A sensation of warmth radiated thrillingly out from the solar plexus to every extremity of the bodies of those who listened; tears came into their eyes; their hearts, their bowels seemed to move within them, as though with an independent life. "Ford!" they were melting, "Ford!" dissolved, dissolved.[58]

When Mond first raises the issue of religion, John hesitates, remembering his own dark night of the soul, and thinking that not even the words of Shakespeare could capture its deepest meaning. But Mond takes the lead, eventually putting forth his own views, assisted by passages from the writings of the British cardinal John Henry Newman and French philosopher Maine de Biran. From Newman, Mond takes the suggestion that we belong not to ourselves, but to our Creator—a fact that becomes more and more apparent with the travails of old age. However, as Biran points out, it is not chiefly infirmity that eventually leads us to God. As the passions ebb and wisdom grows, there is a natural turning from the temporal to those eternal verities that we know deep within ourselves. Mond believes that there may very well be a God. But in a world of prosperity and perpetual youth, God is no longer necessary.

When John speaks of the value of life lived in awareness of God ("God's the reason for everything noble and fine and heroic"), Mond dismisses the notion as a real danger to social stability and happiness. John ultimately insists upon affirming the bad as a condition for the good—on recognizing both our "devils" and our "angels" in the poet Rilke's phrase. When Mond argues that John is claiming his right to be "unhappy," John agrees, proclaiming that he accepts it all—poetry and danger, freedom and fear, goodness and sin, and more:

58. Huxley, *Brave New World*, 83.

the right to grow old and ugly and impotent; the right to have syphilis and cancer; the right to have too little to eat; the right to be lousy; the right to live in constant apprehension of what may happen tomorrow; the right to catch typhoid; the right to be tortured by unspeakable pains of every kind.[59]

To all this the Director simply responds with a shrug and the comment, "You're welcome."

In the discussion with John, Mond has raised a number of vital issues regarding a way of life of which religion is the chief social expression and traditional culture, more broadly, its many manifestations. This way of living takes meaning from large families and small communities, vital arts and close ties to nature, the struggle to survive and the ever-present reality of death. However, meaning is not merely (or even chiefly) a compensation for struggle and suffering. Meaning is a *transformation* whereby experience is elevated beyond the immediate and material into something of "greater and more lasting value." It is meaning in this larger sense—meaning with a large *m*—that Mond finds superfluous and John embraces, despite the suffering and despair that inevitably come with it.

The viewpoint of each man is the reflection of a larger culture. Mond's world is one of firm social order and an ideal of "happiness" that has been etched in the brain from infancy. John's views derive from the meaning-rich world of the Pueblo peoples and the works of Shakespeare. The latter is an extraordinary combination, and reminiscent in some ways of America in the postwar years, when the nation still looked to religion, country, and the great works of the Western tradition for its values. As we have seen, traces of the old language still echoed in the early sixties in John F. Kennedy and Martin Luther King Jr., who evoked the higher aspects of human nature by, respectively, urging listeners to "ask what you can do for your country" or appealing to "content of character." By the end of the sixties all this had changed. Today's politics is a childish fight over who gets the most and who poked his finger in the other's eye. More broadly, ours is a world where words with "higher" resonance (like duty, honor, nobility, virtue, and excellence) have given way to the anti-human language of computers and science, to profane and artless phrases, and to the language of the body—which is now our foremost concern and the chief avenue of satisfaction and fulfillment.

59. Huxley, *Brave New World*, 240.

The conversations with Mond essentially mark the exits of the Director, Bernard, and Watson from the story. While John had hoped to join his friends in exile, Mond has insisted that he remain so that his experiment with the young man may continue. It is nothing less than a death sentence.

John is fortunate for a while in escaping from London and finding a remote lighthouse where he can live. There he prays to the deities he knows: to the Pueblo gods and to Jesus, to the Heavenly Father, and to his guardian animal, the eagle. Sometimes he holds out his hands like Jesus on the cross, standing for hours in pain while asking God to forgive him for his lust. In all this, John reminds us of the fundamental opposition in religion between body and spirit, and of the many debates in recent years that have pitted our embrace of the body's truth against the views of the Pope, the Dalai Lama, and religious conservatives who regard spirit as the higher reality. Indeed, John has a deeply religious nature, and one in which these oppositions have been exacerbated by his enthrallment to poetry and by his love for a creature both whose beauty and capacity for degradation are beyond anything he has known. Thus, like the many gurus who lost their way in America, John's ultimate downfall is assured.

Having purified himself, John lives in peace and solitude for a time. However, he eventually feels remorse for his mistreatment of his mother. This leads him to fashion a whip of knotted chords and to begin to whip himself. It is in this state that he is discovered by reporters. And it is during another act of penance that a group of Brave New Worlders descends upon him, with Lenina among them. The group begins to yell "We-want-the-whip!," hoping to find, in self-inflicted pain, an emotional intensity beyond anything in their experience. However, when Lenina steps forth, John attacks her with the whip as well. Suddenly the chant changes to "Orgy-porgy." Wild dancing ensues and *soma* is freely consumed at an orgy that goes past midnight.

John awakens the next morning and recalls the events of the night. Ashamed of his actions and confronted by a world that lacks any deeper understanding, he returns to the lighthouse and hangs himself, just before an onrush of spectators arrives.

In John we have what I would call "a hero of meaning." Heroes of meaning are different from most heroes. While most heroes return from their quest with some great treasure or boon, the hero of meaning usually

CONCLUSION: AMERICAN DYSTOPIA AND THE HERO OF MEANING

comes back empty handed. Where the former succeeds, the latter most often fails—at least in the eyes of the world. This is not surprising. For the hero of meaning ultimately seeks a world of meaning unattainable on earth.

Heroes of meaning sometimes appear in the tales of traditional societies. In his book *The Human Cycle*, anthropologist Collin Turnbull relates one of these stories as told by the Bushmen of Africa.[60]

The Bushmen tale concerns a small boy who one day spies the reflection of a beautiful bird in a clear watering hole. When he looks up, the bird is gone. From this time forth, the boy devotes himself to searching for the bird, moving from village to village only to learn that the beautiful bird has been spotted but has moved on. This quest consumes his entire life. Finally, in old age, he comes to the foot of Mount Kilimanjaro, where he is told that the bird has been seen on the snowy summit. When the Bushman finally reaches the top of the mountain his strength is gone. He lies down to die, content in the fact that he had once glimpsed beauty and had devoted his life to it. As he closes his eyes for the last time, he calls the name of his mother and stretches out his hand in a last gesture. There, as his life ends, a solitary feather from the bird alights.

Turnbull is careful to point out that the story is highly valued by the Bushmen as evidence of a life well lived. There is no notion that the man has wasted his life by abandoning his social responsibilities. It is enough that he has committed himself to his ideal of beauty and a higher truth. This is an important point. For the hero of meaning exists only as long as meaning is a paramount concern in society. When meaning dies, the hero of meaning must vanish along with it.

The best-known hero of meaning in Western literature is Miguel de Cervantes's fictional creation, Don Quixote, who was born at the dawn of the seventeenth century. Don Quixote is really both a timeless and a timely figure. Timeless because the hero of meaning speaks to a dimension of spiritual striving nearly as old as humanity itself. Timely, because it is this spiritual quality that first began to be threatened when Quixote appeared, and it is this spiritual quality that is rapidly being lost today.

Don Quixote is generally pictured as a half-crazed, skinny old man, who, with his portly aide Sancho Panza, rides the Spanish plains of La Mancha, tilting at windmills and seeking to right all wrongs as a latter-day knight errant. However, Western philosophers have recognized in

60. Turnbull, *Human Cycle*, 265–66.

Cervantes's character a larger story. In a conversation with Bill Moyers, Joseph Campbell pointed this out while drawing attention to certain of philosopher Ortega y Gasset's observations:

> Don Quixote was the last hero of the Middle Ages. He rode out to encounter giants, but instead of giants, his environment produced windmills. Ortega points out 'that this story takes place about the time that a mechanistic interpretation of the world came in, so that the environment was no longer spiritually responsive to the hero.'[61]

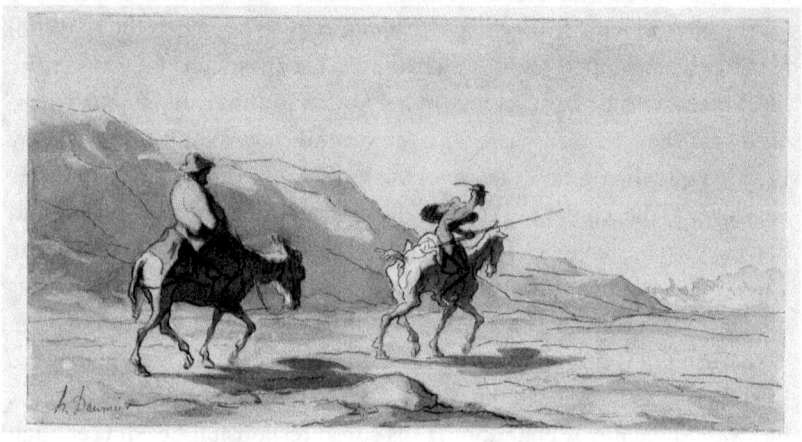

Honoré Daumier, *Don Quixote and Sancho Panza*, 1865–67, pen and ink, brush and ink, and watercolor over graphite on wove paper. Courtesy of Rhode Island School of Design Museum, Providence, RI.

As Campbell suggests, Don Quixote's "tilting at windmills" signifies not only an assault upon technology; it can also be read as an effort to save the richly symbolic language of poetry from the cold reality of prose that was emerging in the new technology's stead.[62] As technology grew in the early seventeenth century, Europeans began to view the world with eyes no longer clouded by those "resemblances and similitudes" (i.e., metaphors and similes) by which the Renaissance had understood nature. A massive windmill, despite its cap and four long "limbs," was clearly not a giant. The world of poetry was coming to an end.

---

61. Campbell and Moyers, *Power of Myth*, 130.
62. Foucault, *Order of Things*, 46–77; Sheridan, *Foucault*, 46–88.

CONCLUSION: AMERICAN DYSTOPIA AND THE HERO OF MEANING   335

Cervantes's contemporary Francis Bacon was among the first of these modern thinkers.[63] Bacon was determined to rid men and women of their habit of understanding nature by means of fanciful parallels and correspondences. His genius lay in looking to the mechanical arts for his epistemology, which helped lay the foundations for the scientific revolution. Following his death, in 1626, England witnessed a literary revolution in which the language of Shakespeare and the King James Bible was pruned of much of its poetry to make way for a sparser style more suitable to scientific discourse.

For more than three centuries, prose and verse maintained a truce through the alliance of the "two cultures." When poetry finally began to lose its hold, in the postwar years, it found a temporary refuge in dreams. However, the poets of the dream, like Sigmund Freud and Carl Jung, eventually gave way to brain technicians who, having lost the capacity for poetry themselves, insisted that dreams were mere gibberish. It is this view that took firm hold in the last two decades of the twentieth century. And it is this view that dominates today, pushing poetry, dreams, religion, metaphysics, and any other manifestation of the "higher" and the "spiritual" further and further to the fringes of culture.

The last significant reincarnation of Don Quixote came in Dale Wasserman's musical *Man of La Mancha*, which opened in New York on November 22, 1965. This was two years to the day after the assassination of President Kennedy—a period, as we have seen, that marked the beginning of a watershed in American culture. The mood of the times was reflected in the reviews. Although most found the work genuinely moving, it had its critics. The same conflicting opinions marked the response to the musical's signature ballad, "The Impossible Dream."

Wasserman's song is a glorious hymn to the noblest of causes, and a reminder of the perils and sacrifices that so often accompany such quests. One line, which speaks of glorious battle, undoubtedly offended some, with an unpopular war in Vietnam already on the horizon. There is also an evocation of the virtues of chastity, which seemed out of date in the era of *Playboy*, James Bond, and Helen Gurney Brown. In fact, the *Playboy* critic was chief among those who found the musical sentimental, though he had nothing but praise for the female lead as one whose neckline "never stops plunging."[64] Still, most were inspired by both ballad

---

63. Bacon, *Novum Organum*, 20.
64. Wasserman, *Impossible Musical*, 135.

and play, with their story of a hero like our Bushman, who gives up not only family, friends, and possessions, but life itself in search of a lofty, unreachable goal.

Man of La Mancha has a complex plot that centers upon a play within a play. It begins with Cervantes, who finds himself imprisoned by the Inquisition in a dark dungeon along with a host of disreputable characters. The story of Don Quixote, which is the real focus of the play, is told to appease the prisoners, who have threatened to destroy Cervantes's manuscript of the tale. It is the prisoners, along with Cervantes and his aide, Sancho Panza, who enact this play within the play.

Wasserman's Don Quixote is an aged country squire, Alonso Quixano, who became so disturbed by reading books that he decided to become the knight Don Quixote de la Mancha. We first see Don Quixote and his aide, Sancho Panza, on the plains of La Mancha, where the old man attacks a windmill he has mistaken for a giant. The story then moves to a dilapidated inn, where the main action occurs. Here, Quixote finds a maid and part-time prostitute, Aldonza, along with a gang of disreputable muleteers. Where the muleteers see only a common prostitute, Quixote sees his exalted lady, Dulcinea. His song to Aldonza is rich in heavenly imagery, which, as we have seen, was still prominent in the early sixties before beginning its decline. When Quixote seeks from the poor girl a scarf as a favor, she flings a wet dishrag, which Quixote regards as sheer gossamer. As Sancho puts it to Aldonza, "Knights have their own language for everything."[65]

Wasserman rightly claimed Aldonza as his great invention, and it is her evolving relationship with Quixote that chiefly drives the action of the story. On the one hand, Aldonza represents what Carl Jung would call an anima figure—that is, a guide to the treasures of the unconscious mind.[66] It is she who assists Quixote in exploits that result in his being "knighted" by the innkeeper. It is Aldonza, too, who eventually reawakens him to his knightly nature when, at the end of the story, Alonso Quixano appears to have been "cured" of his madness, and for a time believes his exploits as Quixote have been nothing but a feverish hallucination. However, if Aldonza is vital to Quixote, he also has an important influence upon her. We first notice this when she tends to the wounds of her enemies, the muleteers, in accordance with Quixote's notion that

---

65. Wasserman, *Impossible Musical*, 266.
66. Jung, *Memories, Dreams, Reflections*, 187–88.

nobility demands it. This influence is evident again at Quixano's death, when Aldonza decides to adopt the name "Dulcinea." Finally, Quixote's impact appears at the very end of the play, in the dungeon, when the prisoner who plays Aldonza's character in the drama leads the others in singing "The Impossible Dream."

The combination of poetry and romantic love that guides Quixote and drives the story reminds us of John. In each, the poetry of romance draws jeers and laughter from others. We have noted this in Hemholtz's reaction to Shakespeare's *Romeo and Juliet*, and we see it again in *Man of La Mancha*, when the muleteers fling Quixote's romantic phrases in Aldonza's face. Both Quixote and John have a capacity to see an exalted beauty where others see merely the physical—to find gossamer where another observes a rag, or an ethereal beauty where others see only "mutton." Both are in search of something "higher," which ultimately expresses itself in the opposition of the fleshly and the spiritual. We observe this in John's Spartan, even abusive, regimen, and in both Quixote's austerities and his gaunt appearance alongside the portly Sancho. Of course, these qualities also appear in the Bushmen hero, whose glimpse of an otherworldly beauty leads him to forswear all earthly joys—only to find himself, at the end, alone and near death at Kilimanjaro's summit.

Wasserman has observed that, while the musical continued to find its audience, it was overshadowed in the late sixties by the surprising success of his theatrical rendering of *One Flew Over the Cuckoo's Nest*—a play that had earlier received scathing reviews. This should come as no surprise.[67] Ken Kesey's novel of the rebellious Randle McMurphy was clearly more in keeping with the political temper of the times.

In fact, over the years, many critics have sought to recast Wasserman's version of Cervantes's hero in political terms, by dramatizing Aldonza's sexual assault, for example, or reconfiguring the dungeon as a ghetto. This may have made some sense in 1965, when the words of Martin Luther King Jr.'s "I have a dream" were still in the minds of many. But how do we now frame as a hero of the Left a man who tilts at windmills, believes in aiding his enemies, and speaks the heavenly language of romance to his beloved? Ours is not a world of poetry, dreams, and ideals but of technology, ideology, and demands. Those contemporary critics who find the musical out of date acknowledge as much.

---

67. Wasserman, *Impossible Musical*, 144–45.

There are many such critics now.[68] Much as John was hopelessly out of place in his new society, Don Quixote is no longer relevant among our Brave New Worlders. We may even say that, today, the injunction to dream "the impossible dream" seems more impossible than ever. I don't mean that the dream itself is more impossible. After all, an "impossible" dream does not become more impossible. No. I mean that we are losing the capacity to dream.

---

68. Saville, "*Man of La Mancha* Review."

Bibliography

ACTA. *What Will They Learn? 2018–19: A Survey of Core Requirements at Our Nation's Colleges and Universities*. ACTA, Sept. 18, 2018. https://www.goacta.org/resource/what-will-they-learn-2018-19-survey-on-core-requirements/.
"All You Need Is Love." Wikipedia, last updated Jan. 29, 2024. https://en.wikipedia.org/wiki/All_You_Need_Is_Love.
Allen, Henry. "The Woman Who Made Single Sexy." *Wall Street Journal*, Apr. 23–24, 2016.
Allyn, David. *Make Love, Not War: The Sexual Revolution: An Unfettered History*. New York: Routledge, 2001.
Altschuler, Glenn C. *All Shook Up: How Rock 'n' Roll Changed America*. Pivotal Moments in American History. Oxford: Oxford University Press, 2003.
Bacon, Francis. *Novum Organum*. Translated and edited by Peter Urbach and John Gibson. Chicago: Open Court, 1994.
Bahrampour, Tara. "Depression Rising for the Young, Study Finds." *Washington Post*, Mar. 17, 2019.
Bailey, Beth L. *From Front Porch to Back Seat: Courtship in Twentieth-Century America*. Baltimore: Johns Hopkins University Press, 1988.
Bailey, Sarah Pulliam. "Church Membership in U.S. Falls below Majority in Seismic Shift." *Washington Post*, Mar. 29, 2021. https://www.washingtonpost.com/religion/2021/03/29/church-membership-fallen-below-majority/.
Bair, Deirdre. *Jung: A Biography*. New York: Back Bay, 2003.
Baja, Morris. *Epiphany in the Modern Novel*. Seattle: University of Washington Press, 1971.
Bakewell, Sarah. *At the Existentialist Café: Freedom, Being, and Apricot Cocktails*. New York: Other, 2016.
Banes, Sally. *Writing Dancing in the Age of Postmodernism*. Hanover, NH: University Press of New England, 1994.
Baragona, Louis. "What's in a Name? You Decide." *Knot* (Summer 2019) 64.
Barnouw, Erik. *Tube of Plenty: The Evolution of American Television*. New York: Oxford University Press, 1975.
Bawer, Bruce. "Poetry and the University." In *Poetry after Modernism*, edited by Robert McDowell, 114–28. Brownsville, OR: Story Line, 1998.
Bayles, Martha. *Hole in Our Soul: The Loss of Beauty and Meaning in American Popular Music*. Culture Studies. Chicago: University of Chicago Press, 1994.
Beattie, John, et al. *The Golden Book of Favorite Songs: A Treasury of the Best Songs of Our People*. Chicago: Hall & McCreary, 1951.

Beauregard, Robert A. *When America Became Suburban*. Minneapolis: University of Minnesota Press, 2006.
Bellah, Robert. *The Broken Covenant: American Civil Religion in Time of Trial*. Culture Studies. Chicago: University of Chicago Press, 1975.
———. "Civil Religion in America." *Daedalus* 96 (1967) 1–21.
Bellow, Saul. *Herzog*. New York: Penguin, 1976.
———. *There Is Simply Too Much to Think About: Collected Nonfiction*. Edited by Benjamin Taylor. New York: Viking Penguin, 2015.
Belton, John, ed. *Movies and Mass Culture*. New Brunswick, NJ: Rutgers University Press, 1996.
Benedek, Laslo, dir. *The Wild One*. Culver City, CA: Columbia, 1954.
Berger, Tom. "What We Lose with the Decline of Cursive." *Edutopia*, Mar. 10, 2017. https://www.edutopia.org/article/what-we-lose-with-decline-cursive-tom-berger/.
Berman, Morris. *The Reenchantment of the World*. New York: Bantam, 1984.
Berry, Wendell. *Another Turn of the Crank: Essays by Wendell Berry*. Washington, DC: Counterpoint, 1995.
———. *Recollected Essays: 1965–1980*. San Francisco: North Point, 1981.
Bertolucci, Bernardo, dir. *Last Tango in Paris*. Beverly Hills, CA: MGM, 1988. DVD. First released 1972.
Bloom, Allan. *The Closing of the American Mind*. New York: Simon & Schuster, 1987.
Boot, Max. "If Schools Stop Teaching History, We're Doomed." *Chicago Tribune*, Feb. 21, 2019. https://www.chicagotribune.com/opinion/commentary/ct-perspec-history-ignorant-study-college-historians-0222-20190221-story.html.
Borger, Julian. "Fires Light Up Washington DC on Third Night of George Floyd Protests." *Guardian*, June 1, 2020. https://www.theguardian.com/us-news.2020/may/31/fires-light-up-washington-dc-on-third-night-of-george-floyd-protests.
Bouselli, Maria. "Your Safari Adventure Awaits." *Knot* (Summer 2019) 129–30.
Bova, Dan. "Power A.M. Routines, Tested." In "Mindfulness: The New Science of Health and Happiness." Special issue, *TIME* (Sept. 2016) 66–71.
Bowman, James. "The Day the Music Died." *Wall Street Journal*, Apr. 12, 2002.
Brand, Gerd. *The Essential Wittgenstein*. Translated by Robert E. Innis. New York: Basic, 1979.
Brenan, Megan. "Nurses Again Outpace Other Professions for Honesty, Ethics." Gallup, Dec. 20, 2018. https://news.gallup.com/poll/245597/nurses-again-outpace-professions-honesty-ethics-aspx.
Brooks, Richard, dir. *The Blackboard Jungle*. New York: Metro-Goldwyn-Mayer, 1955.
Brown, Helen Gurley. *Sex and the Single Girl*. Reprint, Fort Lee, NJ: Barricade, 2003. First published 1962.
Brown, Royal S. "Herrmann, Hitchcock and the Music of the Irrational." In *Alfred Hitchcock's "Psycho": A Casebook*, edited by Robert Kolker, 102–17. Casebooks in Criticism. Oxford: Oxford University Press, 2004.
Bruckner, D. J. R. "The Bollingen Adventure." *New York Times*, June 20, 1982. http://www.nytimes.com/1982/06/20/books/the-bollingen-adventure.html.
Burge, Ryan P. "Mainline Protestants Are Still Declining, But That's Not Good News for Evangelicals." *Christianity Today*, July 13, 2021. https://www.christianitytoday.com/news/2021/july/mainline-protestant-evangelical-decline-survey-us-nones.html.

Burgess, Katherine. "Getting Married? Chances Are It Won't Be in a Church." *Wichita Eagle*, July 24, 2017. https://www.kansas.com/living/religion/article163414458.html.
Burke, Frank. "The Tools of Man." *Pennsylvania Gazette* (Sept./Oct. 2017) 16–18.
Burns, Ken, dir. *The Civil War*. Burbank, CA: Warner, 2004. DVD. First released 1990.
Burns, Tom. *Our Necessary Shadow: The Nature and Meaning of Psychiatry*. New York, Pegasus, 2014.
Burt, Stephanie. "There Is a Poem for Every Reader." *Wall Street Journal*, July 8–9, 2019.
Butterfield, Andrew. "No Photos. Ignore Labels. Just Look." *Wall Street Journal*, Nov. 18–19, 2017.
Caldwell, Simon. "Nearly 500 British Priests Sign Statement in Support of 'Humanae Vitae.'" *National Catholic Reporter*, June 18, 2018. https://www.ncronline.org/news/nearly-500-british-priests-sign-statement-support-humanae-vitae.
Campbell, Joseph, and Bill Moyers. *The Power of Myth*. New York: Doubleday, 1988.
Canaday, John. *Culture Gulch: Notes on Art and Its Public in the 1960's*. New York: Farrar, Straus & Giroux, 1969.
Cannon, Lou. *President Reagan: The Role of A Lifetime*. New York: Public Affairs, 1991.
Carney, Timothy P. *Alienated America: Why Some Places Thrive While Others Collapse*. New York: HarperCollins, 2019.
Carr, Nicholas. *The Shallows: What the Internet Is Doing to Our Brains*. New York: Norton, 2011.
Carrillo, Sequoia. "U.S. Reading and Math Scores Drop to Lowest Level in Decades." NPR, June 21, 2023. https://www.npr.org/2023/06/21/1183445444/u-s-reading-and-math-scores-drop-to-lowest-level-in-decades.
Chamie, Joseph. "The End of Marriage in America?" *Hill*, Aug. 10, 2021. https://thehill.com/opinion/finance/567107-the end-of-marriage-in-america/.
Chapman, James. *License to Thrill: A Cultural History of the James Bond Films*. New York: Columbia University Press, 2000.
Chasar, Mike. *Everyday Reading: Poetry and Popular Culture in Modern America*. New York: Columbia University Press, 2012.
Cherlin, Andrew J. *The Marriage-Go-Round: The State of Marriage and the America Today*. New York: Vintage, 2009.
Chipp, Herschel B., et al. *Theories of Modern Art: A Source Book by Artists and Critics*. Berkeley: University of California Press, 1968.
Cho, Jeena. "Why Are Lawyers So Unhappy?" *Above the Law*, Aug. 1, 2016, https://abovethelaw.com/2016/08/why-are-lawyers-so-unhappy/.
Chua, Amy. *Political Tribes: Group Instinct and the Fate of Nations*. New York: Penguin, 2018.
Church, Forrest. *The American Creed: A Spiritual and Patriotic Primer*. New York: St. Martin's, 2002.
CNN Business. "GM Strike: Nearly 50,000 Workers Walk Out at America's Biggest Automaker." CNN, Sept. 16, 2019; updated Sept. 17, 2019. https://www.cnn.com/business/live-news/gm-workers-strike-uaw-negotiations/synchronous_inspection.
Cooke, Bernard, and Gary Macy. *Christian Symbol and Ritual: An Introduction*. Oxford: Oxford University Press, 2005.
Coomaraswamy, Ananda K. *Christian and Oriental Philosophy of Art*. New York: Dover, 1956.

Coontz, Stephanie. *The Way We Never Were: American Families and the Nostalgia Trap.* New York: Basic, 1992.

Cort, Robert. "Our Love Affair with Movies." *Pennsylvania Gazette* (July/Aug. 2018) 50–55.

Crews, Gordon A., and M. Reid Counts. *The Evolution of School Disturbance in America: Colonial Times to Modern Day.* Westport, CT: Praeger, 1997.

Cross, Gary. *Kids' Stuff: Toys and the Changing World of American Childhood.* Cambridge, MA: Harvard University Press, 1997.

Cross, Sarah H., and Haider J. Warraich. "Changes in the Place of Death in the United States." *New England Journal of Medicine* 381 (2019) 2369–70. https://www.nejm.org/doi/full/10.1056/nejmc1911892.

Csikszentmihalyi, Mihaly. *Finding Flow: The Psychology of Engagement with Everyday Life.* New York: Basic, 1997.

Curtiz, Michael, dir. *Casablanca.* Burbank, CA: Warner Brothers, 2003. DVD. First released 1942.

Dallek, Robert. *An Unfinished Life: John F. Kennedy, 1917–1963.* New York: Back Bay, 2003.

Daurer, Jeremy, and Danny Fingeroth. "The Superhero of the Comics Business." *Wall Street Journal*, Nov. 17–18, 2018.

Davis-Floyd, Robbie E., and Carolyn F. Sargent. *Childbirth and Authoritative Knowledge: Cross-Cultural Perspectives.* Berkeley: University of California Press, 1997.

Day, Chad. "Americans Have Shifted Dramatically on What Values Matter Most." *Wall Street Journal*, Aug. 25, 2019. https://www.wsj.com/articles/americanshaveshifted-dramatically-on-what-values-matter-most-11566738001.

Delbanco, Andrew. *The Death of Satan: How Americans Have Lost the Sense of Evil.* New York: Farrar, Straus & Giroux, 1995.

DeLuca, Dan. "Marsalis Straight, No Chaser." *Philadelphia Inquirer*, Mar. 4, 2007.

De Munck, Victor C., ed. *Romantic Love and Sexual Behavior: Perspectives from the Social Sciences.* Westport, CT: Praeger, 1998.

Denmark, Florence L., et al., eds. *Violence in Schools: Cross-National and Cross-Cultural Perspectives.* New York: Springer, 2005.

Deresiewicz, William. *Excellent Sheep: The Miseducation of the American Elite & the Way to a Meaningful Life.* New York: Free, 2014.

Dias, Elizabeth. "8 Questions: Krista Tippett." *TIME* (Dec. 12, 2016) 72.

Dirda, Michael. "From Beowulf to Batman." *Wall Street Journal*, Apr. 8–9, 2017.

Dirix, Emmanuelle. *Dressing the Decades: Twentieth-Century Vintage Style.* New Haven: Yale University Press, 2016.

Dogster. "Want to Marry Your Pet? There's a Website for That." *Dogster*, Oct. 15, 2015. https://www.dogster.com./lifestyle/this-widow-who-lost-her-cat-husband-plans-to-marry-her-dog. Link discontinued.

Doss, Erika. *Twentieth-Century American Art.* Oxford History of Art. Oxford: Oxford University Press, 2002.

Downing, David. *Marlon Brando.* New York: Stein & Day, 1984.

Dozier, Edward P. *The Pueblo Indians of North America.* Prospect Heights, IL: Waveland, 1983.

Drexler, Peggy. "It's OK for Parents to Feel Ambivalent about Their Children." *Wall Street Journal*, June 22–23, 2019.

Dreyfus, Hubert, and Sean Dorrance Kelly. *All Things Shining: Reading the Western Classics to Find Meaning in a Secular Age.* New York: Free, 2011.

Dunkelman, Marc J. *The Vanishing Neighbor: The Transformation of American Community.* New York: Norton, 2014.

Durrani, Anayat. "What School Choice Is and How it Works." *U.S. News and World Report,* Apr. 14, 2023. https://www.usnews.com/education>k12/articles/what-school-choice-is-and-how-it-works.

Edwards, Emily. "Does Love Really Stink? The 'Mean World' of Love and Sex in Popular Music of the 1980s." In *Adolescents and Their Music: If It's Too Loud, You're Too Old,* edited by Jonathon S. Epstein, 225–49. New York: Garland, 1994.

Ehrenhalt, Alan. "Is Education Reform Worth the Demise of Neighborhood Schools?" *Governing,* Feb. 24, 2015. https://www.governing.com/archive/gov-education-reform-demise-neighborhood-schools-html.

Ehrenreich, Barbara. *Natural Causes: An Epidemic of Wellness, the Certainty of Dying, and Killing Ourselves to Live Longer.* New York: Twelve, 2018.

Elkins, James. *What Happened to Art Criticism?* Chicago: Prickly Paradigm, 2003.

Ellis, Jack C. *A History of Film.* Englewood Cliffs, NJ: Prentice-Hall, 1985.

Ellwood, Robert S. *The Sixties Spiritual Awakening: American Religion Moving from Modern to Postmodern.* New Brunswick, NJ: Rutgers University Press, 1994.

Ephron, Nora, dir. *Sleepless in Seattle.* Culver City, CA: Tri-Star, 2003. DVD. First released 1993.

———. *You've Got Mail.* Burbank, CA: Warner Brothers, 2001. DVD. First released 1998.

Esolen, Anthony. "Free Our Churches from the Ugly and Stupid." *Wall Street Journal,* Feb. 24, 2017. https://www.wsj.com/articles/free-our-churches-from-the-ugly-and-stupid-1487894224.

Esposito, Joseph A. *Dinner in Camelot: The Night America's Greatest Scientists, Writers, and Scholars Partied at the Kennedy White House.* Lebanon, NH: University Press of New England, 2018.

Faulkner, William. *Essays, Speeches & Public Letters.* Edited by James B. Meriwether. New York: Random House, 1965.

Fetters, Ashley, and Kaitlyn Tiffany. "The 'Dating Market' Is Getting Worse." *Atlantic,* Feb. 25, 2020. https://www.theatlantic.com/family/archive/2020/02/modern-dating-odds-economy-apps-tinder-math/606982/.

Fitzgerald, Frances. *The Evangelicals: The Struggle to Shape America.* New York: Simon & Schuster, 2017.

Flaherty, Colleen. "The Evolving English Major." *Inside Higher Ed,* July 18, 2018. https://www.insidehighered.com/news/2018/07/18/new-analysis-english-departments-says-numbers-majors-are-way-down-2012-its-not-death.

Fletcher, Joseph. *Moral Responsibility: Situation Ethics at Work.* Philadelphia: Westminster, 1967.

Florida, Richard L. *The New Urban Crisis.* New York: Basic, 2017.

Foertsch, Jacqueline. *American Culture in the 1940s.* Twentieth-Century American Culture. Edinburgh: Edinburgh University Press, 2008.

Forest, George, and Robert Wright. "Stranger in Paradise." All Musicals, 1953. From *Kismet.* https://www.allmusicals.com/lyrics/kismet/strangerinparadise.htm.

Forrest, Kim. "The Average Wedding Cost, According to Data." *Knot,* updated Dec. 4, 2023. https://www.theknot.com/content/average-wedding-cost.

Fortin, Jacey. "California Tries to Close the Gap in Math, but Sets Off a Backlash." *New York Times*, Nov. 17, 2021. https://www.nytimes.com/2021/11/04/us/california-math-curriculum-guidelines.html.

Foucault, Michel. *The Order of Things: An Archaeology of the Human Sciences*. New York: Vintage, 1973.

Frankl, Viktor E. *Man's Search for Meaning*. Boston: Beacon, 2006.

Franklin, Alison. "New Report Makes the Case for Arts Education: Recommends Access for All." American Academy of Arts & Sciences, Sept. 14, 2021. https://www.amacad.org/news/arts-education-report.

Fried, Martha Nemis, and Morton H. Fried. *Transitions: Four Rituals in Eight Cultures*. New York: Norton, 1980.

Fry, Richard. "The Number of People in the Average U.S. Household Is Going Up for the First Time in over 160 Years." Pew Research Center, Oct. 1, 2019. https://www.pewresearch.org/short-reads/2019/10/01/the-number-of-people-in-the-average-u-s-household-is-going-up-for-the-first-time-in-over-160-years/.

Gablik, Suzi. *Has Modernism Failed?* New York: Thames & Hudson, 1984.

Gallagher, Jacob. "Cut from the Same Cloth." *Wall Street Journal*, Feb. 23–24, 2019.

Galloway, Scott. *Adrift: America in 100 Charts*. New York: Portfolio/Penguin, 2022.

Gambino, Matthew. "Decline in Baptisms, Marriages Seen as Harbinger, Call to Community." *Catholic Philly*, Sept. 24, 2019. https://catholicphilly.com>our-changing-church>decline-in-baptisms-marriages-seen-as-harbinger-call-to-community-2/.

Gardner, John W. *Excellence: Can We Be Equal and Excellent Too?* New York: Norton, 1984.

Gaustad, Edwin, and Leigh Schmidt. *The Religious History of America: The Heart of the American Story from Colonial Times to Today*. New York: HarperOne, 2002.

Gawande, Atul. *Being Mortal: Medicine and What Matters in the End*. New York: Metropolitan, 2014.

Gay, Jason. "America Needs More Kids on Bikes." *Wall Street Journal*, June 15–16, 2019.

———. "The Sweetest Kind of Surrender: Sweatpants." *Wall Street Journal*, Feb. 23–24, 2019.

Genoways, Ted. "The Death of Fiction?" *Mother Jones*, Jan./Feb. 2010. https://www.motherjones.com/media/2010/01/death-of-literary-fiction-magazines-journals/.

Getto, Erica, and Kavish Harjai. "8 Times That a 10 Commandments Monument Had Its Day in Court." MSNBC, July 8, 2015. https://www.msnbc.com/msnbc/8-times-10-commandments-monument-had-its-day-court-msna634566.

Gibson, John. *The War on Christmas: How the Liberal Plot to Ban the Sacred Christian Holiday Is Worse Than You Thought*. New York: Sentinel, 2005.

Gilbert, James. *A Cycle of Outrage: America's Reaction to the Juvenile Delinquent in the 1950s*. New York: Oxford University Press, 1986.

Gilbert, Roger. "Contemporary American Poetry." In *A Companion to Twentieth-Century Poetry*, edited by Neil Roberts, 557–70. Blackwell Companions to Literature and Culture. Oxford: Blackwell, 2003.

Gioia, Dana. "Business and Poetry." In *Poetry after Modernism*, edited by Robert McDowell, 222–54. Brownsville, OR: Story Line, 1998.

Gioia, Ted. *The History of Jazz*. Oxford: Oxford University Press, 2011.

Glass, George S., and David Tabatsky. *The Overparenting Epidemic: Why Helicopter Parenting Is Bad For Your Kids . . . and Dangerous For You, Too!* New York: Skyhorse, 2014.
Glennen, Callum. "The Rise and Fall of the US Mall." *World Finance*, Apr. 7, 2017. http://www.worldfinance.com/markets/the-rise-and-fall-of-the-us-mall.
Goldstein, Richard. "My Students Love Marvel Movies: Now I Do, Too." *Washington Post*, July 8, 2018.
Gompertz, Will. *What Are You Looking At? The Surprising, Shocking, and Sometimes Strange Story of 150 Years of Modern Art*. New York: Penguin, 2012.
Gooder, Lisa Harmon, ed. "The Influencer Issue." Special issue, *Brides* 86 (2019).
Gopnik, Adam. "American Nirvana: Is There a Science of Buddhism?" *New Yorker* (Aug. 7 & 14, 2017) 69–74.
Gopnik, Alison. "The Key to Raising a Confident Child." *Wall Street Journal*, Oct. 26–27, 2019.
Gottfredson, Denise C. *Schools and Delinquency*. Cambridge Studies in Criminology. Cambridge: Cambridge University Press, 2001.
Gottschalk, Jonah. "List of 183 Monuments Ruined Since Protests Began, and Counting." *Federalist*, July 22, 2020. https://thefederalist.com/2020/07/22/list-of-183-monuments-ruined-since-protests-began-and-counting/.
GoWireless. "iPhone XR—Color Flood—Apple." YouTube, Dec. 31, 2018. https://www.youtube.com/watch?v=UfiAr48KyRM.
Gramlich, John. "What We Know about the Increase in U.S. Murders in 2020." Pew Research Center, Oct. 27, 2021. https://www.pewresearch.org/short-reads/2021/10/27/what-we-know-about-the-increase-in-u-s-murders-in-2020.
Grant, Adam. "Three Lies about Meaningful Work." *Huffington Post*, May 7, 2015. https://www.linkedin.com/pulse/three-lies-meaningful-work-adam-grant.
Grant, Gerald. "The World We Created at Hamilton High." *Syracuse University Magazine* 5 (1988) art. 7.
Gray, John. *Feline Philosophy: Cats and the Meaning of Life*. New York: Picador, 2020.
Great American Read. "Read the 100 List." PBS, n.d. https://www.pbs.org/the-great-american-read/books/#/.
Greaves, Ron. "From Divine Light Mission to Elan Vital and Beyond." *Nova Religio* 7 (2004) 45–62.
Green, Dominic. "When Rock Killed Jazz." *Wall Street Journal*, June 11–12, 2016.
Green, Emma. "The Spiritual Significance of a Traditional Church Wedding." *Atlantic*, July 25, 2014. https://www.theatlantic.com/natural/archive/2014/07/how-important-is-it-to-have-a-church-wedding/3.
Greenfield, Briann G. *Out of the Attic: Inventing Antiques in Twentieth-Century New England*. Public History in Historical Perspective. Boston: University of Massachusetts Press, 2009.
Grimes, Ronald L. *Deeply into the Bone: Re-Inventing Rites of Passage*. Life Passages. Berkeley: University of California Press, 2000.
Grundy, Pamela C., and Benjamin C. Rader. *American Sports: From the Age of Folk Games to the Age of the Internet*. 8th ed. New York: Routledge, 2019.
Guralnick, Peter. *Sweet Soul Music: Rhythm and Blues and the Southern Dream of Freedom*. New York: Harper & Row, 1986.
Haberski, Raymond J. *Freedom to Offend: How New York Remade Movie Culture*. Lexington: University Press of Kentucky, 2007.

Hall, Lee. *Common Threads: A Parade of American Clothing.* Boston: Little Brown, 1992.

Halliwell, Martin. *American Culture in the 1950s.* Twentieth-Century American Culture. Edinburgh: Edinburgh University Press, 2007.

Hamburger, Philip. *Separation of Church and State.* Cambridge, MA: Harvard University Press, 2002.

Harari, Yuval Noah. *Homo Deus: A Brief History of Tomorrow.* New York: HarperCollins, 2017.

Hawks, Howard, dir. *Bringing Up Baby.* Burbank, CA: Warner Brothers, 2005. DVD. First released 1938.

Healy, Ben. "Be a Fan: It's Good For You." *Atlantic* (Apr. 2018) 24.

Hedegaard, Holly, et al. *Suicide Mortality in the United States, 1999–2019.* NCHS Data Brief 398, Feb. 2021. https://www.cdc.gov/nchs/data/databriefs/db398-H.pdf.

Hedges, Chris. *War Is a Force That Gives Us Meaning.* New York: Anchor, 2002.

Heelas, Paul. *The New Age Movement: The Celebration of Self and the Sacralization of Modernity.* Oxford: Blackwell, 1996.

Heid, Markham. "Depression and Suicide Rates Are Rising Sharply in Young Americans, New Report Says. This May be One Reason Why." *TIME,* Mar. 14, 2019. https://time.com/5550803/depression-suicide-rates-youth.

Heidegger, Martin. *Poetry, Language, Thought.* Translated by Albert Hofstadter. New York: Harper & Row, 1971.

Heller, Erich. *The Disinherited Mind: Essays in Modern German Literature and Thought.* New York: Harcourt, Brace, Jovanovich, 1975.

Heller, Karen. "Are Gimmicks a Buzzkill for the Yoga Scene?" *Washington Post,* Apr. 1, 2017.

Herd, David. *John Ashbery and American Poetry.* New York: Palgrave, 2000.

Herold, Thomas. "Book Publishing Market Overview for Authors—Statistics & Facts." *Book Ad Report,* Jan. 30, 2019. https://bookadreport.com/book-market-overview-authors-statistics-facts/.

Hidaka, Brandon. "Depression as a Disease of Modernity: Explanations for Increasing Prevalence." *HHS Public Access* (Jan. 12, 2012) 1–16.

Hill, Daniel Delis. *American Menswear: From the Civil War to the Twenty-First Century.* Costume Society of America. Lubbock: Texas Tech University Press, 2011.

Hiller, Arthur, dir. *Man of La Mancha.* New York: United Artists, 1972.

Hine, Stuart K. "How Great Thou Art." How Great Thou Art Official, 1949. https://howgreatthouartofficial.com.

Hitchcock, Alfred. *Hitchcock on Hitchcock: Selected Writings and Interviews.* Edited by Sidney Gottleib. Berkeley: University of California Press, 1995.

———, dir. *Psycho.* Hollywood, CA.: Universal, 1999. DVD. First released 1960.

Hoberman, J. "Bonnie and Clyde." In *Flesh and Blood: The National Society of Film Critics on Sex, Violence, and Censorship,* edited by Peter Keough, 318–23. San Francisco: Mercury, 1995.

Hobsbawm, Eric. *The Jazz Scene.* New York: Pantheon, 1993.

Holden, Jonathan. *The Fate of American Poetry.* Athens: University of Georgia Press, 2008.

Holm, Jean, and John Bowker, eds. *Rites of Passage.* Themes in Religious Studies. London: Pinter, 1994.

Hopkins, Thomas J. *The Hindu Religious Tradition.* Enrico, CA: Dickenson, 1971.

Horton, Donald. "The Dialogue of Courtship in Popular Songs." *American Journal of Sociology* 17 (1957) 569–78.
Howe, Neil. "Are Millennials Giving Up on Democracy?" *Forbes*, Oct. 31, 2017. https://www.forbes.com/sites/neilhowe/2017/10/31/are-millennials-giving-up-on-democracy/.
Huxley, Aldous. *Brave New World*. New York: HarperCollins, 2006.
Hymowitz, Kay S. "The 'L' Word: Love as Taboo." In *Modern Sex: Liberation and Its Discontents*, edited by Myron Magnet, 27–42. Chicago: Dee, 2001.
Ingraham, Christopher. "Nine Days on the Road. Average Commuter Time Reached a New Record Last Year." *Washington Post*, Oct. 7, 2019. https://washingtonpost.com/business/2019/10/07/nine-days-road-average-commute-time-reached-new-record-last-year/.
Jackson, Kenneth T. *Crabgrass Frontier: The Suburbanization of the United States*. New York: Oxford University Press, 1985.
Jain, Andrea R. "Five Myths: Yoga." *Washington Post*, Aug. 16, 2015.
James, William. *The Varieties of Religious Experience: A Study in Human Nature*. New York: Mentor, 1958.
Janik, Allan, and Stephen Toulmin. *Wittgenstein's Vienna*. New York: Touchstone, 1973.
Jefferson, Thomas. "Jefferson's Letter to the Danbury Baptists: The Final Letter, as Sent." Library of Congress, Jan. 1, 1802. https://www.loc.gov/loc/lcib/9806/danpre.html.
Jones, Jeffrey M. "U.S. Church Membership Falls below Majority for First Time." Gallup, Mar. 29, 2021. https://news.gallup.com/poll/341963/church-membership-falls-below-majority-first-time.aspx.
Jung, C. G. *Memories, Dreams, Reflections*. Recorded and edited by Aniela Jaffé. Translated by Richard and Clara Winston. New York: Vintage, 1989.
Junger, Sebastian. *Tribe: On Homecoming and Belonging*. New York: Twelve, 2016.
Kappler, Frank. "Sartre and Existentialsm: A Spurned Nobel Prize Brings the World's Attention to a Lonely Philosophy of Despair." *Life Magazine* 57 (Nov. 6, 1964) 86–100.
Keltner, Dacher, and Jonathan Haidt. "Approaching Awe: A Moral, Spiritual, and Aesthetic Emotion." *Cognition and Emotion* 17 (2003) 297–314.
Kennedy, John F. "Ask Not What Your Country Can Do for You." US History, Jan. 20, 1961. https://www.ushistory.org/documents/ask-not.htm.
Kernan, Alvin. *The Death of Literature*. New Haven: Yale University Press, 1990.
Kierkegaard, Søren. *The Sickness unto Death: A Christian Psychological Exposition for Upbuilding and Awakening*. Edited and translated by Edna H. Hong and Howard V. Hong. Kierkegaard's Writings 19. Princeton, NJ: Princeton University Press, 1980.
King, Martin Luther, Jr. "*I Have a Dream*"; also "*Letter from Birmingham Jail*." Logan, IA: Perfection Learning Corporation, 1990.
Kirsch, Adam. "Poetry for the Pleasure of It." *Wall Street Journal*, Apr. 14–15, 2018.
Klavan, Andrew. "Faith That Upholds Humanity—and Liberty." *Wall Street Journal*, Dec. 29, 2016. https://www.wsj.com/articles/faith-that-upholds-humanityand-liberty-1483053830.
Klemke, E. D., and Steven M. Cahn, eds. *The Meaning of Life: A Reader*. New York: Oxford University Press, 2008.

Kolto-Rivera, Mark E. "Rediscovering the Late Version of Maslow's Hierarchy of Needs: Self-Transcendence and Opportunities for Theory, Research and Unification." *Review of General Psychology* 10 (2006) 302–17.

Kronman, Anthony T. *Education's End: Why Our Colleges and Universities Have Given Up on the Meaning of Life*. New Haven: Yale University Press, 2007.

———. *The Lost Lawyer: Failing Ideals of the Legal Profession*. Cambridge, MA: Belknap, 1993.

Kruse, Kevin M. *One Nation under God: How Corporate America Invented Christian America*. New York: Basic, 2015.

Kübler-Ross, Elisabeth. *On Death and Dying*. New York: Macmillan, 1969.

Kuspit, Donald. *The End of Art*. New York: Cambridge University Press, 2004.

La Cava, Gregory, dir. *My Man Godfrey*. Hollywood, CA: Universal, 2005. DVD. First released 1936.

Lang, Paul Henry, ed. *The Symphony: 1800–1900*. New York: Norton, 1969.

Langton, Simon, dir. *Pride and Prejudice*. New York: New Video, 1995. VHS.

Lasch, Christopher. *The Culture of Narcissism: American Life in an Age of Diminishing Expectations*. New York: Norton, 1979.

Lauer, Claudia. "Bus-Ride Lengths Detailed in Study." *Arkansas Democrat Gazette*, Aug. 17, 2014. https://www.arkansasonline.com/news/2014/aug/17/bus-ride-lengths-detailed-in-study-2014/.

Learning Heroes. "Perspectives of the 2016 Public School Parent: New Study Reveals What Keeps Today's Parents Up at Night." PR Newswire, Apr. 21, 2016. https://www.prnewswire.com/news-releases/perspectives-of-the-2016-public-school-parent-new-study-reveals-what-keeps-todays-parents-up-at-night-300255285.html.

Lee, Joelle. "Is Classical Music Dying?" *Tide*, June 15, 2021. https://thermtide.com/14319/popular/is-classical-music-dying/.

Lee, John Alan. "Ideologies of Lovestyle and Sexstyle." In *Romantic Love and Sexual Behavior: Perspectives from the Social Sciences*, edited by Victor C. de Munck, 33–76. Westport, CT: Praeger, 1998.

Lehman, David, ed. *Beyond Amazement: New Essays on John Ashbery*. Ithaca, NY: Cornell University Press, 1980.

Leppmann, Wolfgang. *Rilke: A Life*. Translated by Russell M. Stockman. Verse translation by Richard Exuer. New York: Fromm, 1984.

Lev, Peter. *American Films of the 70s: Conflicting Visions*. Journal of American Studies. Austin: University of Texas Press, 2000.

Lévi-Strauss, Claude. *The Savage Mind*. Nature of Human Society. Chicago: University of Chicago Press, 1966.

Lewis, Paul. "*Ulysses* at Top as Panel Picks 100 Best Novels." *New York Times*, July 20, 1998. https://www.nytimes.com/1998/07/20/books/ulysses-at-top-as-panel-picks-100-best-novels.html.

Lhamon, W. T., Jr. *Deliberate Speed: The Origins of a Cultural Style in the American 1950s*. Cambridge, MA: Harvard University Press, 1990.

Lindholm, Charles. "The Future of Love." In *Romantic Love and Sexual Behavior: Perspectives from the Social Sciences*, edited by Victor C. de Munck, 17–32. Westport, CT: Praeger, 1998.

Lindner, Christoph. *The James Bond Phenomenon: A Critical Reader*. 2nd ed. Manchester, UK: Manchester University Press, 2009.

Linowitz, Sol. *The Betrayed Profession: Lawyering at the End of the Twentieth Century*. Baltimore: Johns Hopkins University Press, 1994.
Linz, Emily. "Guest Blog: The Value of an English Requirement." *ACTA*, July 27, 2015. https://www.goacta.org/2015/07/guest blog the value of an english requirement/.
Llosa, Mario Vargas. *Notes on the Death of Culture: Essays on Spectacle and Society*. Translated by John King. New York: Farrar, Straus & Giroux, 2012.
Longenbach, James. *The Resistance to Poetry*. Chicago: University of Chicago Press, 2004.
Louv, Richard. *Last Child in the Woods*. Chapel Hill, NC: Algonquin, 2008.
"Love Letters (Song)." Wikipedia, last edited Jan. 13, 2024. https://en.wikipedia.org/wiki/Love_Letters_(song).
Lubitch, Ernst, dir. *The Shop around the Corner*. Beverly Hills, CA: MGM, 2002. DVD. First released 1940.
Lucas, Christopher J. *American Higher Education: A History*. New York: Palgrave Macmillan, 2006.
Lupfer, Jacob. "Fewer Couples Are Marrying in Churches: Does it Matter?" *Religious News Service*, June 7, 2018. https://religion//news.com/2018/06/07/fewer-couples-are-marrying-in-churches-does-it-matter/.
Luscomb, Belinda. "10 Questions: Painter Gerhard Richter on His Work, Escaping from East Germany and Why He Doesn't Collect Art." *TIME* (Oct. 8, 2012) 68.
Lyden, John C. *Film as Religion: Myths, Morals, and Rituals*. New York: New York University Press, 2003.
Magnet, Myron, ed. *Modern Sex: Liberation and Its Discontents*. Chicago: Dee, 2001.
Mailer, Norman. *Advertisements for Myself*. New York: Putnam, 1959.
Man, Glenn. *Radical Visions: American Film Renaissance, 1967–1976*. Westport, CT: Greenwood, 1994.
Manchester, William. *The Glory and the Dream: A Narrative History of America, 1932–1972*. Boston: Bantam, 1979.
March, Segann. "Students, Parents Pay the Price for PTA Membership Declines." *Shreveport Times*, May 6, 2016; updated May 10, 2016. https://www.shreveporttimes.com/story/news/education/2016/05/06/students---and-their-parents---pay-price-pta-membership-declines/83970428.
Martin, Raymond, and John Barresi. *The Rise and Fall of Self and Soul: An Intellectual History of Personal Identity*. New York: Columbia University Press, 2006.
Martin, Richard. "21 Best Funeral Songs for the Older Generation." Music Industry How To, last updated Dec. 27, 2023. https://www.musicindustryhowto.com/funeral-songs-for-the-older-generation/.
Mascaro, Juan, ed. and trans. *The Bhagavad Gita*. New York: Penguin, 1962.
Maslow, Abraham H. *Religions, Values, and Peak-Experiences*. Columbus: Ohio State University Press, 1964.
May, Rollo. *The Cry for Myth*. New York: Delta, 1991.
Maybury-Lewis, David. *Millennium: Tribal Wisdom and the Modern World*. New York: Viking Penguin, 1992.
Mazo, Joseph H. *Prime Movers: The Makers of Modern Dance in America*. 2nd ed. Hightstown, NJ: Princeton, 2000.
McCarey, Leo, dir. *An Affair to Remember*. Los Angeles: Twentieth Century Fox, 2000. DVD. First released 1957.

McCarthy, Anna. *The Citizen Machine: Governing by Television in 1950s America*. New York: New, 2010.
McCartney, Paul, and Stevie Wonder. "Ebony and Ivory." Genius, Mar. 29, 1982. https://genius.com/Paul-mccartney-and-stevie-wonder-ebony-and-ivory-lyrics.
McClatchy, J. D., ed. *The Vintage Book of Contemporary American Poetry: Sixty-Five Outstanding Poets*. New York: Vintage, 1990.
McClory, Robert. *Turning Point: The Inside Story of the Papal Birth Control Commission, and How Humanae Vitae Changed the Life of Patty Crowley and the Future of the Church*. New York: Crossroad, 1997.
McDonough, Megan. "Till Death Do Us Part: A Voodoo-Themed Wedding Celebration at Congressional Cemetery." *Washington Post*, Oct. 26, 2018.
McDowell, Robert, ed. *Poetry after Modernism*. Brownsville, OR: Story Line, 1998.
McGuire, William. *Bollingen: An Adventure in Collecting the Past*. Updated ed. Bollingen. Princeton, NJ: Princeton University Press, 1989.
McKenzie, Shelly. *Getting Physical: The Rise of Fitness Culture in America*. CultureAmerica. Lawrence: University of Kansas Press, 2013.
Medved, Michael. *Hollywood vs. America*. New York: HarperCollins, 1992.
Merken, Sara. "As More Lawyers Return to Office, ABA Finds Stark Split on Remote Work." *Reuters*, Sept. 28, 2022. https://www.reuters.com/legal/legal/industry/more-lawyers-return-office-aba-finds-stark-split-remote-work-2022-09-28/.
Merlock, Ray. "Growing Up with Westerns." In *Rituals and Patterns in Children's Lives*, edited by Kathy Merlock Jackson, 235–51. A Ray and Pat Browne Book. Madison: University of Wisconsin Press, 2005.
Messer, Jeanne. "Guru Maharaj Ji and the Divine Light Mission." In *The New Religious Consciousness*, edited by Charles Y. Glock and Robert Bellah, 52–72. Berkeley: University of California Press, 1976.
Metzgar, Jack. *Striking Steel: Solidarity Remembered*. Critical Perspectives on the Past. Philadelphia: Temple University Press, 2000.
Meyer, Leonard B. *Music, the Arts, and Ideas: Patterns and Predictions in Twentieth-Century Culture*. Chicago: University of Chicago Press, 1967.
Michael, Robert T., et al. *Sex in America: A Definitive Survey*. New York: Warner, 1994.
Midlarsky, Elizabeth, and Helen Marie Klain. "A History of Violence in the Schools." In *Violence in Schools: Cross-National and Cross-Cultural Perspectives*, edited by Florence L. Denmark et al., 37–57. New York: Springer, 2005.
Mitchell, Joni. "Woodstock." Genius, Sept. 13, 1969. https://genius.com/Joni-mitchell-woodstock-lyrics.
Monteith, Sharon. *American Culture in the 1960s*. Twentieth-Century American Culture. Edinburgh: Edinburgh University Press, 2008.
Moody, James. *Life after Life*. New York: Bantam, 1976.
Moore, Alecia, et al. "True Love." Genius, June 28, 2013. https://genius.com/P-nk-true-love-lyrics.
Moorhead, Liz. "Brides Are too Afraid of Becoming 'Bridezilla' to Ask for What They Want." *Washington Post*, Sept. 16, 2018.
Murray, Chris, ed. *Key Writers on Art: The Twentieth Century*. Routledge Key Guides. London: Routledge, 2003.
Myers, Marc. "A Great Day in Harlem, Revisited." *Wall Street Journal*, Nov. 3–4, 2018.
Nation. "Residents of Poor Countries Have Greater Sense of Meaning in Life Than Those in Rich Nations, Research Says." PBS, Dec. 19, 2013. https://www.pbs.org/

newshour/nation/residents-of-poor-countries-have-greater-sense-of-meaning-in-life-than-those-in-rich-nations-researc.
Nelson, S. Katherine, et al. "In Defense of Parenthood: Children Are Associated with More Joy Than Misery." *Psychological Science* 20 (2012) 1–8.
Newcomb, Alyssa. "Dead People Get Life-Like Poses at Their Funerals." *ABC News*, June 13, 2014. https://abcnews.go.com/us/dead-people-life-poses-funerals/story?id=23456853.
Newton-John, Olivia. "Olivia Newton-John-Physical (Official Music Video) [Remastered 2021]." Youtube, Oct. 22, 2021. https://youtu.be/KDGvSZb9syw.
Nichols, Mike, dir. *Biloxi Blues*. Universal City, CA: Universal, 2003. DVD. First released 1988.
———. *The Graduate*. Beverly Hills, CA: MGM, 2007. DVD. First released 1967.
Nietzel, Michael T. "Whither the Humanities: The Ten-Year Trend in College Majors." *Forbes*, Jan. 7, 2019. https://www.forbes.com/sites/michaelnietzel/2019/01/07/whither-the-humanities-the-ten-year-trend-in-college-majors/?sh=c35codo64ad8.
Noonan, Peggy. "The Secrets of a Great Spouse." *Wall Street Journal*, Apr. 21–22, 2018.
Nugent, William R., and Linda Daugherty. "A Measurement Equivalence Study of the Family Bondedness Scale: Measurement Equivalence between Cat and Dog Owners." *Frontiers in Veterinary Science* 8 (2022). https://doi.org/10.3389/fvets.2021.812922.
Nuland, Sherwin B. *How We Die: Reflections on Life's Final Chapter*. New York: Knopf, 1994.
Oates, Stephen B. *Let the Trumpet Sound: A Life of Martin Luther King, Jr.* New York: Harper Perennial, 1994.
O'Loughlin, Michael J. "Poll Finds Many U.S. Catholics Breaking with Church over Contraception, Abortion and L.G.T.B. Rights." *American Magazine*, Sept. 28, 2016. https://www.americanmagazine.org/faith.2016/09/29/poll-finds-many-us-catholics-breaking-church-over-contraception-abortion.
O'Neil, William L. *American High: The Years of Confidence, 1945–1960*. New York: Free, 1986.
Ormsby, Eric. "'The Hebrew Bible' and 'The Art of Bible Translation' Review: An Ear for Scripture." *Wall Street Journal*, Mar. 15, 2019. https://www.wsj.com/articles/the-hebrew-bible-and-the-art-of-bible-translation-review-otherworldly-words-11552659274.
Ortega y Gasset, José. *Meditations on Quixote*. Translated by Evelyn Rugg and Diego Marín. New York: Norton, 1963.
Otto, Rudolf. *The Idea of the Holy*. Translated by John W. Harvey. London: Oxford University Press, 1970.
Parsons, Elsie Clews. *Pueblo Indian Religion*. 2 vols. Reprint, Lincoln: University of Nebraska Press, 1996. First published 1939.
Paul VI, Pope. *Humanae Vitae: Encyclical Letter of His Holiness Pope Paul VI on the Regulation of Birth*. San Francisco: Ignatius, 1998.
PayScale. "The Most and Least Meaningful Jobs." PayScale, n.d. https://www.payscale.com/data-packages/most-and-least-meaningful-jobs.
Peetz, Caitlynn. "The Status of the Teaching Profession Is at a 50-Year Low: What Can We Do about It?" *Education Week*, Nov. 15, 2022. https://www.edweek.org/

teaching-learning/the-status-of-the-teaching-profession-is-at-a-50-year-low-what-can-we-do-about-it/2022/11.

Penn, Arthur, dir. *Bonnie and Clyde*. Burbank, CA: Warner Brothers, 1967.

Pesta, Abigail. "The Survivor." *TIME* (July 29, 2019) 46–52.

Pew Research. "Poll Watch." *The Week* (Jan. 20, 2017) 17.

Pew Research Center. "Parenting in America." Pew Research Center, Dec. 17, 2015. https://www.pewresearch.org/social-trends/2015/12/17/parenting-in-america/.

Phaneuf Funeral Homes & Crematorium. "Popular Funeral Songs and Unusual Funeral Songs." Phaneuf, July 15, 2021. https://phaneuf.net/blog/popular-funeral-songs.

Phelan, Hayley. "Cut From the Same Cloth." *Wall Street Journal*, Feb. 23–24, 2019,.

Phillips, Francis. "The Old Rite Requiem Shows Us the Awe-Inspiring Nature of God." *Catholic Herald*, Oct. 9, 2017. https://catholicherald.co.uk/the-old-rite-requiem-shows-us-the-awe-inspiring-nature-of-death/.

Pierce, Emily. "As Students Return to School, so Does School Violence." *U.S. News and World Report*, Nov. 12, 2021. https.//www.usnews.com.Education.K12.

Piff, Paul K., et al. "Awe, the Small Self, and Prosocial Behavior." *Journal of Personality and Social Psychology* 8 (2015) 883–99.

Pink, Daniel H. *A Whole New Mind: Why Right-Brainers Will Rule the Future*. New York: Riverhead, 2006.

Pinsky, Robert. *The Situation of Poetry: Contemporary Poetry and Its Traditions*. Princeton Essays in Literature. Princeton, NJ: Princeton University Press, 1976.

Pipher, Mary, and Sara Pipher Gilliam. "The Lonely Burden of Today's Teenage Girls." *Wall Street Journal*, Aug. 17–18, 2019.

Poague, Leland, ed. *Conversations with Susan Sontag*. Literary Conversations. Jackson: University Press of Mississippi, 1995.

Pollack, Howard. *Aaron Copland: The Life and Work of an Uncommon Man*. New York: Holt, 1999.

Popenoe, David. *War over the Family*. New Brunswick, NJ: Transaction, 2005.

Porter, Cole. "True Love." Genius, n.d. https://genius.com/Cole-porter-true-love-lyrics.

Post, Emily. *Etiquette: The Book of Social Usage*. New York: Funk & Wagnalls, 1937.

Postman, Neil. *The End of Education: Redefining the Value of School*. New York: Vintage, 1996.

Pott, Leanne. "6 Funeral Trends That Are Changing Death Rituals." AARP, Nov. 20, 2017. https://www.aarp.org/home-family/friends-family/info-2017/funeral-ceremony-trends-fd.html.

Powers, H. Brewster, and James W. Putnam, eds. *Manners Make Men: A Practical and Sparkling Manual of Modern Etiquette Written by University Men in Their Own Style and Designed for Every High School and College Man of the Middle West*. Lawrence, KS: Witen, 1939.

Powers, Stephen, et al. *Hollywood's America: Social and Political Themes in Motion Pictures*. Boulder, CO: Westview, 1996.

Pratt, William, ed. *The Imagist Poem: Modern Poetry in Miniature*. New York: Dutton, 1963.

Putnam, Robert. *Bowling Alone: The Collapse and Revival of American Community*. New York: Simon & Schuster, 2000.

———. "*E Pluribus Unum*: Diversity and Community in the Twenty-First Century." *Scandinavian Political Studies* 30 (2007) 137–74.

———. *Our Kids: The American Dream in Crisis*. New York: Simon & Schuster, 2015.

Radar, Benjamin G. *American Sports: From the Age of Folk Games to the Age of the Spectators*. Englewood Cliffs, NJ: Prentice-Hall, 1983.
Rainer, Tristine. *The New Diary: How to Use a Journal for Self-Guidance and Expanded Creativity*. Los Angeles: Tarcher, 1978.
Randazzo, Sara. "The Flip Side of Making Partner." *Wall Street Journal*, Aug. 10–11, 2019.
Ratcliff, Carter. *Andy Warhol*. New York: Abbeville, 1983.
Ravitch, Diane. *Left Back: A Century of Failed School Reforms*. New York: Simon & Schuster, 2000.
Ray, Nicholas, dir. *Rebel without a Cause*. Burbank, CA: Warner Brothers, 2005. DVD. First released 1953.
Reagan, Ronald. "A Time for Choosing Speech." Reagan Library, Oct. 27, 1964. https://www.reaganlibrary.gov/reagans/ronald-reagan/time-choosing-speech-october-27-1964.
Reese, William J. *America's Public Schools: From the Common School to "No Child Left Behind"; With a New Epilogue on the Continuing Controversy over Federal Education Policy*. Updated ed. Baltimore: Johns Hopkins University Press, 2011.
Reeves, Thomas. "The Collapse of the Mainline Churches." In *Reinventing the American People: Unity and Diversity Today*, edited by Robert Royal, 203–10. Grand Rapids, Eerdmans, 1995.
———. "*Humanae Vitae*: Sex and Authority in the Catholic Church." *National Catholic Reporter*, July 20, 2018. https://www.ncronline.org/news/opinion/signs-times/hymanae-vitae-sex-and-authority-catholic-church.
Reeves, T. Zane. *The Politics of the Peace Corps & Vista*. Tuscaloosa: University of Alabama Press, 1987.
Regan, Pamela. "Romantic Love and Sexual Desire." In *Romantic Love and Sexual Behavior: Perspectives from the Social Sciences*, edited by Victor C. de Munck, 92–112. Westport, CT: Praeger, 1998.
Regnerus, Mark, and Jeremy Uecker. *Premarital Sex in America: How Young Americans Meet, Mate, and Think about Marrying*. New York: Oxford University Press, 2011.
Reilly, Kathie. "Depression on Campus." *TIME* (Apr. 9, 2018) 35–42.
Reiner, Rob, dir. *When Harry Met Sally*. Beverly Hills, CA: 20th Twentieth Century Fox, 2011. DVD. First released 1989.
Remnick, David. *The Bridge: The Life and Rise of Barak Obama*. New York: Knopf, 2010.
Reno, R. R. *Return of the Strong Gods: Nationalism, Populism, and the Future of the West*. Washington, DC: Regnery Gateway, 2019.
Richter, Duncan. *Historical Dictionary of Wittgenstein's Philosophy*. Lanham, MD: Scarecrow, 2004.
Riesman, David, et al. *The Lonely Crowd: A Study of the Changing American Character*. New Haven: Yale University Press, 1950.
Roberts, Paul. *The Impulse Society: America in the Age Of Instant Gratification*. New York: Bloomsbury, 2014.
Rorty, Richard. "The Fire of Life." Poetry Foundation, Nov. 2007. https://www.poetryfoundation.org/poetrymagazine/articles/68949/the-fire-of-life.
Rose, Barbara. *American Art Since 1900*. New York: Praeger, 1975.
———. *Rauschenberg*. New York: Vintage, 1987.
Rose, Brian G. *Television and the Performing Arts: A Handbook and Reference Guide to American Cultural Programming*. New York: Greenwood, 1986.
Rosenberg, Pierre. *Chardin*. Translated by Helga Harrison. Cleveland: World, 1963.

———. *Chardin: 1699–1779*. Cleveland: Cleveland Museum of Art, 1979.

Ross, Alex. *The Rest Is Noise: Listening to the Twentieth Century*. New York: Picador, 2007.

Rothman, Lily. "9 Questions." *TIME* (May 20, 2019) 60.

Rothstein, Richard. *The Way We Were? The Myths and Realities of America's Student Achievement*. New York: Century Foundation, 1998.

Roudané, Matthew C., ed. *Conversations with Arthur Miller*. Literary Conversations. Jackson: University Press of Mississippi, 1987.

Rougemont, Denis de. *Love in the Western World*. Translated by Montgomery Belgion. New York: Harper Colophon, 1956.

Rubenstein, Edwin S. "Life Expectancy Drives U.S. and World Population Growth." Negative Population Growth, Mar. 29, 2022. https://npg.org/library/forum-series/life-expectancy-drives-u-s-and-world-population-growth.html.

Rudd, Melanie, et al. "Awe Expands People's Perception of Time, Alters Decision Making, and Enhances Well-Being." *Psychological Science* 23 (2012) 1030–36. https://doi.org/10.1177/0956797612438731.

Runowicz, John Michael. *Forever Doo-Wop: Race, Nostalgia, and Vocal Harmony*. American Popular Music. Amherst: University of Massachusetts Press, 2010.

Rushdie, Salman. *Two Years Eight Months and Twenty-Eight Nights*. New York: Random House, 2015.

Sabato, Larry J. *The Kennedy Half Century: The Presidency, Assassination, and Lasting Legacy of John F. Kennedy*. New York: Bloomsbury, 2013.

Sahlberg, Pasi, and William Doyle. "To Really Learn, Our Children Need to Play." *Wall Street Journal*, Aug. 10–11, 2019.

Saks, Sam. "Measure for Measure." *Wall Street Journal*, May 12–13, 2018.

Salinger, J. D. *Franny and Zooey*. Boston: Little, Brown, 1961.

Sandler, Irving. *The Triumph of American Painting: A History of Abstract Expressionism*. New York: Harper & Row, 1970.

Satran, Rory. "Seize the Gray." *Wall Street Journal*, Jan. 19–20, 2019.

Saville, Alice. "Man of La Mancha Review." *Time Out*, Apr. 30, 2019. https://www.timeout.com/london/theatre/man-of-la-mancha-review.

Sawhill, Isabel. "20 Years Later, It Turns Out Dan Quayle Was Right about Murphy Brown and Unmarried Moms." *Washington Post*, May 25, 2012. https://www.washingtonpost.com/opinions/20-years-later-it-turns-out-dan-quale-was-right-about-murphy-brown-and-unmarried-moms/2012/05/25/gJQAsNCJqUstory.html.

Schlegel, Rebecca J., et al. "Thine Own Self: True Self-Concept Accessibility and Meaning in Life." *Journal of Personality and Social Psychology* 96 (2009) 473–90.

Schmidt, Leigh Eric. *Restless Souls: The Making of American Spirituality*. New York: HarperCollins, 2005.

Schneider, Kirk. "Towards a Humanistic Positive Psychology." *Journal of Existential Analysis* 22 (2011) 32–38.

Schneider, Kirk J., et al., eds. *The Handbook of Humanistic Psychology: Leading Edges in Theory, Research and Practice*. Thousand Oaks, CA: Sage, 2001.

Schrobsdorff, Susanna. "The Kids Are Not All Right." *TIME* (Nov. 7, 2016) 44–51.

Schulz, Charles M. *The Big Book of Peanuts: All the Daily Strips from the 1960s*. Kansas City: Andrews McMeel, 2015.

Schumacher, E. F. *Small Is Beautiful: Economics as if People Mattered*. New York: Harper Torchbooks, 1973.
Seligman, Martin, and Mihaly Csikszentmihalyi. "Positive Psychology: An Introduction." *American Psychologist* 55 (2000) 5–14.
Selingo, Jeffrey. "The False Promises of Worker Retraining." *Atlantic*, Jan. 8, 2018. https: www.theatlantic.com/education/archive/2018/01/the-false-promises-of-worker-retraining/549398/.
Semuels, Alana. "'They're Trying to Wipe Us off the Map': Small American Farmers Are Nearing Extinction." *TIME*, Nov. 27, 2019. https://time.com/5736789/small-american-farmers-debt-crisis-extinction/.
Sewall, Gibert T. "The Postmodern Schoolroom." In *Dumbing Down: Essays on the Strip-Mining of American Culture*, edited by Katharine Washburn and John Thornton, 57–67. New York: Norton, 1996.
Shea, Courtney. "When Did Naming Your Kid after Yourself Become a Faux Pas?" *Today's Parent*, July 12, 2017. https://www.todaysparent.com/pregnancy/baby-names/when-did-naming-your-kid-after-yourself-become-a-parenting-faux-pas/.
Sheehan, George. *Running & Being: The Total Experience*. New York: Warner, 1978.
Shelton, Ron, dir. *Bull Durham*. Beverly Hills, CA: 20th Century Fox, 1988.
Sheridan, Alan. *Foucault: The Will to Truth*. London: Tavistock, 1980.
Shukla, Aseem. "Yoga: Stolen From the Hindus." *Pittsburgh Post-Gazette*, Apr. 25, 2010. https://www.post-gazette.com/opinion/Op=Ed/2010/04/25/Yoga-stolen-from-the-Hindus/stories/201004250220.
Shumway, David R. *Modern Love: Romance, Intimacy, and the Marriage Crisis*. New York: New York University Press, 2003.
Simon, Cecelia Capuzzi. "Why Writers Love to Hate the M.F.A." *New York Times*, Apr. 9, 2015. https://www.nytimes.com/2015/04/12/education/edlife/12edl-12mfa.html.
Singer, Irving. *Meaning in Life: The Creation of Value*. New York: Free, 1992.
Skolnick, Arlene. *Embattled Paradise: The American Family in an Age of Uncertainty*. New York: Basic, 1991.
Smelser, Neil J. *The Odyssey Experience: Physical, Social, Psychological, and Spiritual Journeys*. Berkeley: University of California Press, 2009.
Smith, Emily Esfahani. *The Power of Meaning: Crafting a Life That Matters*. London: Rider, 2017.
Smith, Huston. *The Religions of Man*. New York: Harper & Row, 1958.
———. *Why Religion Matters: The Fate of the Human Spirit in an Age of Disbelief*. New York: Harper, 2001.
Smith, Jacquelyn. "The Happiest and Unhappiest Jobs in America." *Forbes*, Mar. 22, 2013. https//www.forbes.com/sites/jacquelynsmith/2013/03/22/the-happiest-and-unhappiest-jobs-in-america.
Solomon, Deborah. *Jackson Pollock: A Biography*. New York: Cooper Square, 2001.
Stefancic, Jean, and Richard Delgado. *How Lawyers Lose Their Way: A Profession Fails Its Creative Minds*. Durham, NC: Duke University Press, 2005.
Steiner, George. *In Bluebeard's Castle: Some Notes Towards the Redefinition of Culture*. New Haven: Yale University Press, 1971.
Stelloh, Tim, and Rachel Elbaum. "Tens of Thousands of General Motors Auto Workers Go on Strike." NBC, Sept. 16, 2019. https://www.nbc.com/news/us-news/tens-thousands-general-motors-auto-workers-go-strike-n10.

Stepp, Laura Sessions. *Unhooked: How Young Women Pursue Sex, Delay Love and Lose at Both*. New York: Riverhead, 2007.
Stowe, David W. *Swing Changes: Big-Band Jazz in New Deal America*. Cambridge, MA: Harvard University Press, 1994.
Stroumsa, Guy G. *A New Science: The Discovery of Religion in the Age of Reason*. Cambridge, MA: Harvard University Press, 2010.
Sugarman, Sally. "Playing the Game: Rituals in Children's Games." In *Rituals and Patterns in Children's Lives*, edited by Kathy Merlock Jackson, 124–38. Madison: University of Wisconsin, 2005.
Sullivan, Kaitlin. "Suicide Rates Declined Again in 2020, but Not for All Groups, CDC Reports." NBC, Nov. 3, 2021. https://nbcnews.com/health/mental-health/suicide-rates-declined-2020-not-groups-cdc-report-shows-rcna4363.
Swafford, Jan. *Language of the Spirit: An Introduction to Classical Music*. New York: Basic, 2017.
Sweet, Jacob. "The Loneliness Pandemic." *Harvard Gazette* (Jan./Feb. 2021) 31–35.
Szasz, Thomas. "The Person as Moral Agent." In *The Handbook of Humanistic Psychology: Leading Edges in Theory, Research, and Practice*, edited by Kirk J. Schneider et al., 77–80. Thousand Oaks, CA: Sage, 2001.
Tawa, Nicholas. *The Great American Symphony: Music, The Depression, and War*. Bloomington: University of Indiana Press, 2009.
———. *Supremely American: Popular Song in the 20th Century; Styles and Singers and What They Said about America*. Lanham, MD: Scarecrow, 2005.
Taylor, Eugene I., and Frederick Martin. "Humanistic Psychology at the Crossroads." In *The Handbook of Humanistic Psychology: Leading Edges in Theory, Research, and Practice*, edited by Kirk J. Schneider et al., 21–27. Thousand Oaks, CA: Sage, 2001.
Teachout, Terry. "Films For All Seasons." *Wall Street Journal*, May 5, 2016.
Teaford, Jon C. *The American Suburb: The Basics*. New York: Routledge, 2008.
Tesfamariam, Rahiel. "How the Modern Civil Rights Movement Lost Its Religion." *Washington Post*, Sept. 20, 2015.
Thayer, Kate. "Youth Sports Faces Shortage of Refs Who Don't Want to Stand There and Take Abuse." *Chicago Tribune*, May 2, 2018. https.//www.chicagotribune.com/lifestyles/ct-life-youth-sports-ref-shortage-20180501-story.html.
Thompson, Graham. *American Culture in the 1980s*. Twentieth-Century American Culture. Edinburgh: Edinburgh University Press, 2007.
Thorne, Ashley. "The Drive to Put Western Civ Back in the College Curriculum." *New York Post*, Mar. 29, 2016. https://nypost.com/2016/03/29/the-drive-to-put-western-civ-back-in-the-college-curriculum/.
Thornton, Sarah. *Seven Days in the Art World*. New York: Norton, 2009.
Tocqueville, Alexis de. *Democracy in America*. Edited by Richard D. Heffner. New York, Mentor, 1956.
Tolstoy, Leo. *Anna Karenina*. Edited by Leonard J. Kent and Nina Berberova. Modern Library Classics. New York: Modern Library, 1965.
Troost, Linda, and Sayre Greenfield, eds. *Jane Austen in Hollywood*. Lexington: University of Kentucky Press, 1998.
Turkle, Sherry. "The Attack of the Friendly Robots." *Washington Post*, Dec. 10, 2017.
Turnbull, Colin M. *The Human Cycle*. New York: Simon & Schuster, 1983.

Twenge, Jean M. *iGen: Why Today's Super-Connected Kids Are Growing Up Less Rebellious, More Tolerant, Less Happy—and Completely Unprepared for Adulthood.* New York: Atria, 2017.

Twenge, Jean M., and W. Keith Campbell. *The Narcissism Epidemic: Living in the Age of Entitlement.* New York: Free, 2009.

Tzu, Chuang. *The Complete Works of Chuang Tzu.* Translated by Burton Watson. New York: Columbia University Press, 1968.

Urban, Wayne J., and Jennings L. Wagoner. *American Education: A History.* New York: Routledge, 2009.

Van Gogh, Vincent. *Van Gogh: A Self Portrait; Letters Revealing His Life as a Painter.* Edited by W. H. Auden. Greenwich, CT: New York Graphic Society, 1961.

Van Ogtrop, Kristin. "Why Ambition Isn't Working for Women." *TIME* (Sept. 28, 2015) 53–56.

Wallace, Jennifer Breheny. "Teaching Girls to Be Great Competitors." *Wall Street Journal*, Apr. 13–14, 2019.

———. "Watch TV with Your Family." *Wall Street Journal*, June 12, 2015. https://www.wsj.com/articles/watch-tv-with-your-family-1434120119.

Wang, Wendy. "The U.S. Divorce Rate Has Hit a 50-Year Low." Institute for Family Studies, Nov. 10, 2020. https://ifstudies.org/blog/the-us-divorce-rate-has-hit-a-50-year-low.

Ward, Marguerite. "A Brief History of the 8-Hour Workday, Which Changed How Americans Work." CNBC, May 3, 2017. http://www.cnbc.com/2017/05/03/how-the-8-hour-workday-chsnged-how-americans-work.html.

Washburn, Katharine, and John F. Thornton, eds. *Dumbing Down: Essays on the Strip-Mining of American Culture.* New York: Norton, 1996.

Wasserman, Dale. *The Impossible Musical: The "Man of La Mancha" Story.* New York: Applause Theatre & Cinema, 2003.

Waters, Frank. *Book of the Hopi.* New York: Ballantine, 1963.

Watterson, Bill. *The Days Are Just Packed.* Kansas City: Andrews McMeel, 1992.

Webb, Charles. *The Graduate.* New York: Washington Square, 1991.

Weigel, George. "The Christian Citizen and Democracy." In *Reinventing the American People: Unity and Diversity Today,* edited by Robert Royal, 173–89. Grand Rapids: Eerdmans, 1995.

Wellman, James K., Jr., et al. *High on God: How Megachurches Won the Heart of America.* New York: Oxford University Press, 2020.

White, Kevin. *Sexual Liberation or Sexual License?: The American Revolt against Victorianism.* Chicago: Dee, 2000.

Whyte, William. *The Organization Man.* New York: Simon & Schuster, 1956.

Wiggin, Kate Douglas. *Rebecca of Sunnybrook Farm.* London: Bibliophile, 1994.

Williams, Linda. *Screening Sex.* Durham, NC: Duke University Press, 2008.

Wilson, Sloan. *The Man in the Grey Flannel Suit.* New York: Simon & Schuster, 1955.

Wolf, Susan. *Meaning in Life and Why It Matters.* University Center for Human Values. Princeton, NJ: Princeton University Press, 2010.

Wolfe, Linnie Marsh. *Son of the Wilderness: The Life of John Muir.* Madison: University of Wisconsin Press, 1978.

Wolfe, Tom. "The Me Decade and the Great Awakening." In *"Mauve Gloves & Madmen," "Clutter & Vine," and Other Stories, Sketches, and Essays,* 126–67. New York: Farrar, Straus & Giroux, 1976.

Woodward, Kenneth L. *Getting Religion: Faith, Culture, and Politics from the Age of Eisenhower to the Era of Obama*. New York: Convergent, 2016.

Wordsworth, William. "Preface to the Second Edition of Lyrical Ballads." In *Critical Theory Since Plato*, edited by Hazard Adams, 432–43. San Diego: Harcourt Brace Jovanovich, 1971.

Wright, Joe, dir. *Pride and Prejudice*. Hollywood, CA: Universal, 2005. DVD.

Wrzensniewski, Amy, et al. "Jobs, Careers, and Callings: People's Relations to Their Work." *Journal of Research in Personality* 31 (1997) 21–33.

Wuthnow, Robert. *After the Baby Boomers: How Twenty- and Thirty-Somethings Are Shaping the Future of American Religion*. Princeton, NJ: Princeton University Press, 2007.

———. "From Religion to Spirituality." In *Reinventing the American People: Unity and Diversity Today*, edited by Robert Royal, 191–202. Grand Rapids: Eerdmans, 1995.

Wyaco, Virgil. *A Zuni Life: A Pueblo Indian in Two Worlds*. Edited and translated by J. A. Jones. Albuquerque: University of New Mexico Press, 1998.

Yahr, Emily. "The Rom-Com Is Dead." *Washington Post*, Oct. 9, 2016.

Yeats, William Butler. *The Autobiography of William Butler Yeats*. New York: Collier, 1969.

Young, Terance, dir. *Dr. No*. Los Angeles: United Artists, 2002. DVD. First released 1962.

Zeitlin, Dave. "Wellness Warriors." *Pennsylvania Gazette* (Jan./Feb. 2021) 26–35.

Zelizer, Julian E., ed. *The Presidency of Barack Obama*. Princeton, NJ: Princeton University Press, 2018.

Zimmerman, Fred, dir. *From Here to Eternity*. Culver City, CA: Columbia, 2005. DVD. First released 1953.

Zitner, Aaron. "Americans Pull Back from the Values That Once Defined U.S., WSJ-NORC Poll Finds." *Wall Street Journal*, Mar. 27, 2023. https://www.christianpost.com>voices>americans-pull-back-from-values-that-once-defined-u-s-wsj-nor-poll-finds-d8534cd.

www.ingramcontent.com/pod-product-compliance
Lightning Source LLC
Chambersburg PA
CBHW070616220526
45466CB00001B/13